The Portable Dragon

THE WESTERN MAN'S GUIDE TO THE I CHING

BY R. G. H. SIU

The MIT Press
Massachusetts Institute of Technology
Cambridge, Massachusetts, and London, England

To: Kau Yau King, David R. Schwarz,
Arie Jan Haagen-Smit, and James and Alice Davis

Tenth printing, 1990
First MIT Press paperback edition, 1971

Original edition published under the title
The Man of Many Qualities: A Legacy of the I Ching

Copyright © 1968 by
The Massachusetts Institute of Technology

Printed and bound in the United States of America

ISBN 0 262 19047 8 (hardcover)
ISBN 0 262 69030 6 (paperback)

Library of Congress catalog card number: 68-18242.

PLACE YOUR HAND ON THE I CHING AND PUT A QUESTION
TO IT — secretly or aloud — any question whose
answer can take the form of "the man is . . ." or "the
man will . . ." or "the man should. . . ." Take three
coins of equal denomination, juggle them, and toss
them six times running. Each toss generates one line
of a hexagram, starting from the bottom: more heads
than tails represents an unbroken line; more tails
than heads represents a broken line. A line generated
by a toss yielding all heads or all tails is particularly
strong or significant; the text on the hexagram in the
I Ching pertaining to such lines should be given
especially close scrutiny. (The first statement in the
text pertains to the bottom line, and so on up in
accordance with the progression of events, arriving
finally at the "over-all judgment," a seventh commentary pertinent to the pattern as a whole.) Moreover, the strong lines are "changing lines" — they
evolve into their opposites, creating a new hexagram
which represents a further progression of events
and situations.
After tossing the coins, noting the strong lines (if
any), and drawing the hexagram (and the hexagram
into which it transforms, if any), look up the number
of the hexagram(s) using the index on the following
two pages. Then consult the *I Ching* by looking up
the indicated hexagram(s). There you will find the
answer to your question.

Is the I not the perfect book? –Confucius (551-479 BC)

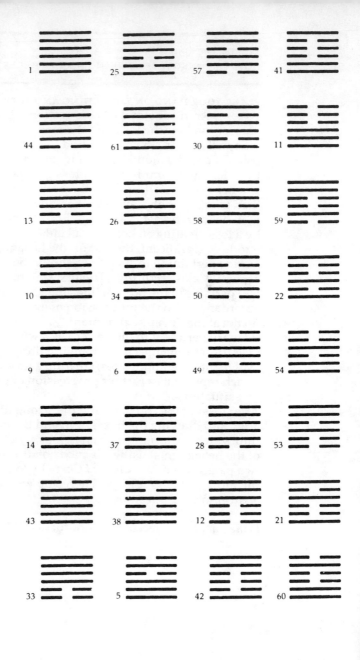

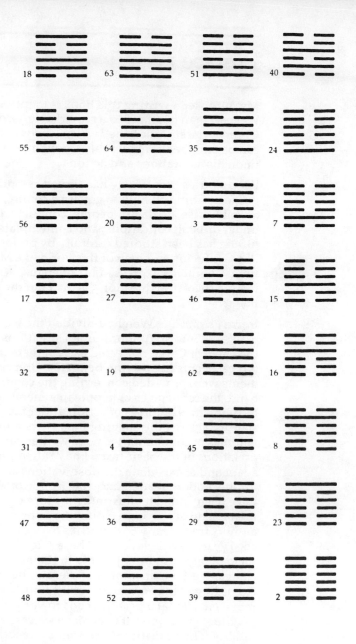

Preface

My purpose in writing this book is to introduce the Western man of affairs to a remarkable 3000-year-old Chinese classic called the *I Ching*. I believe his life can be enriched considerably through its influence upon his aspirations and actions.

For centuries, the *I Ching* has served as a principal guide in China on how to govern a country, organize an enterprise, deal with people, conduct oneself under difficult conditions, and contemplate the future. It has been studied carefully by philosophers like Confucius and men of the world like Mao Tsetung. Confucius expressed his deep respect by asking the rhetorical question "Is the *I* not the perfect book?"

In 1143 B.C., King Wen had divided the working man's life into sixty-four human situations. His son, the Duke of Chou, dissected each of them into six typical events of evolving behavior. Cryptic statements were provided concerning the conditions at hand, the tendencies of people in general, and the recommended courses of action under the circumstances. During the ensuing 1500 years numerous volumes of commentaries were written on the interpretations of the basic texts. I have attempted to adapt and encapsulate the observations and advice for the modern reader. Excerpts from world literature have been added to illustrate the more significant nuances. In all, about 700 quotations by over 650 authors from nearly 60 countries over a period of 6000 years have been used. These selections should, incidentally, also be enjoyable in their own literary right and offer many hours of pleasurable musings. According to the *I Ching*, the sixty-four situations represent all that a person needs to know about his neighbors and himself to achieve success and tranquillity. They constitute a commonsensical framework for day-to-day living, competing, and letting live.

The ultimate purpose of the *I Ching*, however, goes far beyond practical attainments in the competitive world. To achieve this goal, a different orientation is required. The sixty-four situations and responses are no longer regarded as fixed psychological stand-ards of human behavior. Instead, they are intuitively sensed as ever changing transients in the kaleidoscope of living. Nothing is constant, yet nothing secedes from the whole. There is a time and place for the "one-upmanship" of the tycoon, the "sono-mama" of the Buddhist, and the "doing-your-thing" of the hippie. One's actions of the instant are but notes emitted from his ineffable harmony with the totality of nature. This being the case, they cannot help but be ever timely and proper. The man of affairs has become a sage.

R. G. H. Siu
Washington, D.C., 1968

Acknowledgments

The author wishes to express his appreciation to the following, who have granted permission to quote from their works:

Abelard-Schuman, Ltd.: Poem by Juan Chi, reprinted from *Poems of Solitude,* translated from the Chinese by Jerome Ch'en and Michael Bullock. By permission of Abelard-Schuman, Ltd. All Rights Reserved. Copyright 1960 by Jerome Ch'en and Michael Bullock.

The American-Scandinavian Foundation: *Völuspa,* translated by Henry A. Bellows, *The Poetic Edda,* 1923; Knut Hamsun, "The Call of Life," translated by Anders Orbek (ed.), *Norway's Best Stories,* 1927; Einar Benediktsson, "Rain," translated by Watson Kirkconnell, *Icelandic Poems and Stories,* 1943; Odd Nansen, "Grini Prisoner No. 480," *American-Scandinavian Review,* March 1946.

Anderson House: *Key Largo.* Copyright 1939 by Maxwell Anderson. Copyright renewed 1967 by Gilda Anderson, Alan Anderson, Terence Anderson, Quentin Anderson, and Hesper A. Levenstein. All rights reserved. Reprinted by permission of Anderson House.

Bantam Books, Inc.: From "The Sultan of Kembajat" by Bokhari, adapted by Gene Z. Hanrahan, copyright © 1963 by Gene Z. Hanrahan, as it appears in *Fifty Great Oriental Stories,* copyright © by Bantam Books, Inc.

A. S. Barnes and Company, Inc.: Chaim Bialik, "The Last Word," translated in Joseph Leftwich, *The Golden Peacock.* Thomas Yoseloff Inc., 1961.

Behrman House, Inc., and Mr. Maurice Samuel: David Frishman, "For the Messiah." Translated by Maurice Samuel in *Anthology of Modern Jewish Poetry,* published by Behrman House, copyright 1927.

The Bobbs-Merrill Company, Inc.: From *Grant of Appomattox,* by William E. Brooks, copyright 1942 by The Bobbs-Merrill Company, Inc., reprinted by permission of the publishers.

Cambridge University Press: Ibn Shakil, "Ugliness." Translated in A. J. Arberry, *Moorish Poetry,* published by Cambridge University Press.

Jonathan Cape, Ltd., and the Executors of the Laurence Housman Estate: From *Ironical Tales,* by Laurence Housman, 1927.

The Church of Jesus Christ of Latter-Day Saints: Brigham Young, "The Mormon Trek to Utah, 1846." In John A. Widsoe (ed.), *The Discourses of Brigham Young,* 1925.

The Clarendon Press: Swahili folk verse, translated in Lyndon Harries, *Swahili Poetry,* 1962. Reprinted by permission of The Clarendon Press, Oxford.

David McKay Company, Inc.: Muju, "A Cup of Tea" from *101 Zen Stories*, by Nyogen Senzaki and Paul Reps. Philadelphia: McKay, 1939. Used by permission of David McKay Company, Inc.

Mr. Gerard Previn Meyer: Translation of Arthur Rimbaud, "The Poor in Church" in Hubert Creekmore (ed.), *A Little Treasury of World Poetry*, 1952.

Mr. E. G. Morgan: Translation from Eugenio Montale "Portami il girasole ch'io lo trapianti."

John Murray: Translations of Li Po and Han Yü from Soame Jenyns, *Three Hundred Poems of the T'ang Dynasty*, 1944; translation of Yun Sun-do from Peter Hyun, *Voices of the Dawn*, 1960. *Wisdom of the East* series published by John Murray.

The National Council of Teachers of English: Otomo no-Tabito, translated by Younghill Kang and John Morrison in Charlton Laird (ed.), *The World Through Literature*, 1951.

New Directions Publishing Corp.: "The Bird" by Jorge de Lima. Translated in Dudley Fitts, ed., *An Anthology of Latin American Poetry*. Copyright 1942, 1947, by New Directions. "The Toy Cart" by King Shudraka and "The Signet Ring of Rakshasa" by Vishakadatta in *Great Sanskrit Plays in Modern Translation*, by P. Lal. Copyright © 1957, 1959, 1964 by P. Lal. Reprinted by permission of New Directions Publishing Corporation.

The New Yorker: From St. Clair McKelway "Benzoin for the Turbinates." *The New Yorker*, March 22, 1941. Reprinted by permission; copyright © 1941 The New Yorker Magazine, Inc.

Sir Harold Nicolson: From Harold Nicolson, *Good Behaviour*, 1956.

Oxford University Press: From Christopher Fry, *The Dark Is Light Enough*, 1954; Alain Robbe-Grillet, translated by John Weightman in John Cruickshank (ed.), *The Novelist as Philosopher*, 1962; Edwin Muir, "The Good Man in Hell," *Collected Poems*, 1965. Reprinted by permission of Oxford University Press, New York and London.

Pan American Union: Translation of Juan Montalbo, "Pinchincha."

Mr. Robert Payne: Tu Fu, "The Return," translated by Robert Payne, *The White Pony*, 1947.

Peter Pauper Press: Shiki haiku from *The Four Seasons*, 1958.

Frederick A. Praeger, Inc. From Velemir Khlebnikov, "The Refusal." Translated in Vyacheslav Zavalishin, *Early Soviet Writers*, 1958. Reprinted by permission of Frederick A. Praeger, Inc.

Random House, Inc.: From Willa Cather, "Neighbour Rosicky," *Obscure Destinies*, copyright 1930 by Alfred A. Knopf, Incorporated; from Plautus, *The Comedy of Asses*, translated by E. H. Sugden in George E. Duckworth (ed.), *The Complete Roman Drama*, Random House, 1942; from "Phaedre," by Jean Racine, and translated by Robert

the Hungarians," translated by Walter Kirkconnell in
Joseph Kemenyi *et al., World Literature,* 1956.

Vanderbilt University Press: From Jean Campistron,
Andronic, and Thomas Corneille, *The Earl of Essex,* trans-
lated by Lacy Lockert, *The Chief Rivals of Corneille and
Racine,* 1956; Jean de Rotrou, "Cosroes," translated by
Lacy Lockert, *Studies in French-Classical Tragedy,* 1958.
Reprinted by permission of the publisher, Vanderbilt
University Press.

Vanguard Press: Reprinted by permission of the publisher,
The Vanguard Press, from Chekov's play "The Three Sisters," translated by Bernard Guilbert Guerney (copyright
1939, 1943 by Bernard Guilbert Guerney) and contained in
A Treasury of Russian Literature.

Viking Press: From Denis Fonvisin, "Universal Courtier's
Grammar," translated by Bernard G. Guerney, *Portable
Russian Reader,* The Viking Press Inc. 1947.

Contents

I. Introduction to the *I Ching**

The theme of the *I Ching* is the advance and retreat of
the dragon — the symbol of the great man and of the
beneficent forces of nature. Its philosophical prem-
ises evolved during the formative centuries of
Chinese civilization in the central plains of eastern
Asia. In this low-lying tract of land, fed by the
Yellow River and her tributaries, the life of the
Chinese peasant followed the incessant rhythm of
the seasons, century after century.

As the snow melted, sparrows bathed in the first
waters of the year. The *mei hua* blossomed in sheltered places. The peasant looked forward to the
working phase of his own social cycle. With spring
equinox the emperor ceremoniously "desanctified"
the fields from their winter "interdiction." Tilling
followed. The wild geese returned. The song of the
skylark reached up to the clouds. The young sang of
love to each other, and marriages forbidden for the
winter months were now celebrated.

Then came the summer heat, the long day, the
marching columns of ants on the dry ground, the
stately cranes in the water, the grating cicadas in
the trees, and the blooming peonies among the huts.
There was the long anxious waiting for the rain as
the hot winds from the distant desert blew the promising clouds from the skies. Then newly gathered
clouds, welcomed rain, and smiling faces all around.
The crops were saved.

Soon the red dragonfly flew joyously at the coming
of autumn. As the dew became heavy and the moon
full, the geese returned south, the crickets continued
their ceaseless chirping, and the harvest sparrows
blanketed the fields of ripening grain. Then the exciting but sweaty work of harvest, the threshing of
grain outside the front doorways, the winnowing and
casting of chaff to the winds. The grain was finally
put away and the fall festival celebrated. With the
autumnal equinox the closed winter season set in.

* For more details on the *I Ching*, the reader is referred to the excellent translations and notes by James Legge and Richard Wilhelm,
and the lucid lectures by Hellmut Wilhelm. Full bibliographical
information appears in the References.

[1]

The biting winds from the cold desert swept by the withered flowers, the fallen dried stalks and the yellow leaves stubbornly clinging to the bamboo, Peasants huddled on mats of reed in their thatched huts and talked about the events of the past year, while the women mapped their plans for winter weaving. Until middle spring, this was the phase of relative quiescence.

From this biphasic cycle of peasant life arose the fundamental conception of the universe in the Chinese mind. Affairs were grouped according to their tendencies into two general categories. These corresponded to the season dominated by female work, namely the weaving during the closed winter months in the huts, and to the season dominated by male work, namely the hard agricultural labor in the fields. Everything was divided into the two respective modalities of the yin and the yang. Yin originally pertained to shade and yang to light.

In later development, the terms became expanded to encompass the two cosmic principles. Yin stood for cold, softness, contraction, wetness, femininity, and the like. Yang stood for heat, hardness, expansion, dryness, masculinity, and the like.

The opposition, alternation, and interaction of these two forces give rise to all phenomena in the universe, in a continuous advance and regression of the vital forces in nature. Nothing remains static. Good fortune and ill are forever moving against each other according to cosmic rules. It is said that "When the sun reaches the meridian, it declines, and when the moon becomes full, it wanes." As Lao-tzu sums it up, "Reversal is the nature of the Tao."

The art of good living lies in the ordering of one's life in harmony with the cosmological movements of the yin and the yang. This principle applies to specific problems at hand, as well as to the grand generalizations of universal transformations. The simple interaction of the two influences is schematically represented by pairs of divided and/or undivided lines, representing the yin and yang, respectively. The four permutations are

The next-higher yin-yang series consists of the eight

trigrams of three lines each. According to legend, these were devised by Emperor Fu Hsi in 2852 B.C. A name was given to each trigram, symbolizing certain attributes and objects of nature in a state of continual transition. The eight trigrams are

CH'IEN	K'UN	CHEN	K'AN

KEN	SUN	LI	TUI

Doubling of the three lines into six yields sixty-four possible combinations. These form the sixty-four hexagrams of the *I Ching,* which represent the sixty-four assemblages of events to be described in this book. The array is supposed to be inclusive of all human situations in which a person might find himself.

The yin-yang series can be expanded geometrically to provide an infinite progression, namely 128, 256, 512, 1024, ad infinitum. The originators of the *I Ching* judiciously stopped at the practical limit of sixty-four. This number constitutes a classification sufficiently fine so as to provide useful types of situations, against which specific cases can be matched. Yet the subdivisions are not so numerous as to be too cumbersome for a single scheme. This convenient compromise makes the *I Ching* readily applicable by the average person to episodes encountered in his own life.

In 1143 B.C., King Wen systematically organized the sixty-four hexagrams into the cohesive scheme as we know it today. To each hexagram he gave a name and a thematic text, called the *T'uan.* The *T'uan* presents a summary of the hexagram's chief attributes, their expected impact upon the person involved, and related advice. The King's son, the Duke of Chou, added the *Yao,* which is a set of succinct statements concerning the respective constituent lines. The lines represent the evolving behavioral events within the *T'uan,* which result from the movements of the vital yin-yang forces of nature under the conditions of the hexagram. At times, a leitmotiv is carried throughout the six passages of the *Yao.* But frequently the relevancy of the meaning of one line to

[3]

that of the next, or even of the *T'uan* itself, is not quite clear.

Many other additions were made to the basic text over the next 1500 years. Thousands of scholars, philosophers, and men of action have extended the range of meanings and applications of the original *T'uan* and *Yao*. The most important of these commentaries is the *Ten Wings*. This has been ascribed to Confucius (551–479 B.C.), although much of it was undoubtedly the work of others. Another significant addition is the eight apocrypha, or *Wei*, which have been prepared during the late Chou Dynasty (1150–249 B.C.) and the early Han (206 B.C.–220 A.D.). Thus, over a millennium of thought has gone into the development of the full meaning of the *I Ching*. The contributors have included those who have shaped the philosophy of the Chinese people. Its completion paralleled the cultural maturation of China. It is comprehensive and many-sided, containing colorful metaphors, wise advice, practical guidelines, pithy folk sayings, intellectual verses, subtle phraseologies, and speculative ideas.

Because of its multifaceted character the *I Ching* found important uses in a variety of ways. One of the earliest was a reference manual for prophecies. A person interested in his future fortunes would follow standard ceremonial procedures for coming up with an appropriate number, from one to sixty-four, in answer to his question. The two popular techniques of the day were the sorting of forty-nine yarrow stalks and the tossing of three coins. He then looked up the oracular message in the corresponding section of the text.

It is to be noted that no prophet, priest, or oracle is required in the exercise. The person approached the *I Ching* not for the advice of a human intermediary but for the sense of the universal movement itself. He attempted to call forth, through the medium of the yarrow stalks or coins, the hexagram pointing out the appropriate direction for his behavior. The pronounced prophecy is a direct response to a question addressed to the universe itself. Since no human intervention is involved, the principal question concerning the validity of the prophecy is the correspondence mechanism between the seeker's future situation and the issuance of the correct hexagram.

[4]

The Chinese themselves have never attempted to explain in the scientific sense how this correspondence takes place. They take it for granted that everything in the universe is interrelated, that there are general trends and cycles, and that universal assimilation of minor perturbances results in harmonious equilibrium. It has been said that "if I move my hand to the right, everything in the universe also moves." So when a question is ceremoniously posed, the universe responds. It is only natural to do so.

At any given moment, everything fits into the particular pattern of the moment. The fate of the seeker is thus inextricably bound with the cosmic interplay of the yin and the yang. If the suppliant is unfeigned, the *I Ching* will inform him as to the human situation in which he will find himself, through the medium of the ritual stalks or coins. The *I Ching* further assures him that fate is not an awesome fixedness. Considerable latitude exists for personal accommodation and interstitial flexibility. The predictions are therefore accompanied with useful advice regarding proper responses to the auguries on the part of the subject.

The divinational aspects of the *I Ching* do not concern us in this book. They are mentioned purely for historical background. What is of immediate interest is the other equally common usage. Since the sixty-four hexagrams and their supporting literature constitute a comprehensive description of human sentiments and motivations, the text also became a valuable synopsis for meditations on human relationships. It formed the basis of statecraft for many a prime minister of earlier dynasties. It provided the precepts for success and tranquillity. It became a much consulted manual on ethics. It was the source of many proverbs that have guided the lives of the Chinese from the earliest times to this very day.

The directness of the *I Ching's* application to modern man, as well as the universality of its ideas, is indicated by the wide assortment of worldwide quotations used in this book to illustrate its contents.

The prime point to bear in mind in the use of the *I Ching* as a guide to one's dealings with his fellow men is the philosophy forming the basis for its

[5]

counsel. Its central emphasis is on the intuitive grasping of the totality. Specific facts and figures are not constants to be searched out for their own sakes. The whole is ever in continuous flux. No single constituent is without impact upon the others and vice versa. This is clearly taken into account in the evolution of the meaning of the *T'uan* and its relationships to that of the respective lines of the *Yao*.

Depending upon their respective positions and contexts, the individual lines vary greatly in their contributions to the total message of the hexagram. For example, the first (or bottom) and the fourth lines, the second and fifth, and the third and sixth are interdependent pairs. Maximum reinforcement in a pair is brought about by lines of different quality, that is, one undivided and the other divided. This is exemplified by the hexagram containing a fifth undivided line, representing a king or commander in chief. If the second line in the hexagram happens to be divided, representing a minister or an officer, the over-all prognostication of their joint efforts augurs well.

Certain lines are dominating in character and overshadow the influence of other lines in determining the outcome of the hexagram as a whole. When two or more such lines are present in the same hexagram and all signify good omens, the situation bodes well. But when one symbolizes good and the other evil, discord is in the offing.

As a rule, a given kind of line is more favorably placed in certain positions than others. For example, the first, third, and fifth positions are especially propitious for an undivided line; the second, fourth, and sixth for a divided line. Furthermore, certain positions are dominant over the others. A firm, that is, undivided, line in a dominant position, even though ordinarily favorable for a firm line, may result in overfirmness to the detriment of the over-all judgment of the hexagram.

Just as the individual lines within a hexagram affect each other, so do groups of lines. For example, there are four three-line groups in a hexagram. These are lines 1, 2, 3; 4, 5, 6; 2, 3, 4; and 3, 4, 5. The relative positioning of these constituent trigrams also contributes to the interpretation of the over-all image of

[6]

the hexagram. This may be illustrated by the hexagram made up of the trigram of three undivided lines, representing heaven, as the lower half; and the trigram of three divided lines, representing earth, as the upper half. The arrangement connotes a close union. The earth has a tendency to move downward and heaven upward, so that the two forces are moving toward each other. Indeed, the hexagram is *T'ai* or peace. The reversed positioning of the two trigrams gives rise to the hexagram *P'i* or clogging and stagnation. The latter is the situation of noncooperation, lack of prosperity, and heaven and earth moving away from each other.

Not only do the constituent parts of the hexagrams influence each other, but there is also a correspondence between the hexagrams themselves and the time of nature. The affairs of a given month, for example, are subject to the influence of several hexagrams, one of which is sovereign. The twelve sovereign hexagrams are:

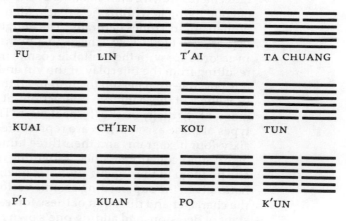

FU   LIN   T'AI   TA CHUANG

KUAI   CH'IEN   KOU   TUN

P'I   KUAN   PO   K'UN

The diagrams depict in a graphic way the waxing and waning of the yin and the yang during the year. The first of the sovereign hexagrams, *Fu*, for example, dominates the eleventh month of the Chinese calendar, the month of the winter solstice. It is the time for reaching the apogee of the yin, or cold, and the initial appearance of the yang, or heat. *Ch'ien* dominates the fourth month, the apogee of the yang. *Kou* is sovereign over the fifth month, during which the summer solstice is followed by rebirth of the yin.

[7]

Finally, *K'un* reigns over the tenth month, just before the rebirth of the yang.

A line of a hexagram, representing a given event in one's life, may be compared to a note in a melody. The note itself possesses at least two potentialities. As an isolated note it exhibits a fixed frequency of a certain number of vibrations per second with a characteristic pitch. But when it is finally expressed in music, an equally important characteristic comes to the fore. It loses its individualism in the orchestral offering. Its pervasiveness becomes significant. The final effect of the note is then determined by its association with other notes and no-notes, with its rendition by particular instruments, with its position relative to the beat rhythm, and many other factors. This is the inherent vitality of music. The hexagrams of the *I Ching* may be looked upon as a comprehensive series of psychic scores covering the spectrum of human responses.

If one has an intuitive appreciation of universal movements during their instants of change, the art of good living is within one's reach. Management of human affairs comes naturally. The enlightenment begins with the *I Ching*'s thesis that humanity moves in accordance with the ineffable cosmic influences, resulting from the interplay of the yin and the yang. It is possible for a person to apprehend the net practical effect of these infinite interactions at any given moment, virtually on the fly, as it were. The prototypes of these assessments are represented by the sixty-four hexagrams and their three hundred and eighty-four constituent lines. Providing the requisite freedom to the organizational elements to react naturally to the superseding cosmic vectors, sensing the character and direction of these forces at the instant of decision, and adding one's own nudge toward selected alternatives permitted by the yin-yang stream will lead to the optimal wholesome balance; one is attuned to nature. Forcing a situation against the gradient circumscribed by the yin-yang cycles engenders crises without resolution; one is antagonistic to nature.

As a person matures to sageness, the explicit knowledge of the formal pronouncements of the hexagrams disappears into his deeper subconscious. Eventually, he becomes oblivious of the very preachings themselves, and the spirit of the *I Ching* merges with his very being. From then on, his actions are no longer heralded by his own learning but evoked by the universal harmony. Being one with nature, he apprehends the all — totally, instantaneously, ineffably. This is the ultimate lesson of the *I Ching*.

Numbers beside the bracketed page number indicate
the hexagram to which the selections on the page refer.

II. Text of the *I Ching*

The sixty-four human situations (hexagrams) of the *I Ching* are presented in the original order of King Wen and the Duke of Chou. The respective constituent events within each evolving pattern *(Yao)* are briefly stated, concluding with the over-all judgment of the human situation as a whole *(T'uan)*. These are printed in italics.

One quotation from world literature is added for each ordinary event of the *Yao* to illustrate some of its principal nuances. Two are provided for a dominating event in the *Yao* and three for the *T'uan*. These literary excerpts are printed in Roman type.

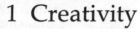

1 Creativity

THE CH'IEN HEXAGRAM

At the outset, the man is unknown, like a dragon lying hidden. The occasion is not yet ripe for his appearance. He is not moved by public opinion and the desire for fame. He bides his time in self-confidence and silence.

Be silent, secret, and conceal
Whate'er you think, whate'er you feel,
Within your soul your dreams should rise
And set like stars that fill the skies
With splendor on their nightly route:
Admire them, scan them, and be mute.

How can a heart at will unfold
Its tale? Can any soul be told
By what it is to live and die?
A thought when spoken is a lie.
The springs men dig for they pollute:
Drink sweet waters and be mute.

Within yourself learn how to live.
Magic that is not fugitive
Lies, a rich treasure, in the mind,
Thoughts that the glare of day will blind
And the wild din without confute:

Heed that low music, and be mute.

FËDOR IVANOVICH TYUTCHEV, RUSSIAN (1803–1873)

A transformation ensues. The man appears among his peers, although not yet in a position of authority. His virtues are displayed, and his goodness becomes known. The prognosis is good for his impact upon the world. It is propitious to see him.

"In Gojam," he [the Prince of Ethiopia] said to me, "every self-respecting man has a war horse except for the priests, and it is wrong that you should be without one." [In the evening the Prince sent d'Abbadie an excellent horse.] . . . My acquaintances now came to congratulate me. I was of course grateful to the Prince for his generosity and courtesy, but as yet I did not understand their meaning, nor the the eagerness of those about me who now adopted a more affectionate familiarity.

In this feudal country, however, men are united by an infinity of ties which would count for nothing in Europe. They live together in a reciprocal dependence and solidarity which they value highly and consider a matter of pride, and which influence all they do. A man freed from all subjection is in their eyes outside the social order; that is how they consider a stranger. In accepting a mule from Dedjasmatch I had already, by the customs of the country, entered into a moral obligation towards him. But in receiving a war horse I became, in the eyes of his men, the man of their master; I was obliged to follow him, and at least for a certain time to share in his fortunes, bad or good. No matter how much good will they might have shown me until now, I had nonetheless been for them like a being apart, like one without any social relationship with them. But from now on I was going to share in their duties and their rights. I was no longer for them a stranger in the old and hostile sense of the word. I became their comrade, their companion.

ARNAULD MICHEL D'ABBADIE, FRENCH (1815–1893)

The man's fame begins to spread. Such periods of transition are always unsettling. There is tension in the air. But the man retains his integrity and avoids being swept along by the masses, which flock to him. He remains active, vigilant, careful, and apprehensive. The prevention of mistakes under perilous circumstances is ever on his mind.

The knight of faith knows . . . that it is beautiful and salutary to be the individual who translates himself into the universal, who edits, as it were, a pure and elegant edition of himself, as free from errors as possible and which everyone can read. . . . But he knows also that higher than this there winds a solitary path, narrow and steep; he knows that it is terrible to be born outside the universal, to walk without meeting a single traveler. . . . The knight of faith knows that to give up oneself for the universal inspires enthusiasm, and that it requires courage, but he also knows that security is to be found in this precisely because it is for the universal. . . . The hero does the deed and finds repose in the universal, the knight of faith is kept in constant tension.

SÖREN AABYE KIERKEGAARD, DANISH (1813–1855)

After a while the man is confronted with a choice for public service in world affairs or solitude in further personal development. Either is appropriate if pursued in virtue and at the proper time.

I find it more agreeable
To contemplate the stars
Than to sign a death warrant.
I find it more agreeable
To listen to the flowers
Whisper "It is he!"
When I walk through the gardens
Than to stroke the rifles
That are to kill those who wish
To take my life.
That is why I shall never —
No, never —
Become a ruler.

VELEMIR VLADIMIROVICH KHLEBNIKOV,
RUSSIAN (1885–1922)

In due time, the man makes his appearance and sets about his work, like the dragon on wing in the heavens.

The fact is that he [André Gide] brings to each a new strength. One of the strongest elements of the influence he exerts is the persuasive and intoxicating encouragement he gives us to persevere, resolutely and happily, each in his own being; and to demand of ourselves the most particular, the most authentic, the best. . . . He has the gift of sharpening each man's critical sense and of increasing his insight, without diminishing his fervor. He does more: he exalts in others — not pride, certainly, and I don't know quite how to put it: an upright vision of self; a confidence, a modest confidence in oneself.
ROGER MARTIN DU GARD, FRENCH (1881–1958)

Confucius visited Lao-tzu, and spoke of charity and duty to one's neighbor.
Lao-tzu said: "The chaff from winnowing will blind a man's eyes so that he cannot tell the points of the compass. Mosquitoes will keep a man awake all night with their biting. And just in the same way this talk of charity and duty to one's neighbor drives me nearly crazy. Sir! Strive to keep the world to its own original simplicity. And as the wind bloweth where it listeth, so let virtue establish itself. Wherefore such undue energy, as though searching for a fugitive with a big drum.

"The snow-goose is white without a daily bath. The raven is black without daily coloring itself. The original simplicity of black and of white is beyond the reach of argument. The vista of fame and reputation is not worthy of enlargement. When the pond dries up and the fishes are left upon dry ground, to moisten them with a little spittle is not to be compared with leaving them in the first instance in their native rivers and lakes."

On returning from this visit to Lao-tzu, Confucius did not speak for three days. A disciple asked him, saying, "Master, when you saw Lao-tzu, in what direction did you admonish him?"

"I saw a dragon," replied Confucius, "a dragon which by convergence showed a body, by radiation became color, and riding upon the clouds of heaven, nourished the two principles of creation. My mouth

[14]1

was agape; I could not shut it. How then do you
think I was going to admonish Lao-tzu?"
CHUANG-TZU, CHINESE (335–275 B.C.)

---

*There is always danger in circumstances of abundance.
The inferior man pushes forward through excessive ambition, thereby losing touch with men of talent and virtue in positions below him. The ruling sage knows when
to display his qualities and to relax, to maintain and to
let go, to win and not to lose.*

Many a clever strategem did he there devise
Until at last he crushed the King of Go
And Kosen could have his revenge.
When by his aid Kosen had regained his realm
And wiped away the shame of Kwaikei,
As minister at Kosen's court,
Duke Toshu could have wielded boundless power,
And gained highest honours and vast possessions.
Yet, since obedient to Heaven's decree
"The wise man should retire
When fame is reached and great deeds done,"
Rowing a boat on the Five Lakes
He found contentment among mists and waters.
KWANZE KOJIRO NOBUMITSU, JAPANESE (1435–1516)

---

*The over-all judgment: creativity comes from awakening
and directing men's higher natures, which originate
in the primal depths of the universe and are appointed
by Heaven. To achieve the high status, the superior
leader displays benevolence, harmony in all that is
right, complete propriety, and perseverance in correct
behavior.*

I Hammurabi, the perfect king,
was not careless (or) neglectful of the blackheaded
   (people)
whom Enlil had presented to me,
(and) whose shepherding Marduk had committed to
   me;
I sought out peaceful regions for them;
I overcame grievous difficulties;
I caused light to rise on them.
With the mighty weapon which Zababa and Inanna
   entrusted to me,
with the insight that Enki allotted to me,
with the ability Marduk gave me,

I rooted out the enemy above and below;
I made an end of war;
I promoted the welfare of the land;
I made the peoples rest in friendly habitations;
I did not let them have anyone to terrorize them.
The great gods called me,
so I became the beneficent shepherd whose scepter is
  righteous;
my benign shadow is spread over my city.
In my bosom I carried the peoples of the land of
  Sumer and Akkad;
they prospered under my protection;
I have governed them in peace;
I have sheltered them in my strength.
In order that the strong might not oppose the weak,
that justice might be dealt the orphan (and) the
  widow,
in Babylon, the city whose head Anum and Enlil
  raised aloft,
in Esagila, the temple whose foundations stand firm
  like heaven and earth,
I wrote my precious words on my stela,
and in the presence of my statue as the king of justice
I set (it) up in order to administer the law of the land,
to prescribe the ordinances of the land,
to give justice to the oppressed.

KING HAMMURABI, BABYLONIAN (1955–1913 B.C.)

Many of you, I fancy, are wondering what on earth
was my purpose in addressing you on the subject of
public safety, as if Athens were in danger or its
affairs in a shaky condition. On the contrary, it has
more than two hundred triremes, it is enjoying peace
on land, and it is supreme at sea.
Furthermore, we have many allies who will aid us
willingly in case of need, and many more who pay
us tribute and take our orders. In these circumstances one might say that it is reasonable for us to
feel confident, convinced that dangers are remote,
and for our enemies to stand in fear and deliberate
on the subject of their own safety.
If you use this line of reasoning, you feel scornful,
I am sure, of what I have come here to tell you, and
you expect to dominate all Hellas by this power of
yours. On the contrary, these are the very reasons,
as it happens, that make me fearful, for in my ex-

perience the cities which think they are in the best condition make the worst plans, those which are the most confident find themselves faced with the greatest multitude of perils.

The cause of this is that neither good nor evil comes to men distinct and unalloyed. Closely allied and concomitant with wealth and princely power is folly, and along with folly comes licentiousness; but with poverty and humility there are joined sobriety and temperance, so that it is hard to decide which of the two portions one would consent to leave as heritage for his own children. From that which is held to be more commonplace we may observe that conditions generally tend in the direction of improvement, while from that which on the surface appears preferable they habitually alter for the worse.
ISOCRATES, GREEK (436–338 B.C.)

Bring me then the plant that points to those bright
Lucidities swirling up from the earth,
And life itself exhaling that central breath!
Bring me the sunflower crazed with the love of light.
EUGENIO MONTALE, ITALIAN (BORN 1896)

2 Responsive Service

THE K'UN HEXAGRAM

At the outset, the man is careful not to overlook the first signs of evil and decay. The threatening dangers are checked before their natural issue and growth.

If an unknown man takes aim at me in the middle of a forest, I am not yet certain that he wishes to kill; must I allow him time to fire in order to be sure of his intent? Is there any reasonable casuist who would deny me the right to forestall the act? But presumption becomes almost equal to certitude if the prince who is about to acquire enormous power has already given evidence of an unbridled pride and ambition. In the imaginary case mentioned above, who would have dared counsel the European states to allow Louis XIV to make such a formidable addition to his power?
EMMERICH VON VATTEL, SWISS (1714–1767)

Nature's way is straight and unerring, foursquare and calm, great and tolerant. Everything is accomplished without the necessity of fabricated purpose. The man's work is equally self-evident. His internal principles are correct; his external acts are righteous; his results are certain.

Sitting quietly, doing nothing,
Spring comes and the grass grows by itself.
ZEN POEM, JAPANESE

You asked me, in brief, what satisfaction I get out of life, and why I go on working. I go on working for the same reason that a hen goes on laying eggs. There is in every living creature an obscure but powerful impulse to active functioning. Life demands to be lived. Inaction, save as a measure of recuperation between bursts of activity, is painful and dangerous to the healthy organism — in fact, it is almost impossible. Only the dying can be really idle.

The precise form of an individual's activity is determined, of course, by the equipment with which he came into the world. In other words, it is determined by this heredity. I do not lay eggs, as a hen does, because I was born without any equipment for it. For the same reason I do not get myself elected to Congress, or play the violon-cello, or teach metaphysics in a college, or work in a steel mill. What I do is simply what lies easiest to my hand. It happens that I was born with an intense and insatiable interest in ideas, and thus like to play with them. It happens also that I was born with rather more than the average facility for putting them into words. In consequence, I am a writer and editor, which is to say, a dealer in them and a concocter of them.

There is very little conscious volition in all this. What I do was ordained by the inscrutable fates, not chosen by me. In my boyhood, yielding to a powerful but still subordinate interest in exact facts, I wanted to be a chemist, and at the same time my poor father tried to make me a business man. At other times, like any other relatively poor man, I have longed to make a lot of money by some easy swindle. But I became a writer all the same, and

shall remain one until the end of the chapter, just
as a cow goes on giving milk all her life, even
though what appears to be her self-interest urges her
to give gin.

HENRY LOUIS MENCKEN, AMERICAN (1880–1956)

*The man wisely keeps his potentialities hidden so that
they can mature without interference. When serving as
an assistant, he remains in the background and lets
glory go to the chief. He manifests himself at the
proper time.*

I have done one braver thing,
  Than all the worthies did;
And yet a braver thence doth spring,
  Which is, to keep that hid.

JOHN DONNE, ENGLISH (1573–1631)

*The man observes the strictest self-restraint and reserve
in dangerous times. In this way he incurs neither injury
from antagonists with designs on pre-eminence nor
obligations to others.*

How do you know I am a diplomat?
By the skilful way you hide your claws.

EDMOND ROSTAND, FRENCH (1868–1918)

*The man does not display his excellence directly. It is
diffused throughout his conduct of affairs.*

In the winter of 1650, I was going into the city of
Chiaochuan from the Little Harbor, accompanied by
a boy carrying a big load of books, tied with a cord
and strengthened with a few pieces of board.

It was toward sunset and the country was covered
with haze. We were about a mile from the city.

"Will we be in time to get into the city before the
gates are closed?" I asked the ferryman.

"You will if you go slowly. But if you run, you will
miss it," replied the ferryman, casting a look at the
boy.

But we walked as fast as possible. About halfway,
the boy fell down. The cord broke and the books fell
on the ground. The boy sat crying. By the time we
had retied the package and reached the city gate, it

was already closed.
I thought of that ferryman. He had wisdom.
CHOU YUNG, CHINESE (1619–1679)

The man is no longer content with his serving role. A bloody contest ensues. Injury to both parties occurs when serving elements attempt to rule.

Who draws his sword against his prince must throw away the scabbard.
JAMES HOWELL, ENGLISH (1594–1666)

The over-all judgment: the mare is commended as the model of docility and strength. The role of the subject is one of unhesitating response and cheerful service to mankind. He requires friends during hours of work but should be alone with his chief when receiving instructions and reporting achievements.

What tormented Ivan Ilych most was the deception, the lie, which for some reason they all accepted, that he was not dying, but was simply ill, and that he only need keep quiet and undergo a treatment and then something very good will result. He however knew that do what they would nothing would come of it, only still more agonizing suffering and death. This deception tortured him — their not wishing to admit what they all knew and what he knew, but wanting to lie to him concerning his terrible condition, and wishing and forcing him to participate in that lie. Those lies — lies enacted over him on the eve of his death and destined to degrade this awful, solemn act to the level of their visitings, their curtains, their sturgeon for dinner — were a terrible agony for Ivan Ilych. And strangely enough, many times when they were going through their antics over him he had been within a hairbreadth of calling out to them, "Stop lying! You know and I know that I am dying. Then at least stop lying about it!" But he had never had the spirit to do it. The awful, terrible act of his dying was, he could see, reduced by those about him to the level of a casual, unpleasant, and almost indecorous incident (as if someone entered a drawing-room diffusing an unpleasant odor) and this was done by that very decorum which he had served all his life long. He saw that no one felt for him, because no one even wished to grasp his position. Only Gerasim recognized it and pitied him. And so Ivan Ilych felt at ease with him. He felt comforted when Gerasim supported his legs (sometimes all night long) and refused to go to bed saying: "Don't you worry, Ivan Ilych. I'll get sleep enough later on," or when he suddenly became familiar and exclaimed: "If you weren't sick it would be another matter, but as it is, why should I grudge a little trouble?" Gerasim alone did not lie; everything showed that he alone understood the facts of the case and did not consider it necessary to disguise them, but simply felt sorry for his emaciated and enfeebled master. Once when Ivan Ilych was sending him away he even said straight out: "We all of us die, so why should I grudge a little trouble?" — expressing the fact that he did not think his work burdensome, because he was doing it for a dying man and hoped someone would do the same for him when his time came.

COUNT LEO NIKOLAEVICH TOLSTOY, RUSSIAN (1828–1910)

JUST. Do what you will, Major, I remain in your service; I must remain.

MAJOR VON TELLHEIM. With your obstinacy, your insolence, your savage boisterous temper toward all who you think have no business to speak to you, your malicious pranks, your love of revenge ——

JUST. Make me as bad as you will, I shall not think worse of myself than my dog. Last winter I was walking one evening at dusk along the river, when I heard something whine. I stooped down, and reached in the direction whence the sound came, and when I thought I was saving a child, I pulled a dog out of the water. That is well, thought I. The dog followed me; but I am not fond of dogs, so I drove him away — in vain. I whipped him away — in vain. I shut him out of my room at night; he lay before the door. If he came too near me, I kicked him; he yelped, looked up at me, and wagged his tail. I have never yet given him a bit of bread with my own hand; and yet I am the only person whom he will obey, or who dares touch him. He jumps about me, and shows off his tricks to me, without my asking for them. He is an ugly dog, but he is a good animal. If he carries it

on much longer, I shall at last give over hating him.
GOTTHOLD EPHRAIM LESSING, GERMAN (1729–1781)

"And yet," demanded Councillor Barlow . . ."what
great cause is he identified with?"
"He is identified," said the speaker, "with the great
cause of cheering us all up."
ARNOLD BENNETT, ENGLISH (1867–1931)

 # 3 Organizational Growth Pains

THE CHUN HEXAGRAM

*At the outset, the man takes stock of the obstacles. He
does not force his advance. He perseveres on the right
course and acquires the appropriate assistants. He continuously rechecks his bearings, as the confusion is
gradually resolved.*

[The Persians] are accustomed to deliberate on matters of the highest moment when warm with wine;
but whatever they in this situation may determine
is again proposed to them on the morrow, in their
cooler moments, by the person in whose house they
had before assembled. If at this time also it meet
their approbation, it is executed; otherwise it is
rejected. Whatever also they discuss when sober, is
always a second time examined after they have been
drinking.
HERODOTUS, GREEK (FIFTH CENTURY B.C.)

We must let you know, that there was a friendship
established by our and your grandfathers; and a
mutual council fire was kindled. In this friendship
all those then under the ground, who had not yet
obtained eyes or faces were included; and it was then
mutually promised to tell the same to their children
and children's children. But so many great men of
your nation have died in so short a time, that none
but youths are left; and this makes us afraid, lest that
treaty, so solemnly established by your ancestors,
should be forgotten by you. We therefore now come
to remind you of it, and renew it; we rekindle the old
fire, and put on fresh fuel.
SCARROOYADY, AMERICAN INDIAN
(EIGHTEENTH CENTURY)

Progress is further inhibited. Someone suddenly appears who is mistaken for a robber at first but actually turns out friendly. His offer of help is not to be accepted. Not being from the right quarter, it may entail undesirable obligations. Things will resume their regular course at the proper time.

"How are you, Hachi? We heard you weren't well and we thought you might be lonely, so we have come to keep you company tonight. Is there anything you would like to eat? Just say the word, and we'll make it for you."

"That's very good of you. A bachelor is pretty helpless when he's ill in bed. Please stay the night and enjoy yourselves."

"Righto, we will. If you want some medicine, or hot water, just tell us."

During the evening the visitors talked and drank sake, and as time went on they lay down one after another and fell asleep. When the sick man awoke he asked for a cup of tea or some hot water, but none of them could he bring out of their stupor. He had to crawl out of bed himself, and then one of them woke and said, "Hey, Hachi, what are you up to?" "Nothing," he said, "I only want some tea," creeping towards the kettle. Then his friend said, "I say, pour me a cup of tea, too, won't you, while you are about it?"

JUPPENSHA IKKU, JAPANESE (1775–1831)

The man wanders aimlessly without adequate guidance, like a hunter without a forester. The superior man knows when going forward will cause regret. He gives up the senseless chase and avoids eventual disgrace.

. . . For me everything disintegrated into parts, these parts again into parts; no longer would anything let itself be encompassed by one idea. Single words floated around me; they congealed into eyes which stared at me and into which I was forced to stare back — whirlpool which gave me vertigo and, reeling incessantly, led me into the void.

HUGO VON HOFMANNSTHAL, AUSTRIAN (1874–1929)

The man lacks sufficient power to discharge his responsibilities. He is like a chariot without a horse. But op-

portunity for help arises. This should be accepted even in the face of self-abnegation.

For more than twenty years, thou knowest well, sir,
'Tis we two that have swayed the Emperor's mind.
Between us he divides his heart and power,
And we dictate the orders that he gives.
To rob thee of the station which thou holdest,
Chagrined and desperate I have oft conspired;
And thou, impelled against me by like envy, —
Thou has assailed my favor and my life.
I feared thee only; thou didst fear me only;
And since we needs must now speak honestly,
It was with reason that, jealous of each other,
Thou fearedest my power and that I feared thine, —
For each of us, appraising well his rival
Quaked lest the other should o'erthrow his fortunes,
Alike assured, fain to destroy each other,
That one of us sufficed to rule the Empire.
    Oft, when our strife was ready to subside,
The Emperor has been careful to maintain it.
Our quarrel hath served him better than our zeal;
Each of us was a faithful minister,
Whose eyes, fixed on a single enemy,
Would keep him ever constant in his duty;
And thus, so long as lived our mutual hatred,
The Emperor has enjoyed the fruit of it.
    It needs must end; the time for that has come.
Thou knowest how matters stand, sir, in this Court:
That the Emperor, nearly two months ago,
By marrying Irene, assumed new ties;
That from his hapless son he snatched this princess,
Breaking the bonds their plighted troth had formed.
To wrath now Andronicus gives his soul up,
And if he spares his father in his rage,
If he respects him still, ah! do not doubt
That he will let its lightnings fall on us.
He thinks that his sad fate was our contrivance;
He thinks that in resolving on a second
Marriage and forming thus a tie that wronged him,
The Emperor followed thy advice and mine.
We stand in equal peril, have fears in common.
Let us unite our hearts, sir, and our fortunes;
And let us hasten to build for our defense
Bulwarks which Andronicus cannot shatter.

JEAN GALBERT DE CAMPISTRON, FRENCH (1656–1723)

*The man attains a position of authority. Premature ex-
pressions of good intentions lead to damaging misinter-
pretations. Time is required for stepwise maturation and
acquisition of general confidence. Consummation cannot
be forced.*

I have played the fool, the gross fool, to believe
The bosom of a friend will hold a secret
Mine own could not contain.
PHILIP MASSINGER, ENGLISH (1583–1640)

A hunter goes into the bush. He finds an old human
skull. The hunter says: "What brought you here?"
The skull answers: "Talking brought me here." The
hunter runs off. He runs to the king. He tells the king:
"I found a dry human skull in the bush. It asks how
its father and mother are."
The king says: "Never since my mother bore me have
I heard that a dead skull can speak." The king sum-
mons the Alkali, the Saba, and the Degi and asks
them if they have ever heard the like. None of the
wise men has heard the like and they decide to send
guards out with the hunter into the bush to find out
if his story is true and, if so, to learn the reason for
it. The guards accompany the hunter into the bush
with the order to kill him on the spot should he have
lied. The guards and the hunter come to the skull.
The hunter addresses the skull: "Skull, speak." The
skull is silent. The hunter asks as before: "What
brought you here?" The skull does not answer. The
whole day long the hunter begs the skull to speak,
but it does not answer. In the evening the guards tell
the hunter to make the skull speak, and when he
cannot they kill him in accordance with the king's
command. When the guards are gone the skull opens
its jaws and asks the dead hunter's head: "What
brought you here?" The dead hunter's head replies:
"Talking brought me here!"
NIGERIAN FOLK TALE

---

*The man fails to overcome the initial difficulties and
despair.*

[This] conclusion . . . will, I regret to think, be highly
distasteful to many. But there can hardly be a doubt
that we are descended from barbarians. The aston-
[25]3

ishment which I felt on first seeing a party of Fuegians on a wild and broken shore will never be forgotten by me, for the reflections at once rushed into my mind — such were our ancestors. These men were absolutely naked and bedaubed with paint, their long hair was tangled, their mouths frothed with excitement, and their expression was wild, startled and distrustful. They possessed hardly any arts, and like wild animals lived on what they could catch; they had no government, and were merciless to any one not of their own tribe. He who has seen a savage in his native land will not feel much shame if forced to acknowledge that the blood of some more humble creature flows in his veins. For my own part I would as soon be descended from that heroic little monkey who braved his dreaded enemy in order to save the life of his keeper, or from that old baboon, who, descending from the mountains, carried away in triumph his young comrade from a crowd of astonished dogs — as from a savage who delights to torture his enemies, offers up bloody sacrifices, practices infanticides without remorse, treats his wives like slaves, knows no decency, and is haunted by the grossest superstitions.

Man may be excused for feeling some pride at having risen, though not through his own exertions, to the very summit of the organic scale; and the fact of his having thus risen, instead of having been aboriginally placed there, may give him hope for a still higher destiny in the distant future. But we are not here concerned with hopes or fears, only with the truth as far as our reason permits us to discover it; and I have given the evidence to the best of my ability. We must, however, acknowledge, as it seems to me, that man, with all his noble qualities, with sympathy which feels for the most debased, with benevolence which extends not only to other men but to the humblest creature, with his godlike intellect which has penetrated into the movements and constitution of the solar system — with all these exalted powers — man still bears in his bodily frame the indelible stamp of his lowly origin.

CHARLES ROBERT DARWIN, ENGLISH (1809–1882)

The over-all judgment: the rise of the state out of disorder is marked by struggles. The period of growth requires caution against premature moves and perseverance to overcome attendant obstacles and confusion. Helpers need be appointed.

The incessant bickering and contests between chief and jealous kinsmen; the weak central power; the divided jurisdictions; the obstinacy with which a man of high birth insists on the proper punctilio to be reciprocated between himself and his Chief — all these are tokens of a free society in the rough.

SIR ALFRED COMYN LYALL, ENGLISH (1835–1911)

ANDROMACHE. Doesn't it ever tire you to see and prophesy only disasters?
CASSANDRA. I see nothing. I prophesy nothing. All I ever do is to take account of two great stupidities: the stupidities of men, and the wild stupidity of the elements.

JEAN GIRAUDOUX, FRENCH (1882–1944)

Nothing can be rushed. Things must grow, they must grow upward, and if the time should ever come for the great work — then so much the better.

We must go on searching.

We have found parts, but not the whole!

We still lack the ultimate strength for: there is no people to sustain us.

But we are looking for a people. We began over there in the Bauhaus. We began with a community to which each one of us gave what we had.

More we cannot do.

PAUL KLEE, SWISS (1879–1940)

---

4 Acquiring Experience

THE MÊNG HEXAGRAM

At the outset, the ignorant youth is being disciplined for the seriousness of life. Care should be exercised against attempts at rigid regimentation of the mind.

   Pretended,
And the cause is manifest.
When she was a girl she showed
[27]4

Candor, and excellent qualities;
But you, wishing to see
Greater perfection in her,
Harshly and inflexibly set out
To correct her slightest faults;
You shouted at her; she did
Nothing that suited you.
Your severity produced in her
Only dissimulation, and cunning;
Your oppression, a greater desire
For freedom. The frequency
Of punishment produced fear,
And lacking true virtues,
Virtues that you were unable
To inspire in her, she
Pretended to possess them.
You made her hypocritical and false;
And as soon as she acquired skill
In deceiving her father,
She deceived him so completely
That only when she had the most vices
Did he believe she was perfect.
LEANDRO FERNÁNDEZ DE MORATÍN,
SPANISH (1760–1828)

The man is tolerant of the ignorant and kind to women. He resembles an official capable of assuming the delegated duties of a prince in directing a large social body with inner strength and outward reserve.

Polly bent over him and wiped the moisture from his face, "Oh, I'm so glad it's over!" she broke out impulsively. "It just broke my heart to see you suffer so, Father."
Rosicky motioned her to sit down on the chair where the tea-kettle had been, and looked up at her with that lively affectionate gleam in his eyes. "You was awful good to me, I won't never forgit dat. I hate it to be sick on you like dis. Down at de barn I say to myself, dat young girl ain't had much experience in sickness, I don't want to scare her, an' maybe she's got a baby comin' or somet'ing."
Polly took his hand. He was looking at her so intently and affectionately and confidingly; his eyes seemed to caress her face, to regard it with pleasure. She frowned with her funny streaks of eyebrows, and

then smiled back at him.

"I guess maybe there is something of that kind going to happen. But I haven't told anyone yet, not my mother or Rudolph. You'll be the first to know."

His hands pressed hers. She noticed that it was warm again. The twinkle in his yellow-brown eyes seemed to come nearer.

"I like mighty well to see dat little child, Polly," was all he said. Then he closed his eyes and lay half-smiling. But Polly sat still, thinking hard. She had a sudden feeling that nobody in the world, not her mother, not Rudolph, or anyone, really loved her as much as old Rosicky did. It perplexed her. She sat frowning and trying to puzzle it out. It was as if Rosicky had a special gift for loving people, some-thing that was like an ear for music or an eye for colour. It was quiet, unobtrusive; it was merely there. You saw it in his eyes, — perhaps that was why they were merry. You felt it in his hands, too. As he dropped off to sleep, she sat holding his warm, broad flexible brown hand. She had never seen another in the least like it. She wondered if it wasn't a kind of gypsy hand, it was so alive and quick and light in its communications, — very strange in a farmer. Nearly all the farmers she knew had huge lumps of fists, like mauls, or they were knotty and bony and uncomfortable-looking, with stiff fingers. But Rosicky's was like quicksilver, flexible, muscular, about the colour of a pale cigar, with deep, deep creases across the palm. It wasn't nervous, it wasn't a stupid lump; it was a warm brown human hand, with some cleverness in it, a great deal of generosity, and something else which Polly could only call "gypsy-like," — something nimble and lively and sure, in the way that animals are.

Polly remembered that hour long afterwards, it had been like an awakening to her. It seemed to her that she had never learned so much about life from any-thing as from old Rosicky's hand. It brought her to herself; it communicated some direct and untrans-latable message.

WILLA SIBERT CATHER, AMERICAN (1873–1947)

CHANDRAGUPTA. And why did they desert me?
CHANAKYA. Bhadrabhata and Purushadatta are notor-ious whorers and drinkers; the first preferred women

[29]4

to elephants, the second liked wine more than horses; they were dismissed and given a subsistence allowance, which it seems they didn't appreciate. They are now in charge of Malayaketu's elephants and horses. Dingarata and Balagupta were after more money—and it seems Malayaketu would pay them better than Your Majesty. Your boyhood servant couldn't stand the strain of too many favors from you; he feared a slump, and Malayaketu seems to have assured him a more balanced regimen. Bhagurayana first frightened Malayaketu out of here by saying I had assassinated Malayaketu's father, then fell under the influence of Chandanadasa and his conspirators, then realized things were too hot for him here; he scuttled to safety with Malayaketu. Malayaketu made him his minister out of gratitude. Rohitaksha and Vijayavarman were jealous; they couldn't endure the granting of favors to Your Majesty's relatives, and they fled.

CHANDRAGUPTA. If you knew all this beforehand, why didn't you take appropriate measures?

CHANAKYA. No action was possible under the circumstances.

CHANDRAGUPTA. You mean you were either weak or had a deeper plan.

CHANAKYA. A minister cannot afford to be weak, Your Majesty.

CHANDRAGUPTA. What was the plan then?

CHANAKYA. A plan that must be not only heard but understood and appreciated. There are only two ways to deal with dissatisfied officials—humor them or punish them. Humoring Bhadrabhata and Purushadatta was out of question: it would have meant reinstating them in positions of dangerous authority. If the elephants and horses fall into unreliable hands, the defense of the kingdom becomes shaky. Humoring Dingarata and Balagupta would have been an even greater headache; their voluptuous greed is so great that giving them a whole kingdom wouldn't satisfy them. Rajasena and Bhagurayana were so fearful of losing all they had that there was no point in humoring *them,* and the same went for the jealous Rohitaksha and Vijayavarman. As for the other alternative—punishing them—I didn't think it advisable. We have just defeated the Nandas, the people are still uneasy—why stir up more trouble by punishing prominent men? Besides, Malayaketu, with Rakshasa's help, is poised to attack us; the Mleccha army is with him, he is infuriated with the assassination of his father. I thought it best, Your Majesty, to let these men escape. . . .

CHANDRAGUPTA. . . . why weren't effective measures taken to prevent Malayaketu from escaping and making trouble for us now?

CHANAKYA. There are two alternatives, Your Majesty. We could have put him in prison; or we could have honored our promise to give him half the kingdom. If we imprison him, think what the people would suspect—first we murder the father, then we imprison the son. We would look like barbarians. But if we give him half the kingdom, we destroy the very purpose of assassinating Parvataka, for the assassination of Parvataka was ordered with the aim of getting his kingdom. So I let Malayaketu escape.

CHANDRAGUPTA. It sounds logical. But why did you let Rakshasa escape?

CHANAKYA. The people respect him. They admire his loyalty and devotion to Nanda. Had he stayed in the city, in prison or out, plots galore would have cropped up, money would have poured in, cells and conspiracies would have festered. Now he can sting us only from the outside, and I can handle him more comfortably.

CHANDRAGUPTA. Couldn't a brave show of force have settled him?

CHANAKYA. Force against a demon like Rakshasa? Yes, and how many men would we lose before we secured him? Besides, there would be no certainty—he might prefer suicide to falling into our hands. And then the loss would be all ours, a first-class brain and a loyal heart gone forever. No, Your Majesty, he has to be tamed as a wild elephant is tamed—with gentle cunning.

VISHAKHADATTA, INDIAN (NINTH CENTURY)

The man guards against the loss of his individuality. He should not imitate persons of senior rank or act like a flippant girl throwing herself at a handsome man. Neither should he accept overtures from such subordinates.

The policy begun by Louis in 1661 was well established and had borne fruit by the time Versailles became the seat of government. Throughout France there was not a single estate of any size the proprietor of which was not at court. The new hotels of the nobility lined the streets near the royal palace, and their owners filled its salons and formed each day a cortège for the king. . . . Each morning when the king went to mass, an obsequious nobility awaited him in the gallery of Versailles. They were all there; all, at least, whose purses were not empty. "Sire," said M. de Verdes to Louis XIV, "away from Your Majesty, one is not only miserable but ridiculous."

But such concentration imposed a heavy load upon the sovereign; it was the price he had to pay for his absolutism. As Taine has well said, "A nobility for useful purposes is not transformed with impunity into a nobility for ornament. . . . The king is expected to keep the entire aristocracy busy, consequently to make a display of himself, to pay back with his own person at all hours. It is the life of an actor who is on the stage the entire day."

The nobility had their price to pay. The cost of living at court ate up their incomes; their continued absence from their estates made their revenues diminish, left their châteaux neglected, and much of their land uncultivated; high play plunged them into debt. A few years brought the inevitable, and they became dependent on the royal bounty. When they looked for support to the salaries attached to their posts at court, and to the king's pensions, the last traces of their independence vanished.

JAMES E. FARMER, AMERICAN (1867–1915)

Clinging to folly inevitably means humiliation. The wise teacher may have to instruct by letting the subject experience the consequences of his errors.

A man after fourteen years of hard asceticism in a lonely forest obtained at last the power of walking over the waters. Overjoyed at this acquisition, he went to his guru, and told him of his grand feat. At this the master replied, "My poor boy, what thou hast accomplished after fourteen years' arduous labor, ordinary men do the same by paying a penny

to the boatman."
SRI RĀMAKRISHNA, INDIAN (1834–1886)

---

*The unassuming youth seeking instruction with humility
gains good fortune.*

It was a fine night on deck, clear, with bright stars
and a faint, quivering circle of the northern lights.
The night was cool, without a breath of wind.
The ship, with her own small lights, was like an
insignificant fragment of a distant world anchored
there in space. The mate took out his pipe and
tinderbox. There was a flash of spark as he expertly
hit the flint against the steel, and then the tinder
glowed.

"Johnny March," he said, "I've kind of got to like
you. Now you listen to what I say. This kind of
spark's all right, but not the kind you were striking
in the cabin. You leave the old man be. He's as good
a master as there is, and he's honest with the owners
and that's all we have to care for. I've sailed with
Griggs before. I don't need to tell you that a master's
king aboard his ship, and you know it makes 'em
queer. I've never seen a skipper yet who liked to be
crossed. You better leave him be."

"Yes sir," said John March.

"And listen, Johnny," the mate said, "the islands are
a fine place. You'll like the islands. The islands are
like heaven, pretty near. The captain will take you
ashore, of course, to make the bargain. You'll see
plenty of funny sights, but keep your mouth shut,
Johnny, except to say 'Yessir', to the captain. We've
got a long way yet to go."

"Yes sir," said John March.

"That's right," said Sprague, "that's right. I like a
tight-lipped boy."

JOHN PHILLIPS MARQUAND, AMERICAN (1893–1960)

"Bring hither a fig from there." "Here it is, sir."
"Break it." "It is broken, sir." "What do you see
there?" "These extremely fine seeds, sir." "Of these,
please break one." "It is broken, sir." "What do you
see there?" "Nothing at all, sir." Then he said to
Shvetaketu: "Verily, my dear, that subtle essence
which you do not perceive—from that very essence,
indeed, my dear, does this great fig tree thus arise.

[33]4

Believe me, my dear, that which is the subtle essence
—this whole world has that essence for its Self;
that is the Real; that is the Self; that art thou,
Shvetaketu."

"Still further may the venerable sir instruct me." "So
be it, my dear," said he.

"Having put this salt in the water, come to me in the
morning." He did so. Then the father said to him:
"That salt which you put in the water last evening—
please bring it hither." Even having looked for it, he
did not find it for it was completely dissolved.
"Please take a sip of water from this end," said the
father. "How is it?" "Salt." "Take a sip from the
middle," said he. "How is it?" "Salt." "Take a sip
from that end," said he. "How is it?" "Salt." "Throw
it away and come to me." Shvetaketu did so thinking
to himself: "That salt, though unperceived, still
persists in the water." Then Āruni said to him:
"Verily, my dear, you do not perceive Being in this
world; but it is, indeed, here only: That which is the
subtle essence—this whole world has that essence
for its Self. That is the Real. That is the Self. That art
thou, Shvetaketu."

CHĀNDOGYA UPANISAD, INDIAN (SIXTH CENTURY B.C.)

The man inflicts penalties not in anger but only as a
preventive against unreasonable excesses.

Hideyoshi was never a man of war. His real genius
was that of statesman. When the need could be met
only by arms, he could be swift and violent; efficient
in this as in other things. Better, however, he loved
the brilliant and intricate intellectual combinations
by which matters could be adjusted without bloodshed, for above all things he admired order and
beauty and the graces of life. Tradition treasures a
tale that reveals the real nature of the man:
After the last and greatest of his battles, having
finally overcome all really serious opposition, he
rode a short way from the field across which he had
furiously and successfully led his forces. Dismount-
ing from his wearied horse he sat himself down in
his armour upon the grass, calmly announcing to
his immediate attendants that he desired to divert
himself by making a flower-arrangement. The astonished retainers explained that there were none of the

appurtenances at hand for the practice of that delicate art. Hideyoshi, pointing out that a horse bucket was close at hand filled with water, directed them to take from his horse's mouth the bit, one ring of which he hung over the single handle of the bucket and then proceeded with his still bloody sword to cut off various grasses and wild flowers which bloomed near his seat. Using the dependent part of the bit as a flower-holder, he spent an hour in composing one of those subtle and delicate combinations of blossoms and foliage which his people have always so much loved. . . .

. . . the underlying purpose of the flower-arrangement is to purify and abstract the mind from all violence and material consideration, to calm the spirit and cleanse it of evil. Hideyoshi explained that he knew he should have to judge and deal with those he had conquered, and that after he had spent so many violent hours in combat, he felt himself in no condition to be either kind or wise until he had entirely cooled the fury and disorder of his emotions by exercising this delicate and exquisite art.
ELIZABETH BISLAND, AMERICAN (1861–1929)

The over-all judgment: there is an inevitability about the progress of youth. The older generation thinks it understands youth, but it does not. Despite the perilous conditions surrounding the inexperienced stage of the young man's life and the intermittent halting of his advances, success will be achieved. Like water overflowing in time, all pitfalls are eventually overcome.

Youth is sharp-sighted and incorruptible. It hangs together and presents an impenetrable front against grown-ups. It is not sentimental, one may approach to it, but one cannot enter into it. Who has been evicted from that paradise can never get back. There is a law of the years. Educationalists who think they can understand the young are enthusiasts. Youth does not want to be understood; it wants to be let alone. It preserves itself immune against the insidious bacillus of being understood. The grown-up who would approach it too importunately is as ridiculous in its eyes as if it had put on children's clothes. We may feel with youth, but youth does not feel with us.

[35]4

That is its salvation.
ERICH MARIA REMARQUE, GERMAN (BORN 1898)

Gay hope is theirs by fancy fed,
    Less pleasing when possest;
The tear forgot as soon as shed,
    The sunshine of the breast:
Theirs buxom health of rosy hue,
Wild wit, invention ever-new,
And lively cheer of vigour born;
The thoughtless day, the easy night,
The spirits pure, the slumbers light
    The fly th' approach of morn.

Alas, regardless of their doom,
    The little victims play!
No sense have they of ills to come,
    Nor care beyond to-day:
Yet see how all around 'em wait
The Ministers of human fate
And black Misfortune's baleful train!
Ah, show them where in ambush stand
To seize their prey, the murderous band!
    Ah, tell them, they are men!

These shall the fury Passions tear,
    The vultures of the mind,
Disdainful Anger, pallid Fear,
    And Shame that sculks behind;
Or pineing Love shall waste their youth,
Or Jealousy with rankling tooth,
That inly gnaws the secret heart,
And Envy wan, and faded Care,
Grim-visag'd comfortless Despair,
    And Sorrow's piercing dart.

Ambition this shall tempt to rise,
    Then whirl the wretch from high,
To bitter Scorn a sacrifice,
    And grinning Infamy.
The stings of Falsehood those shall try
And hard Unkindness' alter'd eye,
That mocks the tear it forc'd to flow;
And keen Remorse with blood defil'd,
And moody Madness laughing wild
    Amid severest woe.

[36]4

Lo, in the vale of years beneath
   A griesly troop are seen,
The painful family of Death,
   More hideous than their Queen:
This racks the joints, this fires the veins,
That every labouring sinew strains,
Those in the deeper vitals rage:
Lo, Poverty, to fill the band,
That numbs the soul with icy hand,
   And slow-consuming Age.

To each his suff'rings: all are men,
   Condemn'd alike to groan;
The tender for another's pain,
   Th' unfeeling for his own.
Yet, ah! why should they know their fate,
Since sorrow never comes too late,
And happiness too swiftly flies?
Thought would destroy their paradise.
No more; where ignorance is bliss
   'Tis folly to be wise.

THOMAS GRAY, ENGLISH (1716–1771)

The soldiers in the castle, seeing our men come on
them with great fury, did all they could to defend
themselves, and killed and wounded many of our
soldiers with pikes, arquebuses, and stones, whereby
the surgeons had all their work cut out for them.
Now I was at this time a fresh-water soldier; I had
not yet seen wounds made by gunshot at the first
dressing. It is true I had read in John de Vigo, first
book, *Of Wounds in General*, eighth chapter, that
wounds made by firearms partake of venomosity, by
reason of the powder; and for their cure he bids you
cauterize them with oil of elders scalding hot, mixed
with a little treacle. And to make no mistake, before
I would use the said oil, knowing this was to bring
great pain to the patient, I asked first before I applied
it, what the other surgeons did for the first dressing;
which was to put the said oil, boiling well, into the
wounds, with tents and setons; wherefore I took
courage to do as they did. At last my oil ran short,
and I was forced instead thereof to apply a digestive
made of the yolk of eggs, oil of roses, and turpentine.
In the night I could not sleep in quiet, fearing some
default in not cauterizing, that I should find the

wounded to whom I had not used the said oil dead from the poison of their wounds; which made me rise very early to visit them, where beyond my expectation I found that those to whom I had applied my digestive medicant had but little pain, and their wounds without inflammation or swelling, having rested fairly well that night; the others, to whom the boiling oil was used, I found feverish, with great pain and swelling about the edges of their wounds. Then I resolved never more to burn thus cruelly poor men with gunshot wounds.

AMBROISE PARÉ, FRENCH (1517–1590)

5 Biding One's Time

THE HSÜ HEXAGRAM

At the outset, there is a suggestion of danger. The man remains calm, concerns himself only with the immediate task at hand, and does not move to counteract remote threats.

HENRI DE CATT. Verses, Sire! And tomorrow Your Majesty will battle!

FREDERICK THE GREAT. Well, what is there so extraordinary in that? Can I not, like anybody else, employ myself on verses and amuse myself by making some, perhaps pretty bad ones? I have given my mind the whole day to the capital affair, which I have turned about in all ways. My plan is made, my decision taken. I may well be permitted, it seems to me, to scribble and rhyme just like anybody else.

DE CATT. Nobody, Sire, will dispute that permission. I say merely that in so critical a moment as must be the moment of giving battle, it is very difficult to find any inclination to versify.

FREDERICK. When you have been accustomed for a long time, as I have been, to all this brawl of battle, you will not think it so strange that, on the eve of the day on which a battle is to be fought, anyone should amuse himself as I am doing. Besides, sir, I am not composing; I am endeavoring to correct an author and to do better than he, if it is possible. When you left me today, I wished to read Rousseau's "Ode to Fortune," and, in opening my book, I fell on "Ode to Count de Sinzendorff," two strophes of which

seemed to me rather ill-written. A moment's patience, sir. I have the last strophe to look over and rewrite. I shall soon be done, and I will show you my fine work. *(Frederick writes.)* . . . Here it is; perhaps, for a day of fatigue as this has been, you will find that the poet has again come off well with his great work.
DE CATT. Yes, Sire, Your Majesty has come off well in such a moment. I doubt whether the generals whom you have and will have to combat ever write verses on the eve of a battle.
FREDERICK. I have a better opinion of them than you have. They would write verses just as I do, if they knew how. This little exercise refreshes your head and your ideas, and I have great need for both my head and my ideas to be fresh.
KING FREDERICK THE GREAT, PRUSSIAN (1712–1786)

The danger approaches with disagreements and unrest. The man remains self-controlled and does not respond to slander.

If any man rail at thee and insult thee, answer him not. Instead be like one who cannot be moved. Even thus shalt thou conquer him. For all who behold shall declare that he who, in spite of provocation, holdeth his tongue is mightier than he who provoketh. So shalt thou be respected by those who have wisdom.
PHARAOH PTAHHOTEP, EGYPTIAN (TWENTY-SEVENTH CENTURY B.C.)

The man attempts a complex undertaking without sufficient capacity for success in one try. He finds himself mired in the intricacies, thereby inviting enemies onto the scene. Caution is required.

Since the devil never sleeps, it happened that one night a big fight got under way in one of the many gambling houses which, contrary to the local ordinances and decrees, abounded in Quintu Mayu Street. A gambler inexperienced at sleight of hand, who wasn't slick enough to get away with the trick, had let three dice fall on a bet with high stakes, when some grouch drew a knife and nailed his hand to the table.
RICARDO PALMA, PERUVIAN (1833–1919)

The man enters the scene of strife and danger in a life-and-death struggle. He accommodates himself to fate, stands fast, and refrains from aggravating the problem.

To endure is greater than to dare; to tire out hostile fortune; to be daunted by no difficulty; to keep heart when all have lost it; to go through intrigue spotless; to forego even ambition when the end is gained— who can say this is not greatness?
WILLIAM MAKEPEACE THACKERAY,
ENGLISH (1811–1863)

The man fortifies his reserve strength by enjoying the intervals of peace between crises. At the same time he maintains his orientation to the ultimate goal with optimistic buoyancy.

Delicate clouds roll up and disappear
The sky is so bright that you cannot see the Milky
   Way;
A pure wind blows through the empty heavens,
The rays of the moon are scattered o'er the waves;
Murmur and shadow fade away on quiet sands and
   still waters.
One cup of wine we shall drink together,
Then you shall sing a song;
The lilt of your song is melancholy and the phrases
   full of bitter thoughts.
One cannot listen to the end before the tears fall like
   rain.
The Tung T'ing (lake) stretches away to the sky,
The Chiu I mountain is high;
Crocodiles and dragons come and go, apes and
   vampires cry,
Nine out of ten die before reaching this official post.
In squalid dark houses we hide ourselves,
When we left our beds we were frightened of snakes,
When we ate we were frightened of poison;
The summer air from the sea was damp and pesti-
   ferous,
The smells rank and rancid.
But there came a day when before the yamen they
   beat the big drum;
A new emperor had succeeded to the sacred line
And had elevated loyal servants.
[40]5

An amnesty travels a thousand miles in a single day;
Those under sentence of death need not die,
The exiled ones were recalled,
The banished could return home.
All strains and impurities were to be things of the
  past.
The new emperor opens a bright new page,
Our senior officials suggest our names, his seniors
  suppress them;
Frustrated, what is left for us but to move to yet more
  barbaric surroundings?
Our present post is small and not to be spoken of,
How can we avoid being trampled and buffeted as
  we lie in the dust?
Most of our contemporaries follow the road back to
  official success,
But that road is dark and dangerous and hard to
  attain.
Your song—come stop it,
Listen to my song.
My sentiments are very different from yours,
Of all the full moons in the year tonight's is the
  brightest.
Man from birth is governed by fate, and nothing
  else,
If you have wine and do not drink it
Will tomorrow be any the better?

HAN YÜ, CHINESE (768–824)

May I say how disappointed I am at some of the talk
in some of the papers—this very gloomy talk, with
petulant letters saying, "What, after all, have we to
celebrate?" Surely right honourable and honourable
Members on this side of the House, at least, will
agree that if, in 1951, we have survived five years of
war, and five years of His Majesty's Government,
then even they will have something they will like
to celebrate, to dance and sing about. "Faith," I think
Mr. G. K. Chesterton said, "is the capacity to believe
in that which is demonstrably untrue." If that is the
only sort of confidence we have in our future, then
let us have that.
I think there are other causes. I am no historian; but
if the House will bear with me for one more minute,
I will present another historical reason why we
should celebrate, not only with the main exhibition,

but with the arrangements set out in this bill. After all, we are emerging from the murky forties into the fifties, and it has been pointed out to me by a better historian than myself that the forties have always been a pretty wretched sort of decade. A hundred years ago there were the Hungry Forties, with the whole of Europe in chaos and revolution, with *The Communist Manifesto,* with crowned heads falling everywhere and rulers taking refuge in this island, and with the Chartists massing on Kennington Common. However, after that period we emerged into what was almost the most prosperous, happy period in this country's history.

In the 1740's, I think, we were at war with France, Spain, and Scotland. A predecessor of mine in this House, Sir Charles Oman, records that when Charles Edward arrived at Derby, "Panic prevailed in London, the King's plate had been sent on shipboard, the Bank of England had paid away every guinea of its reserves, and the citizens of London were fully persuaded that they would be attacked next day by ten thousand wild Scottish clansmen."

In the 1640's there was civil war and King Charles I had his head cut off. In the 1540's, I see, "The time was a very evil one for England." King Henry VIII was marrying too many women, executing too many men, and persecuting everybody else. I need hardly add that we were at war with Scotland, and France as well; but the historian adds, rather woundingly, that "the French War was far more dangerous." In the 1440's we had a weak king, King Henry VI. We were at war with France, and we were gradually losing everything King Henry V had won. . . . In the 1340's we were at war with France, and the Scots invaded the north of England. Also, a small detail, there was the Black Death. In the 1240's we invaded France. In the 1140's we were ruled by an unpleasant woman called Matilda and there was civil war all the time. In the 1040's we were invaded by the Danes.

Now, whatever else may be laid at the door of His Majesty's Government, we are not now at war with France or Scotland or even Denmark, and I do not think that we shall be in 1951; and my hope is that in some way we shall emerge from the 1940's into the fifties in such condition that we shall be justified in celebrating. But if not, even if we are going down, it is not the habit of the British fleet to haul down the ensign when about to begin a doubtful engagement. On the contrary, each ship flies two or three to make sure that one shall be seen. It is in that spirit, I feel, that we ought to go forward with this bold, imaginative, attractive scheme, and show, whether we go up or down, that we can be gracious, gallant, and gay.

SIR ALAN PATRICK HERBERT, ENGLISH (BORN 1890)

The man falls into great complications. Everything looks black. But unexpected help arrives. If he is sensitive to it and accepts it graciously, there will be a happy turn of events.

For fifteen days I struggled to prove that no [mathematical] functions analogous to those I have since called *Fuchsian functions* could exist; I was then very ignorant. Every day I sat down at my work table where I spent an hour or two; I tried a great number of combinations and arrived at no result. One evening, contrary to my custom, I took black coffee; I could not go to sleep; ideas swarmed up in clouds; I sensed them clashing until, to put it so, a pair would hook together to form a stable combination. By morning I had established the existence of a class of Fuchsian functions, those derived from the hypergeometric series. I had only to write up the results, which took me a few hours.

JULES HENRI POINCARÉ, FRENCH (1854–1912)

The over-all judgment: the responses of human beings vary greatly under dangerous circumstances. The strong man advances boldly to meet them head on. The weak man grows agitated. But the superior man stands up to fate, endures resolutely in his inner certainty of final success, and bides his time until the onset of reassuring odds.

When Roland saw the men of France, or dead
Or dying, strewn on every hand, he spake
To Oliver his friend: "God save you, sir,
See you our comrades lying cold in death?
What woe is here for France the beautiful,
Of such men left forlorn! O Charles, great King
And friend, why are you not in Ronceval?
Oliver, comrade, how may we bring word
To Charles the King?" But Oliver spake, and said:

[43]5

"Let be, good friend, I know not. Only this
I know—to yield us would be worse than death."

But Roland answered: "I shall wind my horn,
The King will hear it where he marches down
The strait defiles, and so—I pledge you, friend—
The Franks will turn them back." And Oliver said:
"Shame would it be for you, and lifelong shame
For all your lineage. When I pled with you
To call the King, you would not. Now, alas,
It is too late. The fight is on. If now
You wind your horn, it is not hardihood.
Too late! For both your arms are bathed in blood."
And he replied: "They have dealt winsome blows."
.   .   .   .

And Roland, with a wild and fearful blast
Winded his horn, so that his temples brake
And from his mouth leapt the bright blood. And
    Charles
Heard it, and all his soldiers, as they rode
Down to sweet France through valleys far away.
And the King cried: "It is the horn of Roland!
The Franks are fighting.". . .
.   .   .   .

From Roland's lips flowed blood; his temples brake
With the wild blast and fearful. But the King
And all his soldiers heard it from afar
And the King cried: "The blast is long and strong!"
And Naimon answered: "Ay, for a brave man
Is in distress, is fighting his last fight. . . ."
.   .   .   .

And so the king drew rein, and loud and clear
The clarions rang; the Franks leapt from their pal-
    freys,
And armed themselves with hauberks of fine steel,
With helms and golden-hilted swords, and spears
Astream with pennons white and red and blue;
Then mounted steeds of war, and spurred apace
Through the defiles, and each to the other cried:
"If we but find Count Roland ere he die,
Beside him shall we give good blows." Alas!
To what avail? They will not come in time.
.   .   .   .

And when the King had come to Ronceval
And rode among the dead, he wept, and said

To his chief men: "My lords, rein in your steeds,
For I would fain precede you. Let me find
My nephew Roland ere you follow. Ay—
Years ago, in my vaulted hall at Aix,
Methinks it was a Christmastide—my knights
Were vaunting them of prowess and high deeds
Upon the field of battle, and Roland said
That he should never die in a strange land
Save at the head of all his men, with face
Turned to the foe, and victory in his heart."
He spake, and went before the rest, the space
One throws a spear, and climbed to a high hill.
SONG OF ROLAND, FRENCH (TWELFTH CENTURY)

The precise point at which scales of power turn, like
that of the solstice in either tropic, is imperceptible to
common observation; and, in one case as in the
other, some progress must be made in the new
direction, before the change is perceived. They who
are in the sinking scale, for in the political balance
of power, unlike to all others, the scale that is empty
sinks, and that which is full rises; they who are in the
sinking scale do not easily come off from the habitual
prejudices of superior wealth, or power, or skill, or
courage, nor from the confidence that these prejudices inspire. They who are in the rising scale do not
immediately feel their strength, nor assume that
confidence in it which successful experience gives
them afterwards. They who are the most concerned
to watch the variations of this balance, misjudge
often in the same manner, and from the same prejudices. They continue to dread a power no longer able
to hurt them, or they continue to have no apprehen-
sions of a power that grows daily more formidable.
LORD BOLINGBROKE, ENGLISH (1678–1751)

I speared him with a jest.
ALEXANDER SMITH, SCOTTISH (1830–1867)

 # 6 Strife

THE SUNG HEXAGRAM

---

*At the outset, the man refrains from contention during
the initial stages of strife. He suffers a little. But he*

knows that he needs to walk together with his associates and cannot advance alone.

A prince must also be very wise and not at all times undertake to enforce his own will, although he may have the authority and the very best cause. For it is a far nobler virtue to endure wrong to one's authority than to risk property and person, if it is advantageous to the subjects; since worldly rights attach only to temporal goods.

Hence, it is a very foolish saying: I have a right to it, therefore I will take it by storm and keep it, although all sorts of misfortune may come to others thereby. So we read of the Emperor Octavianus, that he did not wish to make war, however just his cause might be, unless there were sure indications of greater benefit than harm, or at least that the harm would not be intolerable, and said: "War is like fishing with a golden net; the loss risked is always greater than the catch can be." For he who guides a wagon must walk farther otherwise than if he were walking alone; when alone he may walk, jump, and do as he will; but when he drives, he must so guide and adapt himself that the wagon and horses can follow him, and regard that more than his own will. So also a prince leads a multitude with him and must not walk or act as he wills, but as the multitude can, considering their need and advantages more than his will and pleasure. For when a prince rules after his own mad will and follows his own opinion, he is like a mad driver, who rushes straight ahead with horse and wagon, through bushes, thorns, ditches, water, up hill and down dale, regardless of roads and bridges; he will not drive long, all will go to smash.
MARTIN LUTHER, GERMAN (1483–1546)

The man is warned about contending against a superior or more powerful enemy. A conciliatory and timely retreat precludes personal disaster.

The revolutionary parties must complete their education. They have learned how to attack. Now they have to realize that this knowledge must be supplemented with the knowledge of how to retreat properly. They have to realize — that victory is impossible unless they have learned both how to attack and how to retreat properly.

PRESIDENT LENIN, RUSSIAN (1870–1924)

The man lives on income received for services rendered.
He recognizes that works really belonging to oneself
cannot be taken away. He does not engage in perilous
contests over property.

[JUDGE]. Let him say what seems fitting to him.
[GALILEO]. When I had reflected for several days
attentively and continuously on the interrogation put
to me on the sixteenth day of the present month, and
in particular on the question whether I had been
forbidden sixteen years ago by order of the Holy
Office to hold, defend, or teach in any fashion the
view, which at that time already stood condemned,
that the sun is stationary and that the earth moves,
it came to my mind to reread my published *Dialogue*
(as I had not ever done during the three preceding
years) in order to examine carefully whether there
had issued from my pen, against my firmest intention, inadvertently, any statement whereby the
reader or the authorities might argue in me either
some taint of disobedience or anything whatsoever
else which could be conceived as contravening the
orders of the Holy Church; and since by the benign
consent of the authorities I was free to send my
servant forth, I secured a copy of my book; and,
taking it up, I set myself to a careful reading and
detailed study of it. Struck by it, as I was, after so
long an interval, as though by a new thing and the
work of another writer, I freely confess that it seemed
to me at several points written in such a way that a
reader unfamiliar with my inmost thought would
have had some cause for thinking the arguments
brought forth for the false theory, the one I intended
to refute, so drawn as to be more potent in confirm-
ing that theory than easy to rebut; and two of these
in particular, the one concerning sunspots and the
other the flux and reflux of the sea, come to the
reader's ear with qualifications that seem more like
robust and vigorous confirmations than is fitting
from a writer who held them as inconclusive, as in
truth I inwardly and truly held them and hold them
to be, and who desired, as I did, to refute them. And
in order to excuse myself in my own eyes for having

[47]6

fallen into an error so alien to my intention, unable
to satisfy myself fully by remarking that when one
gives the arguments of an adversary with the intention of rebutting them, one is obliged to set them
forth with precision (especially when one writes in
the dialogue form), and must not muffle them so as
to put the adversary at a disadvantage—unable, as I
say, to satisfy myself fully with this excuse, I laid
the blame on the natural complacency any man feels
towards his own subtlety and towards his ability to
show himself sharper than the common run of men,
even to the point of finding ingenious and convinc-
ing demonstrations of probability for false proposi-
tions. Wherefore, although with Cicero I may be
"more avid of glory than is needful for me," if I were
today faced with the task of setting forth the same
arguments, there is no doubt that I should weaken
them in such a way that they could not make an
appearance of having that force which truly and
essentially they lack. My error was, I confess, one of
empty ambition and of pure heedlessness and in-
advertence. And this is what I wished to say on the
subject of the matter that occurred to me in re-
reading my book.

GALILEO GALILEI, ITALIAN (1564–1642)

---

*The man thinks that belligerency toward his weaker
opponents will succeed. But lacking righteousness, he
fails in his endeavors. Returning from the path of strife
to one of inner harmony with the eternal law, he finds
peace and good fortune.*

I should like first to inquire for a little what reason,
what prudence, there is in wishing to glory in the
greatness and extent of the empire, when you cannot
point out the happiness of men who are always rolling, with dark fear and cruel lust, in warlike slaugh-
ters and in blood, which, whether shed in civil or
foreign war, is still human blood; so that their joy
may be compared to glass in its fragile splendour, of
which one is horribly afraid lest it should be suddenly broken in pieces.

SAINT AUGUSTINE, ROMAN (354–430)

---

*The man acts in moderation. By being in the right place,
he is on the road to good fortune. A just and powerful*

[Bishop Fitz-James] . . . tried to excite the Court, with the King at the head, against Colet, having now got hold of another weapon against him. This was that he had openly declared in a sermon that "an unjust peace was to be preferred to the justest war," a war being at that very time in preparation against the French.

. . . The noble young King gave a conspicuous token of his kingly disposition; for he privately encouraged Colet to go on without restraint, and improve by his teaching the corrupt morals of the age, and not to withdraw his light from those dark times.

DESIDERIUS ERASMUS, DUTCH (1466–1536)

King Francis was a hearty king, and loved a royal
   sport,
And one day as his lions fought, sat looking at the
   court.
The nobles filled the benches, and the ladies in their
   pride,
And 'mongst them sat Count de Lorge, with one for
   whom he sighed:
And truly was a gallant thing to see the crowning
   show,
Valor and love, and a king above, and the royal
   beasts below.

Ramped and roared the lions, with horrid laughing
   jaws;
They bit, they glared, gave blows like beams, a wind
   went with their paws;
With wallowing might and stifled roar they rolled on
   one another,
Till all the pit with sand and mane was in a thunder-
   ous smother;
The bloody foam above the bars came whisking
   through the air;
Said Francis then, "Faith, gentlemen, we're better
   here than there."

De Lorge's love o'erheard the King, a beauteous
   lively dame,
With smiling lips and sharp bright eyes, which

[49]6

always seemed the same;
She thought, "The Count, my lover, is brave as brave
can be;
He surely would do wondrous things to show his
love for me;
King, ladies, lovers, all look on; the occasion is
divine;
I'll drop my glove to prove his love; great glory will
be mine."

She dropped her glove, to prove his love, then looked
at him and smiled;
He bowed, and in a moment leaped among the lions
wild;
The leap was quick, return was quick, he has regained his place,
Then threw the glove, but not with love, right in the
lady's face.
"By Heaven," said Francis, "rightly done!" and he
rose from where he sat;
"No love," quoth he, "but vanity, sets love a task
like that."
LEIGH HUNT, ENGLISH (1784–1859)

The man gains repeated rewards from exhaustive con-
flicts. But the happiness does not last. The respect is
undeserved, and the attacks continue without end.

He had, to a morbid excess, that desire to rise which
is vulgarly called ambition, but no wish for the
esteem or the love of his species; only the hard wish
to succeed — not shine, nor serve — succeed, that he
might have the right to despise a world which galled
his self-conceit.
RUFUS WILMOT GRISWOLD, AMERICAN (1815–1857)

The over-all judgment: strife shows itself in various
ways. Open contention occurs when the contender feels
himself to be in the right. When not in the right, he
resorts to blatant impositions or cunning subterfuges.
But carrying conflicts to the bitter end only perpetuates
enmity. The superior man is clear-headed and inwardly
strong, meets opponents halfway, and is ready to submit
his case to authoritative and just arbiters. Difficult enter-
prises are not to be undertaken under such conditions.

There are no snares more dangerous than those which lurk under the guise of duty or the name of relationship. For the man who is your declared foe you can easily baffle by precaution; but this hidden, intestine, and domestic danger not merely exists but overwhelms you before you can foresee and examine it.

MARCUS TULLIUS CICERO, ROMAN (106–43 B.C.)

LIGHTFOOT. Coward! And not only you. *(He rises.)* All of you! Cowards! Maybe, you've courage to die: but not one of you've courage to live.
(Angry murmurs.)
PRIME MINISTER. Francis! The fact that your ideas and ours do not chime . . .
LIGHTFOOT. Ideas! The very substance of our beings doesn't chime. Yours is the Spirit of Yesterday: mine is the Spirit of Tomorrow.
(Murmurs.)
Must I tell you what every Board-school urchin knows? — that, among the myriad orbs of the Milky Way there gyrates, in a minor solar system a negligible planet, and that on this pea of a planet creeps a race of parasites who know themselves for what they are! Isolated! Isolated between the abyss of the unimaginably small, the atom, and the abyss of the unimaginably great, the night about us. In that isolation, what refuge have we but one another? What future but the future of all? What ethic but the good — not of one person, or of one nation — but of Mankind? Answer me that; you can't! The day of the Takers is over, I tell you; the day of the Giver dawns. And I inaugurate it — with the greatest of all possible gifts: mastery over matter. At last, Man is free to enlarge the Kingdom of the Spirit; and so, whether the Sum of Things is justified or not, to justify himself. And do you think, because the Spirit of Yesterday in *you* is afraid, the Spirit of Tomorrow in *me* will run away? *(Pause.)*
ARTHUR. Then . . . you refuse to destroy the secret?
LIGHTFOOT. Utterly!
PRIME MINISTER. Francis! *(Silence.)* I beg you. *(Silence.)* We have been very patient. *(He looks toward Lord Dedham.)*
DUNNE *(intervening)*. One moment. Lightfoot, I'm not
[51]6

a politician. I'm an engineer; your uncle told you. Yes, and what's more, I'm one of your "Boardschool urchins." (*Glancing about the Cabinet.*) I came from the gutter. Well, I planned a great scheme — perhaps you heard of it — the hydroelectrification of the Balkans?

LIGHTFOOT (*interested*). Yes. (*He sits down.*)

DUNNE. My object was peace in the Balkans, by giving them prosperity. I was on the eve of carrying the thing out — when pressure was put on me — this government, that government, all over Europe — yes, and Asia, and America, too — but, above all, *this* government. I told 'em what you've told 'em — the Spirit of Tomorrow, Hope, Courage — against their vicious circle of sophistry and despair. And, in the end, I left 'em talking; and I went ahead. In three weeks an international crisis had developed, which if I hadn't given way, would have led to another war and wrecked civilization. That taught me my lesson. They asked me here — I was useful — to join the Cabinet. And I've been useful! The Dunne Internal Transportation Scheme — you know. Take my advice, Lightfoot, they know better than you or me the nature of the medium they work in.

PRIME MINISTER. I have the concurrence of my colleagues, Francis, in saying that, if you will — er — grant our request, we will put every possible facility for research at your disposal.

(*Cries of "Hear, hear."*)

Your sphere of usefulness — to humanity — will be incalculable. And our facilities are only equaled by our — er — resources.

LIGHTFOOT (*with a queer laugh*). You're trying to bribe me? *Me* — the master of the atom. How — frightfully funny!

(*Angry murmurs.*)

PRIME MINISTER. Francis!

LIGHTFOOT (*suddenly serious; he pushes his chair back, and rises*). To hell with the lot of you. (*He starts to go.*)

DEDHAM. Mr. Lightfoot, I advise you not to leave this room.

LIGHTFOOT. Ho ho! This begins to be interesting. First you cajole; then, you bribe; now, you threaten.

ROBERT MALISE BOWYER NICHOLS (1893–1944)
AND MAURICE BROWNE, ENGLISH

The news of the colt's disappearance soon reached
his owner's ears. He assembled the chiefs of the tribe
and told them what happened. They sent to Jahir,
and he was reproached bitterly. "Jahir," they said,
"you have not suffered, yet have done injustice in
that you carried off that which belonged to another
man." "Say no more," answered Jahir, "and spare
me these reproaches, for, by the faith of an Arab,
I will not return the colt, unless compelled by main
force. I will declare war against you first." At that
moment the tribe was not prepared for a quarrel; and
several of them said to Jahir, "We are too much attached to you to push things to such an extreme as
that; we are your allies and kinsmen. We will not
fight with you, though an idol of gold were at stake."
Then Kerim, son of Wahrab (the latter being the
owner of the mare and colt, a man renowned among
the Arabs for his generosity), seeing the obstinacy
of Jahir, said to him: "Cousin, the colt is certainly
yours, and belongs to you; as for the mare here, accept her as a present from my hand, so that mother
and colt will not be separated, and no one will be able
to accuse me of wronging a kinsman."
The tribe highly applauded this act, and Jahir was
so humiliated by the generosity with which he had
been treated that he returned mare and colt to
Kerim, adding to the gift a pair of male and a pair
of female camels.
ANTAR, ARABIAN (EIGHTH CENTURY)

 7 The Army

THE SHIH HEXAGRAM

*At the outset, a righteous cause, as well as a proper
method for conducting the war, is essential for military
success.*

He asked me what were the usual causes or motives
that made one country go to war with another. I answered they were innumerable; but I should only
mention a few of the chief. Sometimes the ambition
of princes, who never think they have land or people
enough to govern; sometimes the corruption of
ministers, who engage their master in a war in order

to stifle or divert the clamor of the subjects against their evil administration. Difference in opinions hath cost many millions of lives: for instance, whether flesh be bread, or bread be flesh; whether the juice of a certain berry be blood or wine; whether whistling be a vice or a virtue; whether it is better to kiss a post, or throw it into the fire; what is the best colour for a coat, whether black, white, red, or gray; and whether it should be long or short, narrow or wide, dirty or clean; with many more. Neither are any wars so furious and bloody, or of so long continuance, as those occasioned by difference in opinion, especially if it be in things indifferent.

Sometimes the quarrel between two princes is to decide which of them shall dispossess a third of his dominions, where neither of them pretend to any right. Sometimes one prince quarrelleth with another, for fear the other should quarrel with him. Sometimes a war is entered upon, because the enemy is too strong, and sometimes because he is too weak. Sometimes our neighbours want the things which we have, or have the things we want; and we both fight, till they take ours or give us theirs. It is a very justifiable cause of a war to invade a country after the people have been wasted by famine, destroyed by pestilence, or embroiled by factions among themselves. It is justifiable to enter into war against our nearest ally, when one of his towns lies convenient for us, or a territory of land, that would render our dominions round and complete. If a prince sends forces into a nation, where the people are poor and ignorant, he may lawfully put half of them to death, and make slaves of the rest, in order to civilize and reduce them from their barbarous way of living. It is a very kingly, honourable, and frequent practice, when one prince desires the assistance of another to secure him against an invasion, that the assistant, when he hath driven out the invader, should seize on the dominions himself, and kill, imprison, or banish the prince he came to relieve. Alliance by blood or marriage is a frequent cause of war between princes; and the nearer the kindred is, the greater is their disposition to quarrel; poor nations are hungry, and rich nations are proud; and pride and hunger will ever

be at variance.
JONATHAN SWIFT, ENGLISH (1667–1745)

The king's appointment of command is given to the general exclusively. The latter must be in touch with his troops, sharing the good as well as the ill.

The reward of the general is not a bigger tent, but command.
OLIVER WENDELL HOLMES, JR., AMERICAN (1841–1935)

Camões, alone, of all the lyric race,
Born in the angry morning of disaster,
Can look a common soldier in the face:
I find a comrade where I sought a master:
For daily, while the stinking crocodiles
Glide from the mangroves on the swampy shore,
He shares my awning of the dhow, he smiles,
And tells me that he lived it all before.
Through fire and shipwreck, pestilence and loss,
Led by the ignis fatuus of duty
To a dog's death — yet of his sorrows king —
He shouldered high his voluntary Cross,
Wrestled his hardships into forms of beauty,
And taught his gorgon destinies to sing.
ROY CAMPBELL, SOUTH AFRICAN (1901–1957)

Defeat ensues when others interfere with the authority of the chosen leader. Divided command is often fatal.

Has not the famous political fable of the snake, with two heads and one body, some useful instruction contained in it? She was going to a brook to drink, and in her way was to pass through a hedge, a twig of which opposed her direct course; one head chose to go on the right side of the twig, the other on the left; so that time was spent in the contest, and before the decision was completed, the poor snake died with thirst.
BENJAMIN FRANKLIN, AMERICAN (1706–1790)

The man is confronted by a superior enemy. Orderly retreat to preserve the army is his correct course of action.

[Napoleon] spoke of the Russian nobles, who in the

event of war, would fear for their palaces, and, after a good battle, would force the Tsar to conclude a peace.

"Your Majesty is mistaken," [Caulaincourt] replied. . . ." 'If the Emperor Napoleon makes war on me,' the Tsar Alexander said to me, 'it is possible, even probable, that we shall be defeated; assuming that we fight. But that will not mean that he can dictate a peace . . . . We have plenty of room; and our standing army is well-organized, which means, as the Emperor Napoleon has admitted, that we need never accept a dictated peace, whatever reverses we may suffer. What is more, in such circumstances the victor is forced to accept the terms of the vanquished. The Emperor Napoleon made a remark to this effect to Tchernychev in Vienna after the battle of Wagram. He would not have made peace if Austria had not kept an army intact . . . . I shall not be the first to draw my sword, but I shall be the last to sheathe it . . . . The Emperor Napoleon's remark to Tchernychev, in the latest war with Austria, shows clearly enough that the Austrians could have obtained better terms if they had been more persevering. People don't know how to suffer. If the fighting went against me, I should retire to Kamchatka rather than cede provinces and sign, in my capitol, treaties that were really only truces. Your Frenchman is brave; but long privations and a bad climate wear him down and discourage him. Our climate, our winter, will fight on our side. With you, marvels only take place where the Emperor is in personal attendance; and he cannot be everywhere. He cannot be absent from Paris year after year.' "

MARQUIS ARMAND AUGUSTIN LOUIS DE CAULAINCOURT, FRENCH (1772–1827)

Invasion occurs. A seasoned leader is chosen to lead the army to victory and to prevent needless slaughter of the defeated people.

But, O my muse! what numbers wilt thou find
To sing the furious troops in battle join'd!
Methinks I hear the drum's tumultuous sound,
The victor's shouts and dying groans confound;
The dreadful burst of cannon rend the skies,
And all the thunder of the battle rise.

[56]7

'Twas then great Marlborough's mighty soul was
    proved,
That, in the shock of charging hosts unmoved,
Amidst confusion, horror, and despair,
Examined all the dreadful scenes of war;
In peaceful thought the field of death surveyed,
To fainting squadrons sent the timely aid,
Inspired repulsed battalions to engage,
And taught the doubtful battle where to rage.
So when an angel, by divine command,
With rising tempests shakes a guilty land,
Such as of late o'er pale Britannia passed,
Calm and serene he drives the furious blast,
And, pleased the Almighty's orders to perform,
Rides in the whirlwind and directs the storm.
JOSEPH ADDISON, ENGLISH (1672–1719)

As Napoleon and his retinue were riding on ground
so littered with corpses that it was impossible to
avoid stepping on them, one of the horses trod on a
dying soldier and drew a last moan of pain from him.
The Emperor, until then as silent as his victory, terribly depressed by the sight of so many victims, suddenly exploded and relieved his feelings by cries of
indignation and an exaggerated solicitude for the
poor soldier. Someone, to appease him, remarked
that after all it was *only a Russian*. To which Napoleon
replied, "There are no enemies after a victory, but
only men!" Then he scattered the officers who were
following him over the field to succor the wounded
whose cries could be heard on all sides.
PHILIPPE-PAUL DE SÉGUR, FRENCH (1780-1873)

---

*Victory is achieved. The king rewards his supporters.
But he is careful to compensate inferior people with
money instead of land or ruling privileges. Otherwise
power is abused by them.*

Never ennoble anybody in such wise that he may
molest you; and never trust anybody so exclusively
that you lose the capitol and the state to him.
HAN-TZU, CHINESE (280–233 B.C.)

---

*The over-all judgment: discipline in the army is achieved
by the mature and experienced man who gains the support of the ruler and arouses the spirit of the people.*
[57]7

Passions of combat, however, should not lead to cruelty and revenge. Firm-heartedness and correctness should form the basis of action.

The very sight of him [Tiberius] drew tears of joy from the soldiers. They were all eagerness, with a sort of unexampled rapture in their salutation and a passion for touching his hand: they could not restrain themselves from immediately adding "Is it really you, General? Have we got you back in safety?" and then, "*I* was with you in Armenia, General," "*I* was in Raetia," "*I* had a reward from you in Vindelicia," "*I* in Pannonia," "*I* in Germany" — a scene not to be expressed in words, and perhaps scarcely of winning belief.
VELLEIUS PATERCULUS, ROMAN (19 B.C.–30 A.D.)

The punishment most in use in the fleet was flogging on the bare back with the cat-o'-nine-tails. The cat was a short, wooden stick, covered with red baize. The tails were of tough knotted cord, about two feet long. The thieves' cat, with which thieves were flogged, had longer and heavier tails, knotted throughout their length. Flogging was inflicted at the discretion of the captain. It was considered the only punishment likely to be effective with such men as manned the royal ships . . . . It was perhaps the most cruel and ineffectual punishment ever inflicted. The system was radically bad, for many captains inflicted flogging for all manner of offences, without distinction. The thief was flogged, the drunkard was flogged, the laggard was flogged. The poor, wretched topman who got a ropeyard into a buntline block was flogged. The very slightest transgression was visited with flogging. Those seamen who had any pride remaining in them went in daily fear of being flogged. Those who had been flogged were generally callous, careless whether they were flogged again, and indifferent to all that might happen to them. It was a terrible weapon in the hands of the officers. In many cases the officers abused the power, by the infliction of excessive punishment for trifling offences. The sailors like a smart captain. They liked to be brought up to the mark, and if a captain showed himself a brave man, a good seaman, and a glutton for hard knocks, they would stand any punishment he chose
[58]7

to inflict knowing that such a one would not be un-just. They hated a slack captain, for a slack captain left them at the mercy of the underlings, and that, they said, was "hell afloat." But worse than any-thing they hated a tyrant, a man who flogged his whole ship's company for little or no reason, or for the infringement of his own arbitrary rules. Such a man, who kept his crew in an agony of fear, hardly knowing whether to kill themselves or their tyrant, was dreaded by all. He was not uncommon in the service until the conclusion of the Great War. It was his kind who drove so many of our men into the American navy. It was his kind who did so much to cause the mutinies at the Nore and the Spithead, the loss of the *Hermione* frigate, and (to some extent) the losses we sustained in the American War. Lastly, it was his kind who caused so many men to desert, in defiance of the stern laws against desertion. That kind of captain was the terror of the fleet.

JOHN MASEFIELD, ENGLISH (1878–1967)

Nothing in Washington's military career shows the kindliness of his heart and his indifference to per-sonal autocracy more poignantly than an overlooked little memorandum that he ordered destroyed . . . . Realizing that by going south he automatically superseded Greene in command and robbed him of his independence, he tried to soften the blow by a personal message sent with a letter of congratulation following Greene's success at Eutaw Springs . . . . This is the message:

"Col. Morris will inform General Greene in the sin-cerest manner that there are but two motives which can possibly induce Genl. W[ashington] to take the command to the southward: one, the order of C[ornwallis] to repair thither; the other, the French army going there. In the last case Count R[ocham-beau] would command if Genl. W[ashington] did not go in person. General Washington wishes, not only from his personal regard to Genl. Greene, but from principles of generosity and justice, to see him crowned with those laurels which from his un-paralleled exertions he so richly deserves."

RUPERT HUGHES, AMERICAN (1872–1956)

8 Leadership

THE PI HEXAGRAM

*At the outset, the man is filled with sincerity in his
associations with others. He resembles an unadorned
bowl which is full.*

I regret very much that to speak the truth in our day
appears to be bad taste. I find, however, that even at
the risk of seeming to be a boor I must still say what I
truly believe. I believe that time, with infinite understanding, will one day forgive me.

WILLIAM SAROYAN, AMERICAN (BORN 1908)

*The man retains his individuality and dignity in his re-
lationships with others. He is not like the obsequious
office seeker. His convictions are deeply founded.*

The General came before the silent and angry King
and saluting him said: "The village is punished, the
men are stricken to dust, and the women cower in
their unlit homes afraid to weep aloud."

The High Priest stood up and blessed the King and
cried: "God's mercy is ever upon you."

The Clown, when he heard this, burst out laughing
and startled the Court. The King's frown darkened.

"The honor of the throne," said the Minister, "is up-
held by the King's prowess and the blessing of
Almighty God."

Louder laughed the Clown, and the King growled —
"Unseemly mirth!"

"God has showered many blessings upon your
head," said the Clown; "the one he bestowed upon
me was the gift of laughter."

"This gift will cost you your life," said the King,
gripping his sword with his right hand.

Yet the Clown stood up and laughed till he laughed
no more.

A shadow of dread fell upon the Court, for they
heard that laughter echoing in the depth of God's
silence.

SIR RABINDRANATH TAGORE, INDIAN (1861–1941)

The man attempts to cultivate an intimacy with people beyond his proper sphere. But this does not make him a person of greater stature.

What of earls with whom you have supp'd,
    And of dukes that you dined with yestreen?
Lord! a louse, Sir, is still but a louse,
    Though it crawl on the curl of a queen!
ROBERT BURNS, SCOTTISH (1759–1796)

The minister shows open loyalty to his king. This behavior contrasts to that of a person without a post. The latter should remain reserved, so as to retain his personal honor.

Our country! In her intercourse with foreign nations, may she always be in the right; but our country, right or wrong.
STEPHEN DECATUR, AMERICAN (1779–1820)

The superior ruler accepts those who voluntarily come to him and lets others go who care to go. He neither invites nor flatters. Union is based on mutual confidence and appreciation.

LEAR. What dost thou profess? What wouldst thou with us?
KENT. I do profess to be no less than I seem, to serve him truly that will put me in trust, to love him that is honest, to converse with him that is wise and says little, to fear judgment, to fight when I cannot choose, and to eat no fish.
LEAR. What are thou?
KENT. A very honest-hearted fellow, and as poor as the king.
LEAR. If thou be as poor for a subject as he is for a king, thou art poor enough. What wouldst thou?
KENT. Service.
LEAR. Whom wouldst thou serve?
KENT. You.
LEAR. Dost thou know me, fellow?
KENT. No, sir; but you have that in your countenance which I would fain call master.
LEAR. What's that?
KENT. Authority.
WILLIAM SHAKESPEARE, ENGLISH (1564–1616)

Apries having thus been overthrown, Amasis became king. . . . Now at first the Egyptians despised Amasis and held him in no great regard, because he had been a man of the people and was of no distinguished family; but afterwards Amasis won them over to himself by wisdom and not wilfulness. Among innumerable other things of price which he had, there was a foot-basin of gold in which both Amasis himself and all his guests were wont always to wash their feet. This he broke up, and of it he caused to be made the image of a god, and set it up in the city, where it was most convenient, and the Egyptians went continually to visit the image and did great reverence to it. Then Amasis, having learnt that which was done by the men of the city, called together the Egyptians and made known to them the matter, saying that the image had been produced from the foot-basin, into which formerly the Egyptians used to vomit and make water, and in which they washed their feet, whereas now they did to it great reverence; and just so, he continued, had he himself now fared, as the foot-basin; for though formerly he was a man of the people, yet now he was their king, and he bade them accordingly honor him and have regard for him. In such manner he won the Egyptians to himself, so that they consented to be his subjects.

HERODOTUS, GREEK (FIFTH CENTURY B.C.)

The situation bodes ill. No good ending can be expected in the absence of the right beginning. It is too late.

At that moment the boss noticed that a fly had fallen into his broad inkpot, and was trying feebly but desperately to clamber out again. Help! help! said those struggling legs. But the sides of the inkpot were wet and slippery; it fell back again and began to swim. The boss took up a pen, picked the fly out of the ink, and shook it on to a piece of blotting paper. For a fraction of a second it lay still on the dark patch that oozed round it. Then the front legs waved, took hold, and, pulling its small sodden body up it began the immense task of cleaning the ink from its wings. Over and under, over and under, went a leg along a wing, as the stone goes over and under the scythe.

[62]8

Then there was a pause, while the fly, seeming to stand on the tips of its toes, tried to expand first one wing and then the other. It succeeded at last, and, sitting down, it began, like a minute cat, to clean its face. Now one could imagine that the little front legs rubbed against each other lightly, joyfully. The horrible danger was over; it had escaped; it was ready for life again.

But just then the boss had an idea. He plunged his pen back into the ink, leaned his thick wrist on the blotting paper, and as the fly tried its wings down came a great blot. What would it make of that? What indeed! The little beggar seemed absolutely cowed, stunned, and afraid to move because of what would happen next. But then, as if painfully, it dragged itself forward. The front legs waved, caught hold, and, more slowly this time, the task began from the beginning.

He's a plucky little devil, thought the boss, and he felt a real admiration for the fly's courage. That was the way to tackle things; that was the right spirit. Never say die; it was only a question of . . . But the fly had again finished its laborious task, and the boss had just time to refill his pen, to shake fair and square on the new-cleansed body yet another dark drop. What about it this time? A painful moment of suspense followed. But behold, the front legs were again waving; the boss felt a rush of relief. He leaned over the fly and said to it tenderly, "You artful little b. . . ." And he actually had the brilliant notion of breathing on it to help the drying process. All the same, there was something timid and weak about its efforts now, and the boss decided that this time should be the last, as he dipped the pen into the inkpot.

It was. The last blot fell on the soaked blotting-paper, and the draggled fly lay in it and did not stir. The black legs were stuck to the body; the front legs were not to be seen.

"Come on," said the boss. "Look sharp!" And he stirred it with his pen — in vain. Nothing happened or was likely to happen. The fly was dead.

KATHERINE MANSFIELD, NEW ZEALANDER (1888–1923)

The over-all judgment: people's progress results from union around a central figure. The true leader fortifies his sublimity, strength, and perseverance. The hesitant will follow gradually, but the late comers will be left out.

I offer neither pay, nor quarters, nor provisions; I offer hunger, thirst, forced marches, battles and death. Let him who loves his country in his heart and not his lips only, follow me.

GIUSEPPE GARIBALDI, ITALIAN (1807–1882)

... the consent of mankind has always, in spite of the philosophers, given precedence to the soldier.

And this is right.

For the soldier's trade, verily and essentially, is not slaying, but being slain. This, without well knowing its own meaning, the world honours it for. A bravo's trade is slaying; but the world has never respected bravos more than merchants; the reason it honours the soldier is because he holds his life at the service of the State. Reckless he may be — fond of pleasure or of adventure — all kinds of bye-motives and mean impulses may have determined the choice of his profession, and may affect (to all appearance exclusively) his daily conduct in it; our estimate of him is based upon this ultimate fact — of which we are well assured — that put him in a fortress breach, with all the pleasures of the world behind him and only death and his duty in front of him, he will keep his face to the front; and he knows that his choice may be put to him at any moment — and has beforehand taken his part — virtually takes such part continually — does, in reality, die daily.

JOHN RUSKIN, ENGLISH (1819–1900)

Francis, however, was not so easy to break, even if his physique was far from being that of a Viking. He has no beard, neither is he rough-looking. On the contrary, he is clean-shaven and well-groomed. He looks like the kindest man on the earth — and that he well may be. A wholehearted Norwegian more than anyone else. No matter what he may be doing, his manners are always gentle and graceful, and what he says he says mildly and with amiability, even if it is not always meant that way. Francis is far from being "a softy." While he was in prison, often we heard his friends and others outside say, "Poor

Francis!" "What on earth is going to happen to
Francis?" "How is Francis going to endure imprisonment? He isn't very strong, you know,"
and they all shook their worried heads and
thought that this would be the end of Francis.
Never have such words been more unwarranted,
in spite of the fact that his imprisonment lasted
for such a long time. No one kept his colors flying
more bravely the whole time than he. And furthermore he helped thousands of fellow prisoners to
do the same.

Francis had not been long at Grini before he
started his task. Some prisoners wanted him to
tell about Björnson, others about Ibsen or Werge-
land. Some even wanted to hear about Shakespeare,
Dante, Cervantes, and Voltaire; others about the
Greek and Roman classics, and Francis lectured
generously and lavishly. He never said no. Like
everything else at Grini, lecturing was strictly
forbidden. This made, however, no difference to
Francis. On the contrary it made his task all the
more attractive to him. He started one series of
lectures after another. Some of them were given
during working hours on the job where Francis
"worked," others in the barrack rooms at night. No
less than thirteen hundred lectures of this kind
were delivered by Francis during the time of his
imprisonment. In addition to these more formal
lectures he made numerous impromptu speeches.
There were many occasions which called for celebration, such as Christmas, New Year's, the
seventeenth of May, and also the gloomy days
when a prisoner transport left for Germany.
Francis was always on the spot with words for
the day, words that came from the heart, words
that never will be forgotten by those who
heard them.

Outstanding among his speeches was the one he
gave at Christmas 1941, when he talked about Yule
as we find it in Norwegian lyrics, and finished up by
telling the tale of "Jutulen and Johannes Blessom."
One will never forget the last immortal sentence,
which became a catchword to prisoners at Grini,
"You will have to stand it, Blessom."
ODD NANSEN, NORWEGIAN (BORN 1901)

9 Restraint by the Weak

THE HSIAO CH'U HEXAGRAM

At the outset, the man presses forward. When obstacles are encountered, however, he returns to the state of greater choice. By not forcing his way, he eventually gains his objective.

As war is not an act of blind passion, but is dominated by the political objective, therefore the value of that object determines the measure of the sacrifices by which it is to be purchased. . . . As the expenditure of force becomes so great that the political object is no longer equal in value, this object must be given up.

GENERAL KARL VON CLAUSEWITZ,
PRUSSIAN (1780–1831)

The man does not expose himself needlessly to rebuff by pushing forward when the time is not propitious. He retreats with kindred souls.

In the dead of night I have heard, "Lord God,
   Lord God, how long?
I wither, I wither!
Wherefore hast Thou breathed this soul into me?
And wherefore hast Thou planted this heart in me?
To feel all pain, all suffering, all evil,
To bear the burden of all oppression,
All unhappiness and misfortune —
And hast bound my hands that I may not save?
Wherefore hast Thou given me an eye that sees,
And ears that listen,
That I may see the generations and their sighing,
My heart wounded with the wounds of all men,
And hast bound mine hands that I may not save?
Wherefore hast Thou created this sea of
   wretchedness,
And all the evil and all the oppression,
Which mine eyes will look upon for the eternity to
   come,
And hast breathed a spirit into me,
To curse all evil and to blast it —

But hast set a seal upon my lips that I may not curse?
Wherefore these countless multitudes of the unhappy
Which are yet to be until the end of the generations,
With the countless multitudes of their tears
Which will yet be poured into the nether waters,
And wherefore hast Thou made me to hear
The great noise of their weeping which splitteth
  the rocks,
And hast bound mine hands that I may not save?
Wherefore hast Thou given me the strength
To save and to redeem, to help and to rescue,
To comfort those that mourn,
To heal hearts that are broken,
To bind up all sorrows —
And hast laid chains upon mine arm?
Lord God, wherefore hast Thou made me a
  Redeemer,
And hast forbidden me to redeem?"

And in the dead of night there is heard a song of
  storm,
The storm of golden chains,
A storm of links that clash upon each other,
As often as the Messiah strains to burst his bonds,
And tears with the strength of his arm
At the Throne of Glory and the pillars thereof,
And at the heavens and the heaven of heavens —
And an echo is heard against it, in the dead of night,
The sound of a storm of chains of iron
On the face of the earth below.
From end to end of the face of earth below,
And it chances that from amidst the crimson clouds,
From amidst the chrysolite and amber,
From amidst the whiteness of white sapphire,
A Voice is heard answering: "Until a new generation
  arise,
A generation that will understand redemption,
A generation that will desire to be redeemed,
Whose soul will be prepared to be redeemed!
Then wilt thou too achieve thy destiny and be
  redeemed:
Then wilt thou too achieve thy destiny and redeem!"
DAVID FRISHMAN, HEBREW (1861–1922)

The circumstances favor the weak. Progress is frustrated

by external, apparently minor, impediments. The net
effectiveness is that of a wheel without spokes.

Like men with sore eyes: they find the light painful,
while the darkness, which permits them to see nothing, is restful and agreeable.
DIO CHRYSOSTOM, GREEK (40–120)

The man follows the path of righteous flexibility, thereby
eliminating anxieties and averting the dangers of blood-
shed. He is always mindful of the question: what if you
are wrong?

The resolution of Lodovico [to become a Capuchin
monk after killing someone] came very *apropos* for
his hosts, who were in a sad dilemma on his account.
To send him away from the convent, and thus expose
him to justice, that is to say, to the vengeance of his
enemies, was a course on which they would not for a
moment bestow a thought. It would have been to
give up their proper privileges, disgrace the convent
in the eyes of the people, draw upon themselves the
animadversion of all the Capuchins in the universe
for suffering their common rights to be infringed
upon, and arouse all the ecclesiastical authorities,
who at that time considered themselves the lawful
guardians of these rights. On the other hand, the
kindred of the slain, powerful themselves, and strong
in adherents, were prepared to take vengeance, and
denounced as their enemy any one who should put
an obstacle in their way. This history does not tell us
that much grief was felt for the loss of the deceased,
nor even that a single tear was shed over him by any
of his relations; it merely says that they were all on
fire to have the murderer, dead or living, in their
power. But Lodovico's assuming the habit of a
Capuchin settled all these difficulties; he made atone-
ment in a manner, imposed a penance on himself,
tacitly confessed himself in fault, and withdrew from
the contest; he was, in fact, an enemy laying down
his arms. The relatives of the dead could also, if they
pleased, believe and make it their boast that he had
turned friar in despair, and through dread of their
vengeance. But in any case, to oblige a man to re-
linquish his property, shave his head, and walk bare-
foot, to sleep on straw, and to live upon alms, was
[68]9

surely a punishment fully equivalent to the most
heinous offense.

The Superior presented himself with an easy humility to the brother of the deceased, and after a thousand protestations of respect for his most illustrious
house, and of desire to comply with his wishes as
far as was possible, he spoke of Lodovico's penitence,
and the determination he had made, politely making
it appear that his family ought to be therefore satisfied, and insinuating, yet more courteously, and with
still greater dexterity, that whether he were pleased
or not, so it would be. The brother fell into a rage,
which the Capuchin patiently allowed to evaporate,
occasionally remarking that he had too just cause for
sorrow. The Signor also gave him to understand, that
in any case his family had it in their power to enforce satisfaction, to which the Capuchin, whatever
he might think, did not say no; and finally he asked,
or rather required as a condition, that the murderer
of his brother should immediately quit the city. The
Capuchin, who had already determined upon such a
course, replied that it should be as he wished, leaving the nobleman to believe, if he chose, that his
compliance was an act of obedience, and thus the
matter was concluded to the satisfaction of all parties.
ALESSANDRO MANZONI, ITALIAN (1785–1873)

The antagonists of Christ therefore said to the poor:
"You wait patiently for the day of justice: there is no
justice; you wait for the life eternal to achieve your
vengeance: there is no life eternal; you gather
up your tears and those of your family, the cries
of the children and the sobs of the women, to
place them at the feet of God at he hour of death:
there is no God."
Then it is certain that the poor man dried his tears,
and he told his wife to check her sobs, his children
to come with him, and that he stood upon the earth
with the power of a bull. He said to the rich: "Thou
who oppressest me, thou art only man;" and to the
priest: "Thou who hast consoled me, thou hast lied."
That was just what the antagonists of Christ desired.
Perhaps they thought this was the way to achieve
man's happiness, sending him out to the conquest
of liberty.
But, if the poor man, once satisfied that the priests

deceive him, that the rich rob him, that all men have rights, that all good is of this world, and that misery is impiety; if the poor man, believing in himself and his two arms, says to himself some fine day, "War on the rich! for me, happiness here in this life, since there is no other! for me, the earth, since heaven is empty! for me and for all, since all are equal." Oh! reasoners sublime who have led him to this, what will you say to him if he is *conquered?*
ALFRED DE MUSSET, FRENCH (1810–1857)

Partners reinforce each other through loyalty. The man uses both his own resources and those of his neighbors to further their common cause.

"O Wisest One, Mighty God Indra!" he cried, "this hound hath eaten with me, starved with me, suffered with me, loved me! Must I desert him now?"

"Yea," declared the God of Gods, Indra, "all the joys of Paradise are yours forever, but leave here your hound."

Then exclaimed Yudishthira in anguish.
"Can it be that a god can be so destitute of pity? Can it be that to gain this glory I must leave behind all that I love? Then let me lose such glory forever!"

... The brow of Indra darkened.

"It is decreed," he replied sternly. "As you know, the very merit of prayer itself is lost if a dog touches him who is praying. He who enters Paradise must enter pure. Beside the stony highway you left the wife Draupadi and your brothers. Surely for this common creature you will not give up the joys of the Blessed!"

Gently Yudishthira laid his hand upon the hound's head and turned to depart.

"All powerful Indra," he answered quietly, but firmly, "the dead are dead; I could not succor them. There are four deadly sins: to reject a suppliant, to slay a nursing mother, to destroy a Brahman's possessions, and to injure an old friend. But to these I add a fifth, as sinful: to desert the lowliest friend when you pass out of sorrow into good fortune!
[70]9

Farewell, then, Lord Indra. I go — and my hound
with me."
MAHABBARATA, INDIAN
(FIFTH–SECOND CENTURIES B.C.)

Business? It's quite simple — it's other people's
money.
ALEXANDRE DUMAS, FILS, FRENCH (1824–1895)

---

*Bit by bit the man achieves success. This should be
valued but not pushed too far. When the moon is full,
waning is inevitable. Quiescence is in order.*

The wise man does not allow his knowledge and
abilities to be sounded to the bottom, if he desires
to be honored by all. He allows you to know them
but not to comprehend them.
BALTASAR GRACIÁN, SPANISH (1601–1658)

---

*The over-all judgment: the strong element is being re-
strained by the weak. There is hope, but major gains are
not immediately attainable. Ultimate success will be
achieved through friendly persuasion and soothing
gentleness.*

. . . the practice of that which is ethically best — what
we call goodness or virtue — involves a course of
conduct which, in all respects, is opposed to that
which leads to success in the cosmic struggle for existence. In place of ruthless self-assertion, it demands
self-restraint; in place of thrusting aside, or treading
down, all competitors, it requires that the individual
shall not merely respect, but shall help his fellows;
its influence is directed, not so much to the survival
of the fittest, as to the fitting of as many as possible
to survive. It repudiates the gladiatorial theory of
existence. . . . Laws and moral precepts are directed
to the end of curbing the cosmic process, and re-
minding the individual of his duty to the community, to the protection and influence of which he
owes, if not existence itself, at least the life of something better than a brutal savage. . . . Let us understand, once and for all, that the ethical progress of
society depends, not on imitating the cosmic process,
still less in running away from it, but in combating
it. It may seem an audacious proposal thus to pit the
[71]9

microcosm against the macrocosm and to set man to subdue nature to his higher ends; but I venture to think that the great intellectual difference between ancient times and our own day lies in the solid foundation we have acquired for the hope that such an enterprise may meet with a certain measure of success.

The history of civilizations details the steps by which men have succeeded in building up an artificial world within the cosmos. Fragile reed as he may be, man, as Pascal says, is a thinking reed: there lies within him a fund of energy, operating intelligently and so far akin to that which pervades the universe, that it is competent to influence and modify the cosmic process. In virtue of his intelligence, the dwarf bends the Titan to his will.

THOMAS HENRY HUXLEY, ENGLISH (1825–1895)

I think then that the aim of the perfect Courtier . . . is so to win for himself, by means of the accomplishments ascribed to him by these gentlemen, the favour and mind of the prince whom he serves, that he may be able to say, and always shall say, the truth about everything which it is fitting for the prince to know, without fear or risk of giving offence thereby; and that when he sees his prince's mind inclined to do something wrong, he may be quick to oppose, and gently to make use of the favour acquired by his good accomplishments, so as to banish every bad intent and lead his prince into the path of virtue. And thus, possessing the goodness which these gentlemen have described, together with readiness of wit and pleasantness, and shrewdness and knowledge of letters and many other things, — the courtier will in every case be able deftly to show the prince how much honour and profit accrue to him and his from justice, liberality, magnanimity, gentleness, and the other virtues that become a good prince; and on the other hand how much infamy and loss proceed from the vices opposed to them. Therefore I think that just as music, festivals, games, and the other pleasant accomplishments are, as it were, the flower, in like manner to lead or help one's prince toward right, and to frighten him from wrong, are the true fruit of Courtiership. . . .

In this way the Courtier will be able to lead his prince

[72]9

along the thorny path of virtue, decking it as with
shady leafage and strewing it with lovely flowers
to relieve the tedium of the weary journey to one
whose strength is slight; and now with music, now
with arms and horses, now with verses, now with
love talk, and wit with all those means whereof these
gentlemen have told, to keep his mind continually
busied with worldly pleasures, yet always impress-
ing upon him also, as I have said, some virtuous
practice along with these allurements, and playing
upon him with salutary craft; like cunning doctors,
who often anoint the edge of the cup with a sweet
cordial, when they wish to give some bitter-tasting
medicine to sick and over-delicate children.
BALDASSARE CASTIGLIONE, ITALIAN (1478–1529)

A foolish man learning that the Buddha observed the
principle of great love which commends the return
of good for evil, came and abused him. The Buddha
was silent, pitying his folly.
When the man had finished his abuse, the Buddha
asked him, saying: "Son, if a man declined to accept
a present made to him, to whom would it belong?"
And he answered: "In that case it would belong to
the man who offered it."
"My son," said the Buddha, "thou hast railed at me,
I decline to accept thy abuse, and request thee to
keep it thyself. Will it not be a source of misery to
thee? As the echo belongs to the sound, and the
shadow to the substance, so misery will overtake the
evil-doer without fail."
The abuser made no reply, and Buddha continued:
"A wicked man who reproaches a virtuous one is like
one who looks up and spits at heaven; the spittle
soils not the heaven but comes back and defiles his
own person."
GAUTAMA BUDDHA, INDIAN (563–483 B.C.)

10 Stepping Carefully
THE LÜ HEXAGRAM

*At the outset, the man is in a subordinate position with-
out social obligation. Progress will be attained without
blame if he remains content with his simple accustomed
path, making no demands upon others.*
[73]10

Let Homer sing his verse. I listen to this sublime
genius in comparison with whom I, a simple herdsman, a humble farmer, am as nothing. What, indeed,
— if product is to be compared with product, — are
my cheeses and my beans in the presence of his
"Iliad"? But, if Homer wishes to take from me all that
I possess, and make me his slave in return for his
inimitable poem, I will give up the pleasure of his
lays and dismiss him. I can do without his "Iliad,"
and wait, if necessary, for the "Aeneid." Homer cannot live twenty-four hours without my products.
Let him accept, then, the little that I have to offer;
and then his muse may instruct, encourage and
console me.

PIERRE JOSEPH PROUDHON, FRENCH (1809–1865)

The quiet and solitary man apprehends the inscrutable.
He seeks nothing, holds to the mean, and remains free
from entanglements.

I have known the silence of the stars and of the sea,
And the silence of the city when it pauses,
And the silence of a man and a maid,
And the silence for which music alone finds the word
And the silence of the woods before the winds of
    spring begin,
And the silence of the sick
When their eyes roam about the room.
And I ask: For the depths
Of what use is language?
A beast of the field moans a few times
When death takes its young.
And we are voiceless in the presence of realities —
We cannot speak.
A curious boy asks an old soldier
Sitting in front of the grocery store,
"How did you lose your leg?"
And the soldier is struck with silence,
Or his mind flies away
Because he cannot concentrate it on Gettysburg.
It comes back jocosely
And he says, "A bear bit it off."
. .   .   .

There is the silence of a great hatred,
And the silence of a great love,
And the silence of a deep peace of mind,

[74]10

And the silence of an embittered friendship,
There is the silence of a spiritual crisis,
Through which your soul, exquisitely tortured,
Comes with visions not to be uttered
Into a realm of higher life.

. . . .

There is the silence of those unjustly punished;
And the silence of the dying whose hand
Suddenly grips yours.

. . . .

There is the silence of those who have failed;
And the vast silence that covers
Broken nations and vanquished leaders.

. . . .

And there is the silence of age,
Too full of wisdom for the tongue to utter it
In words intelligible to those who have not lived
The great range of life.
EDGAR LEE MASTERS, AMERICAN (1869–1950]

---

*The man recklessly exposes himself to danger, which
exceeds his powers of handling. He invites disaster
thereby.*

The folly of mistaking a paradox for a discovery, a
metaphor for a proof, a torrent of verbiage for a
spring of capital truths, and oneself for an oracle,
is inborn in us.
PAUL AMBROISE VALÉRY, FRENCH (1871–1945)

The strange thing about this crisis of August, 1939
was that the object between Germany and Poland
was not clearly defined, and could not therefore be
expressed as a concrete demand. It was part of Hitler's nature to avoid putting things in a concrete
form; to him differences of opinion were questions
of power and tests of one's nerves and strength.
ERNST VON WEIZSÄCKER, GERMAN (1882–1951)

---

*The man successfully undertakes dangerous enterprises
by proceeding with caution and circumspection.*

Herein consists our distinguishing excellence, that
in the hour of emergency we show the greatest courage, and yet debate beforehand the expediency of
our measures. The courage of others is the result of
[75]10

ignorance; deliberation makes them cowards. And those undoubtedly must be owned to have the greatest souls, who, most acutely sensible of the miseries of war and the sweets of peace, are not hence in the least deterred from facing danger.

PERICLES, GREEK (DIED 429 B.C.)

Peril is evident, as when treading on the tail of a tiger. But the man remains aware and resolute, acting with propriety and humility.

"As far as we personally are concerned, happiness is done with whatever the course of events may be. I know that it is the duty of one king to suffer on behalf of the others, and we are fulfilling that duty well. I hope that someday the fact may be recognized by them all." Too late, Marie Antoinette had grasped in the very depths of her soul that she was destined to become a historical figure, and this need for transcending the limitations of her own time intensified her forces to an extreme. For when a human being begins to plumb his own depths, when he has determined to dig into the inmost recesses of his own personality, he discovers in his own blood the shadowy powers of his ancestors. The fact that she had sprung from the House of Habsburg, that she was descendant and heiress of an ancient imperial line, that she was the daughter of Maria Thérèsa, lifted this weak and unsteady woman as if by magic above her previous limitations. She felt it incumbent upon her to be "digne de Marie Thérèse," to be worthy of her mother, and "courage" became the leitmotiv to her progress toward imminent destruction. Again and again we find such declarations as that "nothing can break my courage"; and when news came from Vienna that her brother Joseph, on an agonizing deathbed, had maintained his composure to the last hour, she felt prophetically that she, too, was foredoomed to die bravely, and she replied with the most self-confident saying of her life: "I venture to declare he died in a way worthy of myself."

STEFAN ZWEIG, AUSTRIAN (1881–1942)

Then one of the chief officers of the King arose, and said: "O King, give up to me the blood of this sage;

for we have not seen him commit any offense against thee; nor have we seen him do aught but cure thee of thy disease, which wearied the other physicians and sages." The King answered: "Ye know not the reason wherefore I would kill the sage. It is this, that if I suffered him to live, I should myself inevitably perish; for he who cured me of the disease under which I suffered by a thing that I held in my hand, may kill me by a thing that I may smell; and I fear that he would do so, and would receive an appointment on account of it; seeing that it is probable he is a spy who hath come hither to kill me; I must therefore kill him, and then shall I feel myself safe."

The sage then said again: "Spare me, and so may God spare thee; and destroy me not, lest God destroy thee."

But he now felt certain that the King would put him to death, and that there was no escape for him; so he said: "O King, if my death is indispensable, grant me some respite, that I may return to my house, and acquit myself of my duties, and give directions to my family and neighbors to bury me, and dispose of my medical books; and among my books is one of the most especial value, which I offer as a present to thee, that thou mayest treasure in thy library." "And what," said the King, "is this book?" He answered: "It contains things not to be enumerated; and the smallest of the secret virtues that it possesses is this: that, when thou hast cut off my head, if thou open this book, and count three leaves, and then read three lines on the page to the left, the head will speak to thee, and answer whatever thou shalt ask." At this the King was excessively astonished, and shook with delight, and said to him: "O Sage, when I have cut off thy head will it speak?" He answered: "Yes, O King, and this is a wonderful thing."

The King then sent him in the custody of guards, and the sage descended to his house, and settled all his affairs on that day; and on the following day he went up to the court; and the Emirs and Viziers, and Chamberlains and Deputies, and all the great officers of the state, went thither also; and the court resembled a flower-garden. And when the sage had entered, he presented himself before the King, bearing an old book, and a small pot containing a powder; and he sat down and said: "Bring me a tray." So they brought him one; and he poured out the powder into it. He then said: "O King, take this book, and do nothing with it until thou hast cut off my head; and when thou hast done so, place it upon this tray, and order some one to press it down upon the powder; and when this is done, the blood will be staunched; then open the book." As soon as the sage had said this, the King gave orders to strike off his head; and it was done. The King then opened the book, and found that its leaves were stuck together; so he put his finger to his mouth, and moistened it with his spittle, and opened the first leaf, and the second, and the third, but the leaves were not opened without difficulty. He opened six leaves, and looked at them; but found upon them no writing. So he said: "O Sage, there is nothing written in it." The head of the sage answered: "Turn over more leaves." The King did so; and in a little while the poison penetrated into his system; for the book was poisoned; and the King fell back and cried: "The poison hath penetrated into me!" — and upon this, the head of the sage Duban repeated these verses:

> They made use of their power, and used it tyran-
> nically; and soon it became as though it never
> had existed.
> Had they acted equitably, they had experienced
> equity; but they oppressed, wherefore fortune
> oppressed them with calamities and trials.
> Then did the case announce to them, This is the re-
> ward of your conduct, and fortune is blameless.

And when the head of the sage Duban had uttered these words, the King immediately fell down dead.
THE THOUSAND AND ONE NIGHTS,
ARABIAN (TENTH CENTURY)

---

*The work is ended and the past course is reviewed.
It if has been appropriate and thorough, good fortune is
assured.*

She walks in beauty, like the night
Of cloudless climes and starry skies,
And all that's best of dark and bright
Meet in her aspect and her eyes;
[78]10

Thus mellow'd do that tender light
Which heaven to gaudy day denies.

One shade the more, one ray the less,
Had half impair'd the nameless grace
Which waves in every raven tress
Or softly lightens o'er her face,
Where thoughts serenely sweet express
How pure, how dear their dwelling-place.

And on that cheek and o'er that brow
So soft, so calm, yet eloquent,
The smiles that win, the tints that glow
But tell of days in goodness spent,
A mind at peace with all below,
A heart whose love is innocent.

GEORGE GORDON (LORD) BYRON, ENGLISH (1788–1824)

The over-all judgment: the situation is difficult, involving wild and intractable people. The strong, however, will not harm the man, who treads with decorum and propriety amid disorder and peril. The hazardous episode will end without damage.

Though you serve richest wines,
Paulus, Rumor opines
    That they poisoned your four wives, I think,
It's of course all a lie;
None believes less than I —
    No, I really don't care for a drink.

MARTIAL, ROMAN (FIRST CENTURY)

In the last year of Yon-san terrible evils were abroad among the people. Such wickedness as the world had never seen before was perpetrated, of which his Majesty was the evil genius. He gave orders to his eunuchs and underlings to bring to him any woman of special beauty. . . .
In these days of trouble there was a young wife of a certain minister, who was very beautiful in form and face. One day it fell about that she was ordered into the Palace. Other women, when called, would cry and behave as though their lives were forfeited, but this young woman showed not the slightest sign of fear. She dressed and went straight into the Palace. King Yon-san saw her, and ordered her to come close to him. She came, and then in a sudden manner the

most terrible odor imaginable was noticeable. The King held his fan before his face, turned aside, spat, and said, "Dear me, I cannot stand this one, take her away," and so she escaped undefiled.

How it came about was thus: She knew that she was likely to be called at any moment, and so had planned a ruse by which to escape. Two slices of meat she had kept constantly on hand, decayed and foul-smelling, but always ready. She placed these under her arms as she dressed and went into the Palace, and so provided this unaccountable odour.

All that knew of it praised her bravery and sagacity.
IM BANG, KOREAN (1640–1722)

Mankind will not be reasoned out of the feelings of humanity.
SIR WILLIAM BLACKSTONE, ENGLISH (1723–1780)

 ## 11 Peace

THE T'AI HEXAGRAM

At the outset, the man brings others of like mind with him as he enters public office during a period of prosperity.

Cortés must have felt by now that Narváez was a poor match for him. He had come all the way from Mexico while the newly arrived general, with his fresh and still untried troops, remained enjoying the delights of Cempoal for no reason other than his usual indolence and carelessness; he was well informed about happenings in Narváez' camp from his own men who came and went, as well as from the men of Narváez who came and sometimes remained, like one Villalobos who, with seven other soldiers, deserted to Cortés as a protest against Ayllón's imprisonment. In this state of mind, he called Juan Velázquez de León. "And as Cortés spoke sometimes very honey-like, and with laughter in his mouth, he said to him half laughing: I had you called because I am told by Andrés de Duero that Narváez says, and it is a general rumour in this camp, that if you go there, I am done with and destroyed, for they believe that you will go over to him; and so, I have decided that, if you love me, you should go thither straight-

way on your good dapple mare, with all your gold,
and your Swaggerer . . . and other small trifles I will
give you; and you will wear the Swaggerer round one
shoulder and arm, and round the other one another
chain still heavier, and you will see what Narváez
wishes of you, and as soon as you come back, I shall
send Diego de Ordás, whom they also wish to see in
their camp."

This scene, vividly recorded by Bernal Díaz, is of the
purest Cortés: a flower of free, spontaneous, humor-
ous and slightly swaggerish life grown out of a root
of coldly calculated caution. It was essential for him
to test the loyalty of these two captains, one-time
leaders of the Velázquez group, *before* the battle and
not *during* battle. . . . The shrewd generosity of Cortés
worked on Velázquez de León at once: he accepted to
go, but refused to take his gold with him. Cortés gave
him one of his servants as an escort — just in case.

SALVADOR DE MADARIAGA, SPANISH (BORN 1886)

---

*The man observes the mean during times of peace. He
is magnanimous toward the uncultivated, ready for
necessary risks, watchful over future possibilities, and
independent of cliques and factions.*

Withal, Father Prospero was a good-natured man and
generous to the poor, of whom he was perhaps the
poorest. What he was paid for funerals, weddings,
and baptisms promptly passed to the hands of others.
He was never absent when people were ill or death
visited a home, and he never lost his kindly
smile and comforting manner. He was unaffected
in his good deeds, devoid of pretension and
solemnity, attaching no importance to his acts of
kindness and passing off allusions to them with
pleasantries — pleasantries that on occasion could be
a little broad.

When a village barkeep refused to accept the price of
a "nip," Father Prospero would jokingly insist:
"Don't put on good manners, man! Take your pen-
nies! You need them to support that mistress of
yours and her kids." Or if some self-righteous village
gossip came to him with a story about so-and-so, he
would say; "But woman, you'd be worse than they are
if you could find a fellow sinner" — and the sting of the

reproof would not be lessened by its joking manner.
JOSÉ RAFAEL POCATERRA, VENEZUELAN (BORN 1890)

[Buddha and Buddhism] are far away from us, and
this we must not forget. For Buddha, insight requires: exercises in meditation, a life of indifference
toward the world and its tasks. It will not suffice to
attempt a scientific experiment and see how much
we can accomplish with a few Yoga exercises. Nor
will it suffice to develop a mood of indifference to the
world and devote ourselves to contemplation. Those
who have not tested the progress of which they are
capable by years of meditative exercises grounded
in the proper faith and way of life, can understand
only as much as is communicable in rational thought.
In Buddha and Buddhism there flows a source which
we Westerners have not tapped, and consequently
there is a limit to our understanding. We must first of
all acknowledge that Buddhism is far removed from
us and renounce all quick, easy ways of coming closer
to it. To participate in the essence of Buddha's truth,
we should have to cease to be what we are. The difference lies not in rational positions but in the whole
view of life and manner of thinking.
But the remoteness of Buddhism need not make us
forget that we are all men, all facing the same questions of human existence. In Buddha and Buddhism
a great solution was found and put into practice. Our
task is to acquaint ourselves with it and as far as
possible to understand it. . . . I believe such an understanding is possible if we avoid excessive haste and
supposedly definitive interpretations. In understanding, we keep alive potentialities that are locked
deep within ourselves, and by understanding we
learn not to take our own historicity for the absolute,
exclusive truth. To my mind everything that is said
in the Buddhist text is addressed to a normal waking
consciousness and must therefore be largely acces-
sible to rational thought.
The fact is that Buddha's life was possible and that
Buddhist life has been a reality in various parts of
Asia down to our own day—this is a great and important fact. It points to the questionable essence of
man. A man is not what he just happens to be; he is
open. For him there is no *one* correct solution.
KARL JASPERS, GERMAN (BORN 1883)

*Change is certain. Peace is followed by disturbances;
departure of evil men by their return. Such recurrences
should not constitute occasions for sadness but realities
for awareness, so that one may be happy in the interim.*

Are we only to look at flowers in full bloom, at the
moon when it is clear?
Nay, to look out on the rain and long for the moon,
to draw the blinds and not to be aware of the passing
of the spring — these arouse even deeper feelings.
There is much to be seen in young boughs about to
flower, in gardens strewn with withered blossom.
Men are wont to regret that the moon has waned or
that the blossoms have fallen, and this must be so;
but they must be perverse indeed who will say,
"This branch, that bough is withered, now there is
nought to see."
YOSHIDA KENKO, JAPANESE (1283–1350)

---

*The man of high rank joins with the lowly in an atmo-
sphere of spontaneity and mutual confidence.*

One might think that a man of genius could browse
in the greatness of his own thoughts and dispense
with the cheap applause of the mob which he de-
spises. But actually he falls a victim to the more
mighty herd instinct; his searching, his findings, and
his call are inexorably meant for the crowd and must
be heard.
CARL GUSTAV JUNG, SWISS (1875–1961)

---

*The example of King I's decree that his younger sister
must obey her outranked husband is presented. The modest union of the high and the low brings real satisfaction.*

"What do you do all day?" he said.

"Teach music; I have another interest too."

"Work!" said old Jolyon, picking up the doll from
off the swing, and smoothing its black petticoat.
"Nothing like it, is there? I don't do any now. I'm
getting on. What interest is that?"

"Trying to help women who've come to grief." Old
Jolyon did not quite understand. "To grief?" he
repeated; then realized with a shock that she meant
exactly what he would have meant himself if he had
[83]11

used that expression. Assisting the Madgalenes of London! What a weird and terrifying interest! And, curiously overcoming his natural shrinking, he asked:

"Why? What do you do for them?"

"Not much. I've no money to spare. I can only give sympathy and food sometimes."

Involuntarily old Jolyon's hand sought his purse. He said hastily: "How d'you get hold of them?"

"I go to a hospital."

"A hospital! Phew!"

"What hurts me most is that once they nearly all had some sort of beauty."

JOHN GALSWORTHY, ENGLISH (1867–1933)

That which is called government, or rather that which we ought to conceive government to be, is no more than some common center in which all parts of society unite. This cannot be accomplished by any method so conducive to the various interests of the community, as by the representative system. It concentrates the knowledge necessary to the interest of the parts, and of the whole. It places government in a state of constant maturity. It is, as has already been observed, never young, never old. It is subject neither to nonage nor dotage. It is never in the cradle nor on crutches. It admits not of a separation between knowledge and power, and is superior, as government always ought to be, to all the accidents of individual man, and is therefore superior to what is called monarchy

THOMAS PAINE, AMERICAN (1737–1809)

The government has long been in disarray. Despite all proclamations to the contrary, ill fortune is at hand. War will only aggravate the situation. The subject should submit to fate, keep inwardly free, and ameliorate the harm done to those nearest him. The bad time will pass.

Parked among benches of oak, in the nooks of the church
Which their breath foully cools, their eyes' red rims
Toward the gilt-streaming choir and precentor's perch

[84]11

Where twenty mouths are bawling the pious hymns,
Inhaling the odor of wax like a perfume of bread,
Happy, like beaten dogs humiliated,
The Poor to their patron and sire, the good God,
Tender their laughable and stubborn *"oremus."*

For the women, it's really fine to smoothe these seats
After six black days of suffering imposed from on
 high.
They cradle here, within their strange capes' pleats,
Caricatures of children, weeping fit to die.

Their unwashed breasts exposed, these topers of
 soup,
A prayer in their eyes, yet never saying a prayer,
Observe parading shabbily a group
Of little street-girls with hats the worse for wear.

Outside, cold, hunger, man the drunken lout.
So it goes! An hour more. Later, nameless ills.
— Meanwhile, there's a whining, shuffling, all about,
From a bandage-swathed collection of old Jills.

The dazed are there, and the epileptics, those
From whom we turned aside in the squares yester-
 day,
And, muzzling ancient missals with the nose,
Those blind folk that a dog guides to an areaway.
All, slobbering faith both beggarly and insane,
Make their complaint to Jesus, infinitely,
Who dreams on high, yellowed by the livid pane,
Far from the scare-crows, the fat bad humanity,

Far from the stench of meat and fusty clothes,
A prostrate farce, sombre with noisome doings;
And prayer, with choice phrases, like a flower,
 grows,
And mysticisms take on the tone of suings,

When, from naves where dies the sun, in folds of silk,
Banal, with green smiles, Ladies, ah, the Daughters
Of Fashion, — O Jesus! — see them, they come, the
 bilious —
Their long yellow fingers kissing the holy waters.
ARTHUR RIMBAUD, FRENCH (1854–1891)

The over-all judgment: heaven and earth are in harmony.
The high and the low are united. The great, strong, and
good elements are entering upon the scene and the small,
weak, and evil departing.

We believe that according to our desire we are able to change the things round about us, we believe this because otherwise we can see no favourable solution. We forget the solution that generally comes to pass and is also favourable: we do not succeed in changing things according to our desire, but gradually our desire changes. The situation that we hoped to change because it was intolerable becomes unimportant. We have not managed to surmount the obstacle, as we were absolutely determined to do, but life has taken us round it, led us past it, and then if we turn round to gaze at the remote past, we can barely catch sight of it, so imperceptible has it become.

MARCEL PROUST, FRENCH (1871–1922)

And as oft in some great concourse, when Sedition lifts her head and the nameless vulgar kindles to rage — when brands and stones are already flying, and fury ministers arms — if they chance to behold a man of reverend goodness and worth, on the instant all are mute; and about him they stand with listening ear, while he sways their spirit by his word and allays their passion: even so sank all that tumult of ocean, when Father Neptune looked forth on the waves, and, floating under a cloudless heaven, guided his steeds and flew outward, giving rein to his speeding car.

VERGIL, ROMAN (70–19 B.C.)

A sweet content
Passing all wisdom or its fairest flower.
RICHARD H. HORNE, ENGLISH (1803–1884)

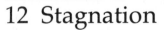

12 Stagnation
THE P'I HEXAGRAM

At the outset, the inferior people are advancing. The man retires from public office in order to preserve his integrity. He brings along his associates, who are like the sod clinging to the uprooted grass.

O, for a draught of vintage! that hath been
  Cool'd a long age in the deep-delved earth,
Tasting of Flora and the country green,

Dance, and Provencal song, and sunburnt mirth!
O for a beaker full of the warm South,
    Full of the true, the blushful Hippocrene,
        With beaded bubbles winking at the brim,
            And purple-stained mouth;
    That I might drink, and leave the world unseen,
        And with thee fade away into the forest dim:

Fade far away, dissolve, and quite forget
    What thou among the leaves hast never known,
The weariness, the fever, and the fret
    Here, where men sit and hear each other groan;
Where palsy shakes a few, sad last gray hairs,
    Where youth grows pale, and spectre-thin, and dies;
        Where but to think is to be full of sorrow
            And leaden-eyed despairs,
    Where Beauty cannot keep her lustrous eyes,
        Or new Love pine at them beyond tomorrow.
JOHN KEATS, ENGLISH (1795–1821)

The man achieves good fortune by patience and obedience to his superior, who resolves his uncertainties. The great man, however, acts independently in meeting the challenge of the circumstances.

This . . . is about the organization man. If the term is vague, it is because I can think of no other way to describe the people I am talking about. They are not the workers, nor are they the white-collar people in the usual, clerk sense of the word. These people only work for The Organization. The ones I am talking about *belong* to it as well. They are the ones of our middle class who have left home, spiritually as well physically, to take the vows of organization life, and it is they who are the mind and soul of our great self-perpetuating institutions. Only a few are top managers or ever will be. In a system that makes such hazy terminology as "junior executive" psychologically necessary, they are of the staff as much as the line, and most are destined to live poised in a middle area that still awaits a satisfactory euphemism. But they are the dominant members of our society nonetheless. They have not joined together into a recognizable elite — our country does not stand still long enough for that — but it is from their ranks that are coming most of the first and second echelons of our leadership, and it is their values which will set the American temper.

The corporation man is the most conspicuous example, but he is only one, for the collectivization so visible in the corporation has affected almost every field of work. Blood brother to the business trainee off to join Du Pont is the seminary student who will end up in the church hierarchy, the doctor headed for the corporate clinic, the physics Ph.D. in a government laboratory, the intellectual on the foundation-sponsored team project, the engineering graduate in the huge drafting room at Lockheed, the young apprentice in a Wall Street law factory.

They are all, as they so often put it, in the same boat. Listen to them talk to each other over the front lawns of their suburbia and you cannot help but be struck by how well they grasp the common denominators which bind them. Whatever the differences in their organization ties, it is the common problems of collective work that dominate their attentions, and when the Du Pont man talks to the research chemist or the chemist to the army man, it is these problems that are uppermost. The word *collective* most of them can't bring themselves to use . . . but they are keenly aware of how much more deeply beholden they are to organization than were their elders. They are wry about it, to be sure; they talk of the "treadmill," the "rat race," of the inability to control one's direction.

But they have no great sense of plight; between themselves and organization they believe they see an ultimate harmony and, more than most elders recognize, they are building an ideology that will vouchsafe this trust.

WILLIAM H. WHYTE, JR., AMERICAN (BORN 1917)

I know perfectly well that success is impossible for me if I cannot write as my heart dictates, free of any outside influence whatsoever, without having to keep in mind that I'm writing for Paris and not for the inhabitants of, say, the moon. Furthermore, the singers would have to sing as I wish, not as they wish, and the chorus, which, to be sure, is extremely capable, would have to show the same goodwill. A single will would have to rule throughout: my own. That may seem rather tyrannical to you, and perhaps it is. But if the work is an organic whole, it is built on a single idea and everything must contribute to the achievement of this unity. You may perhaps say that nothing stands in the way of all that in Paris. No! In Italy it can be done, or at least I can always do it; but in France: no. For example, if I come into the foyer of an Italian theater with a new work, no one ventures to utter an opinion, to pass judgment, before understanding everything thoroughly. And no one would even dare to make inappropriate requests. There is respect for the work and for the composer, and decisions are left to the public.

In the foyer of the Opera, on the other hand, everybody starts to whisper after the first four chords: *Oh, ce n'est pas bon . . . C'est commun, ce n'est pas de bon goût . . . Ce n'ire pas a Paris.* What do such pitiable words as *commun . . . de bon goût . . . Paris* mean, if you're dealing with a real work of art, which should belong to the whole world!

The conclusion from all this is that I'm no composer for Paris.

GIUSEPPE VERDI, ITALIAN (1813–1901)

The man feels inwardly ashamed for having acquired his position illegitimately. But he does not have the strength to carry out his evil purpose.

Do you realize what it is that is causing world chaos? . . . it's Nature hitting back. Not with the old weapons — floods, plagues, holocausts. We can neutralize them. She's fighting back with strange instruments called neuroses. She's deliberately affecting mankind with the jitters. Nature is proving that she can't be beaten — not by the likes of us. She's taking the world away from the intellectuals and giving it back to the apes.

ROBERT EMMET SHERWOOD, AMERICAN (1896–1955)

A turn for the better occurs. To succeed in creating order and making progress, however, the man must be given the requisite authority to do the task. He will fail if he proceeds on his own initiative and judgment.

From the nature of despotic power it follows that the single person, invested with this power, delegates the execution of it also to a single person. A man

[89]12

whose five senses continually inform him that he himself is everything and that his subjects are nothing, is naturally lazy, voluptuous, and ignorant. In consequence of this, he neglects the management of public affairs. But were he to commit the administration to many, there would be continual disputes among them; each would form intrigues to be his first slave; and he would be obliged to take the reins into his own hands. It is, therefore, more natural for him to resign it to a vizier, and to invest him with the same power as himself. The creation of a vizier is a fundamental law of this government.

BARON CHARLES DE SECONDAT DE MONTESQUIEU, FRENCH (1689–1755)

The man brings order and progress to the situation. He exhibits coolheadedness and caution during the transition and maintains contingency plans in readiness.

Oh! 'tis easy
To beget great deeds; but in the rearing of them—
The threading in cold blood each mean detail,
And furze brake of half-pertinent circumstance—
There lies the self-denial.

CHARLES KINGSLEY, ENGLISH (1819–1875)

In old times there was a certain petty monarch of the name of Jayadatta, and there was born to him a son, named Devadatta. And that wise king, wishing to marry his son, who was grown up, thus reflected: "The prosperity of kings is very unstable, being like a courtesan to be enjoyed by force; but the prosperity of merchants is like a woman of good family; it is steady and does not fly to another man. Therefore I will take a wife to my son from a merchant's family, in order that misfortune may not overtake his throne, though it is surrounded with many relations." Having formed this resolve, that king sought for his son the daughter of a merchant in Pataliputra named Vasudatta. Vasudatta for his part, eager for such a distinguished alliance, gave that daughter of his to the prince, though he dwelt in a remote foreign land.

And he loaded his son-in-law with wealth to such an extent that he no longer felt much respect for his father's magnificence. Then King Jayadatta dwelt happily with that son of his who had obtained the daughter of that rich merchant. Now one day the merchant Vasudatta came, full of desire to see his daughter, to the palace of his connection by marriage, and took away his daughter to his own home. Shortly after the King Jayadatta suddenly went to heaven, and that kingdom was seized by his relations, who rose in rebellion; through fear of them his son Devadatta was secretly taken away by his mother during the night to another country.

Then that mother, distressed in soul, said to the prince: "Our feudal lord is the emperor who rules the eastern region; repair to him, my son; he will procure you the kingdom."

When his mother said this to him, the prince answered her: "Who will respect me if I go there without attendants?" When she heard that, his mother went on to say: "Go to the house of your father-in-law, and get money there, and so procure followers; and then repair to the emperor." Being urged in these words by his mother, the prince, though full of shame, slowly plodded on and reached his father-in-law's house in the evening. But he could not bear to enter at such an unseasonable hour, for he was afraid of shedding tears, being bereaved of his father and having lost his worldly splendor; besides, shame withheld him.

So he remained in the veranda of an almshouse nearby, and at night he suddenly beheld a woman descending with a rope from his father-in-law's house, and immediately he recognized her as his wife, for she was so resplendent with jewels that she looked like a meteor fallen from the clouds; and he was much grieved thereat. But she, though she saw him, did not recognize him, as he was emaciated and begrimed, and asked him who he was. When he heard that, he answered: "I am a traveler." Then the merchant's daughter entered the almshouse, and the prince followed her secretly to watch her. There she advanced toward a certain man, and he toward her, and asking why she had come so late, he bestowed several kicks on her. Then the passion of the wicked woman was doubled, and she appeased him, and remained with him on the most affectionate terms.

When he saw that, the discreet prince reflected:

"This is not the time for me to show anger, for I have other affairs in hand; and how could I employ against these two contemptible creatures, this wife of mine and the man who has done me this wrong, this sword which is to be used against my foes? Or what quarrel have I with this adulteress, for this is the work of malignant desire that showers calamities upon me, showing skill in the game of testing my firmness? It is my marriage with a woman below me in rank that is in fault, not the woman herself; how can a female crow leave the male crow to take pleasure in a cuckoo?"

Thus reflecting, he allowed that wife of his to remain in the society of her paramour; for in the minds of heroes possessed with an ardent desire of victory, of what importance is woman, valueless as a straw? But at the moment when his wife ardently embraced her paramour there fell from her ear an ornament thickly studded with valuable jewels. And she did not observe this, but at the end of her interview, taking leave of her paramour, returned hurriedly to her house as she came. And that unlawful lover also departed somewhere or other.

Then the prince saw that jeweled ornament, and took it up; it flashed with many jewel-gleams, dispelling the gathering darkness of despondency, and seemed like a hand-lamp obtained by him to assist him in searching for his lost prosperity. The prince immediately perceived that it was very valuable, and went off, having obtained all he required, to Kanyakubja; there he pledged that ornament for a hundred thousand gold pieces, and after buying horses and elephants went into the presence of the emperor. And with the troops which he gave him he marched, and slew his enemies in fight, and recovered his father's kingdom; and his mother applauded his success.

Then he redeemed from pawn that ornament, and sent it to his father-in-law to reveal that unsuspected secret; his father-in-law, when he saw that earring of his daughter's, which had come to him in such a way, was confounded, and showed it to her. She looked upon it, lost long ago like her own virtue; and when she heard that it had been sent by her husband she was distracted, and called to mind the whole circumstance: "This is the very ornament which I let fall in the almshouse the night I saw that unknown traveler standing there; so that must undoubtedly have been my husband come to test my virtue, but I did not recognize him, and he picked up this ornament."

While the merchant's daughter was going through this train of reflection, her heart, afflicted by the misfortune of her unchastity having been discovered, in its agony, broke. Then her father artfully questioned a maid of hers who knew all her secrets, and found out the truth, and so ceased to mourn for his daughter; as for the prince, after he recovered the kingdom, he obtained as wife the daughter of the emperor, won by his virtues, and enjoyed the highest prosperity.

SOMADEVA, INDIAN (ELEVENTH CENTURY)

Stagnation and disintegration give way to happiness and progress. But they may not last long.

But perhaps by accumulation of this steady, smooth massaging of the nerves, perhaps because, as the dance goes on he comes to less sober tunes, the saxophonist climbs imperceptibly to a new step, the sliding dance becomes more jaunty. Then suddenly I hear the real note of the saxophone, unforgettable, high, and clear, as if from a heart of brass, the new thing, the thing we have come to hear. To me it has quite passed out of humanity, this famous upper register, but it is still near enough for me to understand; piercing, musical, the cry of a faun that is beautiful and hurt. The leader tips his instrument into the air; he blows with all his force but his cheeks remain pale. He is now at the height of his art. The voice of our age has come through his lips through this marvelous instrument. He is a priest possessed with a half-human god, endlessly sorrowful, yet utterly sentimental. Incapable of regret, with no past, no memory, no future, no hope. The sound pricks the dancers, parts their lips, puts spring into their march. These unexpressive, unethical, unthinking men have discovered their unethical, unsentimental reaction to our age.

This is the thing that makes the saxophone great and brings fortune and ruin to its players. But it is a

changeable instrument and can feign many things.
Then, in spite of its nature, the saxophone seems to
brood and almost regret the years that have brought
it to favor, the war, the peace, and this state to which
Europe through its own fault has come; and ghosts
of broken promises and broken soldiers seem sadly
to look over the shoulders of the dancers.
Every beat of the impeccable rhythm is heavy with
the tread of the armies of Somme and Marne, and
under it the heavy echo of the unarmed millions
of Russians marching to Tannenberg. Then the
saxophone seems burdened with an illusory
despair; other days before Europe was ruined rise
up before this assembly of those who were not
ruined.
But this mood is fancy and the saxophone will not
allow it long. It turns with a curve into "I Don't
Care," or "Let's Pretend"; not even regretting our
regrets, absorbed in the present, that owes no debts
either to the irretrievable past or to the incomprehensible future, it strikes up "Rambler Rose," the
latest fox-trot, the march past of our age. That is more
to our taste, we modern Europeans, that oppose to
the dangers with which we are beleaguered not fear,
nor courage, only impossibility; and who have sub-
stituted for human aspiration that needs belief
this innocence of the faun, behind the saxophone.
So, for the supreme expression of our hard, unreflec-
tive joys, we have chosen this instrument. Our
fathers left it uncomprehended; our children will
shiver at it, and discard it again. For the present it
makes audible the spirit of our age.
WILLIAM BOLITHO, SOUTH AFRICAN (1891–1930)

---

*The over-all judgment: there is a want of communica-
tion between those above and those below. Growth is at
an end. The way of the inferior man increases, while that
of the superior man decreases. The latter retires from
the scene to retain his principles.*

The Ephesians would do well to hang themselves,
every grown man of them, and leave the city to
beardless lads; for they have cast out Hermodoros,
the best among them, saying, "We will have none
who is best among us; if there be any such, let him

be so elsewhere and among others."
HERACLITUS, GREEK (SIXTH–FIFTH CENTURY B.C.)

Political corruption is not a matter of men or classes or education or character of any sort; it is a matter of pressure. Wherever the pressure is brought to bear, society and government cave in. The problem, then, is one of discovering and dealing with the cause or the source of the pressure to buy and corrupt.
JOSEPH LINCOLN STEFFENS, AMERICAN (1866–1936)

Chuang-tzu was one day fishing, when the Prince of Ch'u sent two high officials to interview him, saying that His Highness would be glad of Chuang-tzu's assistance in the administration of his government. The latter quietly fished on, and without looking around, replied: "I have heard that in the state of Ch'u there is a sacred tortoise, which has been dead three thousand years, and which the Prince keeps packed up in a box on the altar, in his ancestral shrine. Now do you think that tortoise would rather be dead and have its remains thus honored, or be alive and wagging its tail in the mud?" The two officials answered that no doubt it would rather be alive and wagging its tail in the mud; whereupon Chuang-tzu cried out: "Begone! I, too, elect to remain, wagging my tail in the mud."
CHUANG-TZU, CHINESE (335–275 B.C.)

13 Fellowship
THE T'UNG JÊN HEXAGRAM

At the outset, attempts are made at open friendship.

To sit with the long face
That tries to look wise
Is not congenial
To good fellowship
So much as a loud drinking song.
OTOMO NO-TABITO, JAPANESE (665–731)

Because of special privileges and factions, only a limited fellowship is realized. Regrets and problems result.

"The Jews," replied Lamia, "are profoundly attached
[95]13

to their ancient customs. They suspected you, un-reasonably I admit, of a desire to abolish their laws and change their usages. Do not resent it, Pontius, if I say that you did not always act in such a way as to disperse their unfortunate illusion. It gratified you, despite your habitual self-restraint, to play upon their fears, and more than once have I seen you betray in their presence the contempt with which their beliefs and religious ceremonies inspired you. You irritated them particularly by giving instructions for the sacerdotal garments and ornaments of their high priest to be kept in ward by your legionnaires in the Antonine tower. One must admit that though they have never risen like us to an appreciation of things divine, the Jews celebrate rites which their very antiquity renders venerable."

Pontius Pilate shrugged his shoulders.

"They have very little exact knowledge of the nature of the gods," he said. "They worship Jupiter, yet they abstain from naming him or erecting a statue of him. They do not even adore him under the semblance of a rude stone, as certain of the Asiatic peoples are wont to do. They know nothing of Apollo, of Neptune, of Mars, nor of Pluto, nor of any goddess. At the same time, I am convinced that in the days gone by they worshipped Venus. For even to this day their women bring doves to the altar as victims; and you know as well as I that the dealers who trade beneath the arcades of their temple supply those birds in couples for sacrifice. I have even been told that on one occasion some madman proceeded to overturn the stalls bearing their offerings, and their owners with them. The priests raised an outcry about it, and looked on it as a case of sacrilege. I am of the opinion that their custom of sacrificing turtle-doves was instituted in honor of Venus. Why are you laughing, Lamia?"

"I was laughing," said Lamia, "at an amusing idea which, I hardly know how, just occurred to me. I was thinking that perchance some day the Jupiter of the Jews might come to Rome and vent his fury upon you. Why should he not? Asia and Africa have already enriched us with a considerable number of gods. We have seen temples in honor of Isis and the dog-faced Anubis erected in Rome. In the public square, and even on the race-courses, you may run

across the Bona Dea of the Syrians mounted on an
ass. And did you never hear how, in the reign of
Tiberius, a young patrician passed himself off as the
horned Jupiter of the Egyptians, Jupiter Ammon, and
in this disguise procured the favors of an illustrious
lady who was too virtuous to deny anything to a
god? Beware, Pontius, lest the invisible Jupiter of
the Jews disembark some day on the quay at Ostia!"
ANATOLE FRANCE, FRENCH (1844–1924)

SAXONY. Where am I brought? T'a Roman prison.
  Death!
 Is this the place! Hold, minister of horror,
 Why all this cruelty?
FIRST PRIEST. Ask when you feel it.
SAXONY. Bold slave, is this an answer for a prince?
FIRST PRIEST. Bold prince, is this an answer for a
  priest?
ELKANAH SETTLE, ENGLISH (1648–1724)

---

*Mistrust ensues. The man conceals his weapons, plans
an ambush, but dares not come forth.*

Statesmen have always been eager to accept from the
theologian and the philosopher the correct formula-
tion of the ethical precepts that should guide foreign
policy, and since the seventeenth century all power
politics has, therefore, been presented not as a
crude attempt to survive in a tough world but as a
noble endeavor aimed at the establishment of
political equilibrium and the preservation of
order.
Formulated in those terms the success has not been
overwhelming. We might search for an explanation
in the fact that the process is not guaranteed and that
not all statesmen are good technicians, but it is perhaps safer to explain the result on the theory that
they were not really interested in achieving a balance. There are not many instances in history which
show great and powerful states creating alliances and
organizations to limit their own strength. States are
always engaged in curbing the force of some other
state. The truth of the matter is that states are interested only in a balance which is in their favor. Not an
equilibrium, but a generous margin is their objective. There is no real security in being just as strong

as a potential enemy; there is security only in being a little stronger. There is no possibility of action if one's strength is fully checked; there is a chance for a positive foreign policy only if there is a margin of force which can be freely used.

NICHOLAS JOHN SPYKMAN, AMERICAN (1893–1943)

The man mounts his city wall, but is afraid to embark on aggression. The antagonists consider the difficulties and yield to right and law. Reconciliation is imminent.

Peace through stalemate based on a coincident recognition by each side of the opponent's strength is at least preferable to peace through common exhaustion — and has often provided a better foundation for lasting peace. . . .
Where the two sides are too evenly matched to offer a reasonable chance of early success to either, the statesman is wise who can learn something from the psychology of strategy, if you find your opponent in a strong position costly to force, you should leave him a line of retreat — as the quickest way of loosening his resistance.

BASIL HENRY LIDDELL HART, ENGLISH (BORN 1895)

After considerable difficulties, the man collects his forces and overcomes the obstacles to the union of men. Sadness gives way to joy.

The frightful thing about war is that, as a subject, it's inexhaustible. One's eye is always being caught by some new aspect of the business. My real point is this: that for the men in the trenches — for all of them, that is, who are above the purely animal level, for whom, as you must see for yourself, it is most necessary to find an explanation — the idea that they must stay where they are and get on with their job because there is no real alternative is not enough to keep them in spirits, to prevent their moral collapse. Each one of them has got to find some effective suggestion that will touch him personally, some thought, some fixed idea, the secret of which is known to him alone, the essence of which he can absorb drop by drop. Sometimes he has several among which he can take his choice. No sooner does one begin to lose its potency than he can change over to others. Take my own case, for instance. For quite a while I managed very comfortably on the idea that I was the kind of man who could "rise superior to circumstances" — the circumstances in question being partly composed of mental distress, partly of bodily discomfort. "I'd like," said I, "to see those circumstances to which I could not rise superior!" While shrapnel pattered round me . . . I would recite to myself like a sort of magic formula, those terrific lines of Horace:

Si fractus illabatur orbis
Impavidum ferient ruinae . . .

It really is a magic formula. And then, one day, it no longer worked. My mental distress became too great, my fear became too great, and I just wanted to burst into tears and cry "Mama!" like a little boy. . . . Then take the young second lieutenant fresh from Saint-Cyr, all innocence and splendid bravery, who says to himself: "If France is conquered, life will be impossible. I shall feel personally dishonoured. Far rather would I have my name on a headstone with the words: 'Died on the field of honour,' than live on disgraced." Another example is that of the reservist with a taste for serious reading and an equipment of large-hearted ideals, the kind of man who says to himself: "This is the war that will end war. We are bringing peace to the whole world. Thanks to our sacrifice, our children will be spared knowledge of such horrors." Standing next to him in the same trench will be some fellow who thinks: "This is the end of the world. We're all in for it. What does it matter if I get killed a little sooner or a little later?" Another there may be who believes in a coming reign of justice, who is still convinced that victory for the democracies will mean freedom for the oppressed everywhere in the world, the end of the domination of money and social iniquity, who would be willing even to die if only he could be sure that his death would mean greater happiness for men yet unborn. Then there's the sentimentalist, for whom nothing counts but personal relationships, whose world is made up of just a few dear friends, who argues: "Most of my pals are dead. If they all go, what is there left to live for?" There's the man whose wife left him as soon as he was called up, and ran off with someone else; who gets no letters and no parcels; who feels himself too old to start life afresh, who would just as soon be dead, for whom the very fact of danger is a distraction, because it gives him the illusion that life is still sweet. There is the man who exists in a world of dreams and takes things as they come. "Everything is predestined," says he; "I always knew it. No use fighting against fate. We must just go with the tide." There is the man who never had a chance, who has always felt himself to be the victim of injustice and insult, who has always envied the good fortune of others, who so relishes the taste of equality bred of a general misery that he pays but lip service to the desire for peace with all the bitterness that it will bring for him in its train. Close beside him is another in whom the war has waked a deep-seated strain of pessimism, who thinks sincerely: "The universe is a foul absurdity. It was always pretty obvious, but the war has proved it beyond the shadow of a doubt. Why cling to a foul absurdity?" or: "Humanity is the work of the Devil, a blot on the face of the earth, born for murder and self-slaughter. So much the worse for humanity (and for me, who am part of humanity and so of the whole putrescent mess)." There is the fanatical Catholic, who thinks: "This is God's punishment wrought on a corrupt and faithless generation. If God has decided that I too must pay the penalty, even for the faults of others, who am I to question His will?" There is the gentle Catholic, who carries tucked away in his pack a tiny edition of the *Imitation*, who, when night falls, says his prayers in his shellhole, very quietly, so that no one shall notice him, and murmurs: "Let me suffer, as You suffered, Jesu mine. Why should I be spared, since You suffered a thousand deaths hanging on Your cross? Give me strength that I may be not too unworthy of You." Finally, there is the Man . . . who says: "All that matters to me in this world is the language of France, the cathedrals of our French countryside, the quays of the Seine, landscapes that can be found nowhere else in the world, a way of life that is unique. If all that is to be taken away, life has no longer any point. If, by dying, I can ensure that all these things will live on after me, then death is right and proper. . . ." Picture to yourself trench after trench filled with men thinking such thoughts, and you will find the answer to

your question. . . . That is why Verdun still stands.
JULES ROMAINS, FRENCH (BORN 1885)

"Winning" in a conflict does not have a strictly
competitive meaning; it is not winning relative to
one's adversary. It means gaining relative to one's
own value system; and this may be done by bargaining, by mutual accommodation, and by the avoid-
ance of mutually damaging behavior.
THOMAS C. SCHELLING, AMERICAN (BORN 1921)

---

*The man achieves fellowship, but only with those near-
by. Simply because mankind has not yet attained universal brotherhood, however, is no ground for remorse.*

I was a good Christian; born and bred in the bosom
of the infallible Presbyterian Church. How then
could I unite with this wild idolator in worshiping
his piece of wood? But what is worship? thought I.
Do you suppose now, Ishmael, that the magnanimous God of heaven and earth—pagans and all included—can possibly be jealous of an insignificant
bit of black wood? Impossible! But what is worship?
—to do the will of God—*that* is worship. And what
is the will of God?—to do to my fellow man what I
would have my fellow man do to me—*that* is the will
of God. Now, Queequeg is my fellow man. And what
do I wish that this Queequeg would do to me? Why,
unite with me in my particular form of worship.
Consequently, I must then unite with him in his;
ergo, I must turn idolator.
HERMAN MELVILLE, AMERICAN (1819–1891)

---

*The over-all judgment: the harmonious union among
men is based upon the universal goals of humanity,
openly pursued by a persevering and selfless leader.
Because of this fellowship, difficult enterprises can be
undertaken.*

Except that all its events were happy, this day was
not essentially unlike Feisal's every day. . . . The
roads to Wejh swarmed with envoys and volunteers
and great sheikhs riding in to swear allegiance. . . .
Feisal swore new adherents solemnly on the Koran
between his hands, "to wait while he waited, march
when he marched, to yield obedience to no Turk,

to deal kindly with all who spoke Arabic (whether
Bagdadi, Alleppine, Syrian, or pure-blooded)
and to put independence above life, family, and
goods."

He also began to confront them at once, in his presence, with their tribal enemies, and to compose their
feuds. An account of profit and loss would be struck
between the parties, with Feisal modulating and in-
terceding between them, and often paying the balance, or contributing towards it from his own funds,
to hurry on the pact. During the two years Feisal so
laboured daily, putting together and arranging in
their natural order the innumerable tiny pieces
which made up Arabian society, and combining
them into his one design of war against the Turks.
There was no blood feud left active in any of the
districts through which he had passed, and he was
Court of Appeal, ultimate and unchallenged, for
western Arabia.

He showed himself worthy of this achievement. He
never gave a partial decision, nor a decision so im-
practicably just that it must lead to disorder. No Arab
ever impugned his judgments or questioned his
wisdom and competence in tribal business. By patiently sifting out right and wrong, by his tact, his
wonderful memory, he gained authority over the
Nomads from Medina to Damascus and beyond. He
was recognized as a force transcending tribe, superseding blood chiefs, greater than jealousies. The
Arab movement became in the best sense national,
since within it all Arabs were as one, and for it private interests must be set aside.

THOMAS EDWARD LAWRENCE, ENGLISH (1888–1935)

Whatever opinion is held concerning the vitality of
capitalism itself, whatever the life span predicted
for it, it is bound to withstand the onslaughts of its
enemies and its own irrationality much longer than
essentially untenable export monopolism — untenable even from the capitalist point of view. Export
monopolism may perish in revolution, or it may be
peacefully relinquished; this may happen soon, or it
may take some time and require desperate struggle;
but one thing is certain — it *will* happen. This will
immediately dispose of neither warlike instincts nor
structural elements and organizational forms ori-

ented toward war—and it is to their dispositions and domestic interests that, in my opinion, much more weight must be given in every concrete case of imperialism than to export monopolist interests, which furnish the financial "outpost skirmishes"—a most appropriate term—in many ways. But such factors will be politically overcome in time, no matter what they do to maintain among the people a sense of constant danger of war, with the war machine forever primed for action. And with them, imperialisms will wither and die.
JOSEPH SCHUMPETER, MORAVIAN (1883–1950)

... an energetic myth, a permanent motive to which the mass adheres and which the mass elaborates upon. These solidify vague conceptions into figures, notions into judgments and formulas; and though they may rarely create the language of history, they often create its legends and proverbs.
FRIEDRICH GUNDOLF, GERMAN (1880–1931)

14 Wealth

THE TA YU HEXAGRAM

At the outset, no threats have been received and no challenges met. The man avoids harm by realizing the dangers caused by opulence and exercising appropriate restraint.

You are now entered upon a scene of business, where I hope you will one day make a figure. . . . Business does not exclude (as possibly you wish it did) the usual terms of politeness and good breeding, but, on the contrary, strictly requires them. . . . Be upon your guard against the pedantry and affectation of business, which young people are apt to fall into, from the pride of being concerned in it too young. They look thoughtful, complain of the weight of business, throw out mysterious hints, and seem big with secrets which they do not know. Do you on the contrary never talk of business but to those with whom you are to transact it; and learn to seem *vacuous* and idle when you have the most business. Of all things, the *volto sciolto* and *pensieri stretti* are necessary.
LORD CHESTERFIELD, ENGLISH (1694–1773)

Accumulated virtues and competent helpers enable the man to assume great responsibilities. Like a huge wagon ready for loading, he subordinates strength to humility.

Public opinion cannot be formed without groups and clubs, either open or secret, depending on circumstances. The important thing is that they must have determined ends, and a determined discipline in their work. . . . Methods depend entirely on the outside situation, but such groups are in any case indispensable.
NIKOLAI PLATONOVICH OGAREV, RUSSIAN (1813–1877)

The superior man places his property and talents at the service of the ruler and the public. The inferior man employs them for his own gain.

Our life is not a mutual helpfulness; but rather, cloaked under the due laws-of-war, named "fair competition" and so forth, it is a mutual hostility. We have profoundly forgotten everywhere that *Cash-payment* is not the sole relation of human beings; we think, nothing doubting, that *it* absolves and liquidates all engagements of man. "My starving workers?" answers the rich mill-owner. "Did not I hire them fairly in the market? Did I not pay them, to the last sixpence, the sum covenanted for? What have I to do with them more?" — Verily Mammon-worship is a melancholy need. When Cain, for his own behoof, had killed Abel, and was questioned, "Where is thy brother?" he too made answer, "Am I my brother's keeper?" Did I not pay my brother *his* wages, the thing he had merited from me?
O sumptuous Merchant-Prince, illustrious game-preserving Duke, is there no way of "killing" thy brother but Cain's crude way! . . .
One of Dr. Allison's Scotch facts struck us much. A poor Irish Widow, her husband having died in one of the Lanes of Edinburgh, went forth with her children, bare of all resource, to solicit help from the Charitable Establishments of that City. At this Charitable Establishment and then at that she was refused; referred from one to the other, helped by none; — till she had exhausted them all; till her strength and heart failed her: she sank down in

typhus-fever; died, and infected her Lane with fever, so that "seventeen other persons" died of fever there in consequence. The humane Physician asks thereupon, as with a heart too full for speaking, Would it not have been *economy* to help this poor Widow?
THOMAS CARLYLE, SCOTTISH (1795–1881)

The man discriminates clearly what should be done. He keeps his strength under control, yields not to competition and envy, and does not injure the mild ruler.

The principle which guided him [Montaigne] in his administration was to look only at the fact, at the result, and to grant nothing to noice and outward show: "How much more a good effect makes a noise, so much I abate of the goodness of it." For it is always to be feared that it was more performed for the sake of noise than upon the account of goodness: "Being exposed upon the stall, 'tis half sold." That was not Montaigne's way; he made no show: he employed in a manner useful to all alike gifts of sincerity and conciliation; the personal attraction with which nature endowed him was a quality of the highest value in the management of men. He preferred to warn men of evil rather than to take on himself the honor of repressing it: "Is there any one who desires to be sick that he may see his physician's practice? And would not that physician deserve to be whipped who should wish the plague among us that he might put his art into practice?"
CHARLES AUGUSTIN SAINTE-BEUVE,
FRENCH (1804–1869)

The man and his people are mutually attracted to each other through unaffected sincerity. Benevolence on his part, however, must be accompanied by the proper display of majesty. Otherwise, the people will become insolent and lose their attitude of service.

Who more than Basil honored virtue or punished vice? Who evinced more favor toward the right-doing, or more severity toward offenders — he whose very smile was often praise; whose silence, reproof, in the depths of conscience reaching and arousing the sense of guilt? Grant that he was no light prattler, no jester, no lounger in the markets. Grant that he
[105]14

did not ingratiate himself with the multitude by becoming all things to all, and courting their favor: what then? Should he not, with the right judging, receive praise for this rather than condemnation? Is it deemed a fault in the lion that he has not the look of an ape; that his aspect is stern and regal; that his movements, even in sport, are majestic, and command at once wonder and delight? Or do we admire it as proof of courtesy and true benevolence in actors that they gratify the populace, and move them to laughter by mutual blows on the temple, and by boisterous merriment?

SAINT GREGORY OF NAZIANZUS, ANZANITE (329–389)

I maintain that Democratic manners — typified by the practice of calling the boss by his first name — have reached the point in our country where they conduce not to the preservation of personal dignity but to the abject submission of one man to another. These manners, gradually developed in colonial and post-revolutionary days, worked well in a society largely of self-sufficient farmers. But circumstances have changed, with the usual ironical result.

What happens on the job at the present time? An employee greets the boss by his first name, sits down in his presence, wears the same kind of clothes the boss wears, avoids the use of *sir*, and ostensibly comports himself in general as if he and the boss were as equal as two farmers. But of course he and the boss are not equal, and this inequality must be signalized, first, because the employee is anxious to please the boss, who can advance or impede his fortunes; and secondly, because the boss is anxious that his authority receive recognition, without which he cannot function with any confidence.

In the absence of overt and conventional methods of expressing deference, how then does the American employee acknowledge the boss's superior status? He does so by perfecting a subtle repertoire of body movements and vocal expressions. This repertoire includes the boyish grin, the deprecatory cough, the unfinished sentence, the appreciative giggle, the drooping shoulders, the head-scratch, and the bottom-waggle. But there are employees, the truly gifted ones — as actors, they would adorn the Stanislavski school — who can dispense with these definable

[106]14

maneuvers and simply *live* the part, their whole being radiating a kind of sweet eloquence of submission.
MORTON J. CRONIN, AMERICAN (BORN 1917)

*The man attains the fullness of blessings. He recognizes
the bases for the favorable state of affairs, remains devoted in his actions, and honors the sage who exerted
the beneficent influence.*

There is a beautiful Indian apologue, which says: A
man once said to a lump of clay, "What art thou?"
The reply was, "I am but a lump of clay, but I was
placed beside a rose and I caught its fragrance."
WILLIAM MORLEY PUNSHON, ENGLISH (1824–1881)

*The over-all judgment: strength with elegance is at-
tained. This is in accord with the propitious phase of the
cosmic cycle, which leads to great progress and wealth.
The pride which is likely to be engendered is kept within
bounds.*

The days of palmy prosperity are not those most
favorable to the display of public virtue or the influence of wise and good men. In hard, doubtful, un-
prosperous, and dangerous times, the disinterested
and patriotic find their way, by a species of public
instinct, unopposed, joyfully welcomed, to the control of affairs.
EDWARD EVERETT, AMERICAN (1794–1865)

But the positive side of my mind always assures me
that France is not really herself unless in the front
rank; that only vast enterprises are capable of coun-
ter-balancing the ferments of dispersal which are inherent in her people; that our country, as it is, surrounded by the others, as they are, must aim high
and hold itself straight, on pain of mortal danger. In
short, to my mind, France cannot be France without
greatness.
CHARLES DE GAULLE, FRENCH (BORN 1890)

A pleasant letter I hold to be the pleasantest thing
that this world has to give. It should be good-humoured; witty it may be, but with a gentle diluted
wit. Concocted brilliancy will spoil it altogether. Not
long, so that it will be tedious in the reading; nor
[107]14

brief, so that the delight suffices not to make itself felt. It should be written specially for the reader, and should apply altogether to him, and not altogether to any other. It should never flatter. Flattery is always odious. But underneath the visible stream of pungent water there may be the slightest undercurrent of eulogy, so that it be not seen, but only understood. Censure it may contain freely, but censure which in arraigning the conduct implies no doubt as to the intellect . . . . Then let its page be soiled by no business; one touch of utility will destroy it all . . . . But, above all things, see that it be good-humoured.
ANTHONY TROLLOPE, ENGLISH (1815–1882)

 # 15 Modesty

THE CH'IEN HEXAGRAM

At the outset, the man retains his humility and does not press any claims. As a result he is free from challenges and does not encounter resistance. Difficult enterprises can be undertaken successfully.

But perhaps the desire of the thing called fame will torment thee. —See how soon everything is forgotten, and look at the chaos of infinite time on each side of the present, and the emptiness of applause, and the changeableness and want of judgment in those who pretend to give praise, and the narrowness of the space within which it is circumscribed, and be quiet at last. For the whole earth is a point, and how small a nook in it is this thy dwelling, and how few are there in it, and what kind of people are they who will praise.
EMPEROR MARCUS AURELIUS ANTONINUS, ROMAN (121–180)

Modesty is at the core of the man's being and reveals itself in his outward behavior.

Be your beginning plain: and take good heed
Too soon you mount not on the airy steed,
Nor tell your reader, in a thundering verse,
"I sing the conqueror of the universe."
What can an author after this produce?
The laboring mountain must bring forth a mouse.

[108]15

Much better are we pleased with his address,
Who without making such vast promises,
Says in an easier style and plainer sense,
"I sing the combats of that pious prince
Who from the Phrygian coast his armies bore,
And landed first on the Lavinian shore."
His opening muse set not the world on fire,
And yet performs more than we can require.
Quickly you'll hear him celebrate the fame
And future glory of the Roman name,
Of Styx and Acheron describe the floods,
And Caesars wandering in the Elysian woods.
NICOLAS BOILEAU-DESPRÉAUX, FRENCH (1636–1711)

---

*The man disregards his fame and acknowleged merit but
toils on laboriously and unpretentiously. He is supported
by all the people in bringing his works to a successful
conclusion.*

I am not, brother, a doctor to be looked up to; nor do
I possess all the world's wisdom. But, in one word, I
know enough to distinguish truth from falsehood.
And as I know no character more worthy of esteem
than the truly devout, nor anything in the world
more noble or beautiful than the holy fervor of a sincere piety, so I know nothing more odious than the
whited sepulcher of a pretended zealot, than those
downright imposters, those devotees, for public
show, whose sacrilegious and deceitful grimaces
abuse with impunity, and make a jest, according to
their fancy, of what men hold most holy and sacred;
those men who, from motives of self-interest, make
a trade of piety, and would purchase honor and reputation at the cost of a hypocritical turning up of the
eyes and pretended raptures; those men, I say, whom
we see possessed with such an uncommon ardor for
the next world, in order to make their fortunes in
this; who, with great unction and many prayers,
daily recommend and preach solitude in the midst
of the court; who know how to reconcile their zeal
with their vices; who are passionate, vindictive,
without belief, full of artifice, and would, in order to
destroy a man, insolently cover their fierce resentment under the cloak of Heaven's interests. They are
the more dangerous in their bitter wrath because
they use against us weapons which men reverence

and because their passion, for which they are commended, prompts them to assassinate us with a consecrated blade. One sees too many of those vile characters, but the really devout at heart are easily recognized. Our age has shown us some, brother, who may serve us as glorious examples. Look at Ariston, look at Périandre, Oronte, Alcidamas, Polydore, Clitandre — no one disputes their title. But they do not boast of their virtue. One does not see this unbearable ostentation in them; and their piety is human, is tractable; they do not censure all our doings, they think that these corrections would show too much pride on their part; and, leaving big words to others, they reprove our actions by their own. They do not think anything evil, because it seems so, and their mind is inclined to judge well of others. They have no cabals, no intrigues; all their anxiety is to live well themselves. They never persecute a sinner; they hate sin only, and do not vindicate the interest of Heaven with greater zeal than Heaven itself. These are my people, that is the true way to act; that is, in short, an example to be followed. Your man, to speak plainly, is not of that stamp; you vaunt his zeal with the utmost good faith; but I believe that you are dazzled by a false glare.

MOLIÈRE, FRENCH (1622–1673)

"But why should you, friend, be so very solicitous about the safety of the king?"

"Oh," replied the good man, "because I honor him more than I do any one else, and love him more than myself."

"But what good has he ever done you," asked the king (in disguise), "that you should hold him in high esteem? Methinks you would be rather more comfortably lodged and clothed were you any extraordinary favorite of his."

"Not so," answered the fisherman, "for tell me, Sir Knight, what greater favor can I receive from my honored king, in my humble sphere, than to be protected in the enjoyment of my house and goods, and the little earnings which I make? All I have I owe to his kindness, to the wisdom and justice with which he rules over his subjects, preserving us in peace or protecting us in war from the inroads of the Arabs, as well as all other enemies. Even I, a poor fisherman,

with a wife and little family, am not forgotten, and
enjoy my poverty in peace. He permits me to fish for
eels wherever I please, and take them afterwards to
the best market I can find, in order to provide for my
little ones. At any hour, night or day, I go out or I
come in just as I like, to or fro, in my humble dwelling; and there is not a single person in all these
neighboring woods and valleys who has ever dared
to do me wrong. To whom am I indebted for all this,
but to him for whom I daily offer up my prayers to
God and our holy prophet to watch over his
preservation?"

MATTEO BANDELLO, ITALIAN (1480–1562)

---

*The man maintains his modesty in the proper perspec-
tive. He does not avoid his responsibilities, abuse the
ruler's confidence, or conceal the subordinate's merit.*

He [Dr. Donne] was once, and but once, clouded
with the King's displeasure, and it was about this
time; which was occasioned by some malicious whis-
perer, who had told His Majesty that Dr. Donne had
put on the general humour of the pulpits, and was
becoming busy in insinuating a fear of the King's
inclining to Popery, and a dislike of his government;
and particularly for the King's then turning the evening Lectures into Catechising, and expounding the
Prayer of our Lord, and of the Belief and Command-
ments. His Majesty was the more inclinable to believe this, for that person of Nobility and great note,
betwixt whom and Dr. Donne there had been a great
friendship, was at this very time discarded by the
Court — I shall forbear his name, unless I had a fairer
occasion — and justly committed to prison; which
begot many rumours in the common people, who in
this nation think they are not wise, unless they be
busy about what they understand not, and especially
about religion.
The King received the news with so much discontent
and restlessness, that he would not suffer the sun
to set and leave him under doubt; but sent for Dr.
Donne, and required his answer to the accusation;
which was so clear and satisfactory, that the King
said, "he was right glad he rested no longer under
the suspicion." When the King had said this, Dr.
Donne kneeled down and thanked his Majesty, and

protested his answer was faithful, and free from all collusion, and therefore, "desired that he might not rise till, as in like cases, he always had from God, so he might have from his Majesty, some assurance that he stood clear and fair in his opinion." At which the King raised him from his knees with his own hands, and "protested he believed him; and that he knew he was an honest man, and doubted not but that he loved him truly." And, having thus dismissed him, he called some Lords of his Council into his chamber, and said with much earnestness, "My doctor is an honest man; and, my Lords, I was never better satisfied with an answer than he hath now made me; and I always rejoice when I think that by my means he became a Divine."

IZAAK WALTON, ENGLISH (1593–1683)

The man acts energetically with the use of arms, when necessary, in correcting those who do not submit. Even in severity, however, he retains a considerate demeanor, which attracts devoted followers.

When all those about you say, "This is a man of talents and worth," you may not therefore believe it. When your great officers all say, "This is a man of talents and virtue," neither may you for that believe it. When all the people say, "This is a man of talents and virtue," then examine into the case, and when you find that the man is such, employ him.
When the people all say, "This man won't do," then examine into the case, and when you find that the man won't do, send him away.
When all those about you say, "This man deserves death," don't listen to them. When all your great officers say, "This man deserves death," don't listen to them. When the people all say, "This man deserves death," then inquire into the case, and when you see that the man deserves death, put him to death. In accordance with this we have the saying, "The people killed him."
You must act in this way in order to be the parent of the people.

MENCIUS, CHINESE (372–289 B.C.)

Even though the man's probity is recognized, his aims are not yet achieved. True modesty begins by disciplining

[112]15

one's own ego and the character of one's immediate circle, without being aggressive beyond.

We sit here as the great Council of the King, and in that capacity, it is our duty to take into consideration the state and affairs of the kingdom, and when there is occasion, to give a true representation of them by way of counsel and advice, with what we conceive necessary or expedient to be done.

In this consideration, I confess many a sad thought hath affrighted me, and that not only in respect of our dangers from abroad (which yet I know are great, as they have been often prest and dilated to us), but in respect of our disorders here at home, which do enforce those dangers, and by which they are occasioned. For I believe I shall make it clear to you, that both at first, the cause of these dangers were our disorders, and our disorders now are yet our greatest dangers — that not so much the potency of our enemies as the weakness of ourselves, doth threaten us: . . . Our want of true devotion to heaven — our insincerity and doubting in religion — our want of councils — our precipitate actions — the insufficiency or unfaithfulness of our generals abroad — the ignorance or corruption of our ministers at home — the impoverishing of the sovereign — the oppression and depression of the subject — the exhausting of our treasures — the waste of our provisions — consumption of our ships — destruction of our men — *these* make the advantage to our enemies, not the reputation of their arms; and if in these there be not reformation, we need no foes abroad: *Time itself will ruin us.*

SIR JOHN ELIOT, ENGLISH (1592–1632)

The over-all judgment: the way of heaven is to diminish the prosperous and augment the needy. The superior man gains without boasting.

"He is fainting!" said one of the messmates, "quick! some water!" The steward immediately hurried to the topman with the basin.

Cuticle took the topman by the wrist, and feeling it awhile, observed, "Don't be alarmed, men," addressing the two messmates; "he'll recover presently; this fainting very generally takes place." And

[113]15

he stood for a moment, tranquilly eyeing the patient. Now the Surgeon of the Fleet and the topman presented a spectacle which, to a reflecting mind, was better than a churchyard sermon on the mortality of man.

Here was a sailor, who, four days previous, had stood erect — a pillar of life — with an arm like a royal-mast, and a thigh like a windlass. But the slightest conceivable finger-touch of a bit of crooked trigger had eventuated in stretching him out, more helpless than an hour-old babe, with a blasted thigh, utterly drained of its brawn. And who was it that now stood over him like a superior being, and, as if clothed himself with the attributes of immortality, indifferently discoursed of carving up his broken flesh, and thus piecing out his abbreviated days? Who was it, that, in capacity of surgeon, seemed enacting the part of a Regenerator of life? The withered, shrunken, one-eyed, toothless, hairless Cuticle; with a trunk half dead — a *memento mori* to behold!

HERMAN MELVILLE, AMERICAN (1819–1891)

CAUCHON. . . . But it is not your place to correct the venerable Canon. You forget who you are and who we are. We are your priests, your masters, and your judges. Beware of your pride, Joan.

JOAN (*softly*). I know that I am proud. But I am a daughter of God. If He didn't want me to be proud, why did He send me His shining Archangel and His Saints all dressed in light? Why did He promise me that I shall conquer all the men I have conquered? Why did He promise me a suit of beautiful white armor, the gift of my king? And a sword? And that I should lead brave soldiers into battle while riding a fine white horse? If He had left me alone, I would never have become proud.

CAUCHON. Take care of your words, Joan. You are accusing our Lord.

JOAN (*makes the sign of the Cross*). Oh. God forbid. I say only that His Will be done even if it means making me proud and then damning me for it. That, too, is His Right.

JEAN ANOUILH, FRENCH (BORN 1910)

My God, my God, why hast thou forsaken me?

JESUS, HEBREW (4 B.C.–29 A.D.)

---

16 Contentment

At the outset, the man is enthusiastic and boastful.

As late as 1906 Roosevelt credited Harriman with saying that "he could buy a sufficient number of Senators and Congressmen or State Legislators to protect his interests, and when necessary he could buy the Judiciary."
ARTHUR MEIER SCHLESINGER, SR.,
AMERICAN (BORN 1888)

The man is quiet, but firm as a rock, yet sensitive to the first imperceptible signs of impending changes. He does not delay in taking action.

Mr. Speaker, I smell a rat; I see him forming in the air and darkening the sky; but I'll nip him in the bud.
SIR BOYLE ROCHE, IRISH (1743–1807)

The man looks upward for favors and continues his dependency upon others. He indulges in visions of pleasure and affluence. Unless he changes immediately, he will be sorry.

Perhaps you will say the man is not young; I answer, he is rich; he is not gentle, handsome, witty, brave, good-humoured, but he is rich, rich, rich, rich, — that one word contradicts everything you can say against him.
HENRY FIELDING, ENGLISH (1707–1754)

The man is confident, free of suspicions of others, and sincere in his dedication. He instills harmony and satisfaction among his associates. People gather around him in effective cooperation.

But, friend,
We speak of what is; not of what might be,
And how 'twere better if 'twere otherwise.
I am the man you see here plain enough:
Grant I'm a beast, why, beasts must lead beasts'
    lives!
Suppose I own at once to tail and claws;

[115]16

The tailless man exceeds me; but being tailed
I'll lash out lion fashion, and leave apes
To dock their stump and dress their haunches up.
My business is not to remake myself,
But make the absolute best of what God made.
ROBERT BROWNING, ENGLISH (1812–1889)

To understand all makes us very tolerant.
ANNE LOUISE GERMAINE DE STAËL, FRENCH (1766–1817)

The man is continually complaining. Yet the very strug-
gling against the daily troubles constitutes his immediate
incentive for living.

Now shalt thou rest for aye,
My weary heart. The final error dies
Wherewith I nourished my divinest dreams.
'Tis gone. I feel in me for sweet delusions
Not merely hope, but even desire, is dead.
Rest for all time. Enough
Hath been thine agitation. There is nought
So precious, thou shouldst seek it; and the earth
Deserveth not a sigh. But weary bitterness
Is life, nought else, and ashes is the world.
Be now at peace. Despair
For the last time. Unto our race did Fate
Give nought, save death. Now hold in scorn and hate
Thyself and Nature and the Power Unknown,
That reigns supreme unto the grief of all.
And the vast vanity of this terrestrial hall.
GIACOMO LEOPARDI, ITALIAN (1798–1837)

The man is distracted by pleasure and satisfaction. If he
changes after the events of the day have run their course,
however, the sober awakening will prevent future errors.

It was beginning to grow light this morning when I
awoke. The daylight crept into the room on either
side of the curtain. Ellen was also awake and smiled
toward me. Her arms were white and velvety, her
breast unusually high. I whispered something to her,
and she closed my mouth with hers, mute with tenderness. The day grew lighter and lighter.
Two hours later I was on my feet. Ellen was also up,
busy dressing herself — she had got her shoes on.
Then it was I experienced something which even

now strikes me as a gruesome dream. I was at the wash stand. Ellen had some errand or other in the adjoining room, and as she opened the door I turned around and glanced in. A cold draft from the open window in the room rushed in upon me, and in the center of the room I could just make out a corpse stretched out on a table. A corpse, in a coffin, dressed in white, with a gray beard, the corpse of a man. His bony knees protruded like madly clenched fists underneath the sheet and his face was sallow and ghastly in the extreme. I could see everything in full daylight. I turned away and said not a word.

When Ellen returned I was dressed and ready to go out. I could scarcely bring myself to respond to her embraces. She put on some additional clothes; she wanted to accompany me down as far as the street door, and I let her come, still saying nothing. At the door she pressed close to the wall so as not to be seen.

"Well, good-bye," she whispered.

"Till tomorrow?" I asked, in part to test her.

"No, not tomorrow."

"Why not tomorrow?"

"Not so many questions, dear. I am going to a funeral tomorrow, a relation of mine is dead. Now there — you know it."

"But the day after tomorrow?"

"Yes, the day after tomorrow, at the door here. I'll meet you. Good-bye."

I went.

Who was she? And the corpse? With its fists clenched and the corners of its mouth drooping — how ghastly comic! The day after tomorrow she would be expecting. Ought I see her again?

I went straight down to the Bernina Café and asked for a directory. I looked up the number so and so Gamle Kongevei and — there — there was the name. I waited some little time till the morning papers were out. Then I turned quickly to the announcements of deaths. And — sure enough — there I found hers too, the very first in the list, in bold type: "My husband, fifty-three years old, died today after a long illness." The announcement was dated the day before.

I sat for a long time and pondered.

A man marries. His wife is thirty years younger than he. He contracts a lingering illness. One fair day he dies.

[117]16

And the young widow breathes a sigh of relief.
KNUT HAMSUN, NORWEGIAN (1859–1952)

The over-all judgment: the leading official meets with harmonious obedience. Moving in sympathy and accord with the spirit of the people, he is able to make popular appointments, unite mass movements, and direct military campaigns advantageously.

Here the question arises whether it is better to be loved than feared or feared than loved. The answer is that it would be desirable to be both but, since that is difficult, it is much safer to be feared than to be loved, if one must choose. For on men in general this observation may be made: they are ungrateful, fickle, and deceitful, eager to avoid dangers, and avid for gain, and while you are useful to them they are all with you, offering you their blood, their property, their lives, and their sons so long as danger is remote, as we noted above, but when it approaches they turn on you. Any prince, trusting only in their words and having no other preparations made, will fall to his ruin, for friendships that are bought at a price and not by greatness and nobility of soul are paid for indeed, but they are not owned and cannot be called upon in time of need. Men have less hesitation in offending a man who is loved than one who is feared, for love is held by a bond of obligation which as men are wicked, is broken whenever personal advantage suggests it, but fear is accompanied by the dread of punishment which never relaxes.

Yet a prince should make himself feared in such a way that, if he does not thereby merit love, at least he may escape odium, for being feared and not hated may well go together. And indeed the prince may attain this end if he but respect the property and the women of his subjects and citizens. And if it should become necessary to seek the death of someone, he should find a proper justification and a public cause, and above all he should keep his hands off another's property, for they forget more readily the death of their father than the loss of their patrimony.
NICCOLÒ MACHIAVELLI, ITALIAN (1469–1527)

At the bidding of a Peter the Hermit millions of men hurled themselves against the East; the words of an

hallucinated enthusiast such as Mohamet created a force capable of triumphing over the Graeco-Roman world; an obscure monk like Luther bathed Europe in blood. The voice of a Galileo or a Newton will never have the least echo among the masses. The inventors of genius hasten the march of civilization. The fanatics and the hallucinated create history.
GUSTAVE LE BON, FRENCH (1841–1931)

Now as to politeness . . . I would venture to call it benevolence in trifles.
EARL WILLIAM PITT, ENGLISH (1708–1778)

17 Acquiring Followers
THE SUI HEXAGRAM

At the outset, the man changes his objectives. He will succeed if he remains firm in principle and goes beyond selfish considerations to mingle freely with those who do not share his feelings, as well as those who do.

But Liberty assumes only one shape. Once convinced that each of the molecules which compose a fluid possesses in itself the force by which the general level is produced, we conclude that there is no surer or simpler way of seeing that level realized than not to interfere with it. All, then, who set out with this fundamental principle, that *men's interests are harmonious,* will agree as to the practical solution of the social problem, — to abstain from displacing or thwarting these interests.
FRÉDÉRIC BASTIAT, FRENCH (1801–1850)

There are men who, with clear perceptions, as they think, of their own duty, do not see how too eager a pursuit of one's duty may involve them in the violation of others, or how too warm an embracement of one truth may lead to a disregard of other truths just as important. As I heard it stated strongly, not many days ago, these persons are disposed to mount upon some particular duty, as upon a war horse, and to drive furiously on and upon and over all other duties that may stand in the way. These are men who, in reference to disputes of that sort, are of the opinion that human duties may be ascertained with the ex-
[119]17

actness of mathematics. They deal with morals as with mathematics; and they think what is right may be distinguished from what is wrong with the precision of an algebraic equation. They have, therefore, none too much charity toward others who differ with them. They are apt, too, to think that nothing is good but what is perfect, and that there are no compromises or modifications to be made in consideration of difference of opinion or in deference to other men's judgment. If their perspicacious vision enables them to detect a spot on the face of the sun, they think that a good reason why the sun should be struck down from heaven. They prefer the chance of running into utter darkness to living in heavenly light, if that heavenly light be not absolutely without any imperfection.

DANIEL WEBSTER, AMERICAN (1782–1852)

The man surrounds himself with the incompetent and dismisses the experienced.

Never have a companion who casts you in the shade. The more he does so, the less desirable a companion he is. The more he excels in quality the more in repute: he will always play first fiddle and you second. If you get any consideration, it is only his leavings. The moon shines bright alone among the stars: when the sun rises she becomes either invisible or imperceptible. Never join one that eclipses you, but rather one who sets you in brighter light. By this means the cunning Fabula in Martial was able to appear beautiful and brilliant, owing to the ugliness and disorder of her companions. But one should as little imperil oneself by an evil companion as pay honour to another at the cost of one's own credit. When you are on the way to fortune associate with the eminent; when arrived, with the mediocre.

BALTASAR GRACIÁN, SPANISH (1601–1658)

The man joins with superior people and parts company with the superficial and the inferior.

What a revelation this crisis has been to me in regard to human nature, above all, of the intellectual elite. How quickly and totally have these thinkers, so imbued with the great principles of liberty and human-

ity renounced them and toppled them in the dust! I will not forget it in the sequel when, with peace once more established, I shall be seeing them again professing their ideas, flaunting their spirit, its liberality and its kinships with all that is human.
ROMAIN ROLLAND, FRENCH (1866–1944)

The man acquires followers who flatter, scheme, and act subservient to seek personal gains. There is a chance that he will become dependent on them because of gratifying associations, which will detract from his authority in his position of influence. He must see through such adherents and free himself from egotistical encumbrances.

Question: What is Courtiers' Grammar? *Answer:* Courtiers' Grammar is the Art, or Science, of flattering cunningly, with tongue and pen. *Q:* What is meant by "flattering cunningly"? *A:* It means uttering and writing such untruth as may prove pleasing to those of high station and, at the same time, of benefit to the flatterer. *Q:* What is Courtly Untruth? *A:* It is the expression of a soul inglorious before the soul vainglorious. It consists of shameless praises heaped upon a Great Man for those services which he never performed and those virtues which he never had. *Q:* Into how many categories are the mean-spirited souls divided? *A:* Six. *Q:* What mean-spirited souls constitute the first Category? *A:* Those that have contracted the miserable habit of cooling their heels in the anterooms of Great Gentlemen all day and every day, without the least need therefor. *Q:* What mean-spirited souls constitute the second Category? *A:* Those that, standing in reverent awe in the presence of a Great Man, gaze into his orbs in servility and thirst to anticipate his thoughts, so that they may gratify him by base yea-saying. *Q:* What truly mean-spirited souls constitute the third Category? *A:* Those that, before the face of a Great Man, rejoice, out of sheer pusillanimity, in falsely imputing to themselves all sorts of unheard-of things and in disavowing all things. *Q:* And what mean-spirited souls constitute the fourth Category? *A:* Those that exalt with great praises even such things in Great Gentlemen as honest men ought to despise. *Q:* What truly mean-spirited souls constitute the fifth Category? *A:* Those that, for their servility to the Great, are shameless enough to accept rewards appertaining to meritorious services alone. *Q:* What truly mean-spirited souls, then, constitute the sixth Category? *A:* Those that, through the most contemptible dissembling, deceive the Public: Outside the palace they seem the veriest Catos, they clamor against flatterers, they revile without the least mercy all those before whose mere gaze they tremble, they preach intrepidity and, from their reports, one would gather that they alone, through their firmness, are standing guard over the integrity of the fatherland and warding off ruin from the unfortunate; but, once they set foot within the chambers of the Sovereign, they undergo utter transformation: the tongue that had reviled flatterers prompts them, of itself, to the ignoblest flattery; he is a voiceless slave before the one whom he had reviled but half an hour ago; the preacher of intrepidity is afraid of looking up inopportunely, of inopportunely approaching; the guardian of the integrity of the fatherland will be the first, if he find the chance, to stretch out his hand to plunder the fatherland; the intercessor for the unfortunate rejoices, for the sake of the smallest benefit accruing to him, in sending an innocent man to his ruin.

DENIS IVANOVICH FONVIZIN, RUSSIAN (1745–1792)

The ruler fosters excellence, which brings on good fortune.

I ask not for a larger garden,
But for finer seeds.

RUSSELL HERMAN CONWELL, AMERICAN (1843–1925)

It is a funny thing about life, if you refuse to accept anything but the best you often get it.

WILLIAM SOMERSET MAUGHAM, ENGLISH (1874–1965)

The sage, who is retired, is recalled by the king because of his unique qualifications. The faithful and effective subject is rewarded.

Suppose a ruler wants . . . a garment made from cloth that is difficult to cut properly; he will certainly look for a skilful tailor. . . . To cure a sick horse, he will certainly look for a skilful physician. For all such

[122]17

tasks the ruler will not employ his relatives, nor those who are rich and noble but lack merit, nor those who are merely good-looking, for he understands that they are not capable of performing them.... But when it is a question of governing the state, it is not so. For this task, the ruler selects those who are merely good-looking. ... Does he care less for the state than for a sick horse or a suit of clothes? ...

When the sage-kings of old governed the world, those whom they enriched and ennobled were not necessarily their relatives, or the rich and noble, or the good-looking. Thus Shun had been a farmer ... a potter ... a fisherman ... and a peddler. But Yao discovered him ... made him emperor, and turned over to him the control of the empire and the government of the people.

MO TI, CHINESE (479–381 B.C.)

The over-all judgment: a person must learn to be adaptable and serve others in order to rule. Willing followers are not acquired by force or cunning but through consistency in doing what is human and proper.

Cleverness is serviceable for everything, sufficient for nothing.

HENRI-FRÉDÉRIC AMIEL, SWISS (1821–1881)

... This assumption that she need look for no more devotion now that her beauty had passed proceeded from the fact that she had never realized any love save love as passion. Such love, though it expends itself in generosity and thoughtfulness, though it give birth to visions and to great poetry, remains among the sharpest expressions of self-interest. Not until it has passed through a long servitude, through its own self-hatred, through mockery, through great doubts, can it take its place among the loyalties. Many who have spent a lifetime in it can tell us less of love than the child that lost a dog yesterday.

THORNTON NIVEN WILDER, AMERICAN (BORN 1897)

And the twelve, unblessed, uncaring,
Still go marching on,
Ripe for death and daring,
Pitying none.

[123]17

On, with rifles lifted
At the hidden enemy . . .
Onward, where the snow has drifted
Clutching at the marcher's knee.
ALEKSANDR BLOK, RUSSIAN (1880–1921)

18 Arresting of Decay

THE KU HEXAGRAM

*At the outset, wrongs have arisen which are not yet
deeply rooted and can be remedied. But reforms are
associated with dangers, which should be understood.*

HOST. You, Sir, are demeaning yourself by coming
here. I pray that your honour will return home,
where I shall hasten to present myself before you.
GUEST. I cannot bring disgrace upon you by obeying
this injunction. Be good enough to end by granting
me this interview.
HOST. I do not dare to set an example as to how a
reception of this kind should be conducted, and I
must therefore persist in asking your honour to
return to your own house where I shall call upon you
without delay.
GUEST. It is I who do not dare to make a precedent.
I therefore must persist in asking you to grant me
an interview.
HOST. As for me, as I have failed to obtain your permission to refuse this honour, I shall press my ob-
jection no further. But I hear that your honour is
offering me a present, and this at least I must decline.
GUEST. Without a present, I dare not venture into
your presence.
HOST. I am not sufficiently expert in such ceremonies
and I must persist in declining.
GUEST. Without the support and confidence given me
by my gift, I have not the courage to pay this visit.
I must persist in my request.
HOST. I am also decided in declining. Yet, as I cannot
secure your consent that I should visit you in your
house, how dare I not now respectfully obey?
HAROLD NICOLSON, ENGLISH (BORN 1886)

*The man is gentle in dealing with his mother, even when
duty bound to oppose her. When restoring what has*
[124]18

"Oh, it is true, my friend, man is naturally a serious animal. We must work against this shameful and abominable propensity with all our strength, and attack it from all sides. To that end ambiguities are also good, except that they are so seldom ambiguous. When they are not and allow only one interpretation, that is not immoral, it is only obtrusive and vulgar. Frivolous talk must be spiritual and dainty and modest, so far as possible; for the rest as wicked as you choose."

"That is well enough, but what place have your ambiguities in society?"

"To keep the conversations fresh, just as salt keeps food fresh. The question is not *why* we say them, but *how* we say them. It would be rude indeed to talk with a charming lady as if she were a sexless Amphibium. It is a duty and an obligation to allude constantly to what she is and is going to be. It is really a comical situation, considering how indelicate, stiff and guilty society is, to be an innocent girl."

"That reminds me of the famous Buffo, who, while he was always making others laugh, was so sad and solemn himself."

"Society is a chaos which can be brought into harmonious order only by wit. If one does not jest and toy with the elements of passion, it forms thick masses and darkens everything."

FRIEDRICH VON SCHLEGEL, GERMAN (1772–1829)

The man proceeds too energetically in correcting past errors. This results in some discord and distress. But a trifle too much energy is preferable to a trifle too little, and no great blame will ensue.

The little boat of St. Peter is beaten by many storms and tossed about upon the sea, but it grieves me most of all that, against the orthodox faith, there are now arising, more unrestrainedly and injuriously than ever before, ministers of diabolical error who are ensnaring the souls of the simple and ruining them. With their superstitions and false inventions they are perverting the meaning of the Holy Scriptures and trying to destroy the unity of the Catholic

[125]18

Church. Since . . . this pestilential error is growing in Gascony and the neighboring territories, we wish you and your fellow bishops to resist it with all your might. . . . we give you a strict command that, by whatever means you can, you destroy all these heresies and expel from your diocese all who are polluted by them. . . . if necessary, you may cause the princes and people to suppress them with the sword.

POPE INNOCENT III, ITALIAN (1161–1216)

Indulgence of decay leads to regret.

Well, you see: once upon a time there was a blazing fire inside me. The cold could do nothing against it, a youthfulness, a spring no autumn could touch; a source of light, glowing wells of joy that seemed inexhaustible. Not happiness, I mean joy, felicity, which made it possible for me to live. . . . There was an enormous energy there. . . . A force . . . it must have been the life force, mustn't it? . . . And then it grew weaker and all died away.

EUGÈNE IONESCO, FRENCH (BORN 1912)

With the assistance of able helpers, the man reverses the process of decay of former times. He is praised for it.

Must I then humble my common sense, to the point of submitting it blindly to the decrees of an assembly which is only a crowd? Is it not permitted to me as to Lycurgus to conspire against laws which are inflicting evil on my country? If it pleases the Athenians to decree the penalty of death against any one who proposes to use for the expenses of war the funds intended to put on comedies, will Phocion respect that ridiculous law? Should Demosthenes obey it? And must I, without being either of these great men, go gaily to the spectacle, while Philip is advancing toward our gates? . . .

Nay, nay; Cicero was right; we are agreed, as an incontestable truth, that a citizen must obey the magistrate, and the magistrate the laws; and you may be sure that in a republic where that order is observed the injustice of the laws will never give rise to pernicious quarrels. But these happy republics are rare in this world, since men, always borne along toward tyranny or toward slavery by their passions, are evil or foolish enough to make unjust or absurd laws, what other remedy can we apply to this evil than disobedience? From it will rise some troubles; but why be frightened of that? The trouble is itself a proof that we love order and that we want to restore it. Blind obedience is on the contrary a proof that the doltish citizen is indifferent to good and to evil; and then, what will you hope for? The man who thinks works to strengthen the empire of reason; the man who obeys without thinking throws himself into slavery, because he favors the power of the passions.

GABRIEL BONNE DE MABLY, FRENCH (1709–1785)

Justice may wink a little, but see at last.
THOMAS MIDDLETON, ENGLISH (1570–1627)

The man does not serve his lord, but lets the world go by and cultivates his own character in solitude. In so doing, however, he creates something valuable for the future of mankind.

All true wisdom is only to be learned far from the dwellings of men, out in the great solitudes, and is only to be attained through suffering. Privation and suffering are the only things that can open the minds of men to those things which are hidden from others.
IGJUGARJUK, ESKIMO (1927)

The over-all judgment: great effort is required to arrest decay and restore vigor. One must exercise proper deliberation, plan carefully before making a move, and be alert in guarding against relapse following a renaissance.

It was the human spirit itself that failed at Paris. It is no use passing judgments and making scapegoats of this or that individual statesman or group of statesmen. Idealists make a great mistake in not facing the real facts sincerely and resolutely. They believe in the power of the spirit, in the goodness which is at the heart of things, in the triumph which is in store for the great moral ideals of the race. But this faith only too often leads to an optimism which is sadly and fatally at variance with actual results. It is the realist and not the idealist who is generally justified by

[127]18

events. We forget that the human spirit, the spirit of goodness and truth in the world, is still only an infant crying in the night, and that the struggle with darkness is as yet mostly an unequal struggle. . . . Paris proved this terrible truth once more. It is not Wilson who failed there, but humanity itself. It was not the statesmen that failed so much as the spirit of the peoples behind them.

PRIME MINISTER JAN CHRISTIAAN SMUTS, SOUTH AFRICAN (1870–1950)

You may strip Germany of her colonies, reduce her armaments . . . and her navy. . . . All the same, in the end, if she feels that she has been unjustly treated . . . she will find means of exacting retribution. . . . The maintenance of peace . . . will depend upon there being no cause of exasperation constantly stirring up the spirit of patriotism, of justice, or of fair play to achieve redress.

PRIME MINISTER DAVID LLOYD GEORGE, ENGLISH (1863–1945)

Repentance must be something more than mere remorse for sins: it comprehends a change of nature befitting heaven.

LEW WALLACE, AMERICAN (1827–1905)

 # 19 Getting Ahead

THE LIN HEXAGRAM

At the outset, the man advances with his associates to a higher position. He must remain more prudent than strong in doing right and not be carried away by the popular will.

One of the main lessons to learn from this war is embodied in the homely proverb, "Speak softly and carry a big stick." Persistently only half of this proverb has been quoted in deriding the men who wish to safeguard our National interest and honor. Persistently the effort has been made to insist that those who advocate keeping our country able to defend its rights are merely adopting "the policy of the big stick." In reality, we lay equal emphasis on the fact

that it is necessary to speak softly; in other words, that it is necessary to be respectful toward all people and scrupulously to refrain from wronging them, while at the same time keeping ourselves in condition to prevent wrong done to us. If a nation does not in this sense speak softly, then sooner or later the policy of the big stick is certain to result in war. But what befell Luxemburg six weeks ago, what has befallen China again and again during the past quarter of a century, shows that no amount of speaking softly will save any people which does not carry a big stick.
PRESIDENT THEODORE ROOSEVELT,
AMERICAN (1858–1919)

Many excellent cooks are spoiled by going into the arts.
EUGÈNE HENRI PAUL GAUGIN, FRENCH (1848–1903)

People who are not obedient to the ways of heaven are induced to follow the steadfast man in a high position. The future will be advantageous in every way.

Vocal to the wise; but for the crowd they need interpreters.
PINDAR, GREEK (522–443 B.C.)

It is not from the benevolence of the butcher, the brewer, or the baker that we expect our dinner, but from their regard to their self-interest. We address ourselves, not to their humanity, but to their self-love, and never talk to them of our necessities, but of their advantages.
ADAM SMITH, SCOTTISH (1723–1790)

The man gains power, influence, and comfort. There is danger of relation and carelessness in dealing with others. But if he becomes apprehensive about his actions, he will not continue in his errors and will avoid troubles.

It must be observed that the fact of most significance is the extent to which this deepening and softening of character has progressed *among the power-holding class*. This class is even more affected than the opposing party. The result is peculiar. It is thereby rendered incapable of utilizing its own strength, and consequently of making any effective resistance to the movement which is undermining its position. All

heart is, in fact, taken out of its opposition; men's
minds have become so insensitive to suffering,
misery, wrong, and degradation of every kind, that
it cannot help itself.
BENJAMIN KIDD, ENGLISH (1858–1916)

The man advances to a high place because of the appro-
priateness of his ideas and behavior and the open-
mindedness of a person of high rank who draws men
of competence into service.

Such are all great historical men — whose own particular aims involve those large issues which are
the will of the world-spirit. They may be called
heroes. . . .
Such individuals had no consciousness of the general
Idea they were unfolding, while prosecuting those
aims of theirs; on the contrary, they were practical,
political men. But at the same time they were thinking men, who had an insight into the requirements
of the time — *what was ripe for development.* This was
the very truth for their age, for their world; the
species next in order, so to speak, and which was
already formed in the womb of time. It was theirs to
know this nascent principle; the necessity, directly
sequent step in progress, which their world was to
take; to make this their aim, and to expend their
energy in promoting it.
GEORG WILHELM FRIEDRICH HEGEL,
GERMAN (1770–1831)

The great ruler displays his wisdom in attracting men of
ability to direct his affairs and in providing them freedom
of action.

Man's mind is more treacherous than mountains and
rivers and more difficult to know than the sky. For
with the sky you know what to expect in respect of
the coming of spring, summer, autumn, and winter,
and the alternation of day and night. But man hides
his character behind an inscrutable appearance.
There are those who appear tame and self-effacing,
but conceal a terrible pride. There are those who
have some special ability but appear to be stupid.
There are those who are compliant and yielding but
always get their objective. Some are hard outside but
soft inside, and some are slow without but impatient

within. Therefore a gentleman sends a man to a distant mission in order to test his loyalty. He employs him near by in order to observe his manners. He gives him a lot to do in order to judge his ability. He suddenly puts a question to him in order to test his knowledge and makes a commitment with him under difficult circumstances to test his ability to live up to his word. He trusts him with money in order to test his heart, and announces to him the coming of a crisis to test his integrity. He makes him drunk in order to see the inside of his character, and puts him in female company to see his attitude toward women. Submitted to these nine tests, a fool always reveals himself.

CONFUCIUS, CHINESE (551–479 B.C.)

The sage returns from retirement to teach and help others, who greatly benefit from his experience.

Nan-in, a Japanese master during the Meiji era, received a university professor who came to inquire about Zen.
Nan-in served tea. He poured his visitor's cup full, and then kept on pouring.
The professor watched the overflow until he no longer could restrain himself. "It is overfull. No more will go in!"
"Like this cup," Nan-in said, "you are full of your own opinions and speculations. How can I show you Zen unless you first empty your cup?"

MUJU, JAPANESE (THIRTEENTH CENTURY)

The over-all judgment: the time is propitious for the assertion of authority — to inspect, comfort, and rule. Great progress and success will be realized. But spring does not last forever, and the favorable trend will reverse itself in due time. The wise man foresees evil and handles its threat accordingly.

No man is a warmer advocate for proper restraints and wholesome checks in every department of government than I am; but I have never yet been able to discover the propriety of placing it absolutely out of the power of men to render essential services, because a possibility remains of their doing ill.

PRESIDENT GEORGE WASHINGTON,
AMERICAN (1732–1799)

Just as a single remedy is not suitable to all diseases, and medication varies according to the particular case, so one cannot use for all the heretics of the different sects the same method of questioning, investigation, and examination, but should employ a method particular and appropriate to each case or group. Therefore the inquisitor, as a wise doctor of souls, will proceed with caution in the investigation and questioning, according to the persons he is questioning or in whose company he is conducting the investigation, taking into account their rank, condition, status, malady and with due regard to local conditions.

BERNARD GUI, FRENCH (1261–1331)

Therefore, since the world has still
Much good, but much less good than ill,
And while the sun and moon endure
Luck's a chance, but trouble's sure,
I'd face it as a wise man would,
And train for ill and not for good.
'Tis true, the stuff I bring for sale
Is not so brisk a brew as ale:
Out of a stem that scored the hand
I wrung it in a weary land.
But take it: if the smack is sour,
The better for the embittered hour;
It should do good to heart and head
When your soul is in my soul's stead;
And I will friend you, if I may
In the dark and cloudy day.

There was a king reigned in the East:
There, when kings will sit to feast,
They get their fill before they think
With poisoned meat and poisoned drink.
He gathered all that springs to birth
From the many-venomed earth;
First a little, thence to more,
He sampled all her killing store;
And easy, smiling, seasoned sound,
State the king when healths went round.
They put arsenic in his meat
And stared aghast to watch him eat;
They poured strychnine in his cup
And shook to see him drink it up:
They shook, they stared as white's their shirt:

Them it was their poison hurt.
—I tell the tale that I heard told.
Mithridates, he died old.
ALFRED EDWARD HOUSMAN, ENGLISH (1859–1936)

20 Contemplation

THE KUAN HEXAGRAM

At the outset, the man does not comprehend the nature of prevailing forces nor does he perceive them as a connected whole. This superficial view is acceptable for the masses, but the superior man should know better.

For the most part he [Goncourt] listens and thinks he can hear, he looks and thinks he can see, and then he imagines he can think, and takes the sort of literary trepidation in which he has been indulging these past fifty years for the free flight of ideas. He has the eyes of a fly, eyes with facets, and, like a fly, he alights on everything but penetrates nothing.
ROBERT DE BONNIÈRES, FRENCH (1850–1905)

The housewife is understandably ignorant of worldly affairs. But such a narrow, subjective view of reality is shameful for persons in public life.

It is not by speculating on the abstract relations of ideal nations that men will bring more order and justice into the relations of States; it is by looking at the facts in their reality and seeking, without illusion, without passion, and without surrender, the laws that govern them.
FRANTZ FUNCK-BRENTANO (1862–1947) AND ALBERT SOREL (1842–1906), FRENCH

The man contemplates the effects of his actions in relation to the exigencies of the times rather than indulging in idle speculations. Only in this way is he able to formulate useful guidelines for behavior.

It is of no small benefit on finding oneself in bed in the dark to go over again in the imagination the main outlines of the forms previously studied, or of other noteworthy things conceived by ingenious speculation.
LEONARDO DA VINCI, ITALIAN (1452–1519)

*The person who is aware of the factors leading to the
glory of the nation should be appointed by the king to an
authoritative position. He should be honored rather than
used as a tool.*

One day . . . Mohammed-bin-Nasir set sail for Zan-
zibar to pay his respects to the Seyyid. He landed
first at Mombasa, where he visited the Masrui. They
were holding a durbar: all the leading members of
the clan were there, grouped round the last deposed
governor. When Mohammed entered, the Liwali rose
and bowed to him with marked respect, then he sat
down again, resting his chin on the hilt of his sword.
After a time he raised his head with a deep sigh, and
all the Masrui, as if at a signal, drummed on their
swords with their fingers. Mohammed drew his own
conclusions but cautiously made no comment. He
continued his journey south, and a few days later
was salaaming before Seyyid Said.
"Did you stop at Mombasa?" asked the Seyyid.
"I did."
"What is the news from there?"
"The news is that the Masrui have retaken the fort."
"How," cried the Seyyid angrily, "you are lying. I
have had no word of this. Explain yourself."
"When I passed through Mombasa," said his guest,
"the Masrui were in the town and your soldiers were
in the fort."
"Then how can you say that the Masrui are in the
fort when they are only in the town? What sort of
talk is this?"
Mohammed-bin-Nasir told the story of the durbar . . .
"The meaning is this. When the Liwali rested his
head on his sword and sighed, that sigh came from
the bitterness of his heart as he thought of the fort,
full of your soldiers: and of the Governor, who is
your man. It was as though he spoke to his brothers
and said to them — Alas our fort is lost to us.
"Then all the Masrui replied, tapping their fingers
on their swords. We will retake the fort with our
swords. And such was the drumming and beating
of the swords, that it seemed to me as though they
had beaten on the gates, forced them open and cap-
tured the fort.
"Therefore I said to you, Bwana Mkubwa: that the
Masrui have taken the fort and driven your soldiers
[134]20

away."

The Seyyid Said considered a while, and then he said: "Stay here, you are not permitted to leave. I will send to Mombasa and see if what you say is true. If you are lying to me, I will know that you need a lesson in manners, and you shall then receive it. But if you are right, I will know you for a wise man, and you shall be one of my Councillors."

Three days later came the news of a successful Masrui rising and their capture of Fort Jesus. The Said, even while preparing for an expedition against Mombasa, did not forget Mohammed-bin-Nasir, but gave him honours and money, and sent him on an important mission.

STORY OF SEYYID SAID, ZANZIBARI (1787–1856)

The man in a position of power studies the impact of his life upon the welfare of others. If he so conducts himself that the condition of the people is always good, he will not fall into error.

The quality in which the Roman commonwealth is most distinctly superior, is, in my judgment, the nature of its religion. The very thing that among other nations is an object of reproach — i.e., superstition — is that which maintains the cohesion of the Roman state. These matters are clothed in such pomp, and introduced to such an extent into public and private life, as no other religion can parallel. . . . I believe that the government has adopted this course for the sake of the common people. This might not have been necessary had it been possible to form a state composed of wise men; but as every multitude is fickle, full of lawless desires, unreasoned passion, and violent anger, it must be held in by invisible terrors and religious pageantry.

POLYBIUS, GREEK (205–125 B.C.)

Abou Ben Adhem (may his tribe increase!)
Awoke one night from a deep dream of peace,
And saw within the moonlight in his room,
Making it rich and like a lily in bloom,
An angel writing in a book of gold:
Exceeding peace had made Ben Adhem bold,
And to the presence in the room he said,
"What writest thou?" The vision raised its head,

And, with a look made of all sweet accord,
Answered, "The names of those who love the Lord."
"And is mine one?" said Abou. "Nay, not so,"
Replied the angel. Abou spoke more low,
But cheerily still; and said, "I pray thee, then,
Write me as one that loves his fellow-men."

The angel wrote, and vanished. The next night
It came again, with a great wakening light,
And showed the names whom love of God had
  blessed, —
And, lo! Ben Adhem's name led all the rest!

LEIGH HUNT, ENGLISH (1784–1859)

---

*The sage, who is living outside the routine of the world,
contemplates his own character, not as an isolated ego
manifestation, but in relation to the laws of life. He
judges freedom from blame to be the highest good.*

One day a boy climbed to the heights of Pichincha;
he was only a child, yet he knew where he was, and
had his head and his heart full of the battle. The
mountain in the clouds, with its scarf of mist falling
down to its waist, seemed a masked giant, terrifying.
The city of Quito, at its feet, lifted its thousand
towers to heaven: the green hills of this lovely city,
fresh and graceful, surround her like gigantic uncut
emeralds, set with apparent carelessness in her broad
girdle. Rome, the city of hills, has neither so many
nor more beautiful ones. A sound barely reached the
heights; it was confused, vague, fantastic, that sound
composed [of] a thousand sounds, that voice composed of a thousand voices, always emanating and
ascending from great towns! The ringing of bells, the
beat of hammers, the neighing of horses, the barking
of dogs, the creaking of carts, and the thousand laments coming from no one knows where, sighs of
shadows, uttered perhaps by hunger from its fireless
dwelling and rising on high to mingle with the
daughter of pleasure and infect it with melancholy.
The boy heard, heard with his eyes and with his soul,
heard the silence, as it says in the Scriptures; he heard
the past, he heard the battle. Where had Sucre been?
Perhaps here, on this very spot, on this green stair;
there is where he passed by, farther over is where he

[136]20

broke into a run, and finally, on that side he shot at the fleeing Spaniards.

The boy caught sight of a white bone, a bone half hidden amid the grass and the wildflowers; he went over and picked it up. Had it belonged to one of the royalists? Had it belonged to one of the patriots? Was it a holy or an accursed bone? Child, do not say that! There may have been accursed men; there are no accursed bones. You should know that death, although cold as ice, is a fire which purifies the body; first it corrupts it, decomposes it, dissolves it; then it deodorizes and cleanses it.

The bones of the dead, washed by the rain, shaped by the air, polished by the hand of time, are the remains of the human race, not of this or that man. No, the bones of our enemies are not enemy bones; they are the remains of our fellow men. Child, do not throw this away in disdain. . . . The bones of our fathers who died on Pichincha are now the prize of nothingness; their very dust has taken a more subtle form, turned into spirit, and disappeared into the invisible amphora in which eternity gathers the members of the human race.

JUAN MONTALVO, ECUADORIAN (1832–1889)

He drank off a glass of tea and began in a calmer voice.

"Well, then. My patient kept getting worse and worse. You are not a doctor, my good sir; you cannot understand what passes in a poor fellow's heart, especially at first, when he begins to suspect that the disease is getting the upper hand of him. What becomes of his belief in himself? You suddenly grow so timid; it's indescribable. You fancy then that you have forgotten everything you knew, and that the patient has no faith in you, and that other people begin to notice how distracted you are, and tell you the symptoms with reluctance; that they are looking at you suspiciously, whispering . . . Ah! it's horrid! There must be a remedy, you think, for this disease, if one could find it. Isn't this it? You try—no, that's not it. You don't allow the medicine the necessary time to do good . . . You clutch at one thing, then at another. Sometimes you take up a book of medical prescriptions—here it is, you think! Sometimes, by

Jove, you pick one out by chance, thinking to leave it to fate. . . . But meantime a fellow-creature's dying, and another doctor would have saved him. 'We must have a consultation.' you say; 'I will not take the responsibility on myself.' And what a fool you look at such times! Well, in time you learn to bear it; it's nothing to you. A man has died—but it's not your fault; you treated him by the rules.''

IVAN SERGEEVICH TURGENEV, RUSSIAN (1818–1883)

The over-all judgment: a person should contemplate the workings of the universe with reverence and introspection. In this way expression is given to the effects of these laws upon his own person. This is the source of a hidden power.

Behind the barn was mystery,
The pine trees there were like the sea
When wind was up; but it was more
Than waves upon an unseen shore
That made the boy's heart burn and sing.
He knew well there was a thing
In that spot which bound in one
All splendid things from sun to sun—
Amber jewels of roosters' eyes,
The floating beads of golden flies,
The rainbow's lintel of brief light
Arched across the door of night,
A duck's white feather like a flower
On a pool left by a shower
The hot sound, steady, small, and keen,
Of August mowing by machine.
The cool sound of a scythe, the small
Madness of the cricket's call,
The sudden smell of apples in
October twilight from a bin,
The pleasure, lonely and immense,
Of the hearth-cat's confidence.

The pines behind the barn somehow
Joined the lowing of a cow
To the moon that marched through crowds
Of angels of fair-weather clouds.
The pines possessed the ancient right
Of opening doorways in the night
To let the day and cockcrow through,
They built a fire in the dew.

[138]20

Laid the hand of East in West's,
Filled the eggs in robins' nests
With thunder rolling deep below
The earth at night. They mingled snow
Of Junetime daisies with December's,
And built the roses in the embers.

It took a boy of ten to see
Such a tremendous unity.

ROBERT PETER TRISTRAM COFFIN,
AMERICAN (1892–1955)

One day an eagle said with pride: "None can soar up
    like me!
Sick shivering and giddiness reign where I dare
    to go.
My Adriatic is the air, my gondola the cloud,
My canopy a background like purple satin's glow."
.   .   .   .   ,   ,

She spoke and looked again upon her ornaments of
    power,
And shook her wings as shakes a queen her mantle,
    royally.
"No other can soar up like me!" Into the clouds she
    flew,
Repeating ever while she rose: "None can soar up
    like me!"

"Who art thou?"
  "A dry leaf."
    "And whence?"
      "I come from far above."

"And hast thou wings?"
  "Nay!"
    "Wingless leaf that in my path I find,
Who has breathed into thee this breath which gives
    the power to rise
Yet higher in the ether than my sovereignty?"
    "The wind!"

You hear it, O ye ragged men in yonder neighboring
    street!
Take courage, all ye foolish ones! Be faint of heart
    no more,
Ye ignorant! When o'er the world a strong, mad
    whirlwind sweeps,

[139]20

Then higher than the eagles, the dry leaves rise and
   soar!

SANTIAGO ARGÜELLO BARRETO,
NICARAGUAN (1872–1942)

Rikiu was watching his son Shoan as he swept and
watered the garden path. "Not clean enough," said
Rikiu, when Shoan had finished his task, and bade
him try again. After a weary hour the son turned to
Rikiu: "Father, there is nothing more to be done. The
steps have been washed for the third time, the stone
lanterns and the trees are well sprinkled with water,
moss and lichens are shining with a fresh verdure;
not a twig, not a leaf have I left on the ground."
"Young fool," chided the tea-master, "that is not the
way a garden path should be swept." Saying this,
Rikiu stepped into the garden, shook a tree and scattered over the garden gold and crimson leaves, scraps
of the brocade of autumn! What Rikiu demanded
was not cleanliness alone, but the beautiful and the
natural also.

KAKUZO OKAKURA, JAPANESE (1862–1913)

21 Punishment

THE SHIH HO HEXAGRAM

*At the outset, the man receives a mild sentence as a
warning for a small offense.*

BURGOMASTER. All *I* can see is that you are again seeking an outlet for your pugnacity. You want to make
an onslaught on your superiors—that is an old habit
of yours. You cannot endure any authority over you;
you look askance at anyone who holds a higher post
than your own; you regard him as a personal enemy
—and then you care nothing what kind of weapon
you use against him. But now I have shown you how
much is at stake for the town, and consequently for
me too. And therefore I warn you, Thomas, that I am
inexorable in the demand I am about to make to you!
DR. STOCKMANN. What demand?
BURGOMASTER. As you have not had the sense to refrain from chattering to outsiders about this delicate

business, which should have been kept an official secret, of course it cannot now be hushed up. All sorts of rumors will get abroad, and evil-disposed persons will invent all sorts of additions to them. It will therefore be necessary for you publicly to contradict these rumors.

STOCKMANN. I! How? I don't understand.

BURGOMASTER. We expect that, after further investigation, you will come to the conclusion that the affair is not nearly so serious or pressing as you had at first imagined.

STOCKMANN. Aha! So you expect that?

BURGOMASTER. Furthermore, we expect you to express your confidence that the Board of Directors will thoroughly and conscientiously carry out all measures for the remedying of possible defects.

STOCKMANN. Yes, but that you'll never be able to do, so long as you go on tinkering and patching. I tell you that, Peter, and it's my deepest, sincerest conviction —

BURGOMASTER. As an official, you have no right to hold any individual conviction.

STOCKMANN (starting). No right to — ?

BURGOMASTER. As an official, I say. In your private capacity, of course, it is another matter. But as a subordinate official of the Baths, you have no right to express any conviction at issue with that of your superiors.

STOCKMANN. This is too much! I, a doctor, a man of science, have no right to — ?

BURGOMASTER. The matter in question is not a purely scientific one; it is a complex affair; it has both a technical and an economic side.

STOCKMANN. What the devil do I care what it is! I will be free to speak my mind upon any subject under the sun!

BURGOMASTER. As you please — so long as it does not concern the Baths. With them we forbid you to meddle.

STOCKMANN (shouts). You forbid — ! You! A set of —

BURGOMASTER. I forbid it — I your chief; and when I issue an order, you have simply to obey.

HENRIK IBSEN, NORWEGIAN (1828–1906)

The hardened sinner must be punished severely to secure the desired ends. Although indignation often goes

[141]21

too far in meting out punishment, it may still be just.

In his own grease I made him fry.
GEOFFREY CHAUCER, ENGLISH (1340–1400)

The man lacks sufficient power and authority and the culprit does not submit to him. It is like biting through old dried meat and coming upon something poisonous. Some humiliation results but no blame.

It is not a man's duty, as a matter of course, to devote himself to the eradication of any, even the most enormous wrong; he may still properly have other concerns to engage him; but it is his duty, at least, to wash his hands of it.
HENRY DAVID THOREAU, AMERICAN (1817–1862)

Great obstacles in the form of strong opponents require the man to make difficult judgments. All goes well if he cautiously perseveres.

Hope nothing from foreign governments. They will never be really willing to aid you until you have shown that you are strong enough to conquer without them.
GIUSEPPE MAZZINI, ITALIAN (1805–1872)

A clear-cut case meets with difficulty because of a tendency to be lenient. The man must be as true as gold and as impartial as the mean.

On January 20, I had an audience with the Tsar.
"From my second report, Your Majesty may have seen that I regard the situation as worse than ever. The frame of mind of the country is such that very serious outbreaks may be expected. Political divisions no longer exist, but Russia, as one, demands a change in Government, and the appointment of a responsible Prime Minister who has the confidence of the country. It is necessary to work in agreement with the legislative bodies and public organizations in order to organize the rear and conquer the enemy. To our great shame in these war times, everything is in disorder. There is no government, no system, and no cooperation between front and rear. Wherever one looks he sees only disorder and betrayal. . . . The

[142]21

idea spreads that everything is done that harms Russia and benefits the enemy. Strange rumors circulate about traitors and spies in the rear of the army. There is not one honest man in your entourage; all decent people have either been sent away or have left. . . . It is no secret that the Empress issues State orders without consulting you; that Ministers go to her with their reports; and that at her will those she disapproves of are removed and are replaced by others who are totally unfit. . . . She is regarded as a partisan of Germany, which she protects. Even the common people speak of it.''. . .

I then turned the conversation to the front and recalled how I had pleaded with him not to take the supreme command and that now, after the failure on the Rumanian front, all blame fell upon him.

"Do not bring about a situation, Your Majesty, which will force your subjects to choose between you and the good of the country. Until now, Tsar and country have been one, but lately a distinction has been made."

The Tsar pressed his head with his hands and said: "Is it possible that for twenty-two years I have tried to do some good, and that for twenty-two years I have failed?"

It was a trying moment.

"Yes, Your Majesty, for twenty-two years you have followed the wrong trail."

MIKHAIL RODZIANKO, RUSSIAN (1859–1924)

A wise government knows how to enforce with temper or to conciliate with dignity.
GEORGE GRENVILLE, ENGLISH (1712–1770)

The man is deaf to repeated warnings. Evil accumulates, as he thinks, "Small sins do no harm." His guilt grows until it cannot be pardoned.

Everybody is talkin' these days about Tammany man growin' rich on graft, but nobody thinks of drawin' the distinction between honest graft and dishonest graft. There's all the difference in the world between the two. Yes, many of our men have grown rich in politics. I have myself. I've made a big fortune out of the game, and I'm gettin' richer every day, but I've not gone in for dishonest graft — black-mailin' gamblers, saloon-keepers, disorderly people, etc. — and neither has any of the men who have made big fortunes in politics.

There's an honest graft, and I'm an example of how it works. I might sum up the whole thing by sayin': "I seen my opportunities and I took 'em."

Just let me explain by examples. My party's in power in the city, and it's goin' to undertake a lot of public improvements. Well, I'm tipped off, say, that they're going to lay out a new park at a certain place.

I see my opportunity and I take it. I go to that place and I buy up all the land I can in the neighborhood. Then the board of this or that makes its plan public, and there is a rush to get my land, which nobody cared particular for before.

Ain't it perfectly honest to charge a good price and make a profit on my investment and foresight? Of course, it is. Well, that's honest graft. . . .

Now, in conclusion, I want to say that I don't own a dishonest dollar. If my worst enemy was given the job of writin' my epitaph when I'm gone, he couldn't do more than write:

"George W. Plunkitt. He Seen His Opportunities, and He Took 'Em."

GEORGE WASHINGTON PLUNKITT,

AMERICAN (1842–1924)

The over-all judgment: force and energetic efforts are needed to remove talebearers, traitors, and others who impede unity. The lasting solution, however, is based on clarity of thinking, gentleness, hardness, as well as enthusiasm in fitting proportions.

We must crush both the interior and exterior enemies of the Republic, or perish with her. And in this situation, the first maxim of your policy should be to conduct the people by reason and the enemies of the people by terror. If the spring of popular government during peace is virtue, the spring of popular government in rebellion is at once both virtue and terror; virtue, without which terror is fatal! terror, without which virtue is powerless! Terror is nothing else than justice, prompt, secure, and inflexible! It is therefore an emanation of virtue; it is less a particular principle than a consequence of the general principles of democracy, applied to the most urgent want of the country.

MAXIMILIEN FRANÇOIS DE ROBESPIERRE,
FRENCH (1758–1794)

Nothing was spared to enhance the effect of the auto-de-fé of Trinity Sunday, May 21, 1559, in which the first portion of the Valladolid prisoners were to suffer. It was solemnly proclaimed fifteen days in advance, during which the buildings of the Inquisition were incessantly patrolled, day and night, by a hundred armed men, and guards were stationed at the stagings in the Plaza Mayor, for there were rumors that the prison was to be blown up and that the stagings were to be fired. Along the line of the procession palings were set in the middle of the street, forming an unobstructed path for three to march abreast. . . . Every house-front along the line and around the plaza had its stagings; people flocked in from thirty and forty leagues around and encamped in the fields. . . .

The procession was headed by the effigy of Leonor de Vivero, who had died during trial, clad in widow's weeds and bearing a mitre with flames and appropriate inscriptions, and followed by a coffin containing her remains to be duly burnt. Those who were to be relaxed in person numbered fourteen, of whom one, Gonzalo Baez, was a Portuguese convicted of Judaism. Those admitted to reconciliation, with penance more or less severe, were sixteen in number, including an Englishman variously styled Anthony Graso or Bagor — probably Baker — punished for Protestantism, like all the rest, excepting Baez. When the procession reached the plaza, Augustin Cazalla was placed in the highest seat, as the conspicuous chief of the heresy, and next to him his brother, Francisco de Vivero. Melchor Cano at once commenced the sermon, which occupied an hour, and then Valdés and the Bishops approached the Princess Juana and Prince Carlos, who were present, and administered to them the oath to protect and aid the Inquisition, to which the multitude responded in a mighty roar, "To the death!" Cazalla, his brother

[145]21

and Alonzo Pérez, who were in orders, were duly degraded from the priesthood, the sentences were read, those admitted to reconciliation made the necessary adjurations and those condemned to relaxation were handed over to the secular arm. Mounted on asses, they were carried to the Plaza de la Puerta de Campo, where the requisite stakes had been erected, and there they met their end. . . .

Of these there were only two or three who merit special consideration. Cazalla, on his trial, had at first equivocated and denied that he had dogmatized, asserting that he had only spoken of these matters to those already converted. As a rule, all the prisoners eagerly denounced their associates; he may have been more reticent at first, for he was sentenced to torture *in caput alienum,* but when stripped he promised to inform against them fully, which he did, including Carranza among those who had misled him as to purgatory. He recanted, professed conversion and eagerly sought reconciliation . . . . He declared that, when opportunity offered in the auto, he would curse and detest Lutheranism and persuade everyone to do the same, with which purpose he took his place in the procession.

So great was his emotional exaltation that he fulfilled this promise with such exuberance during the auto that he had to be checked . . . . On the way to the brasero he continued to exhort the people and directed his efforts especially to the heroic Herrezuelo, who had steadfastly refused to abandon his faith and was to be burnt alive . . . .

It was otherwise with Herrezuelo, the only martyr in the group. He avowed his faith and resolutely adhered to it, in spite of all effort to convert him and of the dreadful fate in store for him. On the way to the brasero, Cazalla wasted on him all his eloquence. He was gagged and could not reply, but his stoical endurance showed his unyielding pertinacity. When chained to the stake, a stone thrown at him struck him in the forehead, covering his face with blood but, as we are told, it did him no good. Then he was thrust through the belly by a pious halberdier, but this moved him not and, when the fire was set, he bore his agony without flinching and, to the general surprise, he thus ended diabolically. Illescas, who stood so near that he could watch every expres-

[146]21

sion, reports that he seemed as impassive as flint but, though he uttered no complaint and manifested no regret, yet he died with the strangest sadness in his face, so that it was dreadful to look upon him as on one who in a brief moment would be in hell with his comrade and master, Luther . . . .

The remainder of the Valladolid reformers were reserved for another celebration, October 8th, honored with the presence of Philip II, who obediently took the customary oath, with bared head and ungloved hand. It was, if possible, an occasion of greater solemnity than the previous one. A Flemish official, who was present, estimates the number of spectators at two hundred thousand and, though he must have been hardened to such scenes at home, he cannot repress an expression of sympathy with the sufferers. Besides a Morisco who was relaxed, a Judaizer reconciled and two penitents for other offences, there were twenty-six Protestants. The lesson was the same as in the previous auto, that few had the ardor of martyrdom. Thirteen had made their peace in time to secure reconciliation or penance. Even Juana Sánchez, who had managed to bring with her a pair of scissors and had cut her throat, recanted before death, but her confession was considered imperfect and she was burnt in effigy . . . . only in two cases did this withstand the test of fire. Carlos de Seso was unyielding to the end and, when we are told that he had to be supported by two familiars to enable him to stand when hearing his sentence, we can guess the severity of the torture endured by him. Juan Sánchez was likewise pertinacious; when the fire was set it burnt the cord fastening him to the stake; he leaped down and ran in flames; it was thought that he wanted to confess but, when a confessor was brought, he refused to listen to him; one account says that the guards thrust him back into the flames, another, that he looked up and saw Carlos de Seso calmly burning and himself leaped back into the blazing pile . . . . Thus was exterminated the nascent Protestantism of Valladolid.

HENRY CHARLES LEA, AMERICAN (1825–1909)

Well, even in a beaten army when every tenth man is felled by the club, the lot falls also on the brave. There is some injustice in every great precedent, which, though injurious to individuals, has its compensation in the public advantage.

GAIUS CASSIUS LONGINUS, ROMAN (DIED 42 B.C.)

22 Public Image

THE PI HEXAGRAM

At the outset, the man is tempted to create a falsely flattering public image for himself. A simple demeanor is more gracious and fitting to his position.

Aunt Alicia slipped the large square-cut emerald on one of her thin fingers and was lost in silence.
"Do you see," she said in hushed voice, "that almost blue flame darting about in the depths of the green light? Only the most beautiful emeralds contain that miracle of elusive blue."
"Who gave it to you, Aunt?" Gilberte dared to ask.
"A king," said Aunt Alicia simply.
"A great king?"
"No. A little one. Great kings do not give very fine stones."
"Why not?"
For a fleeting moment, Aunt Alicia proffered a glimpse of her tiny white teeth.
"If you want my opinion, it's because they don't want to. Between ourselves, the little ones don't either."
"Then who does give great big stones?"
"Who? The shy. The proud, too. And the bounders, because they think that to give a monster jewel is a sign of good breeding. Sometimes a woman does, to humiliate a man . . . ."

SIDONIE-GABRIELLE COLETTE, FRENCH (1873–1954)

The man seeks adornment for its own sake, without regard to his inner spiritual qualities, which it should enhance.

"The hat, my boy, the hat, whatever it may be, is in itself nothing—makes nothing, goes for nothing; but, be sure of it, everything in life depends upon the cock of the hat." For how many men—we put it to your own experience, reader—have made their way through the thronging crowds that beset fortune,

not by the innate worth and excellence of their hats,
but simply, as Sampson Piebald has it, by "the cock
of their hats"? The cock's all.
DOUGLAS WILLIAM JERROLD, ENGLISH (1803–1857)

I did not understand his meaning; his discourse was
so obscured by solemnity, grandeur, and majesty.
MICHEL EYQUEM DE MONTAIGNE, FRENCH (1533–1592)

---

*The man is enjoying a charmed life, and is given many
honors. He should guard against convivial indolence and
be aware of its consequences.*

If daily drinkers felt the headache first,
Before the tasting, few would feel athirst!
But now alas! comes pleasure first, then pain,
Too late to teach that abstinence is gain.
CLEARCHUS, GREEK (FIFTH CENTURY B.C.)

---

*The man is faced with the choice between a life of bril-
liance and one of simplicity. All considerations suggest
simplicity. Renouncing potential comforts may seem
disappointing at first, but peace of mind will be attained
through proper relationship with the sincere supporter.*

How vainly men themselves amaze,
To win the palm, the oak, or bays,
And their incessant labours see
Crown'd from some single herb or tree.
Whose short and narrow verged shade
Does prudently their toils upbraid;
While all the flow'rs and trees do close
To weave the garlands of repose!

Fair quiet, have I found thee here,
And innocence, thy sister dear!
Mistaken long, I sought you then
In busy companies of men.
Your sacred plants, if here below,
Only among the plants will grow;
Society is all but rude
To this delicious solitude.
ANDREW MARVELL, ENGLISH (1621–1678)

---

*The man meets someone whom he wishes to befriend and
feels ashamed at his meager gifts. But his natural sincerity overcomes the difficulties and good fortune ensues.*

A poor man knows not   how to eat with a rich man
  if he begins to eat fish   he eats the head.
Invite a poor man and he comes disreputably   he
  comes licking his lips   he is an upsetter of the
  platter.
The poor man has no reserve   if he is called he
  comes   with the blood of lice   in his finger-nails.
The face of a poor man   is furrowed   by hunger and
  thirst that is in his vitals.
Poverty is no state   fit for mortal man   it makes
  him a beast   to be fed upon the grass.
Poverty is no right thing when a man gets it though
  he be nobly born   he has no power with God.
SWAHILI FOLK VERSE

The man reaches the peak of his development, and dis-
plays perfect grace through the true expression of his
character without pretensions. He understands the
patterns of human frailties.

EDWARD. Now, George, it rests I gratify thy worth;
And therefore here I do bequeath to thee,
In full possession, half that Kendal hath;
I give it frankly unto thee forever,
Kneel down, George.
GEORGE. What will your majesty do?
EDWARD. Dub thee a knight, George.
GEORGE. I beseech your grace, grant me one thing.
EDWARD. What is that?
GEORGE. Then let me live and die a yeoman still.
So was my father, so must live his son.
For 'tis more credit to men of base degree
To do great deeds than men of dignity.
ROBERT GREENE, ENGLISH (1560–1592)

He had thought more than other men, and in matters
òf the intellect he had that calm objectivity, that certainty of thought and knowledge, such as only really
intellectual men have, who have no axe to grind, who
never wish to shine, or to talk others down, or to
appear always in the right.
I remember an instance of this in the last days he was
here, if I can call a mere fleeting glance he gave me
an example of what I mean. It was when a celebrated

historian, philosopher, and critic, a man of European fame, had announced a lecture in the school auditorium. I had succeeded in persuading the Steppenwolf to attend it, though at first he had little desire to do so. We went together and sat next to each other in the lecture hall. When the lecturer ascended the platform and began his address, many of his hearers, who had expected a sort of prophet, were disappointed by his rather dapper appearance and conceited air. And when he proceeded, by way of introduction, to say a few flattering things to the audience, thanking them for their attendance in such numbers, the Steppenwolf threw me a quick look, a look which criticized both the words and the speaker of them — an unforgettable and frightful look which spoke volumes! It was a look that did not simply criticize the lecturer, annihilating the famous man with its delicate but crushing irony. That was the least of it. It was more sad than ironical; it was indeed utterly and hopelessly sad; it conveyed a quiet despair, born partly of conviction, partly of a mode of thought which had become habitual with him. This despair of his not only unmasked the conceited lecturer and dismissed with its irony the matter at hand, the expectant attitude of the public, the somewhat presumptuous title under which the lecture was announced — no, the Steppenwolf's look pierced our whole epoch, its whole overwrought activity, the whole surge and strife, the whole vanity, the whole superficial play of a shallow, opinionated intellectuality. And alas! the look went still deeper, went far below the faults, defects and hopelessness of our time, our intellect, our culture alone. It went right to the heart of all humanity, it bespoke eloquently in a single second the whole despair of a thinker, of one who knew the full worth and meaning of man's life. It said: "See what monkeys we are! Look, such is man!" and at once all renown, all intelligence, all the attainments of the spirit, all progress towards the sublime, the great and the enduring in man fell away and became a monkey's trick!

HERMANN HESSE, GERMAN (1877–1962)

The over-all judgment: the ceremonial observances of society are stimulating to the workings of the govern-

ment. However, they are not to be relied upon in decisions of consequence. The basic attitude must be firm, abiding, and correct.

"I have had a look at the dossier," he [the young lawyer] told the rebel. "The charges are pretty stiff, but in extenuation there is your extreme youth at the time of the revolution. A misguided youth of twenty, a mere child . . . . We will concentrate on that. And, of course, on your having returned of your own free will. I have not the slightest idea what made you do it, but we will say that you were longing to do penance."
The rebel made a wry face.
"Must we?" he hesitated. "It may sound sacrilegious to your ears, but I do not feel particularly guilty, I have no sense of guilt at all, I am afraid. My case is simply that I want to live at home and if the price is a few years in prison I am willing to pay it."
"We had better speak of repentance," the young lawyer advised him. "Of repentance and expiation. These soulful things go down all right if they are handled impressively."
YOLANDA FOELDES, HUNGARIAN (BORN 1903)

The maiden who listens, like the town that negotiates, is halfway toward surrender.
COUNT ADRIEN DE MONTLUC, FRENCH (1589–1646)

My idea was then and still is that if a man did his work well, the price he could get for that work, the profits, and all financial matters would care for themselves.
HENRY FORD, AMERICAN (1863–1947)

23 Intrigue
THE PO HEXAGRAM

At the outset, the superior men around the ruler are being undermined by the slander and intrigue of inferior men on their destructive path. All that can be done is to be patient while the evil continues.

You belittle slander, sir? You scarcely know what you are making light of. I have seen the most respectable people very near to being overwhelmed by it. There is no silly piece of malice, no abomination, no absurd story that we could not get taken up and repeated by the idlers of a big city, provided we go about it the right way. And we have in Seville such skilled people in affairs of that kind — To start with a low sound, skimming the ground like the swallow before the storm, *pianissimo*, very softly it murmurs, spreads swiftly, and hurls while running the poisoned dart. Here such and such a mouth takes it up, and *piano, piano* it slips easily into your ear. The evil is done; it trails; it winds; and *rinforzando*, from mouth to mouth it goes the dance of a pace; then suddenly, no one knows how, you see slander rear itself, hiss, swell, and grow before your eyes. It hurls itself forward, enlarges its flight, whirls, envelops, uproots, thunders, and becomes, thanks to heavens, a universal cry, a public *crescendo*, a general chorus of hatred and condemnation. What the devil could resist it?

PIERRE AUGUSTIN DE BEAUMARCHAIS,
FRENCH (1732–1799)

The inferior men grow stronger. No help is in sight.
Great caution and stubborn adherence to personal con-
victions are required.

I am a man, a discerning one, yet who respects me
  prospers not,
My righteous word has been turned into a lie,
The man of deceit has covered me with the South-
  wind, I am forced to serve him,
Who respects me not has shamed me before you.
You have doled out to me suffering ever anew,
I enter the house, heavy is the spirit,
I, the man, went out to the street, oppressed is the
  heart,
With me, the valiant, the righteous shepherd has
  become angry and looked upon me inimically,
My herdsman has sought out evil forces against me
  who am not his enemy,
My companion says not a true word to me,
My friend gives the lie to my righteous word.
The man of deceit has conspired against me,
And you, O my god, do not thwart him!

SUMERIAN INSCRIPTION (2000 B.C.)

Because of circumstances beyond his control, the man finds himself associating with evil men. His inner relationship with a superior man enables him to retain his righteous stability, leading to opposition from inferior people.

The ceremonial welcome reached its high point about midnight. Huge chunks of the roasted cow were brought in to us, and we gnawed at the almost raw meat between swigs of liquor. Outside, there was muted drumming. Voices were growing louder and louder.

Suddenly, in the midst of a long-winded speech by an immensely dignified Masai chief from a neighboring and friendly tribe, Kenyatta jumped up, grabbed his heavy cane and half staggered to the door.

"Come, Peter," he called.

Everybody was startled. I hesitated. He raised his cane and beckoned to me with it. I knew that this would be a dreadful breach of tribal etiquette.

"Come, man!" he snapped.

I got up, aware of the sudden silence that had descended on the huge gathering. By some strange magic everybody seemed to know something had gone wrong.

"Jomo," I said.

"I can't stand any more," he snapped. "Come!"

I followed him to the door. I knew the discourtesy we were inflicting on the tribe. I also knew that my friend was at the breaking point. We walked through the crowd of people, got into Kenyatta's car and drove off into the night. The African moon was big and yellow, bathing the land in a soft light that almost achieved the clarity of daylight.

He took me to his house. It was a big, sprawling, empty place on the brow of a hill. Inside, it had nothing to make for comfort. There were hard wooden chairs, a few tables and only the bed in the bedroom. There were no books, none of the normal amenities of western civilization. When we arrived two women emerged from somewhere in the back and hovered about in the shadows. They brought in liquor, but I never got a clear glimpse of either of them. My friend's anguish of spirit was such that I did not want to ask questions. We sat on the veranda and drank steadily and in silence until we were both miserably, depressingly drunk.

And then Kenyatta began to speak in a low, bitter voice of his frustration and of the isolated position in which he found himself. He had no friends. There was no one in the tribe who could give him the intellectual companionship that had become so important to him in his years in Europe. The things that were important to him — consequential conversation, the drink that represented a social activity rather than the intention to get drunk, the concept of individualism, the inviolability of privacy — all these were alien to the tribesmen in whose midst he lived. So Kenyatta, the western man, was driven in on himself and was forced to assert himself in tribal terms. Only thus would the tribesmen follow him and so give him his position of power and importance as a leader.

PETER ABRAHAMS, SOUTH AFRICAN (BORN 1919)

Calamity is imminent. Neither warning nor protection is forthcoming. The man is at the mercy of destroyers.

DIABOLUS. Come, show me the agreement you've drawn up
Between me and my darling. Read the terms,
For you're a perfect artist in this kind.
PARASITE. 'Twill make the mother tremble when she reads.
DIABOLUS. Well, read it to me.
PARASITE. Are you listening?
DIABOLUS. Yes.
PARASITE *(reading)*. "Diabolus, the son of Glaucus, gives
Cleareta the sum of twenty minae,
That he may have Philaenium, her daughter,
And keep her night and day for one whole year."
DIABOLUS. She mustn't see another man.
PARASITE. Must that be in?
DIABOLUS. It must, and write it plain!
PARASITE. "She shall not ever see another man,
Though she should say he is her friend or patron,
Or feign that he's the sweetheart of her friend;
Her doors must be fast closed to all but you,
And she must always say she's not at home.
Then, though she say it's come from foreign parts,
[155]23

No letter shall be found in all the house,
Nor a wax tablet; also any picture
From which wax might be got for writing letters,
She now shall sell; and if they are not sold
Within four days from when she gets the money,
They shall be yours, to burn them, if you like,
That she may have no wax wherewith to write.
She shall invite no guest; you shall do that.
If she catch sight of any other man,
She instantly shall look the other way.
She shall not drink from any one but you;
Shall take the cup from you and hand it back;
Nor drink a single drop without your knowledge."
DIABOLUS. That's well.
PARASITE. "To turn suspicion from herself,
She shall not tread on anybody's foot
When she gets up or crosses the next couch.
Nor in descending shall she give a hand.
She shall not give her ring to anyone
To look at, nor shall ask his in return,
Nor shall she challenge anyone but you
To play at dice; and she shall name your name,
And not say, 'Thee,' when challenging to throw.
And only goddesses shall she invoke,
And no male god; but if she must do so,
She shall tell you, and you shall do it for her.
She shall not nod, or wink her eye, or beckon
To any man; and if the light goes out,
She shall not move a limb until it's lit."
DIABOLUS. First-rate! But in her room, I'd rather have
Her move her limbs a bit. Cut out that clause;
For she shan't say the contract does forbid.
PARASITE. I know; you fear a catch.
DIABOLUS. True!
PARASITE. I'll remove
That clause. Now hear the rest.
DIABOLUS. All right; read on.
PARASITE. "She shall not utter an ambiguous word,
Or speak in any language but her own.
If she perchance must cough, she shall not cough
So as to put her tongue out when she coughs.
If she pretends she wants to clean her lips,
She shall not do it so; it would be better
For you to wipe her lips yourself than suffer
That she should show her open mouth to men.
Her mother shall never drop in to dinner,

[156]23

Nor start to make complaints; and if she does,
Her punishment shall be to have no wine
For twenty days."
DIABOLUS. Bravo! A clever bond!
TITUS MACCIUS PLAUTUS, ROMAN (254–184 B.C.)

---

*The dark forces undergo change, yielding to the strong
influence of the basic goodness of men.*

Remorse goes to sleep during a prosperous period
and wakes up in adversity.
JEAN JACQUES ROUSSEAU, SWISS (1712–1778)

---

*The evil finally brings about its own demise, and good
times return. The man acquires fresh vigor, and the
sovereign is strengthened by public support.*

A Wolf, once upon a time, resolved to disguise himself, thinking that he should thus gain an easier
livelihood. Having, therefore, clothed himself in a
sheep's skin, he contrived to get among a flock of
Sheep, and feed along with them, so that even the
Shepherd was deceived by the imposture. When
night came on and the fold was closed, the Wolf was
shut up with the Sheep, and the door made fast. But
the Shepherd, wanting something for his supper,
and going in to fetch out a sheep, mistook the Wolf
for one of them and killed him on the spot.
AESOP, GREEK (SIXTH CENTURY B.C.)

In the reign of King Giovanni d'Atri, there was
ordered to be erected a certain great bell for the
especial use of individuals who might happen to
meet with any grievous injuries, when they were to
ring as loudly as they could, for the purpose of obtaining redress. Now it so fell that the rope in the
course of time was nearly worn away, on which a
bunch of snake-weed had been fastened to it, for the
convenience of the ringers. One day a fine old cour-
ser belonging to a knight of Atri, which being no
longer serviceable, had been turned out to run at
large, was wandering near the place. Being hard
pressed by famine, the poor steed seized hold of the
snake-weed with his mouth, and sounded the bell
pretty smartly. The council, on hearing the clamor,
immediately assembled, as if to hear the petition of

the horse, whose appearance seemed to declare that he required justice. Taking the case into consideration, it was soon decreed that the same cavalier whom the horse had so long served while he was young should be compelled to maintain him in his old age; and the king even imposed a fine in similar instances to the same effect.

BELL OF ATRI, ITALIAN (THIRTEENTH CENTURY)

The over-all judgment: the decay of the body politic has set in. Inferior men are on the aggressive rise. The time is not favorable for the lonely superior man to undertake anything. The law of heaven dictates cycles of rise and fall, fullness and emptiness. It cannot be countermanded. It is prudent to submit and wait.

FAMUSOV. [You should] take a government position.
CHATSKI. I should gladly serve, but I hate to be subservient.
FAMUSOV. That's it! You are all a haughty lot! Ask how your fathers have done! Learn from your elders. Let us take, for example, my deceased uncle, Maksim Petrovich: he used to dine not upon silver, but upon gold; a hundred servants were at his beck; he was all covered with decorations; he traveled all the time in a procession, was all the time at Court, and at what Court! It was not then as now: he served under Empress Catherine! In those days there was some weight in dignity: bow all you please to them, they would not nod their heads. A dignitary was not an ordinary mortal: he drank and ate quite differently. And my uncle, — what is your prince, your count? He had such a serious look, such a haughty mien, — but when it was necessary to be subservient, he knew how to limber up his joints. Once he by chance made a misstep during audience at Court: he fell, and almost hurt his occiput. The old man groaned, — his hoarse voice provoked her Majesty's smile, she deigned to laugh. What did he do? He rose, arranged his clothes, wanted to make a bow, and fell down again, but this time on purpose. The laughter was louder than before, — he repeated his feat. Well, how is that according to your own ideas? According to ours he was shrewd: he fell down in pain, he rose quite well. Who was oftenest invited to whist? Who heard a kind word at Court? Maksim Petrovich!

[158]23

That's no trifle! Who conferred ranks, and gave pensions? Maksim Petrovich!
ALEKSANDR SERGEEVICH GRIBOEDOV,
RUSSIAN (1795–1829)

That is why I speak of hyperdemocracy. . . . The characteristic of the hour is that the commonplace mind, knowing itself to be commonplace, has the assurance to proclaim the rights of the commonplace and to impose them wherever it will.
JOSÉ ORTEGA Y GASSET, SPANISH (1883–1955)

When winter comes, a crow perches even on a scarecrow.
KIKAKU ENOMOTO, JAPANESE (1661–1707)

24 Recovery
THE FU HEXAGRAM

At the outset, the man returns to the original course of goodness after a minor setback. There is no cause for remorse since the evil is put aside quickly.

In fact there is a great deal to be said for getting fired from the first job. . . . getting fired from the first job is the least painful and the least damaging way to learn how to take a setback. And whom the Lord loveth he teacheth early how to take a setback.
Nobody has ever lived, I daresay, who has not gone through a period when everything seemed to have collapsed and when years of work and life seemed to have gone up in smoke. No one can be spared this experience; but one can be prepared for it. The man who has been through earlier setbacks has learned that the world has not come to an end because he lost his job—not even in a depression. He has learned that he will somehow survive. He has learned, above all, that the way to behave in such a setback is not to collapse himself.
PETER FERDINAND DRUCKER, AMERICAN (BORN 1909)

No, no, I do not want a throne befouled
With blood, the very blood whence I took life.
Trusting that passion common in great spirits,
I against nature heard ambition's voice,
[159]24

I deemed my tenderness of heart false virtue;
With sovereignty the stake, my heart was silent;
But when a father must be sacrificed,
Ambition speaks no more and sonship counsels.
JEAN ROTROU, FRENCH (1609–1650)

*The man makes an admirable comeback through an act
of self-mastery. This is made easier by the example of a
good man.*

The sun was already dropping low, and in the dead
stillness only the twittering of the birds was audible,
and the crackle of the dead wood under his feet. As
he walked along rapidly, he fancied he heard the
clang of iron striking iron, and he redoubled his
pace. There was no repair going on in his section.
What did it mean? He emerged from the woods, the
railway embankment stood high before him; on the
top a man was squatting on the bed of the line busily
engaged in something. Semyon commenced quietly
to crawl up towards him. He thought it was some one
after the nuts which secure the rails. He watched,
and the man got up, holding a crow-bar in his hand.
He had loosened a rail, so that it would move to one
side. A mist swam before Semyon's eyes; he wanted
to cry out, but could not. It was Vasily! Semyon
scrambled up the bank, as Vasily with crow-bar and
wrench slid headlong down the other side.
"Vasily Stepanych! My dear friend, come back! Give
me the crow-bar. We will put the rail back; no one
will know. Come back! Save your soul from sin!"
Vasily did not look back, but disappeared into the
woods.
Semyon stood before the rail which had been torn
up. He threw down his bundle of sticks. A train was
due; not a freight, but a passenger-train. And he had
nothing with which to stop it, no flag. He could not
replace the rail and could not drive in the spikes
with his bare hands. It was necessary to run, absolutely necessary to run to the hut for some tools.
"God help me!" he murmured.
Semyon started running toward his hut. He was out
of breath, but still ran, falling every now and then.
He had cleared the forest; he was only a few hundred
feet from his hut, not more, when he heard the distant hooter of the factory sound—six o'clock! In two

minutes time No. 7 train was due. "Oh, Lord! Have pity on innocent souls!" In his mind Semyon saw the engine strike against the loosened rail with its left wheel, shiver, careen, tear up and splinter the sleepers — and just there, there was a curve and the embankment seventy feet high, down which the engine would topple — and the third-class carriages would be packed . . . little children . . . All sitting in the train now, never dreaming of danger. "Oh, Lord! Tell me what to do! . . . No, it is impossible to run to the hut and get back in time."

Semyon did not run on to the hut, but turned back and ran faster than before. He was running almost mechanically, blindly; he did not know himself what was to happen. He ran as far as the rail which had been pulled up; his sticks were lying in a heap. He bent down, seized one without knowing why, and ran on farther. It seemed to him the train was already coming. He heard the distant whistle; he heard the quiet, even tremor of the rails; but the strength was exhausted, he could run no farther, and came to a halt about six hundred feet from the awful spot. Then an idea came into his head, literally like a ray of light. Pulling off his cap, he took out of it a cotton scarf, drew his knife out of the upper part of his boot, and crossed himself, muttering, "God bless me!"

He buried the knife in his left arm above the elbow; the blood spurted out, flowing in a hot stream. In this he soaked his scarf, smoothed it out, tied it to the stick and hung out his red flag.

He stood waving his flag. The train was already in sight. The driver would not see him — would come close up, and a heavy train cannot be pulled up in six hundred feet.

And the blood kept on flowing. Semyon pressed the sides of the wound together so as to close it, but the blood did not diminish. Evidently he had cut his arm very deep. His head commenced to swim, black spots began to dance before his eyes, and then it became dark. There was a ringing in his ears. He could not see the train or hear the noise. Only one thought possessed him. "I shall not be able to keep standing up. I shall fall and drop the flag; the train will pass over me. Help me, O Lord!"

All turned black before him, his mind became a blank, and he dropped the flag; but the bloodstained
[161]24

banner did not fall to the ground. A hand seized it
and held it high to meet the approaching train.
The engineer saw it, shut the regulator, and reversed
steam. The train came to a standstill.
People jumped out of the carriages and collected in a
crowd. They saw a man lying senseless on the foot-
way, drenched in blood, and another man standing
beside him with a blood-stained rag on a stick.
Vasily looked around at all. Then, lowering his head,
he said: "Bind me. I tore up a rail!"
VSEVOLOD MIKHAILOVICH GARSHIN,
RUSSIAN (1855–1888)

---

*The man is changeable, departing time after time from
the right course because of his uncontrolled desire for
apparent advantages and returning to it for seemingly
better solutions. No great blame will be attached to him,
but there is some danger.*

We think so because other people all think so;
Or because — or because — after all, we do think so;
Or because we were told so, and think we must think
  so;
Or because we once thought so, and think we still
  think so;
Or because having thought so, we think we *will*
  think so.
HENRY SIDGWICK, ENGLISH (1838–1900)

---

*The man is superficially connected with inferior people
but more deeply attached to a noble friend.*

From childhood, I have been — only a thief. . . .
Always I was called Waska, the pick-pocket, the son
of a thief! See, it was of no consequence to me, as
long as they would have it so . . . so they would have
it. . . . I was a thief, perhaps, only out of spite . . .
because nobody came along to call me anything
except — thief. . . . You call me something else,
Natasha. . . .
MAKSIM GORKY, RUSSIAN (1868–1936)

---

*The man makes a noblehearted recovery by squarely
facing his own shortcomings rather than leaning on
trivial excuses.*

Tsou Chi, the prime minister of Ch'i, was over eight feet tall and had a very handsome face and figure. One day as he was putting on his court robes and cap and looking at himself in the mirror, he said to his wife, "Who do you think is better looking, I or Lord Hsü of Ch'eng-pei?" His wife replied, "You are much better looking! How could Lord Hsü compare to you?" Lord Hsü of Ch'eng-pei was one of the handsomest men in the state of Ch'i.

Tsou Chi was not entirely confident, however, and so he put the same question to his concubine. "Who is better looking, I or Lord Hsü?" "Lord Hsü could never compare to you!" she replied.

The next morning a guest came to call and while Tsou Chi was sitting and chatting with him, he asked, "Who is better looking, Lord Hsü or I?" "Lord Hsü is nowhere near as good looking as you!" said the guest.

The following day Lord Hsü himself came to visit. Tsou Chi stared very hard at Lord Hsü and realized that his own looks could not compare, and when he went and looked in the mirror it was obvious that the difference between them was great indeed.

That night when he went to bed he thought over the incident. "My wife says I am better looking because she is partial to me, my concubine says I am better looking because she is afraid of me, and my guest says I am better looking because he hopes to get something out of me!" he declared.

The next time he went to court and had an audience with King Wei, he said, "I am certainly not as good looking as Lord Hsü. And yet my wife, who is partial to me, my concubine, who is afraid of me, and guest of mine, who wants something from me, all have told me that I am better looking than Lord Hsü. Now the state of Ch'i is a thousand *li* square and contains a hundred and twenty cities. In this vast realm, there are none of the palace ladies and attendants who are not partial to Your Majesty, none of the court ministers who do not fear you, and no one within the four borders who does not hope to get something from you. If that is so, think how great must be the deception you face!"

"You are right," said the king, and issued a notice saying that, to any one of the officials or people of the state who would attack his faults to his face, he would give first prize; to anyone who would submit a letter of reprimand, he would give second prize; and to anyone who would spread critical rumors in the market so that they reached his ears, he would give third prize. When the notice was first issued, the officials who came forward with criticisms packed the gate of the palace until it looked like a market place. After several months, there were still people who came forward with criticisms from time to time. But by the end of the year, though the king might beg for reprimand, no one could any longer find anything to criticize.

INTRIGUES OF THE WARRING STATES,
CHINESE (480–222 B.C.)

The man attempts to gain his objectives by force. His blind obstinacy leads to calamity. The use of armies under these conditions will result in a great defeat and a long-lasting disaster for the state.

Rubashov stared through the bars of the window at the patch of the blue above the machine-gun tower. Looking back over his past, it seemed to him now that for forty years he had been running amuck—the running-amuck of pure reason. Perhaps it did not suit man to be completely freed from old bonds, from the steadying brakes of "Thou shalt not" and "Thou mayst not," and to be allowed to tear along straight toward the goal.

ARTHUR KOESTLER, HUNGARIAN (BORN 1905)

The over-all judgment: The time of darkness is past, in conformity with the cyclic course of nature. Society is harmonious. Friends come. Nothing stands in the man's road to progress.

... the ailing civilization pays the penalty for its failing vitality by being disintegrated into a dominant minority, which rules with increasing oppressiveness but no longer leads, and a proletariat (internal and external) which responds to this challenge by becoming conscious that it has a soul of its own and by making up its mind to save its soul alive. The dominant minority's will to repress evokes in the proletariat a will to secede; and a conflict between

[164]24

these two wills continues while the declining civilization verges towards its fall, until, when it is *in articulo mortis,* the proletariat at length breaks free from what was once its spiritual home but has now become a prison-house and finally a City of Destruction. In this conflict between a proletariat and a dominant minority, as it works itself out from beginning to end, we can discern one of those dramatic spiritual encounters which renew the work of creation by carrying the life of the Universe out of the stagnation of autumn through the pains of winter into the ferment of spring.

ARNOLD JOSEPH TOYNBEE,
ENGLISH (BORN 1889)

"Promise [said Saint Francis to the wolf of Gubbio] thou wilt never play me, thy bondsman, false." Then the wolf, lifting up his right paw, placed it in the hand of Saint Francis. Whereat . . . there was such marvel and rejoicing among all the people — not only at the strangeness of the miracle, but because of the peace made with the wolf — that they all began to cry aloud to heaven.

STORY OF SAINT FRANCIS OF ASSISI,
ITALIAN (1182–1226)

Cliffs of scarlet cloud gleam in the west;
The sun's feet are sinking beneath the earth.
By the rustic gate sparrows are twittering.
The stranger returns to his home from a thousand li.
My wife is astonished that I still exist.
No longer bewildered, she wipes away her tears.
I was drifting sand in the wind of the world's anger.
It is just fate that has brought me back alive.
The fence gate is filled with neighbors' faces,
Sighing and shedding a few tears.
In the deep night we light a new candle
And see each other face to face as in a dream.

TU FU, CHINESE (712–770)

25 Instinctive Goodness

THE WU WANG HEXAGRAM

At the outset, the man follows the original pure impulses of his heart. His aims will be achieved.

When the heart dares to speak, it needs no preparation.
GOTTHOLD EPHRAIM LESSING, GERMAN (1729–1781)

If you are looking for an easy and simple choice, the
most peaceful, the most practical way of navigating
in the sea of art is to float with the tide — be it in the
calm of a carefree day when the waters are quiet and
clear to the point of boredom, or in the nightmarish
turbulence of a night of raging waves surrounded by
darkness and impenetrable turmoil. But if such a
course offers you little challenge, and you wish to
choose your own course in the direction of your own
goal — if you are ready to challenge the struggle and
sufferings confronting you, the elements do not
frighten you, you do not require favorable weather,
you do not have to inquire about favorable trade
winds — you can boldly set your course against the
tide.
MICHEL FOKINE, RUSSIAN (1880–1942)

---

*The man succeeds in everything he undertakes. He does
not proceed with mercenary or selfish interests in mind
but does good things for their own sake. Unsought
wealth will come his way.*

A Vinaya teacher once asked a Zen master, "How do
you discipline yourself in your daily life?"
The master said, "When I am hungry I eat, when I
feel tired I sleep."
Teacher: "That is what everybody generally does.
Could he be said to be disciplining himself as much
as yourself?"
Master: "No, not in the same way."
Teacher: "Why not the same?"
Master: "When they eat, they dare not eat, their
minds are filled with all kinds of contrivances.
Therefore, I say, not the same."
DAISETZ TEITARO SUZUKI, JAPANESE (1870–1966)

---

*Undeserved calamity comes to the sincere person. Un-
expected misfortunes of this kind, however, do not
throw the superior man off stride.*

We lived in Illinois from 1839 to 1844, by which time
they again succeeded in kindling the spirit of perse-
[166]25

cution against Joseph and the Latter-day Saints.
Treason! Treason! they cried, calling us murderers,
thieves, liars, adulterers, and the worst people on the
earth. And this was done by the priests, those pious
dispensers of the Christian religion whose charity
was supposed to be extended to all men, Christian
and heathen; they were joined by drunkards, gamblers, thieves, liars, in crying against the Latter-day
Saints. They took Joseph and Byrum, and as a guar-
antee for their safety, Governor Thomas Ford pledged
the faith of the State of Illinois. They were imprisoned, on the pretense of safe keeping, because
the mob was so enraged and violent. The Governor
left them in the hands of the mob, who entered the
prison and shot them dead. . . . After the mob had
committed these murders, they came upon us and
burned our houses and grain. When the brethren
would go out to put out the fire, the mob would lie
concealed under fences, and in the darkness of the
night, they would shoot them. At last they succeeded
in driving us from the state of Illinois. . . .
We left Nauvoo in February, 1846. There remained
behind a few of the very poor, the sick and the aged,
who suffered again from the violence of the mob;
they were whipped and beaten, and had their houses
burned. We traveled west, stopping in places, building settlements, where we left the poor who could
not travel any farther with the company. Exactly
thirty years today myself, with others, came out of
what we named Emigration Canyon; we crossed the
Big and Little mountains, and came down the valley
about three quarters of a mile south of this. We
located, and we looked about, and finally we came
and camped between the two forks of City Creek,
one of which ran southwest and the other west. Here
we planted our standard on this temple block and the
one above it; here we pitched our camps and determined that here we would settle and stop. . . .
We wish strangers to understand that we did not
come here out of choice, but because we were obliged to go somewhere, and this was the best place
we could find. It was impossible for any person to
live here unless he labored hard and battled and
fought against the elements. . . . We came here penni-
less in old wagons, our friends back [home] telling us
to "take all the provisions you can, for you can get no

more! Take all the seed grain you can, for you can get none there!'' We did this, and in addition to all this we have gathered all the poor we could, and the Lord has planted us in these valleys, promising that he would hide us up for a little season until his wrath and indignation passed over the nations. Will we trust in the Lord? Yes.
BRIGHAM YOUNG, AMERICAN (1801–1877)

What really belongs to the man cannot be lost to him. As long as he remains steadfast to his own nature, he will commit no error.

'Tis not in mortals to command success,
But we'll do more, Sempronius: we'll deserve it.
JOSEPH ADDISON, ENGLISH (1672–1719)

Unexpected evil comes to the man through no fault of his own. He should not anxiously resort to hasty remedies. Nature will overcome the evil in her own way and at her own pace.

  Sick unto death
I have no desire
  For medicine
But people are so pertinacious,
  Urging me to take it!
AKEMI TACHIBANA, JAPANESE (1811–1868)

Time is the great physician.
PRIME MINISTER BENJAMIN DISRAELI,
ENGLISH (1804–1881)

The time is not ripe for further progress. The man keeps still. Activities in opposition to fate will not help him in any way.

Who is there that can make muddy water clear? But if allowed to remain still, it will gradually become clear of itself. Who is there that can secure a state of absolute repose? But let time go on, and the state of repose will gradually arise.
LAO-TZU, CHINESE (604–531 B.C.)

The over-all judgment: heaven endows man with innate goodness. Instinctive devotion to this spirit leads to success, though conscious purpose jeopardizes nature's
[168]25

innocence. But even with instinctive sincerity, action must be in accord with the will of heaven.

If men suddenly see a child about to fall into a well, they will all without exception experience a feeling of alarm and distress. They will feel so not as a ground on which they may gain favor of the child's parents, nor as a ground on which they may seek the praise of their neighbors and friends, nor from a dislike to the reputation of having been unmoved by such a thing.
MENCIUS, CHINESE (372–289 B.C.)

When I look back on my life, with its successes and its failures, its endless errors, its deceptions and its fulfillments, its joys and miseries, it seems to me strangely lacking in reality. It is shadowy and un-substantial. It may be that my heart, having found rest nowhere, had some deep ancestral craving for God and immortality which my reason would have no truck with. In default of anything better it has seemed to me sometimes that I might pretend to myself that the goodness I have not so seldom after all come across in many of those I have encountered on my way had reality. It may be that in goodness we may see, not a reason for life nor an explanation of it, but an extenuation. In this indifferent universe, with its inevitable evils that surround us from the cradle to the grave, it may serve not as a challenge or a reply, but as an affirmation of our own indepen-dence. It is the retort that humour makes to the tragic absurdity of fate. Unlike beauty, it can be perfect without being tedious, and, greater than love, time does not wither its delight. But goodness is shown in right action and who can tell in this meaningless world what right action is? It is not action that aims at happiness; it is a happy chance if happiness re-sults. Plato, as we know, enjoined upon his wise men to abandon the serene life of contemplation for the turmoil of practical affairs and thereby set the claim of duty above the desire for happiness; and we have all of us, I suppose, on occasion adopted a course because we thought it right though we well knew that it could bring us happiness neither then nor in the future. When then is right action? For my own part the best answer I know is that given by Fray
[169]25

Luis de Leon. To follow it does not look so difficult that human weakness quails before it as beyond its strength. With it I can end my book. The beauty of life, he says, is nothing but this, that each should act in conformity with his nature and his business.
WILLIAM SOMERSET MAUGHAM, ENGLISH (1874–1965)

Love as long as you can,
Suffer as long as you can,
Forgive as long as you can,
And God be your judge!
NIKOLAI ALEKSEEVICH NEKRASOV,
RUSSIAN (1821–1877)

 ## 26 Restraint by the Strong

THE TA CH'U HEXAGRAM

At the outset, the man is confronted with dangerous obstacles. He should not attempt to advance rashly but remain composed.

I have been sent to you by God.
He has seen how you are downtrod. . . .
.   .   .   .

Your life will be a burden to you,
One long, long night without a star.
The wind will carry off your groaning,
God will not listen to your moaning.
Your torment will be vast and dread,
As vast and dread as your sins are.
And you will wish that you were dead.

Yet long for life, yet long to live.
But neither life nor death the Lord will give.
And when you plead, and when you sue,
Your own heart will not trust you,
And you will strive to rise, be free,
Too late your efforts then will be.
This is a grave in which you lie
Buried alive, but will not die.
This is a hell, from which there is no flying,
And endless hell, but without dying.

God said: "Now, to the potter go,
And buy a pot. Take it, and throw
It crashing into fragments on the ground.

And loudly let your voice resound:
'Even so will you be broken!'
And then, when these words have been spoken,
Stand with bowed head, silent and dumb.
The day draws near, the day will come."
CHAIM NACHMAN BIALIK, HEBREW (1873–1934)

---

*The opposition is decisively stronger. The man should
wait while storing energy for his next move.*

Now I shall tell a tale for princes, however wise they
be. A hawk clutched with his talons a gaily-colored
nightingale and bore her aloft into the clouds. When
she wailed piteously, pierced by the crooked claws,
the hawk said arrogantly to her: "Wretch! Why do
you shriek? One much stronger now holds you and
you must go wherever I take you, singer though you
are. I shall make a dinner of you, if I so wish, or I
shall let you go! But foolish is he, who sets himself
against the stronger, for not only can he not win, but
suffering is added to his shame." So spoke the fleet,
long-winged hawk.
HESIOD, GREEK (EIGHTH CENTURY B.C.)

---

*The man is joined by strong allies who are going in the
same direction. The obstacles begin to give way. But the
dangers are not over. He must remain alert, well prepared, and farsighted.*

Then Gunther sought Siegfried and said: "Now
counsel me in this. On the morrow our guests ride
forth, and they desire of me and mine a lasting cove-
nant. What they offer I will tell thee: as much gold as
five hundred horses may carry, they will give me to
go free."
And Siegfried answered: "That were ill done. Send
them forth without ransom, that they ride no more
hither as foeman. And they shall give thee the hand
thereon for surety."
STORY OF THE NIBELUNGS,
AUSTRIAN (TWELFTH CENTURY)

---

*The man retrains the wild force by timely preventive
acts and extraordinary precautions, like fastening a
headboard on the growing horns of a young bull.*

Speak not ill of a great enemy, but rather give him good words, that he may use you the better if you chance to fall into his hands. The Spaniard did this when he was dying. His confessor told him (to work him to repentance) how the devil tormented the wicked that went to hell; the Spaniard, replying, called the devil, "my lord": "I hope my lord the devil is not so cruel." His confessor reproved him. "Excuse me," said the Don, "for calling him so; I know not into what hands I may fall, and if I happen into his I hope he will use me the better for giving him good words."

JOHN SELDEN, ENGLISH (1584–1654)

The man dissipates the wild force by controlling its basic source.

Calpurnius . . . having raised an army, chose for his officers men of family and intrigue, hoping that whatever faults he might commit, would be screened by their influence; and among these was Scaurus, of whose disposition and character we have already spoken. There were, indeed, in our consul Calpurnius, many excellent qualities, both mental and personal, though avarice interfered with the exercise of them; he was patient of labor, of a penetrating intellect, of great foresight, not inexperienced in war, and extremely vigilant against danger and surprise.

The troops were conducted through Italy to Rhegium, from thence to Sicily, and from Sicily into Africa; and Calpurnius's first step, after collecting provisions, was to invade Numidia with spirit, where he took many prisoners, and several towns, by force of arms.

But when Jugurtha (of Numidia) began, through his emissaries, to tempt him with bribes, and to show the difficulties of the war which he had undertaken to conduct, his mind, corrupted with avarice, was easily altered. His accomplice, however, and manager in all his schemes, was Scaurus; who, though he had at first, when most of his party were corrupted, displayed violent hostility to Jugurtha, yet was afterwards seduced, by a vast sum of money, from integrity and honor to injustice and perfidy. Jugurtha, however, at first sought only to purchase a suspension of hostilities, expecting to be able, during the interval, to make some favorable impression, either by bribery or by interest, at Rome; but when he heard that Scaurus was cooperating with Calpurnius, he was elated with great hopes of regaining peace, and resolved upon a conference with them in person respecting the terms of it. In the meantime, for the sake of giving confidence to Jugurtha, Sextus the quaestor was dispatched by the consul to Vaga, one of the prince's towns; the pretext for his journey being the receiving of corn, which Calpurnius had openly demanded from Jugurtha's emissaries, on the ground that a truce was observed through their delay to make a surrender. Jugurtha, then, as he had determined, paid a visit to the consul's camp, where, having made a short address to the council, respecting the odium cast upon his conduct, and his desire for a capitulation, he arranged other matters with Bestia and Scaurus in secret; and the next, as if by an evident majority of voices, he was formally allowed to surrender. But, as was demanded in the hearing of the council, thirty elephants, a considerable number of cattle and horses, and a small sum of money, were delivered into the hands of the quaestor. Calpurnius then returned to Rome to preside at the election of magistrates, and peace was observed throughout Numidia and the Roman army.

GAIUS SALLUSTIUS CRISPUS, ROMAN (86–34 B.C.)

In the Western Hemisphere we have always endeavored to preserve the unique position of the United States as a predominant power without rival. We have not been slow in recognizing that our predominance was not likely to be effectively threatened by any one American nation or combination of nations acting without support from outside the hemisphere. This peculiar situation has made it imperative for the United States to isolate the Western Hemisphere from the political and military policies of non-American nations. The interference of non-American nations in the affairs of the Western Hemisphere, especially through the acquisition of territory, was the only way in which the predominance of the United States could have been challenged from within the hemisphere itself. The Monroe Doctrine and the policies implementing it express that permanent national interest of the United States in the Western Hemisphere.

Since a threat to our national interest in the Western Hemisphere can only come from outside — historically, from Europe — we have always striven to prevent the development of conditions in Europe which would be conducive to a European nation's interfering into the affairs of the Western Hemisphere or contemplating a direct attack upon the United States. These conditions would be most likely to arise if a European nation, its predominance unchallenged within Europe, could look across the sea for conquest without fear of being menaced at the center of its power; that is, in Europe itself.

It is for this reason that the United States has consistently — the War of 1812 is the sole major exception — pursued policies aiming at the maintenance of the balance of power in Europe. It has opposed whatever European nation — be it Great Britain, France, Germany, or Russia — was likely to gain that ascendancy over its European competitors which would have jeopardized the hemispheric predominance and eventually the very independence of the United States. Conversely, it has supported whatever European nation appeared capable of restoring the balance of power by offering successful resistance to the would-be conqueror.

HANS JOACHIM MORGENTHAU, AMERICAN (BORN 1904)

The man eventually removes all obstacles and attains progress and honor.

The blockade went on notwithstanding. The corn was giving out, and what there was cost a very high price, and Porsinna was beginning to have hopes that he would take the City by sitting still, when Gaius Mucius, a young Roman noble, thinking it a shame that although the Roman people had not, in the days of their servitude when they lived under kings, been blockaded in a war by any enemies, they should now, when free, be besieged by those same Etruscans whose armies they had so often routed, made up his mind that this indignity must be avenged by some great and daring deed. At first he intended to make his way into the enemy's camp on his own account. Afterwards, fearing that if he should go unbidden by the consuls and without anyone's knowing it, he might chance to be arrested by the Roman sentries and brought back as a deserter — a charge which the state of the City would confirm — he went before the senate. "I wish," said he, "to cross the river, senators, and enter, if I can, the enemy's camp — not to plunder or exact reprisals for their devastations: I have in mind to do a greater deed, if the gods grant me their help." The Fathers approved. Hiding a sword under his dress, he set out. Arrived at the camp, he took up his stand in the thick of the crowd near the royal tribunal. It happened that at the moment the soldiers were being paid; a secretary who sat beside the king, and wore nearly the same costume, was very busy, and to him the soldiers for the most part addressed themselves. Mucius was afraid to ask which was Porsinna, lest his ignorance of the king's identity should betray his own, and following the blind guidance of Fortune, slew the secretary instead of the king. As he strode off through the frightened crowd, making a way for himself with his bloody blade, there was an outcry, and thereat the royal guards came running in from every side, seized him and dragged him back before the tribunal of the king. But friendless as he was, even then, when Fortune wore so menacing an aspect, yet as one more to be feared than fearing, "I am a Roman citizen," he cried; "men call me Gaius Mucius. I am your enemy, and as an enemy I would have slain you; I can die as resolutely as I could kill: both to do and to endure valiantly is the Roman way. Nor am I the only one to carry this resolution against you: behind me is a long line of men who are seeking the same honour. Gird yourself therefore, if you think it worth your while, for a struggle in which you must fight for your life from hour to hour with an armed foe always at your door. Such is the war we, the Roman youths, declare on you. Fear no serried ranks, no battle; it will be between yourself alone and a single enemy at a time." The king, at once hot with resentment and aghast at his danger, angrily ordered the prisoner to be flung into the flames unless he should at once divulge the plot with which he so obscurely threatened him. Whereupon Mucius, exclaiming, "Look, that you may see how cheap they hold their bodies whose eyes are fixed upon renown!" thrust his hand into the fire that was kindled for the sacrifice. When he allowed his hand to burn as if his spirit were unconscious of sensation, the king was almost beside himself with wonder. He bounded from his seat and bade them remove the young man from the altar. "Do you go free," he said, "who have dared to harm yourself more than me. I would invoke success upon your valour, were that valour exerted for my country; since that may not be, I release you from the penalties of war and dismiss you scatheless and uninjured." Then Mucius, as if to requite his generosity, answered, "Since you hold bravery in honour, my gratitude shall afford you the information your threats could not extort: we are three hundred, the foremost youths of Rome, who have conspired to assail you in this fashion. I drew the first lot; the others, in whatever order it falls to them, will attack you, each at his own time, until Fortune shall have delivered you into our hands."

The release of Mucius, who was afterwards known as Scaevola, from the loss of his right hand, was followed by the arrival in Rome of envoys from Porsinna. The king had been so disturbed, what with the hazard of the first attack upon his life, from which nothing but the blunder of his assailant had preserved him, and what with the anticipation of having to undergo the danger as many times more as there were conspirators remaining, that he voluntarily proposed terms of peace to the Romans. In these terms Porsinna suggested, but without effect, that the Tarquinii should be restored to power, more because he had been unable to refuse the princes this demand upon their behalf than that he was ignorant that the Romans would refuse it. In obtaining the return of their lands to the Veientes he was successful; and the Romans were compelled to give hostages if they wished the garrison to be withdrawn from Janiculum. On these terms peace was made, and Porsinna led his army down the Janiculum and evacuated the Roman territory. The Fathers bestowed on Gaius Mucius, for his bravery, a field across the Tiber, which was later known as the Mucian Meadows.

TITUS LIVIUS, ROMAN (59 B.C.–17 A.D.)

When the star Mao T'ao fell into darkness, the
  message — victory — was quickly dispatched.
Now at the Golden Gate the runners await their
  reward, official robes.
This general astride his white horse always defeats
  his enemy. . . .
But when will the drafted soldiers fighting at the
  Yellow Dragon return?
WANG WEI, CHINESE (699–759)

*The over-all judgment: the times are such that the chief
executive entrusts strong personalities with leadership.
In harmony with the heavenly cycle, the superior men
should embark upon public office. Even great undertakings will succeed.*

It occurred to me that I should find much more truth
in the reasonings of each individual with reference to
the affairs in which he is personally interested, and
the issue of which must presently punish if he has
judged amiss, than in those conducted by a man of
letters in his study, regarding speculative matters
that are of no practical moment, and followed by no
consequences to himself.
RENÉ DESCARTES, FRENCH (1596–1650)

It is the freeman who must win freedom for the slave;
it is the wise man who must think for the fool; it is
the happy who must serve the unhappy.
JEAN PAUL FRIEDRICH RICHTER, GERMAN (1763–1825)

There is a story about Diderot, the Encyclopaedist
and materialist, a foremost figure in the intellectual
awakening which immediately preceded the French
Revolution. Diderot was staying at the Russian court,
where his elegant flippancy was entertaining the
nobility. Fearing that the faith of her retainers was at
stake, the Tsaritsa commissioned Euler, the most
distinguished mathematician of the time, to debate
with Diderot in public. Diderot was informed that a
mathematician had established a proof of the existence of God. He was summoned to court without
being told the name of his opponent. Before the assembled court, Euler accosted him with the following
pronouncement, which was uttered with due gravity:
"$a + b^n/n = x$, donc Dieu existe. Répondez!" Algebra

was Arabic to Diderot. Unfortunately he did not realize that was the trouble. Had he realized that algebra is just a language which we use to describe the *sizes* of things in contrast to the ordinary languages which we use to describe the *sorts* of things in the world, he would have asked Euler to translate the first half of the sentence into French. Translated freely into English, it may be rendered: "A number x can be got by first adding a number a to a number b multiplied by itself a certain number of times, and then dividing the whole by the number of b's multiplied together. So God exists after all. What have you got to say now?" If Diderot had asked Euler to illustrate the first part of his remark for the clearer understanding of the Russian court, Euler might have replied that x is 3 when a is 1 and b is 2 and n is 3, or that x is 21 when a is 3 and b is 3 and n is 4, and so forth. Euler's troubles would have begun when the court wanted to know how the second part of the sentence follows from the first part. Like many of us, Diderot had stagefright when confronted with a sentence in size language. He left the court abruptly amid the titters of the assembly, confined himself to his chambers, demanded a safe conduct, and promptly returned to France.
SIR LANCELOT THOMAS HOGBEN, ENGLISH (BORN 1895)

 ## 27 Sagacious Counsel

THE I HEXAGRAM

At the outset, the man is envious of the prosperity of others.

I am like a frog trying to outvie the crickets.
THEOCRITUS, GREEK (THIRD CENTURY B.C.)

The man does not provide for his own support. He improperly takes what he needs from below and also cravenly begs for it from above. Such unworthiness leads to misfortune.

"Dad, I'm going t'own a mortgage 'fore I die; mind what I say."
"Hope ye will, Zury," his father replies. "Yew'll have a holt of the right end of the poker then; 'n't t'other

feller, he'll have a holt o' the hot part, same's we've
got naow."
"You bet! An' it'll sizzle his hands, tew, afore I'll ever
let up on him."
JOSEPH KIRKLAND, AMERICAN (1830–1894)

---

*Instead of solid accomplishments, the man pursues
pleasures and self-gratification. He will never achieve
anything so long as he is surrounded by dissipating temptations.*

In forty ways, friend Punnamukha, does a woman
accost a man: She yawns, she bows down, she makes
amorous gestures, she pretends to be abashed, she
rubs the nails of one hand or foot with the nails of
the other hand or foot, she places one foot on another foot, she scratches on the ground with a stick.
She causes her boy to leap up, she causes her boy to
leap down, she dallies with her boy and makes him
dally with her, she kisses him and makes him kiss
her, she eats food and makes him eat food, she gives
and begs for gifts, she imitates whatever he does.
She talks in a loud tone, she talks in a low tone; she
talks as in public, she talks as in private. While dancing, singing, playing musical instruments, weeping,
making amorous gestures, adorning herself, she
laughs and looks. She sways her hips, she jiggles her
waist-gear, uncovers her thigh, covers her thigh,
displays her breast, displays her armpit, and displays
her navel. She buries the pupils of her eyes, lifts her
eyebrows, scratches her lips, and dangles her tongue.
She takes off her loin-cloth, puts on her loin-cloth,
takes off her turban, and puts on her turban.
DHAMMAPADA, INDIAN (THIRD CENTURY B.C.)

---

*The man in a high position recognizes the need for able
helpers to pursue his lofty aims for the good of the people. He looks for the required talent with the searching
glare of a hungry tiger.*

You may meet a man who speaks smoothly, who is
talented in all things, and is very agreeable to you.
Yet, if the pupils of his eyes are not right do not make
a friendship with him, lest you may afterwards reap
regret and remorse. Especially in choosing subjects
is this important. Chikurei foresaw the treason of

Anrokuzan by the latter's appearance. It is safest to employ honest men, even though they may not be the cleverest.

EKKEN KAIBARA, JAPANESE (1630–1714)

The man realizes his personal deficiencies in strength and knowledge to discharge his assigned responsibilities. He seeks and follows the advice of a spiritual superior, who is unknown to the public. Persevering under such guidance will bring success. But he must recognize his dependency and not assume great undertakings alone.

O for a living man to lead!
That will not babble when we bleed;
O for the silent doer of the deed!
One that is happy in his height,
And one that in a nation's night
Hath solitary certitude of light.

STEPHEN PHILLIPS, ENGLISH (1868–1915)

I know how to listen when clever men are talking. That is the secret of what you call my influence.

HERMANN SUDERMANN, GERMAN (1857–1928)

The sage educates others. Heavy responsibilities accompany such a position. Awareness of the situation enables the man to accept great challenges with success to the benefit of the people.

"The foolish crowd is accustomed to place
an equal value on the good and the bad:
I give it the worst, for that is what it praises."
  In this manner a writer of indecent farces
was wont to excuse his errors;
and a sly poet who heard him
answered in the following way:
  A master gave straw to his
humble ass and said to him:
"Take this, since with this you are content."
He said this so many times that one day
the ass became angry, and answered, "I take
what you are willing to give me; but, unjust man,
do you think that I like nothing but straw?
Give me grain and you will see whether I eat it."
  Let those who work for the public know
that perhaps they blame the public in vain;
for if it eats straw when they give it straw,
[180]27

when they give it grain, it eats grain.
TOMAS DE IRIATE, SPANISH (1750–1791)

'Tis a great foolery to teach our children the knowledge of the stars and the motion of the eighth sphere,
before their own.
Anaximenes writing to Pythagoras, "To what purpose," said he, "should I trouble myself in searching
out the secrets of the stars, having death or slavery
continually before my eyes?" for the kings of Persia
were at that time preparing to invade his country.
Every one ought to say thus, "Being assaulted, as I
am by ambition, avarice, temerity, superstitution,
and having within so many other enemies of life,
shall I go cudgel my brains about the world's revolutions?"
MICHEL DE MONTAIGNE, FRENCH (1533–1592)

---

*The over-all judgment: the sage promotes men of talent
and virtue and through them sustains the entire people.
The right people are developed, the proper sides of their
natures encouraged, and the right ways of achieving
goals passed on.*

In order that people may be happy in their work,
these three things are needed: They must be fit for
it: They must not do too much of it: And they must
have a sense of success in it.
JOHN RUSKIN, ENGLISH (1819–1900)

We need never fear that any philosophic sentiment
can destroy the religion of a country. It is in vain that
our mysteries are contrary to our demonstrations,
they are not the less revered by our Christian philosophers, who know that the objects of reason and of
faith are of a different nature. Philosophers will never
form a religious sect. Why? Because they do not
write for the people, and because they are without
enthusiams. Divide the human race into twenty
parts, there will be nineteen made up of those who
work with their hands, and who will never know
whether there has been a M. Locke in the world. In
the twentieth part that remains how few men do we
find who read? And among those who read, there are
twenty who read novels for one who studies philosophy. The number of those who think is excessively
[181]27

small, and they do not think about troubling the world.

It is not Montaigne, or Locke, or Bayle, or Spinoza, or Hobbes, or Lord Shaftesbury, or Mr. Collins, or Mr. Toland, or Fludd, or Becker, or the Comte de Boulainvilliers, etc., who have carried the torch of discord in their country. It is for the most part the theologians, who having first had the ambition to become head of sects, have soon had that of being heads of parties. What am I saying? All the books of modern philosophers put together will never make even as much noise in the world as was made in the past by the dispute of the Capuchins about the form of their sleeves and their hoods.

VOLTAIRE, FRENCH (1694–1778)

Let them teach who can do nothing better, whose qualities are laborious application, sluggishness of mind, muddiness of intellect, prosiness of imagination, chill of blood, patience to bear the body's labors, contempt of glory, avidity for petty gains, indifference to boredom . . . . Let them watch boys' fidgety hands, their wandering eyes, their *sotto voce* whisperings who delight in that task, who enjoy dust and noise and the clamor of mingled prayers and tears, and whimperings under the rod's correction. Let them teach who love to return to boyhood, who are shy of dealing with them and shamed by living with equals, who are happy to be set over their inferiors, who always want to have someone to terrify, to afflict, to torture, to rule, someone who will hate and fear them. That is a tyrannical pleasure, such as, according to the story, pervaded the fierce spirit of that old man of Syracuse, to be the evil solace of his deserved exile. But you, a man of parts, merit a better occupation. . . . Since you can follow the Roman masters, Cicero and Virgil, would you choose Orbilius, Horace's "flogging master"?

FRANCESCO PETRARCA, ITALIAN (1304–1374)

28 Great Gains

At the outset, the man displays considerable care in embarking upon an important enterprise.

It is not enough to have great qualities; we must know how to husband them.
DUKE FRANÇOIS DE LA ROCHEFOUCAULD, FRENCH (1613–1680)

An extraordinary reinvigoration occurs. During unusual occasions it may be desirable to join the lowly in order to permit a new outlook and growth.

I think, I could turn and live with animals, they are
  so placid and self-contain'd,
I stand and look at them long and long.

They do not sweat and whine about their condition,
They do not lie awake in the dark and weep for their
  sins
They do not make me sick discussing their duty to
  God.
Not one is dissatisfied, not one is demented with the
  mania of owning things,
Not one kneels to another, nor to his kind that lived
  thousands of years ago,
Not one is respectable or unhappy over the whole
  earth.

So they show their relations to me and I accept them,
They bring me tokens of myself, they evince them
  plainly in their possession.
I wonder where they get those tokens
Did I pass that way huge times ago and negligently
  drop them?

WALT WHITMAN, AMERICAN (1819–1892)

A one-foot waterfall—
  it too makes noises, and at night
  the coolness of it all!
KOBAYASHI ISSA, JAPANESE (1763–1827)

The man becomes overconfident in his limited strength. He rushes ahead in opposition to advice from those in a

*position to help. This leads to the loss of voluntary sup-
port. His burdens increase, and he proves unequal to the
task.*

Then rush'd to meet the insulting foe;
They took the spear — but left the shield.
PHILIP MORIN FRENEAU, AMERICAN (1752–1832)

---

*The man becomes the master of the difficult situation by
refusing the assistance of weak men. He relies on his own
strength of character.*

Better make a weak man your enemy than your
friend.
JOSH BILLINGS, AMERICAN (1818–1885)

Paying no heed to the great Army deployed there,
firmly guarding the gates, he [Lord Mitsuyori] entered (the Palace grounds), with (his men) loudly
clearing the way for him. The soldiers were over-
awed and, lowering their bows and turning aside
their arrows, let him pass.
Passing behind the Shiskinden (the central hall of
the Palace), he went around the Courtier's Room,
looking in. Lord Nobuyori was in the highest place,
and all the high officials present had been placed below him. "This is indeed a strange affair," thought
Lord Mitsuyori. "No matter how others conduct
themselves, since he is Colonel of the Gate Guards
of the Right and I the Colonel of the Gate Guards of
the Left, I should certainly not come below him."
Then, saluting the great Controller of the Left and
Consultant, Lord Nagakata, who was in the lowest
place among the consultants, with "Today's seating
appears to be an extremely disorderly affair," he
walked up sedately and placed himself determinedly
above Lord Nobuyori.
Since Mitsuyori was not only the maternal uncle of
Nobuyori but also a man of great force, he was regarded with particular awe. (Mitsuyori) sat down on
(Nobuyori's) right sleeve, and (the latter) lowered
his eyes and grew pale, while the nobles seated there
looked on aghast. Then Lord Mitsuyori, after readjusting the train of his underrobe, tidying his
clothing, readjusting his wand of authority, and
composing his features, said, "Today, the Colonels
[184]28

of the Guards seem to be occupying the head places. I have heard something to the effect that those who do not come (to court) when summoned are to be executed, and so I have come. Now, what are your orders?'' Nobuyori, however, said nothing, and the nobles seated there had not a word (to say) in reply. How much the less could they conduct the conference. After some time Lord Mitsuyori rose abruptly and said, "I have come at a bad time." Then he walked out calmly.

HEIKE MONOGATARI, JAPANESE (THIRTEENTH CENTURY)

Notwithstanding promising potentialities the man gives up his alliances with the people below him and seeks the company only of those of higher rank. An unstable arrangement results. Instead of greater security, there will be less. No renewal occurs after the flower saps the tree's remaining energy.

A partnership with men in power is never safe.

PHAEDRUS, ROMAN (FIRST CENTURY)

The man pursues his objectives for the public good, regardless of consequences and danger. Misfortune results. But no blame is attached to his conduct, because there are certain things more important than life itself.

I, John Brown, am now quite *certain* that the crimes of this guilty *land* will never be purged away but with blood. I had *as I now think* vainly flattered myself that without *very much* bloodshed it might be done.

JOHN BROWN, AMERICAN (1800–1859)

The over-all judgment: unusual periods of greatness and misfortune require extraordinary talent in the conduct of affairs. When the weight begins to exceed the carrying capacity of the beam, quick transition and action are required.

Nahum Ish Gamzu, one of Rabbi Akiba's teachers, narrated the following experience: I was once traveling to the house of my father-in-law, taking with me three donkey-loads of food and drink. A starving man asked me for food. I answered that I would give him some when I unloaded, but before I could do so, he fell dead. I greatly grieved over his death and prayed that the Lord send sufferings upon me in expiation for my sin. I should not have delayed my help, but should have cut through the load and given him food at once.

TALMUD, HEBREW (450)

If we withdraw the confidence we placed
In these our present statesmen, and transfer it
To those whom we mistrusted heretofore,
This seems I think our fairest chance for safety:
If with our present counsellors we fail,
Then with their opposites we might succeed.

ARISTOPHANES, GREEK (446–380 B.C.)

My center is giving way, my right is in retreat; situation excellent. I will attack.

MARSHAL FERDINAND FOCH, FRENCH (1851–1929)

29 Danger

THE K'AN HEXAGRAM

At the outset, the man is hopelessly in danger. As a consequence of allowing himself to grow accustomed to evil, he has lost the right way. His efforts will only embroil him more deeply.

Lies full of calumny, hatred long fostered, shameful love affairs, calculated crimes of avarice and hate, all this was reshaped in her as a cruel image of a dream is reshaped in the state of waking.
The crowd, swarming before her mind's eye, a moment earlier when she had recognized all those of her family, shrank accordingly. Faces were superimposed one upon the other; they now formed only one single face, which was the face of vice. Confused gestures became fixed in one single attitude, which was the gesture of crime. The avaricious ones made a mass of living gold, the voluptuous ones a heap of bowels. Everywhere sin burst its wrappings and disclosed the mystery of its generation: Scores of men and women bound by the fibers of the same cancer, and the hideous fetters retracted like the cut-off arms of an octopus to the very heart of the monster, the initial sin . . .
[186]29

And she understood that the hour had come to herself.

GEORGES BERNANOS, FRENCH (1888–1948)

A person in danger should not try to escape at one stroke. He should first calmly hold his own, then be satisfied with small gains, which will come by creative adaptations.

Nothing is accomplished all at once, and it is one of my great maxims . . . that nature makes no leaps. . . . This law of continuity declares that we pass from the small to the great — and the reverse — through the medium, in degree as well as in parts.

GOTTFRIED WILHELM VON LEIBNIZ, GERMAN (1646–1716)

When Kutsugen was dismissed from office he went to Kotan, and sat sighing by the river. He looked like a skeleton, so paled and emaciated was he. A fisherman seeing him there, said to him: "Are you not the Prime Minister? What may you be doing here?" Kutsugen replied: "The whole world is filthy; I alone am clean. Everybody is drunk; I alone am sober. This is the reason I was dismissed." The fisherman said: "A sage is not bound to things, is not the slave of circumstances, but follows them, acts in accordance with them. If the whole world is filthy, you must jump in the muddy water and splash about in it. If all men are drunk, drink with them. What is the good of meditating so profoundly and idealistically?" Kutsugen said: "I have heard that when a man has washed himself he dusts his hat, and when a man has bathed his body, he shakes his clothes. How can he who has purified himself put on his old dirty clothes again? I would rather jump in this river and feed my body to the fishes. I will not allow my purity to be sullied by the defilements of this world!"
The smiling fisherman gave a chuckle, and rowed away; he sang, keeping time with his oar.
"If the water of Soro is clear, I will wash the ribbon of my hat;
If it is dirty, I will wash my feet in it."
This was all he said, and was gone.

KUTSUGEN, CHINESE (THIRD CENTURY B.C.)

The man becomes entangled in danger at every turn. He should refrain from action, which only worsens the situation, and wait until the solution reveals itself.

More than two thousand years ago the wise Epicurus said: "Either God wants to prevent evil, and cannot do it; or he can do it and does not want to; or he neither wishes to nor can do it, or he wishes to and can do it. If he has the desire without the power, he is impotent; if he can and has not the desire, he has a malice which we cannot attribute to him; if he has neither the power nor the desire, he is both impotent and evil, and consequently is not God; if he has the desire and the power, whence then comes evil, or why does he not prevent it?" For more than two thousand years the best minds have been waiting for a rational solution of these difficulties, and our doctors teach us that they will be removed only in a future life.
BARON PAUL HENRI DIETRICH D'HOLBACH,
FRENCH (1723–1789)

The man is without a sponsor because of the lack of impressive gifts. Ceremonial forms and expensive gifts are unnecessary, however, during periods of great urgency. Spurred on by unostentatious sincerity, he presents his thoughts directly to the chief. No error will result from this honest request for mutual help during times of peril.

Should there be no valiant spirit?
Must we always feel what we say?
Are we never to say what we feel?
FRANCISCO GÓMEZ DE QUEVEDO Y VILLEGAS,
SPANISH (1580–1645)

The man is almost extricated, but remains in danger because of excessive ambition. He does not learn from the water's example of rising only to the lowest point of the rim to flow out of a ravine. He should not attempt great and apparently unattainable things but should only try to escape danger by following the path of least resistance.

Dreams and fables I call into being. And even as I put them on paper and adorn them, so much do they
[188]29

become a part of myself that (foolish as I am!) I weep
and rage at the ills I invent.
PIETRO METASTASIO, ITALIAN (1698–1782)

. . . If you place in a bottle half a dozen bees and the
same number of flies, and lay the bottle down hori-
zontally, with its base to the window, you will find
that the bees will persist, till they die of exhaustion
or hunger, in their endeavor to discover an issue
through the glass; while the flies, in less than two
minutes, will all have sallied forth through the neck
on the opposite side. . . . It is their [the bees'] love of
light, it is their very intelligence, that is their un-
doing in this experiment. They evidently imagine
that the issue from every prison must be there where
the light shines clearest; and they act in accordance,
and persist in too logical action. To them glass is a
supernatural mystery they never have met in nature;
they have had no experience of this suddenly impenetrable atmosphere; and, the greater their intelligence, the more inadmissible, more incomprehensible, will the strange obstacle appear. Whereas
the feather-brained flies, careless of logic as of the
enigma of crystal, disregarding the call of the light,
flutter wildly hither and thither, and meeting here
the good fortune that often waits on the simple, who
find salvation there where the wiser will perish,
necessarily end by discovering the friendly opening
that restores their liberty to them.
MAURICE MAETERLINCK, BELGIAN (1862–1949)

---

*The man is hopelessly enmeshed in his own faults after
missing the proper course. No chances of escape are
apparent.*

They recognize the lofty and beautiful only in books,
and that not always; in life and reality they recognize
neither the one nor the other, and because of this are
quickly disillusioned (their pet expression!), grow
chilly in the soul, grow old in the flower of their
years, stop in mid-journey, and end . . . by becoming
reconciled with reality. . . . That is, whatever they do
they fall straight from the clouds into the mud; or
they become mystics, misanthropes, lunatics, or
sleepwalkers. Usually they are ludicrous or pitiful . . .
but sometimes they are not at all pitiful but dreadful
[189]29

because of their reconciliation with reality.
VISSARION GRIGORIEVICH BELINSKY,
RUSSIAN (1811–1848)

The over-all judgment: the superior man proceeds with
the integrity and goodness of his heart. As in the case of
water constantly flowing and filling all depths, he shrinks
from no danger and eventually escapes from all ravines.
His mind is sharpened and made penetrating from its
brushes with danger. Progressing consistently is the only
way to liberation.

Calmness and irony are the only weapons worthy of
the strong.
ÉMILE GABORIAU, FRENCH (1835–1873)

Out of the night that covers me,
  Black as the pit from pole to pole,
I thank whatever gods may be
  For my unconquerable soul.

In the fell clutch of circumstance
  I have not winced nor cried aloud.
Under the bludgeonings of chance
  My head is bloody, but unbowed.

Beyond this place of wrath and tears
  Looms but the horror of the shade,
And yet the menace of the years
  Finds and shall find me unafraid.

It matters not how strait the gate,
  How charged with punishments the scroll,
I am the master of my fate:
  I am the captain of my soul.
WILLIAM ERNEST HENLEY, ENGLISH (1849–1903)

I *will* be as harsh as truth, and as uncompromising as
justice. On this subject, I do not wish to think, or
speak, or write, with moderation. No! No! Tell a man
whose house is on fire, to give a moderate alarm; tell
him to moderately rescue his wife from the hands of
the ravisher; tell the mother to gradually extricate her
babe from the fire into which it has fallen; — but urge
me not to use moderation in a cause like the present.
I am in earnest — I will not equivocate — I will not

excuse — I will not retreat a single inch — AND I WILL
BE HEARD.

WILLIAM LLOYD GARRISON, AMERICAN (1805–1879)

30 The Cosmic Mean

THE LI HEXAGRAM

*At the outset, the man is initially confused amid the
bustle of life. He will avoid error by careful attention to
the central issue at stake.*

If a good man were ever housed in Hell
  By needful error of the qualities,
Perhaps to prove the rule or shame the devil,
  Or speak the truth only a stranger sees,

Would he, surrendering quick to obvious hate,
  Fill half eternity with cries and tears,
Or watch beside Hell's little wicket gate
  In patience for the first ten thousand years,

Feeling the curse climb slowly to his throat
  That, uttered, dooms him to a rescindless ill,
Forcing his praying tongue to run by rote,
  Eternity entire before him still?

Would he at last, grown faithful in his station,
  Kindle a little hope in hopeless Hell,
And sow among the damned doubts of damnation,
  Since here someone could live and could live well?

One doubt of evil would bring down such a grace,
  Open such a gate, all Eden could enter in,
Hell be a place like any other place,
  And love and hate and life and death begin.

EDWIN MUIR, ENGLISH (1887–1959)

*The man occupies the central position of reasonableness,
which results in enduring good fortune.*

This innocent word *Trimmer* signifieth no more than
this. That if men are together in a boat, and one part
of the company would weigh it down on one side,
another would make it lean as much to the contrary;
it happeneth there is a third opinion of those, who
conceive it would do as well, if the boat went without
endangering the passengers. Now 'tis hard to im-

agine by what figure in language, or by what rule in sense, this cometh to be a fault, and it is much more a wonder it should be thought a heresy.

MARQUIS GEORGE SAVILLE, ENGLISH (1633–1695)

Dined with Goethe. "Within the last four days, since I saw you," said he, "I have read many things; especially a Chinese novel, which occupies me still and seems to me very remarkable."

"Chinese novel!" said I, "that must look strange enough."

"Not so much as you might think," said Goethe, "the Chinamen think, act, and feel almost exactly like us; and we soon find that we are perfectly like them, except that all they do is more clear, pure, and decorous, than with us.

"With them all is orderly, citizen-like, without great passion or poetic flight; and there is a strong resemblance to my *Hermann and Dorothea,* as well as to the English novels of Richardson. They likewise differ from us in that with them external nature is always associated with the human figures. You always hear the goldfish splashing in the pond; the birds are always singing on the bough; the day is always serene and sunny; the night is always clear. There is much talk about the moon; but it does not alter the landscape, its light is conceived to be as bright as day itself; and the interior of the houses is as neat and elegant as their pictures. For instance: 'I heard the lovely girls laughing, and when I got sight of them they were sitting on cane chairs.' There you have, at once, the prettiest situation; for cane chairs are necessarily associated with the greatest lightness and elegance. Then there is an infinite number of legends which are constantly introduced into the narrative and are applied almost like proverbs: as, for instance, one of a girl who was so light and graceful in the feet that she could balance herself on a flower without breaking it; and then another, of a young man so virtuous and brave that in his thirtieth year he had the honor to talk with the Emperor; then there is another of two lovers who showed such great purity during a long acquaintance that, when they were on one occasion obliged to pass the night in the same chamber, they occupied the time with conversation and did not approach one another.

"There are innumerable other legends, all turning upon what is moral and proper. It is by this severe moderation in everything that the Chinese empire has sustained itself for thousands of years, and will endure hereafter."

JOHANN PETER ECKERMANN, GERMAN (1792–1854)

The man reaches his declining years and recalls the transitoriness of life. Instead of enjoying the ordinary pleasures while they last, he groans in melancholy.

I am growing so peevish about my writing. I am like a man whose ear is true but who plays falsely on the violin: his fingers refuse to reproduce precisely those sounds of which he has the inward sense. Then the tears come rolling down from the poor scraper's eyes and the bow falls from his hand.

GUSTAVE FLAUBERT, FRENCH (1821–1880)

The man forges upward too abruptly in his restlessness. Others cannot bear his unseemly manner, and he consumes himself like the fire.

An itching humour or a kind of longing to see that which is not to be seen, to do that which ought not to be done, to know that secret which should not be known, to eat of the forbidden fruit.

ROBERT BURTON, ENGLISH (1577–1640)

The man reaches the zenith of life. After experiencing certain disappointments, he recognizes the vanity of human behavior. If he modifies his value system and mood, good fortune will eventually be realized.

There is something sad about a man who has reached the summit of the fame a writer can acquire in his lifetime. He is as it were uninterested in his career. He knows that a new book leaves him where he is and takes him no further forward. Out of a certain artistic pride, out of the love of beauty that is in him, he goes on doing his best, but the whiplash of success no longer has the power to drive him on. He is rather like a soldier who has reached the highest rank he can attain in a particular service and who goes on performing brilliant feats of arms without any en-

thusiasm but simply because he is a gallant fighter.
EDMOND (1822–1896) AND JULES (1830–1870)
DE GONCOURT, FRENCH

For to what purpose is all the toil and bustle of this
world? What is the end of avarice and ambition, of
the pursuit of wealth, of power, and pre-eminence?
Is it to supply the necessities of nature? The wages of
the meanest laborer can supply them. We see that
they afford him food and clothing, the comfort of a
house, and of a family. If we examine his economy
with rigour, we should find that he spends a great
part of them upon conveniences, which may be regarded as superfluities, and that, upon extraordinary
occasions, he can give something even to vanity and
distinction. What then is the cause of our aversion
to this situation, and why should those who have
been educated in the higher ranks of life, regard it as
worse than death, to be reduced to live, even without
labour, upon the same simple fare with him, to dwell
under the same lowly roof, and to be clothed in the
same humble attire? Do they imagine that their
stomach is better, or their sleep sounder, in a palace
than in a cottage? The contrary has been so often
observed, and, indeed, is so very obvious, though it
had never been observed, that there is nobody
ignorant of it. From whence, then, arises that emula-
tion which runs through all the different ranks of
men, and what are the advantages which we propose
by that great purpose of human life which we call
bettering our condition? . . . It is the vanity, not the
ease, or the pleasure, which interests us. But vanity
is always founded upon the belief of our being the
object of attention and approbation. The rich man
glories in his riches, because he feels that they naturally draw upon him the attention of the world. . . . At
the thought of this, his heart seems to swell and
dilate itself within him, and he is fonder of his
wealth, upon this account, than for all the other
advantages it procures him. The poor man, on the
contrary, is ashamed of his poverty. . . . The poor
man goes out and comes in unheeded, and when in
the midst of a crowd is in the same obscurity as if
shut up in his own hovel. . . . The man of rank and
distinction, on the contrary, is observed by all the
world. Everybody is eager to look at him, and to
[194]30

conceive, at least by sympathy, that joy and exulta-
tion with which his circumstances naturally inspire
him. His actions are the objects of the public care. . . .
It is this, which, notwithstanding the restraint it im-
poses, notwithstanding the loss of liberty with which
it is attended, renders greatness the object of envy,
and compensates, in the opinion of mankind, all that
toil, all that anxiety, all those mortifications which
must be undergone in the pursuit of it; and what is of
yet more consequence, all that leisure, all that ease,
all that careless security, which are forfeited for ever
by the acquisition.
ADAM SMITH, SCOTTISH (1723–1790)

---

*The man is employed by the ruler to conduct punitive
expeditions. He kills the ringleaders of the enemy but
spares the followers. He roots out the bad but tolerates
the relatively harmless. He avoids excessive punishments.*

As for me, conscript fathers, I look on all tortures as
far short of what these criminals deserve. But most
men remember best what happened last; and, forget-
ting the guilt of wicked men, talk only of their punishment, if more severe than ordinary.
GAIUS JULIUS CAESAR, ROMAN (100–44 B.C.)

---

*The over-all judgment: those who provide guidance and
cheer must possess a continuing and persevering principle in order not to be extinguished. As the sun and the
moon cling to the heavens, so the superior man complies
with docile humility to the dictates of the beneficent
forces of the cosmos.*

The man who is angry at the right things and with
the right people, and, further, as he ought, when he
ought, and as long as he ought, is praised. This will
be the good-tempered man. . . . For the good-tempered man tends to be unperturbed and not to be led
by passion, but to be angry in the manner, at the
things, and for the length of time, that the rule
dictates.
ARISTOTLE, GREEK (384–322 B.C.)

A thousand heartfelt thanks, particularly for being so gentle and kind in telling confidentially
and at once about Maria's engagement before I

learnt of it from Father's letter. In return, I think I may
confidently say that your expectations of the way
I am taking the whole matter will not be disappointed.

I am indeed — why should I deny it? deeply affected
by what has happened. I had already built my castle
in the air — and it all collapses so unmercifully. There
are still sad times ahead of me, for the greater the
good, the more bitter the resignation becomes. One
thing has, however, given me strength and support,
even in the first moment of sighs and bitter tears, and
that is the realization that she is destined for one
whom I can recognize without loss of respect as a
better man than I am. . . . Though I am promising to
be resigned to my fate in the first moments of grief,
I hope I shall be able to meet Hufeland without con-
straint (or at least give that appearance), for during
the few moments when I first met him, he won my
entire respect, and he will make Maria happier than
I, a man of strong passions, could ever have done.
JACOB BURCKHARDT, SWISS (1818–1897)

Who knows, when raindrops are descending,
Which thirsty seed will highest grow?
Who knows, when Sabbath knees are bending,
Where God will greatest grace bestow?
EINAR BENEDIKTSSON, ICELANDIC (1864–1940)

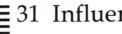

31 Influencing to Action

THE HSIEN HEXAGRAM

---

*At the outset, something is beginning to happen which is
not yet apparent to everyone.*

Will the wise man do things that the laws forbid,
knowing that he will not be found out? A simple
answer is not easy to find.
EPICURUS, GREEK (342–270 B.C.)

---

*The influence of the man increases, yet it is not obvious.
He is eager to act but should wait for more favorable
circumstances.*

By entrusting you with the government of Our Kingdom of Italy, we have given proof of the respect your

conduct has inspired us. But you are still at an age
when one does not realize the perversity of men's
hearts; I cannot therefore too strongly recommend to
you prudence and circumspection. Our Italian subjects are more deceitful by nature than the citizens of
France. The only way in which you can keep their
respect, and serve their happiness, is by letting no
one have your complete confidence, and by never
telling anyone what you really think of the ministers
and high officials of your court. Dissimulation, which
comes naturally at a maturer age, has to be emphasized and inculcated at yours. . . .
The less you talk, the better: you aren't well enough
educated, and you haven't enough knowledge, to
take part in informal debates. Learn to listen, and
remember that silence is often as effective as a display of knowledge. Don't be ashamed to ask questions. . . . So long as a prince holds his tongue, his
power is incalculable; he should never talk, unless
he knows he is the ablest man in the room.
EMPEROR NAPOLEON BONAPARTE, FRENCH (1769–1821)

A person should refrain from running after those he
would like to influence, yielding to the whims of his
master, and acquiescing to the moods of his own heart.
Personal inhibition should constitute the basis for the
enjoyment of granted freedom.

At last, we are no longer friends.

You walk easily, lightly,
In the labyrinth of complications.
What subtlety! What dancing grace! . . .
It is true that there always remains
Some dust from your wings
On the branches, on the thorns,
Even I also noticed several times
That your wings are ragged at the edges . . .
But the essential thing, the important thing,
Is that despite the raggedness you can still fly.

I am not like that.
I am heavy, I am rather clumsy,
I have no wings and not much breeding.
I need a broad and straight road.
If I lack space, I break everything,
I get hurt, I get tired . . . I finally fall.
[197]31

In the middle of the wood I stop, unable to go on.
I cannot stand it any longer.

You . . . you may still call me a friend. . . .
Although you lose a bit of your wing,
You sit on my thorn bush and can still fly.
Yet I, I suffer it is true,
But I am no longer your friend.
You are friend of the sea, you are friend of the river. . . .
MARIO DE ANDRADE, BRAZILIAN (1893–1945)

No harm has yet been incurred from a selfish wish to influence. But neither is the man's power of any great consequence. He is too indecisive and unsure of himself to move anyone beyond his own circle of friends.

When the mind is in a state of uncertainty the smallest impulse directs it to either side.
TERENCE, ROMAN (185–159 B.C.)

"What about these injections that are supposed to prevent colds?" I asked. "I see by this medical paper that some chimpanzees that have been given the injections have colds just the same and some don't."
"They have not been entirely successful," the doctor said. "They are designed to attack the causes of secondary and tertiary infections which follow the initial infection or irritation known as the common cold. In many cases they seem to make the cold milder for this reason. The idea is that, whatever causes the initial inflammation, it weakens the general resistance of the mucous membrane, and the pneumococcus, various kinds of streptococcus, and other known germs or viruses rush right in. The injections cause a purely chemical reaction which for some reason tends to counteract the general irritation or infection. Like codeine. Codeine really seems to have some specific effect on a cold, but it doesn't always have it, and when it does have it, we don't know why it does. There's another preparation made from a cold vaccine which is taken internally, like a pill. I think it was forty per cent of a group of people who reported a great improvement after taking this, but forty per cent of another group who were given pills containing nothing at all also reported great improvement. One reason we are beginning to think a cold isn't caused by a germ is that a cold, unlike

most infectious diseases, seems to develop no immunity. You can have one cold on top of another, as you know. We're up a tree, as I said before."

"This business of the common cold not being caused by a germ at all sort of strikes at the foundations of American civilization, doesn't it?"

"Don't get me wrong," the doctor said. "The no-germ theory hasn't been proved, any more than the germ theory. The thing is we just don't know. There's a great deal to be said for the germ theory, although it seems right now that there is more to be said for the no-germ theory. And anyway, influenza is a contagious disease definitely caused by a germ, so the precautions people usually take to keep from giving other people their colds are just as well. The funny thing about influenza is that the turbinates don't seem to be particularly affected by it. You don't get the same acute sniffling or stuffed-up feeling with influenza that you do with the common, grippy cold, yet with influenza you are a whole lot sicker than you are with a common cold."

"I guess I ought to get out of here tomorrow," I said.

"No reason why you shouldn't," he said. "You've had no fever for two days and there doesn't seem to be any serious bronchial infection. You'll cough a little for a day or two, and then you ought to be O.K." The doctor sneezed suddenly.

"I hope I haven't given you my cold," I said.

"You may have," he said. "If there *are* common cold germs, I have doubtless picked some of them up from you. On the other hand, it is probably just the turbinates seeing ghosts. Of course, a piece of dust or something may have got up my nose just then and made me sneeze, the sneeze being a reflex action designed by nature to clear the nose of any irritating substance. But this reflex action isn't absolutely dependable either, any more than the turbinates are. I suspect that what happened just now was that the turbinates, for some reason known only to themselves, got excited and worked up an overabundant amount of moisture; this moisture, trickling through my nose, fooled my sensory nervous system into thinking that there was some irritating substance in there and caused me to sneeze. Sneezing, incidentally, isn't such a good method of ridding the nose of an irritating substance because sneezing itself irritates the nose."

"And perhaps causes or contributes to an inflammation of the mucous membrane of the upper respira-
tory tract?"

"Exactly," he said.

ST. CLAIR MCKELWAY, AMERICAN (BORN 1905)

---

*The man's goals are trivial, although free from selfish
motives.*

An ugly bride may be praised as handsome in order
to enhance the bridegroom's affection.

TALMUD, HEBREW (450)

The best historians of later times have been seduced
from truth, not by their imagination, but by their
reason. They far excel their predecessors in the art of
deducing general principles from facts. But unhap-
pily they have fallen into the error of distorting facts
to suit general principles. They arrive at a theory
from looking at some of the phenomena; and the
remaining phenomena they strain or curtail to suit
the theory. For this purpose it is not necessary that
they should assert what is absolutely false; for all
questions are questions of comparison and degree.
Any proposition which does not involve a contradic-
tion in terms may possibly be true; and if all the circumstances which raise a probability in its favor be
stated and enforced, and those which lead to an
opposite conclusion be omitted or lightly passed
over, it may appear to be demonstrated. In every
human character and transaction there is a mixture of
good and evil: a little exaggeration, a little suppres-
sion, a judicious use of epithets, a watchful and
searching skepticism with respect to the evidence on
one side, a convenient credulity with respect to every
report or tradition on the other, may easily make a
saint of Laud (Archbishop of Canterbury), or a tyrant
of Henry IV.

BARON THOMAS BABINGTON MACAULAY,
ENGLISH (1800–1859)

---

*The man resorts to superficial ways of influencing others
through nothing but talk. The results are negligible.*

Arias has read and seen everything, at least he would
lead you to think so; he is a man of universal knowl-

edge, or pretends to be, and would rather tell a falsehood than be silent or appear to ignore anything. Some person is talking at mealtime in the house of a man of rank of a northern court; he interrupts and prevents him telling what he knows: he goes hither and thither in that distant country as if he were a native of it; he discourses about the habits of its court, the native women, the laws and customs of the land; he tells many little stories which happened there, thinks them very entertaining, and is the first to laugh loudly at them. Somebody presumes to contradict him, and clearly proves to him that what he says is untrue. Arias is not disconcerted; on the contrary, he grows angry at the interruption, and exclaims: "I aver and relate nothing but what I know on excellent authority; I had it from Sethon, the French ambassador at that court, who only a few days ago came back to Paris, and is a particular friend of mine; I asked him several questions, and he replied to them all without concealing anything." He continues his story with greater confidence than he began it, till one of the company informs him that the gentleman whom he has been contradicting was Sethon himself, but lately arrived from his embassy.
JEAN DE LA BRUYÈRE, FRENCH (1645–1696)

The over-all judgment: meaningful influence depends upon mutual respect. It is proper for a young man to place himself in a position inferior to that of a weak girl and show appropriate deference. Similarly, the superior man frees his mind from self-indulgence and opens it to the influence of others.

The wish to be independent of all men, and not to be under obligation to any one is the sure sign of a soul without tenderness.
JOSEPH JOUBERT, FRENCH (1754–1824)

I must not omit an important subject, and mention of a mistake which princes can with difficulty avoid, if they are not very prudent, or if they do not make a good choice. And this is with regard to flatterers, of which the courts are full, because men take such pleasure in their own things and deceive themselves about them that they can with difficulty guard against this plague; and by wishing to guard against it they run the risk of being contemptible. Because there is no other way of guarding one's self against flattery than by letting men understand that they will not offend you by speaking the truth; but when everyone can tell you the truth, you lose their respect. A prudent prince must therefore take a third course, by choosing for his council wise men, and giving these alone full liberty to speak the truth to him, but only of those things that he asks and of nothing else; but he must ask them about everything and hear their opinion, and afterwards deliberate by himself in his own way, and in these councils and with each of these men comport himself so that everyone may see that the more freely he speaks, the more he will be acceptable. Beyond these he should listen to no one, go about the matter deliberately, and be determined in his decisions.

NICCOLÒ MACHIAVELLI, ITALIAN (1469–1527)

. . . it is the part of a good and wise man to give a free rein to the liberty of others and to accent with patience the words of free speaking, whatever they may be. Nor does he oppose himself to its works so long as these do not involve the casting away of virtue. For since each virtue shines by its own proper light, the merit of tolerance is resplendent with a very special glory.

Once a certain man of Privernum, when asked how the captives from his city would keep the peace if they were granted amnesty, replied to the Roman consul: "If you grant them an advantageous peace, they will keep it forever; if a disadvantageous one, they will not keep it long." By these bold words, freely spoken, it came to pass that the citizens of Privernum obtained not only pardon for their rebellion, but the benefits of Roman citizenship besides, because one man of them had dared to speak out thus boldly in the Senate.

JOHN OF SALISBURY, ENGLISH (1120–1180)

32 Enduring

At the outset, the man wants to endure. Whatever endures must be gradually matured. There is no advantage in precipitous action.

Being a man, ne'er ask the gods for life set free from grief, but ask for courage that endureth long.
MENANDER, GREEK (343–291 B.C.)

The man endures by keeping his force of character within the bounds of available power.

The enemies of Fabius thought they had sufficiently humiliated and subdued him by raising Minucius to be his equal in authority; but they mistook the temper of the man, who looked upon their folly as not his loss, but like Diogenes, who, being told that some persons derided him, made answer, "But I am not derided," meaning that only those were really insulted on whom such insults made an impression, so Fabius, with great tranquility and unconcern, submitted to what happened, and contributed a proof to the argument of the philosophers that a just and good man is not capable of being dishonoured.
PLUTARCH, GREEK (46–120)

It is time to be old,
To take in sail: —
The gods of bounds,
Who sets to seas a shore
Came to me in his fatal rounds,
And said, "No more!

No farther shoot
Thy broad ambitious branches, and thy root
Fancy departs: no more invent;
Contract thy firmament
To compass of a tent . . ."

As the bird trims her to the gale,
I trim myself to the storm of time,
I man the rudder, reef the sail,
Obey the voice at eve obeyed at prime;

"Lowly faithful, banish fear,
Right onward drive unharmed;
The port, well worth the cruise, is near,
And every wave is charmed."

RALPH WALDO EMERSON, AMERICAN (1803–1882)

The man does not maintain an inner consistency of character. His vicissitudes lead to troubles from unforeseen quarters.

The priest began to tell stories about the uncertainty of this life and the retributions of the life to come. Genji was appalled to think how heavy his own sins had already been. It was bad enough to think that he would have them on his conscience for the rest of his present life. But then there was also the life to come. What terrible punishments he had to look forward to! And all the while the priest was speaking Genji thought of his own wickedness. What a good idea it would be to turn hermit, and live in some such place! . . . But immediately his thoughts strayed to the lovely face which he had seen that afternoon; and longing to know more of her he asked, "Who lives with you here?"

LADY MURASAKI SHIKIBU, JAPANESE (978–1015)

Perseverance alone does not assure success. No amount of stalking will lead to game in a field that has none.

He diggy, diggy, diggy, but no meat dar!

JOEL CHANDLER HARRIS, AMERICAN (1848–1908)

The man is faithful to tradition and submits meekly. These are desirable virtues for a wife but not for a man of affairs. He should be flexible and assertive, according to the demands of duty and the tenor of the times.

Suppose you have seen some persons escaping from the hands of marauders and hiding in a thick forest; and the marauders, who follow them with naked swords in their hands stand before you and ask you where those people are! What answer will you give? Will you speak the truth or will you save the lives of the unoffending and innocent people? I ask this question because preventing the murder of innocent people is according to the Shastras a religion as highly important as Truth itself . . . . The Blessed Lord

Shri Krishna who understood the meaning of all laws
says to Arjuna . . . "If you can escape without speaking, then do not speak under any circumstances; but
if it is necessary to speak, or if by not speaking you
may rouse suspicion in the mind (of another), then,
telling a lie has been found, after mature deliberation, to be much better than speaking the truth."
BAL GANGADHAR TILAK, INDIAN (1856–1920)

The man in a high position is perpetually excited and
restless. As a result he does not have the inner com-
posure necessary for positive contributions. His motive
power is soon exhausted by violent efforts.

There is no time,
No time,
There is no time,
Not even for a kiss,
Not even for this,
Not even for this rhyme. ,

It is May
And blossoms sway
In sifted snow
Under the moon.
I only know
That I can not stay,
For today is May
And tomorrow June.

An arrow shot
From an idiot's bow,
That is my lot
And I must go.

There is no time,
No time,
There is no time,
Not even for a kiss,
Not even for this,
Not even for this rhyme, —
    No . . .!

ROBERT SILLIMAN HILLYER, AMERICAN (1895–1961)

The over-all judgment: one should act out the law of
one's being in consonance with the way of heaven and
earth, which is enduring and eternal. The superior man

*perseveres long in his course, adapts to the times, but
remains firm in his direction and correct in his goals.*

The ruler's first of virtues is to hold the rule.
CARL SPITTELER, SWISS (1845–1924)

Your Excellency's kind consideration in honouring
me with a letter assures me, to my great joy, of your
unchanged feelings to me, and this I have for many
years regarded as one of my great fortunes. How
could the august generosity of our incomparable
Empress, which I enjoy through your fatherly inter-
cession, divert me from my love and zeal to the
sciences, when extreme poverty, which I have endured voluntarily for the sake of science, has not
been able to distract me from it? Let not your Excellency think it self-praise of me, if I am bold to present
to you my defence.

When I was studying in the School of the Redeemer, I
was surrounded on all sides with powerful obstacles
that made against science, and in those years the influence of these tendencies was almost insurmount-
able. On the one hand, my father, who had never had
any other children but me, said that in leaving him
I, being his only son, had left all his possessions
(such as they were in those parts), which he had
acquired for me in the sweat of his brow, and which
strangers would carry away after his death. On the
other hand, I was confronted with unspeakable
poverty: as I received but three kopeks a day, all I
dared spend a day for food was half a kopek for bread
and half a kopek for kvas, while the rest went for
paper, shoes and other necessities. In this way I
passed five years, and did not abandon study. On
one hand, they wrote to me that, knowing the well-
being of my father, well-to-do people of my village
would give me their daughters in marriage, and in
fact they proposed them to me, when I was there;
on the other hand, the small schoolboys pointed
their fingers at me, and cried: "Look at the clod-
hopper who has come to study Latin at the age of
twenty!" Soon after that I was taken to St. Peters-
burg, and was sent abroad, receiving an allowance
forty times as large as before. But that did not divert
my attention from study, but proportionately in-

creased my eagerness, though there is a limit to my strength. I must humbly beg your Excellency to feel sure that I will do all in my power to cause all those who ask me to be wary in my zeal to have no anxiety about me, and that those who judge me with malicious envy should be put to shame in their unjust opinion, and should learn that they must not measure others with their yardstick, and should remember that the Muses love whom they list.

MIKHAIL VASILIEVICH LOMONOSOV,
RUSSIAN (1711–1765)

What is the course of the life
Of mortal men on the earth? —
Most men eddy about
Here and there — eat and drink,
Chatter and love and hate,
Gather and squander, are raised
Aloft, are hurl'd in the dust,
Strive blindly, achieving
Nothing; and then they die —
Perish; — and no one asks
Who or what they have been,
More than he asks what waves,
In the moonlit solitudes mild
Of the midmost Ocean, have swell'd,
Foam'd for a moment, and gone,
And there are some, whom a thirst
Ardent, unquenchable, fires,
Not with the crowd to be spent,
Not without aim to go round
In an eddy of purposeless dust,
Effort unmeaning and vain.
Ah yes! some of us strive
Not without action to die
Fruitless, but something to snatch
From dull oblivion, nor all
Glut the devouring grave!
We, we have chosen our path —
Path to a clear-purposed goal,
Path of advance! — but it leads
A long, steep journey, through sunk
Gorges, o'er mountains in snow.
Cheerful, with friends, we set forth —
Then, on the height, comes the storm.

[207]32

Thunder crashes from rock
To rock, the cataracts reply,
Lightnings dazzle our eyes.
Roaring torrents have breach'd
The track, the stream-bed descends
In the place where the wayfarer once
Planted his footstep — the spray
Boils o'er its borders! aloft
The unseen snow-beds dislodge
Their hanging ruin; alas
Havoc is made in our train!
Friends, who set forth at our side,
We, we only are left!
With frowning foreheads, with lips
Sternly compress'd we strain on,
Falter, are lost in the storm.
On — and at nightfall at last
Come to the end of our way,
To the lonely inn 'mid the rocks;
Where the gaunt and taciturn host
Stands on the threshold, the wind
Shaking his thin white hairs —
Holds his lantern to scan
Our storm-beat figures, and asks:
Whom in our party we bring?
Whom we have left in the snow?

Sadly we answer: We bring
Only ourselves! we lost
Sight of the rest in the storm.
Hardly ourselves we fought through,
Stripp'd, without friends, as we are.
Friends, companions, and train,
The avalanche swept from our side.
MATTHEW ARNOLD, ENGLISH (1822–1888)

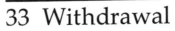

33 Withdrawal

THE TUN HEXAGRAM

*At the outset, the man is in a perilous position at the end
of the retreating column still in contact with the enemy.
No action should be undertaken under such circumstances.*

"Please reserve a room for my wife," he said to the nurse.

"Just a minute!" she replied.

"But there isn't a minute to lose!"

The nurse returned to the telephone. "I am sorry, doctor," she said. "There's no free room."

"I don't understand. This is Dr. Endre Kovacs speaking."

"I know, doctor. But we have instructions. All our rooms must be kept free for German soldiers."

"Then give me a bed in one of the wards."

"I am sorry but there isn't even a bed."

Dr. Kovacs called up the director of the hospital. In the adjoining room his wife was groaning with pain. The director got in touch with the German Commissioner. After a few minutes, which seemed an eternity to Dr. Kovacs, the director rang him back.

"I am sorry, my friend. You can imagine my despair at being obliged to tell you this. But I was unable to obtain the necessary permit."

"Then my wife must die?"

"We are a defeated country."

HANS HABE, HUNGARIAN (BORN 1911)

It is a case without parallel in history that our allies and friends should impose conditions upon us which are usually imposed upon vanquished enemies. It is not a lack of courage that induced our Government to take the decision which grips our hearts. . . . God knows that more courage is needed for living than for committing suicide. . . . We shall not blame those who left us in the lurch, but history will pronounce a judgment about these days.

HUGO VAVRECKA, CZECH (1938)

The man holds fast to the purpose of withdrawal but with due moderation.

I will not serve that in which I no longer believe, whether it calls itself my home, my fatherland, or my church.

JAMES JOYCE, IRISH (1882–1941)

Seeing at Madrid that the republic of letters is a republic of wolves each snarling at the other; and that the contempt caused by this ridiculous bitterness

made it easy for all the insects, the mosquitoes, the
gnats, the crawling things, the envious, the hack
writers, the publishers, the censors, — the whole pack
of wolves which fastens itself to the skins of the unfortunate men of letters, to bite to pieces and suck
dry the little substance left them; tired of writing,
bored with myself, disgusted with others, buried
under debts, light of purse, at last convinced that the
tangible revenue of the razor is preferable to the
empty honors of the pen, I left Madrid: and my pack
on my back, philosophically traveling about through
the two Castiles, La Mancha, Estremadura, Sierra-
Morena, and Andalusia, welcomed in one town, imprisoned in another, and everywhere rising above
events; praised by some, harshly criticized by others;
making the best of good and bad weather, putting
up with misfortune, making fun of fools, defying the
wicked, laughing at my misery, and shaving everybody.
PIERRE AUGUSTIN DE BEAUMARCHAIS,
FRENCH (1732–1799)

---

*The man loses his freedom of action during retreat. The
hangers-on impede and fetter his movements. The expedient course of action is to employ them in such a way
as to retain the initiative. But he must maintain an appropriate distance from them and not rely on expedient
actions of this kind in dealing with important matters.*

At bottom the world isn't a joke. We only joke about
it to avoid an issue with someone to let someone
know he's there with his questions: to disarm him by
seeming to have heard and done justice to his side of
the standing argument. Humor is the most engaging
cowardice. With it I myself have been able to hold
some of my enemy in play far out of gunshot.
ROBERT LEE FROST, AMERICAN (1874–1963)

---

*The man withdraws, despite his desire to do otherwise.
The superior man can retreat in a friendly way, adjusting to the situation, and retaining his convictions. The
inferior man is unable to do this.*

This will be my valediction:
"In the meanwhile . . . Well, then
Afterwards . . ."
[210]33

If on the cherry tree left behind
The blossoms are fragrant.
CHIKAMATSU MONZAEMON, JAPANESE (1653–1725)

The man recognizes the proper time for an admirable
retirement with necessary amenities and without dis-
agreeableness. Firmness in the rectitude of his purpose is
necessary to guard against being misled by irrelevant
issues.

There was living at that time, a few leagues from El
Ombú, one Valerio de la Cueva, a poor man, whose
all consisted of a small flock of three or four hundred
sheep and a few horses. He had been allowed to
make a small rancho, a mere hut, to shelter himself
and his wife Donata and their one child, a boy
named Bruno; and to pay for the grass his few sheep
consumed he assisted in the work at the estancia
house. This poor man, hearing of El Ombú, where
he could have house and ground for nothing, offered
himself as occupant, and in time came with wife and
child and his small flock, and all the furniture he
possessed — a bed, two or three chairs, a pot and
kettle, and perhaps a few other things. Such poverty
El Ombú had not known, but all others had feared to
inhabit such a place on account of its evil name, so
that it was left for Valerio, who was a stranger in
the district.
Tell me señor, have you ever in your life met with a
man, who perhaps poor, or even clothed in rags, and
who yet when you had looked at and conversed with
him, has caused you to say: Here is one who is like
no other man in the world? Perhaps on rising and going out, on some clear morning in summer, he looked
at the sun when it rose, and perceived an angel
sitting in it, and as he gazed, something from that
being fell upon and passed into and remained in
him. Such a man was Valerio. I have known no other
like him.
"Come, friend Nicandro," he would say, "let us sit
down in the shade and smoke our cigarettes, and
talk of our animals. Here are no politics under this
old ombú, no ambitions and intrigues and ani-
mosities — no bitterness, except in these green leaves.
They are our laurels — the leaves of the ombú. Happy
Nicandro, who never knew the life of cities! I wish
[211]33

that I, too, had seen the light on these quiet plains, under a thatched roof. Once I wore fine clothes and gold ornaments, and lived in a great house where there were many servants to wait on me. But happy I have never been. Every flower I plucked changed into a nettle to sting my hand. Perhaps that maleficent one, who has pursued me all my days, seeing me now so humbled and one with the poor, has left me and gone away. Yes, I am poor, and this frayed garment that covers me will I press to my lips because it does not shine with silk and gold embroidery. And this poverty which I have found will I cherish, and bequeath it as a precious thing to my child when I die. For with it is peace."
WILLIAM HENRY HUDSON, ENGLISH (1841–1922)

When it so happens that the things a man's got to love gits fewer and smaller, they gits more valuable, Airnest, in his sight; for he knows mighty well, if he loses them, that he's just like an old bird that comes back to the tree when the blossoms and the flowers have all dropped off, and are rotting under it. It's mighty nigh to winter in his heart then, Airnest — mighty nigh — and the sooner he begins to look out for a place to sleep in, the wiser man you may take him to be.
WILLIAM GILMORE SIMMS, AMERICAN (1806–1870)

No doubt exists as to the need for retirement. The man resigns in a gracious manner.

The weary Mole also was glad to turn in without delay, and soon had his head on his pillow, in great joy and contentment. But ere he closed his eyes he let them wander round his old room, mellow in the glow of the firelight that played or rested on familiar and friendly things which had long been unconsciously a part of him, and now smilingly received him back, without rancor. He was now in just the frame of mind that the tactful Rat had quietly worked to bring about in him. He saw clearly how plain and simple — how narrow, even — it all was; but clearly, too, how much it all meant to him, and the special value of some such anchorage in one's existence. He did not at all want to abandon the new life and its splendid spaces, to turn his back on sun and air and
[212]33

all they offered him and creep home and stay there; the upper world was all too strong, it called to him still, even down there, and he knew he must return to the larger stage. But it was good to think he had this to come back to, this place which was all his own, these things which were so glad to see him again and could always be counted upon for the same simple welcome.

KENNETH GRAHAME, ENGLISH (1859–1932)

The over-all judgment: the times favors the small men. Retreat is proper for the superior man. The right moment needs be selected, so as to control the nature of the withdrawal and to prepare for the countermove. Eventually the hostile forces are brought to a standstill through dignified detachment.

"Listen, man-cub," said the Bear, and his voice rumbled like thunder on a hot night. "I have taught thee all the Law of the Jungle for all the peoples of the jungle — except the Monkey Folk who live in the trees. They are outcaste. They have no speech of their own, but use the stolen words which they overhear when they listen, and peep, and wait up above in the branches. Their way is not our way. They are without leaders. They have no remembrance. They boast and chatter and pretend that they are a great people about to do great affairs in the jungle, but the falling of a nut turns their minds to laughter and all is forgotten. We of the jungle have no dealings with them. We do not drink where the monkeys drink; we do not go where the monkeys go; we do not hunt where they hunt; we do not die where they die."

RUDYARD KIPLING, ENGLISH (1865–1936)

Give me a nobler, wider sphere
   Where I, at least, can bleed to death.
Oh, do not let me stifle here
   Among these hucksters. Give me breath!

They eat and drink with greedy pride
   Dull and complacent as the mole;
Their generosity is wide —
   As wide as, say, the poor-box hole.

Cigar in mouth they stroll along;
   Their hands are fat with many a gem;
Their stomachs are both huge and strong.

But who could ever stomach *them!*

They deal in spices, but the air
   Is filled, alas, with something else;
Their souls pollute the atmosphere,
   And foul it with their fishy smells.

If they but had some human vice,
   Some lust too terrible to see —
But not these virtues, not this nice
   Flabby and smug morality.

Ye clouds above, take me away
   To Africa or furthest North;
Even to Pomerania. Pray
   Carry me with you, bear me forth.

Take me away . . . They pass me by.
   The clouds are wise; they do not heed. `
For when they see this town they fly,
   And anxiously increase their speed.

HEINRICH HEINE, GERMAN (1797–1856)

Chancing a Nightingale to meet,
Thus did an Ass the songstress greet,
"Whither in such a hurry winging?
I'm told, my dear, you're famed for singing.
My curiosity I fain would satisfy,
So if you'll condescend to gratify,
Come! for a specimen of your rare skill,
And let me hear how featly you can trill!"
Forthwith the Nightingale began,
And through her cadences she ran,
How tender and most soft,
Anon her voice she raised aloft;
While all around in silence hushed
Listened to her melting strain,
As it sweetly gushed,
And floated over dale and plain;
Hardly breathed the enraptured swain
As drank his ear of sound the stream,
And as he mused on the varying theme.
Caused the songstress, the critic Ass
His sentence thus began to pass,
"Upon my word! 'tis not amiss!
Yet you should hear
Friend Chanticleer.
From him some lessons you'd do well to take.
His mode of singing well I know,

[214]33

Nor can there finer be, I trow.
Yes! He is clever;
And you, my dear, should by all means endeavor
Like him to crow!
He has a voice — a shake —
That really keeps folks quite awake.
Yet after all you do not sing amiss."
On hearing this,
Far away the song-bird flew.
IVAN ANDREEVICH KRYLOV, RUSSIAN (1768–1844)

34 Great Vigor
THE TA CHUANG HEXAGRAM

At the outset, the man in a lowly station possesses great energy. Seeking advancement through force, however, will bring misfortune.

Europe has no such class of men; the early knowledge they [Americans] acquire, the early bargains they make, give them a great degree of sagacity. As free-men, they will be litigious; pride and obstinacy are often the cause of lawsuits. . . . As citizens it is easy to imagine, that they will carefully read the news-papers, enter into every political disquisition, freely blame or censure governors and others. As farmers, they will be careful and anxious to get as much as they can, because what they get is theirs. . . . As Christians, religion curbs them not in their opinions. . . . Industry, good living, selfishness, litigiousness, country politics, the pride of freemen, religious in-difference, are their characteristics.
ST. JEAN DE CRÈVECOEUR, AMERICAN (1735–1813)

The way begins to open for growth and progress. Exuber-ant self-confidence needs be tempered by continued inner equilibrium in the use of power.

"I am cramped and crushed! I want to escape!" This cry destroys and fructifies the bowels of the earth eternally. It leaps from body to body, from genera-tion to generation, from species to species, becoming always stronger and more carnivorous. All parents shout: "I want to give birth to a son greater than I!"
NIKOS KAZANTZAKIS, GREEK (1883–1957)

The situation becomes entangled and perilous. The inferior man in power applies full force and gets himself irretrievably enmeshed. He is like a goat butting against a hedge and getting its horns entangled. The superior man renounces empty display of force and retains the secure middle position.

I had nothing to eat for a day and a night, and just before we set out the Master gives me a wash under the hydrant. Whenever I am locked up until all the slop-cans in our alley are empty, and made to take a bath, and the Master's pals speak civil and feel my ribs, I know something is going to happen. And that night, when every time they see a policeman under a lamp-post, they dodged across the street, and when at the last one of them picked me up and hid me under his jacket, I began to tremble; for I knew what it meant. It means I was to fight again for the Master.

I don't fight because I like fighting. I fight because if I didn't the other dog would find my throat, and the Master would lose his stakes, and I would be very sorry for him, and ashamed. Dogs can pass me and I can pass dogs, and I'd never pick a fight with one of them. When I see two dogs standing on their hind legs in the streets, clawing each other's ears, and snapping for each other's windpipes, or howling and swearing and rolling in the mud, I feel sorry that they should act so, and pretend not to notice. If he'd let me, I'd like to pass the time of day with every dog I meet. But there's something about me that no nice dog can abide. When I trot up to nice dogs, nodding and grinning, to make friends, they always tell me to be off. "Go to the devil!" they bark at me. "Get out!" And when I walk away they shout "Mongrel!" and "Gutter dog!" and sometimes, after my back is turned, they rush me. I could kill most of them with three shakes, breaking the backbone of the little ones and squeezing the throat of the big ones. But what's the good? They *are* nice dogs; that's why I try to make up to them: and, though it's not for them to say it, I *am* a street-dog, and if I try to push into the company of my betters, I suppose it's their right to teach me my place.

RICHARD HARDING DAVIS, AMERICAN (1864–1916)

The man removes all obstacles through quiet persever-
ance. Unseen power can move heavy loads.

He knew, sly and subtle as he was, that if he went to
her plainly and said: "Miss March, I love you and
want you to marry me," her inevitable answer would
be: "Get out. I don't want any of that tomfoolery." . . .
He would have to go gently. He would have to catch
her as you catch a deer or a wood-cock when you go
out shooting. It's no good walking out into the forest
and saying to the deer: "Please fall to my gun." No,
it is a slow, subtle battle. When you really go out to
get a deer, you gather yourself together, you coil
yourself inside yourself, and you advance secretly,
before dawn, into the mountains. It is not so much
what you do, when you go out hunting, as how you
feel. You have to be subtle and cunning and absolutely fatally ready. It becomes like a fate. Your own
fate overtakes and determines the fate of the deer you
are hunting. First of all, even before you come in
sight of your quarry, there is a strange battle, like
mesmerism. Your own soul, as a hunter, has gone out
to fasten on the soul of the deer, even before you see
any deer. And the soul of the deer fights to escape.
Even before the deer has any wind of you, it is so. It
is a subtle, profound battle of wills, which takes place
in the invisible. And it is a battle never finished until
your bullet goes home. When you are *really* worked
up to the true pitch, and you come at last into range,
you don't then aim as you do when you are firing a
bottle. It is your own *will* which carries the bullet
into the heart of the quarry. The bullet's flight home
is a sheer projection of your own fate into the fate of
the deer. It happens like a supreme wish, supreme
act of volition, not as a dodge of cleverness.
DAVID HERBERT LAWRENCE, ENGLISH (1885–1930)

The mightiest men have hitherto always bowed
reverently before the saint, as the enigma of self-
subjugation and utter voluntary privation — why did
they thus bow? They divined in him — and as it were
behind the questionableness of his frail and wretched
appearance — the superior force which wished to test
itself by such a subjugation; the strength of will, in
which they recognised their own strength and love of

power, and knew how to honour it: they honoured
something in themselves when they honoured the
saint. In addition to this, the contemplation of the
saint suggested to them a suspicion: such an enor-
mity of self-negation and anti-naturalness will not
have been coveted for nothing—they have said, in-
quiringly. There is perhaps a reason for it, some very
great danger, about which the ascetic might wish to
be more accurately informed through his secret inter-
locutors and visitors? In a word, the mighty ones of
the world learned to have a new fear before him,
they divined a new power, a strange still unconquered enemy:—it was the "Will to Power" which
obliged them to halt before the saint. They had to
question him.

FRIEDRICH WILHELM NIETZSCHE, GERMAN (1844–1900)

---

*The man has lost his alertness and strength because of
the ease of his position.*

A grammarian once embarked in a boat. Turning to
the boatman with a self-satisfied air he asked him:
"Have you ever studied grammar?"
"No," replied the boatman.
"Then half your life has gone to waste," the grammarian said.
The boatman thereupon felt very depressed, but he
answered him nothing for the moment. Presently
the wind tossed the boat into a whirlpool. The boatman shouted to the grammarian:
"Do you know how to swim?"
"No," the grammarian replied, "my well-spoken,
handsome fellow."
"In that case, grammarian," the boatman remarked,
"the whole of your life has gone to waste, for the
boat is sinking in these whirlpools."

JALAL AL-DIN RUMI, PERSIAN (1207–1273)

---

*The man goes too far and reaches a deadlock with neither
the capability to advance nor the opportunity to retreat.
If he recognizes his weakness and is not obstinate, he will
not compound the error.*

In quarrels between countries, as well in those between individuals, when they have risen to a certain
height, the first cause of dissension is no longer re-

membered, the minds of the parties being wholly engaged in recollecting and resenting the mutual expressions of their dislike. When feuds have reached that fatal point, all considerations of reason and equity vanish; and a blind fury governs, or rather confounds all things. A people no longer regards their interest, but the gratification of their wrath.
JOHN DICKINSON, AMERICAN (1732–1808)

The over-all judgment: the great man with vigor should also demand the rightness of things, the timeliness of action, and the propriety of method. In this way, power does not degenerate into sheer force.

Among those who aspire to power he is the best who is naturally intelligent and discerning; who has acquired a knowledge of what happens in the world of changing times and tumbling empires; who is adroit at negotiating with the enemy and who can keep a secret; for he is the pillar of politics.
IBN AL TIQTAQA, ARABIAN (THIRTEENTH CENTURY)

The practical politician must inevitably submit himself to a discipline of compromise — continuously say less than he would like to say in order to keep in step with his colleagues — be content with a sort of highest common factor of truth, because his purpose is to get something done.
CHRISTOPHER HOLLIS, ENGLISH (BORN 1902)

The years I spent in Siberia taught me many lessons. . . . I soon realized the absolute impossibility of doing anything really useful for the mass of the people by means of the administrative machinery. With that illusion I parted forever. Then I began to understand not only men and human character, but also the inner springs of the life of human society. The constructive work of the unknown masses, which so seldom finds any mention in books, and the importance of that constructive work in the growth of forms of society, fully appeared before my eyes. . . . to live with natives, to see at work all the complex forms of social organization which they have elaborated far away from the influence of any civilization, was, as it were, to store up floods of light which illuminated my subsequent

[219]34

reading. . . .

Having been brought up in a serf-owner's family, I entered active life . . . with a great deal of confidence in the necessity of commanding, ordering, scolding, punishing, and the like. But when, at an early age, I had to manage enterprises and to deal with men, and when each mistake would lead at once to heavy consequences, I began to appreciate the difference between acting on the principle of command and discipline and acting on the principle of common understanding. The former works admirably in a military parade, but it is worth nothing where real life is concerned, and the aim can be achieved only through the severe effort of many converging wills. Although I did not then formulate my observations in terms borrowed from party struggles, I may say now that I lost in Siberia whatever faith in state discipline I had cherished before.

PËTR ALEKSEEVICH KROPOTKIN, RUSSIAN (1842–1921)

 ## 35 Progress

THE CHIN HEXAGRAM

At the outset, the man's desire to advance has not met with official confidence. He should maintain a calm and generous attitude.

I'm nobody! Who are you?
Are you nobody, too?

EMILY ELIZABETH DICKINSON, AMERICAN (1830–1886)

The man appears to be advancing but is grieving because he is prevented from making contacts with men in authority. His perseverance in adhering to correct principles will be rewarded by blessings from the mild ruler.

The Emperor — so it (the parable) goes — has sent a message to you, the humble subject, the insignificant shadow cowering in the remotest distance before the imperial sun; the Emperor from his death-bed has sent a message to you alone. He has commanded the messenger to kneel down by the bed, and has whispered the message to him: so much store did he lay on it that he ordered the messenger to whisper it back into his ear again. Then by a nod of the head he has confirmed that it is right. Yes, before the assembled spectators of his death — all the obstructing walls have been broken down, and on the spacious and loftily mounting open staircases stand in a ring the great princes of the Empire — before all these he had delivered his message. The messenger immediately sets out on his journey: a powerful, an indefatigable man; now pushing with his right arm, now with his left, he cleaves a way for himself through the throng; if he encounters resistance he points to his breast, where the symbol of the sun glitters; the way, too, is made easier for him than for any other man. But the multitudes are so vast; their numbers have no end. If he could reach the open fields how fast he would fly, and soon doubtless you will hear the welcome hammering of his fists on your door. But instead how vainly does he wear out his strength; still he is only making his way through the chambers of the innermost palace; never will he get to the end of them; and if he succeeded in that nothing would be gained; he must fight his way next down the stair; and if he succeeded in that nothing will be gained; the courts would still have to be crossed; and after the courts the second outer palace; and once more stairs and courts; and once more another palace; and so on for thousands of years; and if at last he should burst through the outermost gate — but never, never can that happen — the imperial capital would lie before him, the centre of the world, crammed to bursting with its own refuse. Nobody could fight his way through here even with a message from a dead man. — But you sit at your window when evening falls and dream it to yourself.

FRANZ KAFKA, AUSTRIAN (1883–1924)

The man moves forward with the trust and support of all around him.

It's a simple formula: do your best and somebody might like it.

DOROTHY BAKER, AMERICAN (BORN 1907)

The man advances like a marmot. But such machinations are always uncovered.

ISOBEL. Nearly seventy years ago there were two young men, boys almost, twenty-three perhaps, living together in rooms in Islington. Both poor, both eager, ambitious, certain of themselves, very certain of their destiny. But only one of them was a genius. He was a poet, this one; perhaps the greater poet because he knew that he had not long to live. As the lark sings, so he sang. The poetry came bubbling out of him, and he wrote it down feverishly, quick, quick before the hand became cold and the fingers could no longer write. That was all his ambition. He had no thoughts of present fame; there was no time for it. He was content to live unknown, so that when dead he might live forever. His friend was ambitious in a different way. He wanted the present delights of fame. So they lived together there, one writing and writing, always writing; the other writing and then stopping to think how famous he was going to be, and envying those who were already famous, and then regretfully writing again. A time came when the poet grew very ill, and lay in bed, but still writing, but still hurrying, hurrying to keep pace with the divine music in his brain. Then one day there was no more writing, no more music. The poet was dead. *(She is silent for a little.)*

WILLIAM *(as her meaning slowly comes to him)*. Isobel, what are you saying?

MARION. I don't understand. Who was it?

OLIVER. Good Lord!

ISOBEL *(in the same quiet voice)*. The friend was left — with the body of the poet — and all that great monument which the dead man had raised for himself. The poet had no friends but this one; no relations of whom he had ever spoken or who claimed him now. He was dead, and it was left to his friend to see that he won now that immortality for which he had given his life. . . . His friend betrayed him.

SEPTIMA. I say!

WILLIAM. I *won't* believe it! It's monstrous!

MARION. I don't understand.

ISOBEL *(wearily)*. One can see the temptation. There he was, this young man of talent, of great ambition, and there were these works of genius lying at his feet, waiting to be picked up — and fathered by him. I suppose that, like every other temptation, it came suddenly. He writes out some of the verses, scribbled down anyhow by the poet in his mad hurry, and sends them to the publisher; one can imagine the
[222]35

publisher's natural acceptance of the friend as the true author, the friend's awkwardness in undeceiving him, and then his sudden determination to make the most of the opportunity given him. . . . Oh, one can imagine many things — but what remains? Always and always this. That Oliver Blayds was not a poet; that he did not write the works attributed to him; and that he betrayed his friend. *(She stops and then says in an ordinary matter of fact voice.)* That is why I thought he ought not to be buried in the Abbey.

ALAN ALEXANDER MILNE, ENGLISH (1882–1956)

The man occupies an influential position with the intelligent sovereign. He remains gentle and reserved in his dealings. Let him not reproach himself for not obtaining all possible gains or regretfully take failures to heart. His beneficent influence will eventually be crowned with success.

Hsiang, king of Ch'u, was feasting in the Orchid-tower Palace, with Sung Yü and Ching Ch'ai to wait upon him. A gust of wind blew in and the king bared his breast to meet it, saying: "How pleasant a thing is this wind which I share with the common people." Sung Yü answered: "This is the Great King's wind. The common people cannot share it." The king said: "Wind is a spirit of Heaven and Earth. It comes widespread and does not choose between noble and base or between high and low. How can you say 'This is the king's wind'?" Sung answered: "I have heard it taught that in the crooked lemon tree birds make their nests and to empty places winds fly. But the wind-spirit that comes to different things is not the same." The king said: "Where is the wind born?" and Sung answered: "The wind is born in the ground. It rises in the extremities of the green p'ing-flower. It pours into the river-valleys and rages at the mouth of the pass. It follows the rolling flanks of Mount T'ai and dances beneath the pine-trees and cypresses. In gusty bouts it whirls. It rushes in fiery anger. It rumbles low with a noise like thunder, tearing down rocks and trees, smiting forests and grasses.

"But at last abating, it spreads abroad, seeks empty places and crosses the threshold of rooms. And so growing gentler and clearer, it changes and is dispersed and dies.

"It is this clear Man-Wind that, freeing itself, falls and rises till it climbs the high walls of the Castle and enters the gardens of the Inner Palace. It bends the flowers and leaves with its breath. It wanders among the osmanthus and pepper-trees. It lingers over the fretted face of the pond, to steal the soul of the hibiscus. It touches the willow leaves and scatters the fragrant herbs. Then it pauses in the courtyard and turning to the North goes up to the Jade Hall, shakes the hanging curtains and lightly passes into the inner room.

"And so it becomes the Great King's wind.

"Now such a wind is fresh and sweet to breathe and its gentle murmuring cures the diseases of men, blows away the stupor of wine, sharpens sight and hearing and refreshes the body. This is what is called the Great King's wind."

The king said: "You have well described it. Now tell me of the common people's wind." Sung said: "The common people's wind rises from narrow lanes and streets, carrying clouds of dust. Rushing to empty places it attacks the gateway, scatters the dust-heap, sends the cinders flying, pokes among foul and rotting things, till at last it enters the tiled windows and reaches the rooms of the cottage. Now this wind is heavy and turgid, oppressing man's heart. It brings fever to his body, ulcers to his lips and dimness to his eyes. It shakes him with coughing; it kills him before his time.

"Such is the Woman-Wind of the common people."

SUNG YÜ, CHINESE (FOURTH CENTURY B.C.)

You will probably be desired to intercede for the favors of the Pope on particular occasions. Be cautious, however, that you trouble him not too often; for his temper leads him to be most liberal to those who weary him least with their solicitations. This you must observe, lest you should give him offense, remembering also at times to converse with him on more agreeable topics; and if you should be obliged to request some kindness from him, let it be done with that modesty and humility which are so pleasing to his disposition.

LORENZO DE MEDICI, ITALIAN (1449–1492)

The man uses force in punishing the rebellious people of his own city. This is permissible. Continuation of the offensive, especially against strangers, however, will bring occasion for regret.

For seven years I conformed. But he, at the bidding of his deity and of his council, sought to destroy me. . . . breaking with him, I did not do so treacherously, rebelling against him in chariot or in house; instead I declared war on him: "Thou hast picked a quarrel with me. Thou art the Great King, whereas I possess only the one stronghold which thou hast left me. Well, the goddess Ishtar of Samuha and the storm-god of Nerik will decide between us!" When I wrote thus to Urhi-Teshub, someone might have said to me: "Why didst thou in the first place set him on the throne, and now thou writest to him to depose him?" But if he had not picked a quarrel with me, would the gods have permitted a great king to be defeated by a little king? It is because he picked a quarrel with me that the gods by their judgment brought him to defeat at my hands.
KING HATTUSILIS III,
HITTITE (THIRTEENTH CENTURY B.C.)

The over-all judgment: the great leader does not take unfair advantage of the people's support but uses it for his country's welfare. Progress depends upon an enlightened ruler with an obedient servant.

What is a minority? The chosen heroes of this earth have been in a minority. There is not a social, political, or religious privilege that you enjoy today that was not bought for you by the blood and tears and patient suffering of the minority. It is the minority that has stood in the van of every moral conflict, and achieved all that is noble in the history of the world.
JOHN B. GOUGH, AMERICAN (1817–1886)

Some men attain power by legal science, some by eloquence, some by military achievement; but he [Cato the Elder] was a person of such versatile talents, that let him be doing what he would, you would have said that it was the very thing for which nature had designed him.
TITUS LIVIUS, ROMAN (50 B.C.–17 A.D.)

Tell me yourself, I challenge you — answer. Imagine
that you are creating a fabric of human destiny with
the object of making men happy in the end, giving
them peace and rest at last, but that it was essential
and inevitable to torture to death only one tiny
creature — that baby beating its breast with its fist,
for instance — and to found that edifice on its un-
avenged tears, would you consent to be the architect
on those conditions? Tell me, and tell the truth.
FËDOR MIKHAILOVICH DOSTOEVSKY, RUSSIAN (1821–1881)

 # 36 Intelligence Unappreciated

THE MING I HEXAGRAM

*At the outset, the man encounters hostility and derision
in his attempt to soar above all obstacles. He does not
compromise but perseveres in his thinking and remains
true to his principles. People do not understand him.*

He is weary of sharing the shame of this immense
crowd who secretly abhor as much as he does, but
who approve and encourage, at least by their silence,
atrocious men and abominable actions. Life is not
worth so much opprobrium. When the booths, the
taverns and houses of debauchery vomit by the
thousand legislators, magistrates and army generals
who rise out of the mire for the good of their country,
he has another ambition, and he does not think himself undeserving of his country, if some day he
makes her say: This country, which at that time
produced so many prodigies of imbecility and baseness, also produced a small number of men who
renounced neither their reason nor their conscience;
witnessing the triumphs of vice, they remained
friends of virtue and did not blush to be honorable
men. In these times of violence they dared to question; in these times of the most abject hypocrisy, they
did not feign to be wicked in order to buy their repose at the price of oppressed innocence; they did
not conceal their hatred from villains who, to reward
their friends and punish their enemies, spared nothing, for it cost nothing but crimes, and a certain A. C.
(André Chénier) was among those five or six whom
neither the general frenzy, nor avidity, nor fear,
could induce to bend the knee before crowned assas-

[226]36

sins, to touch hands stained by murders, and to sit
down to a table where they drink human blood.
ANDRÉ MARIE DE CHÉNIER, FRENCH (1762–1794)

*The man is injured but is not disabled. He recovers and
pursues his good purpose with the strength of a horse.*

Please read this sentence over twice, and believe it.
Healing is a living process, greatly under the influence of mental conditions. It has often been found
that the same wound received in battle will do well
in the soldiers that have beaten, that would prove
fatal in those that have just been defeated.
OLIVER WENDELL HOLMES, AMERICAN (1809–1894)

The sages, of blessed memory, frequently allude to
persecutions in the following manner: "once the
wicked government passed the following degree
of persecution," or, "they decreed so and so."
After a while God would make the decree null
and void by destroying the power which issued it.
It was this observation that led the rabbis of blessed
memory to affirm that persecutions are of short
duration.
The divine assurance was given to Jacob our father,
that his descendants would survive the people who
degraded and discomfited them as it is written:
"And thy seed shall be like the dust of the earth."
That is to say, although his offspring will be abased
like dust that is trodden under foot, they will ultimately emerge triumphant and victorious, and as
the simile implies, just as the dust settles finally upon
him who tramples upon it, and remains after him, so
shall Israel outlive its persecutors.
MOSES MAIMONIDES, HEBREW (1135–1204)

*The man encounters the chief of disorder and captures
him. Despite swift victory, he is not overly eager to put
all things in order in one fell swoop. Only gradualness is
effective in correcting the long-standing evils.*

Be calm in arguing, for fierceness makes
Error a fault, and truth discourtesy.
GEORGE HERBERT, ENGLISH (1593–1633)

*The man is in close proximity to the leader of the evil
forces. Knowing the latter's secret thoughts, he recog-*

nizes that there is no hope for improvement. He therefore
leaves the scene before the disastrous storm.

But one sees it all day long; this thing is not a miracle. . . . Do you not see that when a person becomes mayor, commissary, purveyor, custom-house officer, judge, notary, bursar, he at once ceases to have human habits, and takes on those of a wolf, or a fox, or some sort of vulture?
LUDOVICO ARIOSTO, ITALIAN (1474–1533)

The man recalls the manner in which Prince Chi preserved his convictions by feigning insanity when trapped in the court of the tyrant Chou Hsin. In coping with danger during times of darkness, he exhibits an invincibility of spirit, coupled with unusual caution.

Harden thyself against all subordinates.
The people give heed to him who terrorizes them;
Approach them not alone.

Fill not thy heart with a brother,
Know not a friend,
Nor make for thyself intimates,
Wherein there is no end.
When thou sleepest, guard for thyself thine own heart;
For a man has no friend
In the day of evil.

PHARAOH AMENEMHET I, EGYPTIAN (2000–1970 B.C.)

This senator was the tool and the slave, the little puppet of a gross, uneducated machine boss, so was this governor and this supreme court judge; and all three rode on railroad passes. This man, talking soberly and earnestly about the beauties of idealism and the goodness of God, had just betrayed his comrades in a business deal. This man, a pillar of the church and heavy contributor to foreign missions, worked his shop girls ten hours a day on a starvation wage and thereby directly encouraged prostitution. . . .
It was the same everywhere, crime and betrayal, betrayal and crime — men who were alive, but who were neither clean nor noble, men who were clean and noble but who were not alive. Then there was a great, hopeless mass, neither noble nor alive, but merely clean. It did not sin positively nor deliber-
[228]36

ately; but it did sin passively and ignorantly by acquiescing in the current immorality and profiting by it. Had it been noble and alive it would not have been ignorant, and it would have refused to share in the profits of betrayal and crime.

I discovered that I did not like to live on the parlor floor of society. Intellectually I was bored. Morally and spiritually I was sickened. I remembered my intellectuals and idealists, my unfrocked preachers, broken professors, and clean-minded, class-conscious workingmen. I remembered my days and nights of sunshine and starshine, where life was all a wild sweet wonder, a spiritual paradise of unselfish adventure and ethical romance. And I see before me, ever blazing and burning, the Holy Grail.

So I went back to the working-class, in which I had been born and where I belonged. I care no longer to climb. The imposing edifice of society above my head holds no delights for me. It is the foundation of the edifice that interests me. There I am content to labor, crowbar in hand, shoulder to shoulder with intellectuals, idealists, and class-conscious workingmen, getting a solid pry now and again and setting the whole edifice rocking. Some day, when we get a few more hands and crowbars to work, we'll topple it over, along with all its rotten life and unburied dead, its monstrous selfishness and sodden materialism. Then we'll cleanse the cellar and build a new habitation for mankind, in which all the rooms will be bright and airy, and where the air that is breathed will be clean, noble, and alive.

JACK LONDON, AMERICAN (1876–1916)

There is only darkness. The ruler opposes officers capable of good and intelligent service. He does not shower blessings upon his people but ignores his duties and responsibilities for increasing the common good.

He is a man of splendid abilities, but utterly corrupt. He shines and stinks like rotten mackerel by moonlight.

JOHN RANDOLPH, AMERICAN (1773–1833)

It was a competition of ingenuity in the elaboration of intrigue and in the refinement of reprisals. The customary meaning of words was arbitrarily distorted to cover the conduct of those who employed them. Reckless irresponsibility was treated as courageous loyalty, cautious reserve as cowardice masked under a high-sounding name, restraint as a cloak for poor-spiritedness, and the policy of reason as a policy of *laissez faire*. A frenzied fanaticism was the popular ideal of conduct, while intrigue that took no risks was regarded as a legitimate method of self-defense. Violence of feeling was a warrant of honesty, deprecation of violence a signal for suspicion. Success in intrigue was the test of intelligence and the detection of intrigue a testimonial to superior cleverness, while anyone who so shaped his policy as to dispense with such methods was pilloried as a nihilist toward his own group and a weakling in face of their opponents. In short, approbation was reserved for those who forestalled their enemies in striking a blow or who implanted that suggestion in minds which had not previously conceived it. The ties of party actually became closer than kinsmen . . . and the associations in question were formed, not to secure the benefits of established institutions, but to gain illegitimate advantages by violating them. Complicity in crime was a more effective sanction for loyalty to engagements than a solemn oath. A fair offer from opponents was received as a signal for practical precautions by the dominant party of the moment, instead of evoking any generous response. The exaction of reprisals was valued more highly than an immunity from wrongs demanding them. The rare covenants of reconciliation were only entered into on either side as a momentary last resort and only observed so long as no alternative resource presented itself. Anyone who spied a weak spot in his adversary's armor and had the nerve to seize his opportunity took more satisfaction in obtaining his revenge by treachery than in obtaining it in fair fight, the dominating considerations being the elimination of risk and the added halo of intellectual brilliance investing the triumphs of perfidy.

THUCYDIDES, GREEK (471–400 B.C.)

The over-all judgment: the capable minister is serving his country under a weak and unsympathetic sovereign. The difficulties of the situation should be appreciated. The superior man hides his light under such circum-

stances. He appears outwardly yielding and tractable,
but inwardly steadfast to his own convictions.

The king [Sigismund III] reigns but does not rule.
GENERAL JAN ZAMOYSKI, POLISH (1541–1605)

The contrast has long been remarked in the west that
subsisted between all the sultans before Soliman and
all those after him . . . Selim II [1566–1574] . . . who
preferred the society of eunuchs and of women, and
the habits of the serai to the camp, who wore away
his days in sensual enjoyments, in drunkenness and
indolence . . . With him begins the series of those
inactive sultans, in whose dubious character we may
trace one main cause of the decay of the Ottoman
fortunes. . . .
There existed among the Ottomans an institution
fitted to prevent the effects of incapacity in the sultan, the institution . . . of the grand vizier. This
officer they were accustomed to style an unlimited
deputy. . . . A great portion of the public weal depended on him . . . and when the sultan was incapable the whole executive power (was) in his
hands. . . .
The consequence of this new practice was that
whilst the head of the government was constantly
changed, the manner and course of the administration, and the principles and usages of the higher
functionaries were unsettled and subjected to no
fewer changes. . . .
What constantly befalls Oriental despotisms occurred in this case likewise; here, too, caprice called
up someone who was able to master it. A new system
of government grew up, situated in the hands of
favorites within the palace, such as the sultan's
mother, or his wives, or his eunuchs. . . . In this way
there arose, within the walls of the harem, an
interest opposed to the vizier, and by which he was
himself ruled, and placed and displaced; not a
general interest of the empire, nor a personal one of
the sultan, but an interest of women and of eunuchs, who now assumed the head of this warlike
state. . . .
They began to cover their seats with cloth of gold;
they slept in summer on the finest silk, and in winter
wrapped in costly furs. . . . In lieu of the simple fare
[231]36

of Soliman's time they outdid all the delicacies of
Italy . . . to do or suffer everything for gold. . . .
Justice was venal; every office had its price.
LEOPOLD VON RANKE, GERMAN (1795–1886)

"Well," Coffe answered coldly, "the minister offers
you his arm when you leave the Opera. Your fortune
is envied by magistrates on duty at the State Council,
by prefects on leave and deputies handling ware-
houses of tobacco. This is the other face of the coin.
It's that simple."
"Your composure is enough to drive me mad," said
Lucien, beside himself with rage. "Those indignities!
That atrocious remark: 'His soul is on his face'! That
mud!"
"That mud is for us the noble stain of the field of
honor. That public uproar will weigh in your favor.
These are the shining deeds of the career you have
chosen and into which my poverty and gratitude
have moved me to follow you."
"You mean that you would not be here if you had an
income of 1200 francs."
"If I had only three hundred, I should not be serving
a minister who keeps thousands of poor devils
locked up in the dungeons of Mount Saint-Michel
and Clairvaux."
STENDHAL (MARIE HENRI BEYLE), FRENCH (1783–1842)

 ## 37 Family Life

THE CHIA JÊN HEXAGRAM

At the outset, the man establishes firm rules of order and
relationships in the household. Overindulgence of a
young child leads to the difficult task of breaking the
child's will later on.

In the autumn the deer are lured within reach of the
hunters by the sounds of the flute, which resemble
the sounds of the voices of their mates, and so are
killed.
Almost in like manner, one of the five most beautiful
girls in Yedo, whose comely face charmed all the
capital even as the spring-blossoming of cherry trees,
cast away her life in the moment of blindness caused

by love.

When, having wrought a vain thing, she was brought before the Mayor of the city of Yedo, that high official questioned the young criminal, asking: "Are you not O-Shichi, the daughter of the *Yaoya?* And being so young, how came you to commit such a dreadful crime as incendiarism?"

Then O-Shichi, weeping and wringing her hands, made this answer: "Indeed that was the only crime that I ever committed; and I had no extraordinary reason for it, but this:

"Once before, when there had been a great fire — so great a fire that nearly all Yedo was consumed, — our house also was burned down. And we three — my parents and I, — knowing no other where to go, took shelter in a Buddhist temple, to remain there until our house could be rebuilt.

"Surely that destiny, that draws two young persons to each other is hard to understand! . . . In that temple there was a young acolyte, and love grew up between us.

"In secret we met together, and promised never to forsake each other, — we pledged ourselves to each other by sucking blood from small cuts we made in our little finger, and by exchanging written vows that we should love each other forever.

"Before our pillows had yet become fixed our new house in Hondo was built and made ready for us.

"But from that day when I bade a sad farewell to Kichizisama, whom I had pledged myself for the time of two existences, never was my heart consoled by even one letter from the acolyte.

"Alone in my bed at night, I used to think and think, and at last in a dream there came to me the dreadful idea of setting fire to the house, — as the only means of again being able to meet my beautiful lover.

"Then, one evening I got a bundle of dry rushes, and placed inside it some pieces of live charcoal, and I secretly put the bundle into a shed at the back of the house.

"A fire broke out, and there was a great tumult, and I was arrested and brought here — oh! how dreadful it was.

"I will never, never commit such a fault again. But whatever happens, O pray save me, my *Bugyo* —

O pray take pity on me!"
Ah! the simple apology! But what was her age? — not
twelve? — not thirteen? — not fourteen? Fifteen comes
after fourteen. Alas! she was fifteen and could not be
saved!
Therefore O-Shichi was sentenced according to the
law. But first she was bound with strong cords and
was for seven days exposed to public view on the
bridge called Nihonbashi. Ah! what a piteous sight
it was!
Her aunts and cousins, — even Bekurai and Kaku-
suke, the house servants, had often to wring their
sleeves, — so wet were their sleeves with tears.

But because the crime could not be forgiven, O-Shichi
was bound to four posts, and fuel was kindled, and
the fire rose up! . . . And poor O-Shichi in the midst
of that fire.
Even so the insects of summer fly to the flame.

BALLAD OF O-SHICHI, JAPANESE

---

*The good fortune of the family lies primarily in the un-
assuming role of the wife, who looks after the welfare of
the family and food for the sacrifice. Similarly, in gov-
ernmental affairs the state of public welfare depends
primarily upon the unassuming civil servant who confines himself to the duties at hand.*

In the days when my hair first fell over my forehead
And in play I plucked flowers before the door,
You came riding to me on a bamboo horse.
Throwing blue plums, we chased each other round
  the bed.
Together we lived in the hamlet of Ch'ang Kan,
In those days we were both young and innocent.
At the age of fourteen I became your wife.
So bashful I dared not look up,
I hung my head in the darkest corners.
A thousand times you called me, but I did not
  answer.
At the age of fifteen I began to come to my senses
And plighted my troth to you till we should be dust
  and ashes together.
We kept faith as he who clung [despite the rising
  waters] to the post of old.
How should I dally on the tower seeking a hus-

band's return?
When I was sixteen you went on a far journey.
In the gorges of Ch'u Tang foaming rapids defy the
    traveller.
In the fifth month they cannot be passed in (safety).
The monkeys lift their melancholy howls in the
    distant heights.
Before the door I gaze where your parting feet have
    trodden.
Little by little the green moss covers them,
Deep green moss that cannot be brushed away.
Already the leaves are falling in the autumn wind.
In the eighth month the yellow butterflies come;
They flutter in pairs over the flowers of the western
    garden.
These matters touch my heart with emotion
As I sit lonely while my bloom fades to age.
Sooner or later you must return down the Three
    Gorges.
Do not forget to send a letter informing me of your
    arrival,
Then I will meet you nor fear the distant road
Even to the Long Wind Beach.
LI PO, CHINESE (705–762)

Every man who strikes blows for power, for influence, for institutions, for the right, must be just as
good an anvil as he is a hammer.
JOSIAH GILBERT HOLLAND, AMERICAN (1819–1881)

---

*A proper balance must be struck between indulgence and
severity. However, severity, despite occasional mistakes,
is preferable to a lack of discipline.*

The ultimate result of shielding men from the effects
of folly is to fill the world with fools.
HERBERT SPENCER, ENGLISH (1820–1903)

---

*The woman of the family balances the income and ex-
penditures, enriching the well-being and peace of the
family. The faithful steward performs the same service
for public welfare.*

I think as I talk to you, that I belong to a dead age. I
wonder if you think that? In my day, we considered
a girl immensely courageous and independent who
taught school or gave music lessons. Nowadays, girls

sell real estate and become scientists and think nothing of it. Give us our due, Christina. We weren't
entirely bustles and smelling salts, we girls who did
not go into the world. We made a great profession
which I fear may be in some danger of vanishing
from the face of the earth. We made a profession of
motherhood. That may sound old-fashioned to you.
Believe me, it had its value. I was trained to be a
wife that I might become a mother. . . . Your father
died of his investigations of a dangerous disease.
You called that splendid of him, didn't you? Would
you say any less of us who gave our lives to being
mothers?
SIDNEY COE HOWARD, AMERICAN (1891–1939)

---

*The father is not feared by the family. Like a richly en-
dowed king, he governs through mutual affection and
tempers the display of his powers.*

And down in the horrible tower I heard the door
   Locked up. Without a word I looked anew
   Into my sons' faces, all the four.
I wept not, so to stone within I grew.
   They wept; and one, my little Anselm, cried:
   "You look so, Father, what has come on you?"
But I shed not a tear, neither replied
   All that day nor the next night, until dawn
   Of a new day over the world rose wide.
A cranny of light crept in upon the stone
   Of that dungeon of woe; and I saw there
   On those four faces the aspect of my own.
I bit upon both hands in my despair.
   And they, supposing it was in the excess
   Of hunger, rose up with a sudden prayer,
And said: "O Father, it will hurt much less
   If you of us eat; take what once you gave
   To clothe us, this flesh of our wretchedness."
Thereon I calmed myself, their grief to save.
DANTE ALIGHIERI, ITALIAN (1265–1321)

The King is dead, by millions mourned,
That bared their heads, or wept, or sighed;
The dog, that waited for him in vain,
Has broken its heart, and died.
So end two lives, and one so small thing—

It never knew its Master was a King.
WILLIAM HENRY DAVIES, ENGLISH (1871–1940)

It is the father's character which eventually determines
order and unity in the family. He should be sincere and
majestic.

I wouldn't say that Father and Mother really disliked
Roman, or that they took a dim view of our marriage.
On the contrary, they were rather impressed by their
educated, well-bred son-in-law, and Father gladly
discussed international politics with him.
One thing, however, my parents could never forgive
Roman: his failure to share their reverence for
"things." A material possession, in our household,
meant everything; it was the measure of attained
wealth and social standing, the repository of ambitions and dreams, the symbol of a happy family life,
the goal and crowning glory of all efforts. A possession was a moral idea, character was judged by the
quality of a person's possessions, and his attitude
toward possessions determined whether or not he
could be trusted. We lived simply. Father had no expensive vices; he didn't smoke or drink. But after
almost every payday a new object appeared in our
room: a silver sugar bowl, a pillow, a lamp. On the
thirty-fifth anniversary of his employment at the
factory, the worker's committee gave Father a phono-
graph — and Father was proud to have been worthy
of such a splendid gift.
Roman never ridiculed this passion of my parents —
he considered it understandable and natural — but he
was just a little too quick in taking for granted each
new acquisition, or, once in a while, he would
absent-mindedly bump into some of the objects
arranged around the room. What's more, he sometimes spent money on flowers or theater tickets, and
when Mother and Father would begin enumerating
all the "lasting" things he could have bought instead, he just shrugged his shoulders.
When, during the First World War, Roman was called
up, Father gave him his old watch — a very good
watch, foreign-made. Roman thanked him, put the
watch in his pocket, and said nothing more about it.
But a few weeks later Father spoke up at dinner:
"Mark my words, he's bound to lose it somewhere in

the trenches."

More time went by, and then again Father remarked:
"A sloppy fellow, that hubby of yours. I'd bet my
boots someone swiped his watch without him knowing a thing about it."

After this, there were long daily discussions — that
one didn't really need a watch at the front, and that a
reasonable man would have left it at home. And besides, there were watches and watches; one should
realize this, but, regrettably, some people didn't
seem to. And, surely, there must be something behind the fact that Roman never mentioned in his
letters whether the watch was running well, whether
perhaps it needed fixing, or even whether he still
had it.

A year later Roman came home on leave. When asked
about the watch, he took it out of his pocket and put
it on the table.

"You know," said my father, "we're adults, all of us;
we understand what war is. Should, God forbid, anything happen to you . . ."

"Dad!" I exclaimed.

"Father is right," said Roman indifferently. "I'll
leave the watch at home."

"You see!" cried Father, delighted. "Roman is more
sensible than you."

Roman went back to the front, and a month later we
were notified that he had been killed in action.

I haven't spoken to Mother and Father since.

WIKTOR WOROSZYLSKI, POLISH (BORN 1927)

---

*The over-all judgment: the family prospers when the
father is indeed father, son son, elder brother elder
brother, younger brother younger brother, husband
husband, and wife wife. The principal cooperative
sphere is that between man and wife. These social relations also carry over into the public domain, such as the
faithfulness of a prince to his lord, the loyalty of a friend
to a friend, and the deference of a person of lower rank
to one of higher rank.*

The lady, by his garb beguiled,
With fearless innocence looked up and smiled.
She bade the seeming Brahman to a seat,
And gave him water for his weary feet;
And still intent on hospitable care,

Brought forth the choicest of her woodland fare. . . .
"And now," she said, "declare thy name and race,
And why thou roamest to this gloomy place."
She spoke. The stranger thundered in reply:
"Terror of men and gods and world am I,
Ravan, whose will the giant hosts obey.
Since I have seen thee, lovely one, today,
Clad in silk rainment, bright as burnished gold,
My love for all my wives is dead and cold.
Though countless dames of perfect beauty, torn
From many a pillaged realm, my home adorn.
Come fairest, come, my queen and darling be;
Among a thousand I will love but thee.
My city, Lanka, like a glittering crown,
Looks from the high brow of a mountain down
On restless ocean, which with flesh and foam
Beats with wild rage against my island Home.
There pleasant gardens shall thy steps invite
With me to wander when the moon is bright;
There in new joys thy breast shall ne'er retain
One faint remembrance of this place of pain."
Then from her breast the noble fury broke,
With flashing eyes and quivering lip she spoke:
"Me! me! the faithful wife of Rama! him
Before whose glory Indra's fame is dim;
Rama, who fails not in the battle-shock,
Fierce as the ocean steed, fast as the rock!
Rama, the Lord of each auspicious sign;
Rama, the glory of his princely line.
Me, Rama's wife — the dear, fond wife of him;
Him of the eagle eye, the lordly limb —
Me dost thou dare with words of love to press,
A jackal suing to a lioness?
As far above thy impious reach am I
As yonder sun that blazes in the sky. . . .
Thou win his wife! With lighter labor try
To pluck the sun from yonder sky;
Safer to wrap within thy robe the flame
Than woo to folly Rama's faithful dame!"
RAMAYANA, INDIAN (1000 B.C.)

No grander, more admirable, or more useful project
has occupied the human mind than that of a perpetual and universal peace among all the European
peoples; and no author has better merited the attention of the public than he who advances means of

carrying this project into effect. Indeed such an affair
is not likely to leave a sensitive and virtuous man
without some modicum of enthusiasm; and perhaps
the illusion of a truly humane heart, whose zeal
makes all things appear easy, is to be preferred to
that harsh and negative intellect which always finds
in its own indifference the first obstacle to everything which can promote the public good.
ABBÉ DE SAINT-PIERRE, FRENCH (1658–1743)

After he had completed the conquest of the Shang
people, in the second year, King Wu fell ill and was
despondent. The two lords, the duke of Shao and
T'ai-wang Kung said, "For the king's sake let us
solemnly consult the tortoise oracle." But the duke
of Chou (King Wu's younger brother, named Tan)
said, "We must not distress the ancestors, the former
kings!"
The duke of Chou then offered himself to the ancestors, constructing three altars within a single compound. Fashioning one altar on the southern side
facing north, he took his place there, holding a jade
disc and grasping a baton of jade. Then he made this
announcement to the Great King, to King Chi, and
to King Wu, his great grandfather, grandfather, and
father, and the scribe copied down the words of his
prayer on tablets:
"Your chief descendant So-and-so (King Wu's personal name is tabooed) has met with a fearful disease
and is violently ill. If you three kings are obliged to
render to Heaven the life of an illustrious son, then
substitute me, Tan, for So-and-so's person. I am
good and compliant, clever and capable. I have much
talent and much skill and can serve the spirits. Your
chief descendant has not as much talent and skill as
I and cannot serve the spirits! . . ."
Then he divined with three tortoises, and all were
auspicious. He opened the bamboo receptacles and
consulted the documents, and they too indicated an
auspicious answer. The duke of Chou said to the
king, "According to the indications of the oracle, you
will suffer no harm."
(The king said) "I, the little child, have obtained a
new life from the three kings. I shall plan for a distant end. I hope that they will think of me, the solitary man."
[240]37

After the duke of Chou returned, he placed the tablets containing the prayer in a metal-bound casket. The next day the king began to recover.

(Later, King Wu died and was succeeded by his infant son, King Ch'eng. The duke of Chou acted as regent and was slandered by King Wu's younger brothers. The young king was forced to punish the duke.)

In the autumn, when a plentiful crop had ripened but had not yet been harvested, Heaven sent great thunder and lightning accompanied by wind. The grain was completely flattened and even large trees were uprooted. The people of the land were in great fear. The king and his high ministers donned their ceremonial caps and opened the documents of the metal-bound casket and thus discovered how the duke of Chou had offered himself as a substitute for King Wu. The two lords and the king then questioned the scribe and various other functionaries, and they replied, "Yes, it is true. But his lordship forbade us to speak about it."

The king grasped the document and wept. "There is no need for us to make solemn divination about what has happened," he said. "In former times the duke of Chou toiled diligently for the royal house, but I, the youthful one, had no way of knowing it. Now Heaven has displayed its terror in order to make clear the virtue of the duke of Chou. I, the little child, will go in person to greet him, for the rites of our royal house approve such action."

When the king came out to the suburbs to meet the the duke of Chou, Heaven sent down rain and reversed the wind, so that the grain all stood up once more. The two lords ordered the people of the land to right all the large trees that had been blown over and to earth them up. Then the year was plentiful.

SHU CHING, CHINESE (400 B.C.)

38 Alienation

THE K'UEI HEXAGRAM

At the outset, the man slips into avoidable mistakes during times of opposition. When members of his own fold are estranged, he should not run after them; he should let them come back of their own accord. On the

Mr. Cobden . . . was a sensitive agitator. Generally, an agitator is a rough man of the O'Connell type, who says anything himself, and lets others say anything. "You peg into me and I will peg into you, and let us see which will win," is his motto. But Mr. Cobden's habit and feeling were utterly different. He never spoke ill of anyone. He arraigned principles, but not persons. We fearlessly say that after a career of agitation of thirty years, not one individual has — we do not say a valid charge, but a producible charge — a charge he would wish to bring forward against Mr. Cobden. You cannot find the man who says, "Mr. Cobden said this of me, and it was not true." This may seem trivial praise, and on paper it looks easy. But to those who know the great temptations of actual life it means very much. . . . Very rarely, if even ever in history, has a man achieved so much by his words — been victor in what was thought at the time to be a class struggle — and yet spoken so little evil as Mr. Cobden. There is hardly a word to be found perhaps, even now, which the recording angel would wish to blot out. We may on other grounds object to an agitator who lacerates no one, but no watchful man of the world will deny that such an agitator has vanquished one of life's most imperious and difficult temptations.
WALTER BAGEHOT, ENGLISH (1826–1877)

Misunderstanding prevents people who share an inner affinity from meeting together in the normal way. A casual meeting between the man and his master under informal circumstances proves useful.

It is when we try to grapple with another man's intimate need that we perceive how incomprehensible, wavering, and misty are the beings that share with us the sight of the stars and the warmth of the sun.
JOSEPH CONRAD, POLISH (1857–1924)

Having heard it devours the snake,

How horrid sounds the pheasant's voice.
MATSUO BASHO, JAPANESE (1644–1694)

Things look completely hopeless. The man is opposed and dishonored. But if he clings to what he believes to be right, the ending will be good.

The wintry wind blows away the snow
And knocks on the mountain window.
The bitter draught from the door
Withers the sleeping plum-blossoms,
But however much it despoils the flower,
Can it prevent the spring coming?
YUN SUN-DO, KOREAN (1587–1666)

The man finds a like-minded person among the opposition. They blend their honest desires and achieve a common goal.

Because an all-powerful police tried to force us to hold our tongues, every word took on the value of a declaration of principles. Because we were hunted down, every one of our gestures had the weight of a solemn commitment.
JEAN PAUL SARTRE, FRENCH (BORN 1905)

The true nature of the companion is revealed by looking beneath the surface. The man joins with him to deal effectively with the disunion.

Few persons have courage enough to appear as good as they really are.
JULIUS CHARLES (1795–1855) AND AUGUSTUS WILLIAM (1792–1834) HARE, ENGLISH

Cunning must be he and knavish, who would go beyond thee in all manner of guile, aye, though it were a god that met thee. Bold man, crafty in counsel, insatiate in deceit, not even in thine own land, it seems, wast thou to cease from guile and deceitful tales, which thou lovest to the bottom of thine heart. But come, let us no longer talk of this, being both well versed in craft. . . . Now am I come hither to weave a plan for thee.
HOMER, GREEK (SIXTH CENTURY B.C.)

---

*The man misjudges his friend unfairly because of mis-
understandings. But he realizes his mistake and relieves
the tension.*

Coming back from England one day I met Ysaye on
the ship. He said he had something important to tell
me, so we went to the smoking lounge and he said:
"Do you remember when we met in Berlin once and
you told me to play a composition by Moore which
left me cold?" "Yes, I remember." "And when you
asked me again at some other time, I was still very
unwilling." "I had noticed it, but did not want to
bother you further with my suggestion." "Well, I
must tell you now that as time goes on, I admire
Moore's music more and more. I have just been on
tour in England, during which I played his Violin
Concerto nine times, and my liking for it has increased so much that when I played it last night at
Plymouth I began to think it was as fine as the Beet-
hoven Concerto."
PABLO CASALS, SPANISH (BORN 1876)

*The over-all judgment: great undertakings cannot suc-
ceed during periods of division and mutual alienation.
The superior man recognizes the circumstances, does
not become impatient, and sets about achieving gradual
improvements in small matters.*

A vice-president of one Eastern corporation not long
ago plugged the carburetor in the auto of a new rival
to make him late for his first executive meeting.
A high executive of a conservative Pennsylvania corporation planted rumors that his principal rival had
"fallen for a New Dealish line," thus ruining his
chances for the presidency.
An elevator company executive waited for his rival's
special project to flop, then submitted to the boss a
series of memos (carefully backdated) to show he'd
opposed the project all along.
These businessmen were practicing the most delicate
of all arts of self-advancement—throat cutting.
WALL STREET JOURNAL, AMERICAN (1957)

It is dangerous to mention ropes
In the house of a man who was hanged.
CRISTÓBAL DE CASTILLEJO, SPANISH (1490–1550)

For what is the Holy See in relation to the masses of Catholics, and where does its strength lie? It is the organ, the mouth, the head of the Church. Its strength consists in its agreement with the general conviction of the faithful. When it expresses the common knowledge and sense of the age, or of a large majority of Catholics, its position is impregnable. The force it derives from this general support makes direct opposition hopeless, and therefore disedifying, tending only to division and promoting reaction rather than reform. The influence by which it is to be moved must be directed first on that which gives its strength, and must pervade the members in order that it may reach the head. While the general sentiment of Catholics is unaltered, the course of the Holy See remains unaltered too. As soon as that sentiment is modified, Rome sympathizes with the change. The ecclesiastical government, based upon the public opinion of the Church, and acting through it, cannot separate itself from the faithful, and keep pace with the progress of the instructed minority. It follows slowly and warily, and sometimes begins by resisting and denouncing what in the end it thoroughly adopts. Hence a direct controversy with Rome holds out the prospect of great evils, and at best a barren and unprofitable victory. The victory that is fruitful springs from that gradual change in the knowledge, the ideas, and the convictions of the Catholic body, which, in due time, overcomes the natural reluctance to forsake a beaten path, and by insensible degrees constrains the mouthpiece of tradition to conform itself to the new atmosphere with which it is surrounded. The slow, silent, indirect action of public opinion bears the Holy See along, without any demoralizing conflict or dishonourable capitulation.

BARON JOHN EMERICH ACTON, ENGLISH (1834–1902)

 # 39 Obstruction

THE CHIEN HEXAGRAM

At the outset, the man forges ahead in the face of an impasse and is overwhelmed by complications. He should wait for a favorable moment.

Boldness is a mask for fear, however great.
LUCAN, ROMAN (39–65)

---

*When duty bound, the man should seek out the danger
and deliberately face the opposition. This is especially
important for officials in the government.*

Early this morning the enemy came in sight, marching in regular order, and displaying their strength
to the greatest advantage, in order to strike us with
terror. But that was no go; they'll find that they have
to do with men who will never lay down their arms
as long as they can stand on their legs. We held a
short council of war, and finding that we should be
completely surrounded, and overwhelmed by numbers, if we remained in the town, we concluded to
withdraw to the fortress of the Alamo, and defend it
to the last extremity. We accordingly filed off, in good
order, having some days before placed all the surplus
provisions, arms, and ammunition in the fortress.
We have had a large national flag made; it is composed of thirteen stripes, red and white, alternately,
on a blue ground, with a large white star, of five
points, in the centre, and between the points the
letters T E X A S. As soon as all our little band, about
one hundred and fifty in number had entered and
secured the fortress in the best possible manner,
we set about raising our flag on the battlements . . . .
The enemy marched into Bexar, and took possession
of the town, a blood-red flag flying at their head, to
indicate that we need not expect quarters if we
should fall into their clutches. In the afternoon a
messenger was sent from the enemy to Colonel
Travis, demanding an unconditional and absolute
surrender of the garrison, threatening to put every
man to the sword in case of refusal. The only answer
he received was a cannon shot, so the messenger left
us with a flea in his ear, and the Mexicans commenced firing grenades at us . . . .
DAVID CROCKETT, AMERICAN (1786–1836)

---

*Under certain circumstances, however, it is the duty of
the man to refrain from dealing with obstructions.
Should the father, for example, fail to return from his*

It is better to live   than to lie a corpse,
  The live man catches the cow;
I saw flames rise   for the rich man's pyre,
  And before his door he lay dead.

The lame rides a horse,   the handless is herdsman,
  The deaf in battle is bold;
The blind man is better   than one that is burned,
  No good can come of a corpse.
VÖLUSPA, ICELANDIC (TWELFTH CENTURY)

The man charges ahead, only to fall back because of insufficient strength. He needs to gather trustworthy associates for the venture before it can succeed.

"Pray, look better, sir," quoth Sancho. "Those things yonder are not giants, but windmills, and the arms you fancy, are their sails, which, being whirled about the wind, make the mill go."
"It is a sign," cried Don Quixote, "thou art but little acquainted with adventures. I tell thee they are giants; and therefore, if thou art afraid, get thee aside and say your prayers, for I am resolved to engage in fierce and unequal combat against them all."
This said, he clapped spurs to his horse Rozinante, without giving ear to his squire Sancho, who bawled out to him, and assured him that they were windmills, and not giants. But he was so fully possessed with a strong conceit of the contrary that he did not so much as hear his squire's outcry, nor was he sensible of what they were, although he was already near them; far from that. "Stand, cowards," cried he as loud as he could; "stand your ground, ignoble creatures, and fly not basely from a single knight, who dares encounter you all."
At the same time the wind rising, the mill-sails began to move, which, when Don Quixote spied, "Base miscreants," cried he, "though you move more arms that the giant Briareus, ye shall pay for your arrogance." He most devoutly recommended himself to his Lady Dulcinea, imploring her assistance in this perilous adventure; and so, covering himself with

his shield, and couching his lance, he rushed with
Rozinante's utmost speed upon the first windmill
he could come at, and, running his lance into the
sail, the wind whirled about with such swiftness
that the rapidity of the motion presently broke the
lance into shivers, and hurled away both knight and
horse along with it, till down he fell, rolling a good
way off in the field. Sancho Panca ran as fast as his
ass could drive to help his master, whom he found
lying and not able to stir, such a blow he and Rozinante had received. "Mercy on me!" cried Sancho,
"did I not give your worship fair warning? Did not
I tell you they were windmills, and that nobody
could think otherwise, unless he had also windmills
in his head?"
"Peace, friend Sancho," replied Don Quixote, "there
is nothing so subject to the inconstancy of fortune as
war. I am verily persuaded, that cursed necromancer
Freston, who carried away my study and books, has
transformed these giants into windmills, to deprive
me of the honour of the victory; such is his inveterate
malice against me; but in the end, all his pernicious
wiles and stratagems shall prove ineffectual against
the prevailing edge of my sword."
MIGUEL DE CERVANTES SAAVEDRA,
SPANISH (1547–1616)

The man meets the obstruction head-on in an emer-
gency. His spirit attracts able helpers.

Ferdinand Lasalle, the brilliant social revolutionist,
once said that the war against capitalism was not a
rose water affair . . . . It is rather of the storm and
tempest order . . . . All kinds of attacks must be expected and all kinds of wounds will be inflicted . . . .
You will be assailed within and without, spat upon
by the very ones that you are doing your best to
serve, and at certain crucial moments find yourself
isolated, absolutely alone as if to compel surrender,
but in those moments, if you have the nerve you become supreme.
EUGENE VICTOR DEBS, AMERICAN (1855–1926)

What is the end of all government? Certainly the
happiness of the governed. Others may hold other
opinions, but this is mine, and I proclaim it. What

are we to think of a government whose good fortune is supposed to spring from the calamities of its subjects, whose aggrandizement grows out of the miseries of mankind? This is the kind of government exercised under the East India Company upon the natives of Hindustan; and the subversion of that infamous government is the main object of the bill in question. But in the progress of accomplishing this end, it is objected that the charter of the company should not be violated; and upon this point, sir, I shall deliver my opinion without disguise. A charter is a trust to one or more persons for some given benefit. If this trust be abused, if the benefit be not obtained, and its failure arise from palpable guilt, or (what in this case is full as bad) from palpable ignorance or mismanagement, will any man gravely say that that trust should not be resumed and delivered to other hands, more especially in the case of the East India Company, whose manner of executing this trust, whose laxity and languor, have produced, and tend to produce, consequences diametrically opposite to the ends of confiding that trust, and of the institution for which it was granted? I beg of gentlemen to be aware of the lengths to which their arguments upon the intangibility of this charter may be carried. Every syllable virtually impeaches the establishment by which we sit in this House, in the enjoyment of this freedom, and of every other blessing of our government. These kinds of arguments are batteries against the main pillar of the British Constitution. Some men are consistent with their own private opinions, and discover the inheritance of family maxims, when they question the principles of the Revolution; but I have no scruple in subscribing to the articles of that creed which produced it. Sovereigns are sacred, and reverence is due to every king; yet, with all my attachments to the person of a first magistrate, had I lived in the reign of James II, I should most certainly have contributed my efforts and borne part in those illustrious struggles which vindicated an empire from hereditary servitude, and recorded this valuable doctrine, "that trust abused is revocable."
CHARLES JAMES FOX, ENGLISH (1749–1806)

The man cannot go forward. He needs to remain where
[249]39

he is and serve the great man in order to achieve meri-
torious deeds.

God alone knows, how difficult it was to accustom
myself to this life He gave me; to go each day along
the desolate road of despair, each day to squander
feelings, to feel, to faint away; each day abandoning
the wonderful land of phantoms to return among the
reptiles and not to hiss; each day to begin a single
thought of despair, to pray with this thought — and
not to curse.
JULIUSZ SLOWACKI, POLISH (1809–1849)

---

*The over-all judgment: governing a large organization
requires timely activity and discreet inactivity on the
part of the chief executive. One must be particularly sensitive to promising circumstances, talented men, and the
right objectives.*

In every dark hour of our national life a leadership of
frankness and vigor has met with that understanding and support of the people themselves which is
essential to victory. I am convinced that you will
again give that support to leadership in these critical
days.
In such a spirit on my part and on yours we face our
common difficulties. They concern, thank God, only
material things. Values have shrunken to fantastic
levels; taxes have risen; our ability to pay has fallen;
government of all kinds is faced by serious curtail-
ment of income; the means of exchange are frozen
in the currents of trade; the withered leaves of industrial enterprise lie on every side; farmers find no markets for their produce; the savings of many years in
thousands of families are gone.
More important, a host of unemployed citizens face
the grim problem of existence, and an equally great
number toil with little return. Only a foolish optimist
can deny the dark realities of the moment . . . .
I am prepared under my constitutional duty to recommend the measures that a stricken nation in the
midst of a stricken world may require.
These measures, or such other measures as the Congress may build out of its experience and wisdom,
I shall seek, within my constitutional authority, to
bring to speedy adoption.
[250]39

But in the event that the Congress shall fail to take
one of these two courses, and in the event that
the national emergency is still critical, I shall not
evade the clear course of duty that will then confront me.
I shall ask the Congress for the one remaining instrument to meet the crisis — broad executive power to
wage a war against the emergency as great as the
power that would be given to me if we were in fact
invaded by a foreign foe.
For the trust reposed in me I will return the courage
and the devotion that befit the time. I can do no less.
PRESIDENT FRANKLIN DELANO ROOSEVELT,
AMERICAN (1882–1945)

Take, for example, the American Revolution, which
destroyed the political unity of the English race. You
will often hear this event treated simply as if it were
simply due to the wanton tyranny of an English government, which desired to reduce its colonies to servitude by taxing them without their consent. But if
you will look closely into the history of that time —
and there is no history which is more instructive —
you will find that this is a gross misrepresentation.
What happened was essentially this. England, under
the guidance of the elder Pitt, had been waging a
great and most successful war, which left her with
an enormously extended Empire, but also with an
addition of more than seventy millions to the National Debt. That debt was now nearly £400 millions, and England was reeling under the taxation
it required. The war had been waged largely in
America, and its most brilliant result was the conquest of Canada, by which the old American colonies
had benefited more than any other part of the Empire, for the expulsion of the French from North
America put an end to the one great danger which
hung over them. It was, however, extremely probable
that if France ever regained her strength, one of her
first objects would be to recover her dominion in
America.
Under these circumstances the English government
concluded that it was impossible that England alone,
overburdened as she was by taxation, could undertake the military defense of her greatly extended
Empire. Their object, therefore, was to create sub-

sidiary armies for its defense. Ireland already raised by the vote of the Irish Parliament, and out of exclusively Irish resources, an army consisting of from twelve to fifteen thousand men, most of whom were available for the general purpose of the Empire.

In India, under a despotic system a separate army was maintained for the protection of India. It was the strong belief of the English Government that a third army should be maintained in America for the defense of the American colonies and of the neighboring islands, and that it was just and reasonable that America should bear some part of the expense of her own defense. She was charged with no part of the interest of the National Debt; she paid nothing toward the cost of the navy which protected her prosperous portion of the Empire; she was the part which benefited most by the late war, and she was the part which was most likely to be menaced if the war was renewed. Under these circumstances Grenville determined that a small army of ten thousand men should be kept in America, under the distinct promise that it was never to serve beyond that country, and the West Indian Isles, and he asked America to contribute 10,000 pounds a year, or about a third part of its expense.

But here the difficulty arose. The Irish army was maintained by the vote of the Irish Parliament; but there was no single parliament representing the American colonies, and it soon became evident that it was impossible to induce thirteen legislatures to agree upon any scheme for supporting an army in America. Under these circumstances Grenville in an ill-omened moment resolved to revive a dormant power which existed in the Constitution, and levy this new war-tax by Imperial taxation. He at the same time guaranteed the colonists that the proceeds of this tax should be expended solely in America; he intimated to them in the clearest way that if they would meet his wishes by themselves providing the necessary sum, he would be abundantly satisfied, and he delayed the enforcement of the measure for a year in order to give them ample time for doing so.

Such and so small was the original cause of difference between England and her colonies. Who can fail to see that it was a difference abundantly susceptible of compromise, and that a wise and moderate statesmanship might easily have averted the catastrophe?

WILLIAM EDWARD LECKY, IRISH (1838–1903)

Govern a great nation as you would fry a small fish.

LAO-TZU, CHINESE (604–531 B.C.)

---

40 Eliminating Obstacles

THE CHIEH HEXAGRAM

At the outset, the man is freed from obstacles and is recuperating in peace.

While I, the son of Su, was sitting up one night a rat began gnawing. I knocked on the bed to stop it. It stopped for a time and then commenced again. I called the boy to bring a candle, and, after a search we found an empty sack from the interior of which came all the hullaballoo. "Ah!" I exclaimed, "This rat has got shut up here and cannot get out." So we opened the sack and looked inside. There was nothing to be seen. But, on holding up the candle we discovered there a dead rat. The boy cried out in amazement, "Can that which was just now gnawing die so quickly? Whence came the noise? Surely it was not its ghost?" Saying which he turned the rat out. Directly it touched the ground it ran off so quickly that even the sharpest-witted could not have caught it!

"How strange," said I, with a sigh, "is the artfulness of this rat. Although shut in a sack too strong for it to break through by gnawing, yet it gnaws to attract attention by the noise, and 'dies' to affect its escape under the pretense of death! I have heard it said that amongst living beings man is the most intelligent. He has tamed the Dragon, conquered the Monster, subdued the Tortoise, and hunted the Unicorn. He has, in fact, made all creatures to serve him — the master. And yet — here we have him deceived by the cunning of a solitary rat which unites the speed of a fleeing hare with the temperament of a young girl! Wherein, I wonder, lies his intelligence?"

SU TUNG-PO, CHINESE (1036–1101)

The man proceeds at a proper pace and with moderation to remove the designing individuals, who influence the ruler through flattery and obstruct public progress.

Coming into contact with barbarian peoples, you have nothing more to fear than touching the left horn of a snail. The only things one should be really anxious about are the means of mastery of the waves of the sea—and, worst of all dangers, the minds of those avid for profit and greedy of gain.
CHANG HSIEH, CHINESE (SEVENTEENTH CENTURY)

An external enemy, a privileged oppressor, can be attacked and vanquished far more easily than an internal enemy, whose forces are spread everywhere in a thousand different shapes, elusive and invulnerable, harassing us on all sides, poisoning our lives, giving us no rest. . . . This internal enemy cannot be combated with ordinary weapons; we can liberate ourselves from him only by dispelling the raw, foggy atmosphere of our lives in which he was born, grew up and gained strength, and by surrounding ourselves with an atmosphere in which he will be unable to breathe.
NIKOLAI ALEKSANDROVICH DOBROLYUBOV,
RUSSIAN (1836–1861)

The man has obtained material goods and comfort and seeks a life of ease which does not suit his nature. Like a woman's self-adornment which excites to lust, this way of life merely invites robbers and leads to humiliation.

Their [the new middle class] grandparents or even their own parents went hungry and ill clothed, and it will take some time for these people to have their fling, to eat all they want and to wear fine raiment, and flaunt authority. They must get to a state, and by slow stages too, where there is going to be something fit for education. . . . The trouble is to us old-fashioned New Englanders that "the cheap streak" so often spoils what is of good inheritance, and the wrong side of our great material prosperity is seen almost everywhere.
SARAH ORNE JEWETT, AMERICAN (1849–1909)

The man removes the inferior people who have attached

themselves to him and have even become indispensable in some respects. This is a necessary prelude to great attainments. Their departure will enable him to cultivate friends with similar views and mutual confidence.

What is it you would have of me, Doctor? Can you reasonably desire that I should make you one of the chief Omrahs of my court? Let me tell you, if you had instructed me as you should have done, nothing would be more just; for I am of this persuasion, that a child well educated and instructed is as much, at least, obliged to his master as to his father. But where are those good documents you have given me? In the first place, you have taught me that all Frangistan was nothing but I know not what little island, of which the greatest king was he of Portugal, and next to him he of Holland, and after him he of England; and as to the other kings, as those of France and Andalusia, you have represented them to me as our petty rajas, telling me that the kings of Indostan were far above them altogether, that they (the kings of Indostan) were . . . the great ones, the conquerors and kings of the world; and those of Persia and Usbec, Kashgar, Tartary and Cathay, Pegu, China and Matchina did tremble at the name of the kings of Indostan. Admirable geography! You should rather have taught me exactly to distinguish all those states of the world, and well to understand their strength, their way of fighting, their customs, religions, governments, and interests; and by the perusal of solid history, to observe their rise, progress, decay; and whence, how, and by what accidents and errors those great changes and revolutions of empires and kingdoms have happened. I have scarce learned of you the name of my grandsires, the famous founders of this empire; so far were you from having taught me the history of their life, and what course they took to make such great conquest. You had a mind to teach me the Arabian tongue, to read and to write. I am much obliged, forsooth, for having made me lose so much time upon a language that requires ten or twelve years to attain to its perfection; as if the son of a king should think it to be an honor to him to be a grammarian or some doctor of the law, and to learn other languages than of his neighbors when he can well be without them; he, to whom time is so pre-

cious for so many weighty things, which he ought by times to learn. As if there were any spirit that did not with some reluctancy, and even with a kind of debasement, employ itself in so sad and dry an exercise, so longsome and tedious, as is that of learning words.
KING AURANGZEB, INDIAN (1618–1707)

The man drives away inferior people through an inner resolve and makes a complete mental and spiritual break. They recognize his earnestness, withdraw of their own accord, and even extend begrudging approval.

Yes, I am grieved to the backbone; Mr. _____, whom you would just now meet in the carriage road and who proposes to be enchanted and in raptures with the works of God's creation, has just left the house; and — what do you think — he cooly turned up his nose at my Bahia toad, calling it an ugly brute.

That a gentleman, avowing himself a lover of natural history, and pretending an anxiety to work in the same vineyard with me, should profanely designate one of God's creatures "an ugly brute," was enough to put me out for a week, so I left him in the staircase to his own cogitations.
CHARLES WATERTON, ENGLISH (1782–1865)

My mind is fully made up. I will not indulge in the tomfoolery of *Proschit* [purification ceremony]. No, not even if I die for it. I have been provoked and have been dragged from my seclusion into public notice. But my enemies will find me a hard nut to crack. I know what your *biradari* [caste] is and if necessary, in self-defense, I will ruthlessly and mercilessly lay bare the tattered fabric of its existence and tear it into the minutest possible shreds. I am only waiting for some foeman worthy of my steel to take the field and will then be ready to break a lance with him. . . . So long as H and others of his ilk howl and bark I will pass them by with the most studied indifference and contemptuous silence.
PUNDIT MOTILAL NEHRU, INDIAN (1861–1931)

Using hitherto concealed, ready, and perfect instruments, the man removes the powerful promoter of obstruction and rebellion.

A certain jackal, as he was roaming about the borders of a town, just as his inclinations led him, fell into a dyer's vat; but being unable to get out, in the morning he feigned himself dead. At length, the master of the vat, which was filled with indigo, came, and seeing a jackal lying with his legs uppermost, his eyes closed, and his teeth bare, concluded that he was dead, and so, taking him out, he carried him a good way from the town, and there left him. The sly animal instantly got up, and ran into the woods; when, observing that his coat was turned blue, he meditated in this manner: "I am now of the finest color! What great exaltation may I not bring about for myself?" Saying this, he called a number of jackals together, and addressed them in the following words: "Know that I have lately been sprinkled king of the forests, by the hands of the goddess herself who presides over these woods, with a water drawn from a variety of choice herbs. Observe my color, and henceforward let every business be transacted according to my orders." The rest of the jackals, seeing him of such a fine complexion, prostrated themselves before him, and said: "According to Your Highness' commands!" By this step he made himself honored by his own relations, and so gained the supreme power over those of his own species, as well as all the other inhabitants of the forests. But after a while, finding himself surrounded by a levee of the first quality, such as the tiger and the like, he began to look down upon his relations; and, at length, he kept them at a distance. A certain old jackal, perceiving that his brethren were very much cast down at this behavior, cried: "Do not despair! If it continue thus, this imprudent friend of ours will force us to be revenged. Let me alone to contrive his downfall. The lion, and the rest who pay him court, are taken by his outward appearance; and they obey him as their king, because they are not aware that he is nothing but a jackal; do something then by which he may be found out. Let this plan be pursued: Assemble all of you, in a body about the close of the evening, and set up one general howl in his hearing; and I'll warrant you, the natural disposition of his species will incline him to join in the cry; for

Whatever may be the natural propensity of anyone is very hard to be overcome. If a dog were

[257]40

made king, would he not gnaw his shoe straps?
And thus the tiger, discovering that he is nothing but
a jackal, will presently put him to death." The plan
was executed, and the event was just as it had been
foretold.
HITOPADESA, INDIAN (FOURTEENTH CENTURY)

*The over-all judgment: the tension eases. The sooner
things return to their accustomed ways the better. The
new masters should not change the existing manners and
customs. Loose ends should be tied together as soon as
possible, so as to begin a new slate.*

The Roman state stands by ancient customs and its
manhood.
QUINTUS ENNIUS, ROMAN (239–169 B.C.)

"Is Lee over there?" pointing up the road.
"Yes, he is in that brick house, waiting to surrender
to you."
"Well, then, we'll go over," said Grant.
. . . Lee had been waiting there, in a high-backed
armchair by the window, for a half-hour before Grant
came. He arose as Grant entered with extended hand,
saying "General Lee." They shook hands and began
talking of the days when they had met before, in
Mexico. The *Memoirs* go on with the story: "Our
conversation grew so pleasant that I almost forgot the
object of our meeting. After conversation had run on
in this style for some time General Lee called my
attention to the object of our meeting."
Grant had stated his terms, that Lee's army "should
lay down their arms, not to take them up again" unless properly exchanged. Again the talk wandered off
into other fields and again Lee had to interrupt with
the suggestion that Grant write out the terms he
proposed. Paroles were to be given that officers and
men were not to take up arms against the United
States until properly exchanged; all arms and public
property were to be surrendered. "This will not embrace the side-arms of the officers, nor their private
horses or baggage. This done, each officer and man
will be allowed to return to their homes, not to be
disturbed by United States authority so long as they
observe their paroles and the laws in force where
they may reside."
[258]40

As Grant finished writing Lee took from his pocket a pair of steel-rimmed spectacles, pushed some books aside on the table beside him, and carefully read what had been written. When he came to the last sentence he showed his appreciation and, with some degree of warmth in his manner, said: "This will have a very happy effect on my army."

When Grant asked him for suggestions he pointed out that the horses of the calvary and artillery belonged to the men who used them, and he was immediately told that the parole officers would be instructed "to let all the men who claim to own a horse or mule take the animals home with them to work their little farms."

Then Grant asked about his need of rations, remembering that Sheridan had the cars that should have reached Amelia, and when Lee told him of this situation he gave orders that sufficient should be turned over to answer all their need.

The letters containing the terms and their acceptance were signed, the last formalities were over, and Lee left the room. He signaled to his orderly to bridle his horse, and standing on the steps of the porch he looked out over the valley where his army lay, smiting the glove he carried in his right hand on his left, in an absent sort of a way, and seeming to see nothing till his horse was led in front of him; then mounted and rode away. As he was going Grant came to the door and saluted him in silence.

. . . And when the firing of salutes began to sound from his own lines he stopped them with the words, "The war is over; the rebels are our countrymen again; and the best sign of rejoicing after the victory will be to abstain from all demonstrations in the field."

WILLIAM E. BROOKS, AMERICAN (BORN 1875)

We have a maxim in the House of Commons, and written on the walls of our house, that old ways are the safest and surest ways.

SIR EDWARD COKE, ENGLISH (1552–1634)

At the outset, the man disregards his own interests to help his superior. The latter should be sensitive to the amount of such help that can be accepted without harm to the subordinate. Neither should a subordinate give without due consideration.

Living in extreme poverty, Federigo was seldom in a state to receive any one in his house, and this morning being less prepared than usual, and finding nothing to show respect to a lady in whose honor he had entertained such numbers of people, he was grieved beyond measure, and stood in great perplexity, inveighing against his evil fortune as a man bereft of his senses, and running hither and thither, and finding neither money nor provisions and the hour being late, and his desire being great to show the lady some mark of attention, happening to cast his eyes on his favorite falcon, which was resting on its perch in his chamber, and seeing no other resource, he seized the poor bird, and finding it fat and in good condition thought it would be a dish worthy of the lady, without further hesitation he wrung its neck, and giving it to a girl, ordered her to pluck it and place it on the spit and carefully roast it. He then spread on his table a napkin of snowy whiteness, one of the few things which yet remained to him of his former possessions, and after some time, with a cheerful aspect returned into the garden to the lady and told her that a dinner, the best he could provide, was prepared for her. On this the lady with her companion went and sat themselves at the table, where Federigo with great courtesy waited on them, whilst they unknowingly ate his favorite falcon. When they had risen from the table, after some agreeable conversation, it seemed to the lady to be now a proper time to make known the purpose of her visit, and turning politely to Federigo, she thus spoke: "Calling to recollection your past life, Federigo, and remembering my reserve, which you perhaps esteemed hard-heartedness and cruelty, I doubt not that you will wonder at my presumption when you learn the

object of my visit; but if you now had, or ever had
had children, and know the strength of a parent's
affection, I feel assured that you would in some measure pardon me; and though you have none, I, who
have a dear and beloved son, cannot yet forego the
common affections of a mother. I am, then, by maternal love and duty compelled to ask you the gift of
a possession which I know is indeed very dear to
you, and justly so, since your evil fortune has left
you no other comfort in your adversity. The gift then
I ask is your falcon, which my son is so desirous of
possessing, that if I do not obtain it for him, I fear it
will so aggravate the illness under which he labors,
that I shall lose him."

GIOVANNI BOCCACCIO, ITALIAN (1313–1375)

---

*The man renders faithful service without sacrificing
himself. Forfeiting one's dignity and personality to do
the bidding of a person of high rank is shameful.*

A prowling wolf, whose shaggy skin
(So strict the watch of dogs had been)
  Hid little but his bones,
Once met a mastiff dog astray.
A prouder, fatter, sleeker Tray
  No human mortal owns.
  Sir Wolf, in famished plight,
  Would fain have made a ration
  Upon his fat relation:
  But then he first must fight;
  And well the dog seemed able
  To save from the wolfish table
  His carcass snug and tight.
So, then in civil conversation,
The wolf expressed his admiration
Of Tray's fine case. Said Tray, politely,
"Yourself, good Sir, may be as sightly:
Quit but the woods, advised by me;
For all your fellows here, I see,
Are shabby wretches, lean and gaunt,
Belike to die of haggard want.
With such a pack, of course, it follows,
One fights for every bit he swallows.
  Come, then, with me and share
On equal terms our princely fare."
  "But what with you

Has one to do?"
Inquires the wolf. "Light work indeed,"
Replies the dog; "you only need
To bark a little now and then,
To chase off duns and beggar-men, —
To fawn on friends that come or go forth,
Your master please, and so forth;
  For which you have to eat
  All sorts of well-cooked meat —
Cold pullets, pigeons, savory messes —
Besides unnumbered fond caresses."
  The wolf, by force of appetite,
  Accepts the terms outright,
  Tears glistening in his eyes;
  But faring on, he spies
A galled spot on the mastiff's neck.
"What's that?" he cries. "Oh, nothing but a speck."
"A speck?" — "Ay, ay, 'tis not enough to pain me.
Perhaps the collar's mark by which they chain me."
"Chain! chain you! What! run you not, then,
  Just where you please and when?"
"Not always, Sir; but what of that?"
"Enough for me, to spoil your fat!
It ought to be a precious price
Which could do servile chains entice;
For me, I'll shun them while I've wit."
So ran Sir Wolf, and runneth yet.
FELIX MARIA DE SAMANIEGO, SPANISH (1745–1801)

---

*A close bond is possible only between two persons. A
group of three engenders jealousy. The lone man finds
a complementary companion.*

They asked me: "Are you happy
To love her, though her teeth are gappy?"
I said: "I am delighted
With pools that other men have slighted.

"For when, within your knowing,
Were mosses found on waters growing
Where people every minute
Come down, to dip their buckets in it?"
IBN SHAKIL, MOORISH (THIRTEENTH CENTURY)

The King of Wei sent the King of Ch'u a beautiful
girl. The king was delighted with her, and his con-
sort, Cheng Hsiu, aware of the king's infatuation,

treated the girl with special affection. . . . When she was sure that the king would not suspect her of jealousy, she said to the new girl, "The king is much taken with your beauty but he does not seem to care for your nose. I suggest you always keep your nose covered." Accordingly, whenever the new girl visited the king, she would cover her nose.

"I notice," said the king to Cheng Hsiu, "that when the new girl is with me she covers her nose. Why is that, I wonder?"

"I could tell you why —" said Cheng Hsiu.

"If you know, then tell me, no matter how bad it is," the king insisted.

"It would seem," said Cheng Hsiu, "that she does not like the way you smell."

"What insolence!" exclaimed the king. "Let her nose be cut off at once!" he ordered. "See that there is no delay in carrying out the command!"

INTRIGUES OF THE WARRING STATES,
CHINESE (480–222 B.C.)

As a consequence of giving up his bad habits, the man attracts the help of well-disposed friends.

He who bends to himself a Joy
Does the winged life destroy;
But he who kisses the Joy as it flies
Lives in Eternity's sunrise.

WILLIAM BLAKE, ENGLISH (1757–1827)

Fate has marked the man for good fortune. Nothing opposes him. He needs fear nothing.

To all men thou dost slander me;
To all men I speak well of thee;
How sad to think we're dubbed a pair of arrant liars
  everywhere.

BERNARD DE LA MONNOIE, FRENCH (1641–1728)

Mohammed, Emir of Granada, kept
His brother Yusuf captive in the hold
Of Salobrina. When Mohammed lay
Sick unto death, and knew that he must die,
He wrote with his own hand, and sealed the scroll
With his own seal, and sent to Khaled, "Slay
  Thy prisoner, Yusuf."

[263]41

At the chess-board sat,
Playing the game of kings, as friend with friend,
The captive and his gaoler, whom he loved.
Backward and forward swayed the mimic war;
Hither and thither glanced the knight across
The field—the Queen swept the castles down, and
     passed
Trampling through the ranks, when in her path
A castle rose, threatened a knight in flank—
"Beware, my lord—or else I take the Queen!"
Swift, on his word, a knocking at the gate.
"Nay, but my castle holds the King in check!"
And in the doorway stood a messenger,
"Behold!—a message from my lord the King!"
And Khaled stood upon his feet, and reached
His hand to take the scroll, and bowed his head
O'er the King's seal.
     "Friend, thou hast ridden fast?"
The man spake panting, and the sweat ran down
His brow and fell like raindrops on the flags—
"I left Granada at the dawn—the King
Had need of haste."
     And Khaled broke the seal
And read with livid lips, and spake no word,
But thrust the scroll into his breast. . . . Then turned
And bade the man go rest, and eat, and drink. . . .
But Yusuf smiled, and said: "O friend—and doth
My brother ask my head of thee?" Then he
Whose wrung heart choked the answer gave the
     scroll
To Yusuf's hand, but spake not. Yusuf read
Unto the end, and laid the parchment down,
"Yet there is time—shall we not end the game?
Thy castle menaces my King—behold!
A knight has saved the King!"
     But Khaled's knees
Were loosed with dread, and white his lips; he fell
Back on the couch, and gazed on Yusuf's face
Like one astonished. Yusuf's fearless eyes
Smiled back at his, unconquered. "Brother, what
So troubles thee? What can Mohammed do,
Save send me forth to find—only, maybe,
A little sooner than I else had gone—
The truth of those things whereof thou and I
Have questioned oft? Tomorrow at this time
I shall know all Aflatoun knew, and thou

Shalt know one day. And, since we have this hour,
Play we the game to the end."
    Then Khaled moved
A pawn with trembling fingers.
    "See — thy Queen
Is left unguarded. Nay! — thy thought had strayed —
I will not take her."
    Khaled cast himself
Down on his face, and cried, like one in pain:
"Be thou or more or less — I am but man!
For me to see thee go unto thy death
Is not a morning's pastime."
    "Nay — and yet
Were it not well to keep this thought of me
In this last hour together, as if our
Mohammed could not conquer? — I perchance
May yet look back. . . . But hark — Who comes?
    Aloud
The thundering hoofs upon the drawbridge rang
Of Andalusian stallions; and a voice
Cried: "Hail! King Yusuf!" — drowned in answering
    shouts
And hammering lance-shafts thick upon the gate
Then Khaled, trembling, stood, with ashen lips,
Listening, as in a dream. And unto him
Came Yusuf — caught him in his arms. "Heart friend!
Fear not, all's well. The king shall not forget
Who loved him, even to the brink of death!
Look up, beloved!
    "See, thou hast swept the men
From the board. 'Twas writ in heaven, we two
Should never play that game unto the end!"
LONDON SPEAKER, ENGLISH (NINETEENTH CENTURY)

---

*The man increases in power and dispenses blessings to
the world without diminishing his own resources. Everyone willingly serves him because he does not siphon off
resources to his private advantage.*

(Trajan knew that) the goodness of government is
shown both in its earnest aspects and its amuse-
ments; and that whilst neglect of serious business
was harmful, neglect of amusement caused discontent; even distributions of money were less
desired than games; further largesses of corn and
money pacified only a few or even individuals only,
[265]41

but games the whole people.
MARCUS CORNELIUS FRONTO,
ROMAN (SECOND CENTURY)

"Child," Lord Arglay said, "I am an old man and I have known nothing all my life farther or greater than the work I have taken to do. I have never seen a base for any temple nor found an excuse to believe in the myths that are told there. I will not say *believe* or *do not believe*. But there is one thing only of which I have wondered at times, and yet it seemed foolish to think of it. It will happen sometimes when one has worked hard and done all that one can for the purpose before one — it has happened then that I have stood up and been content with the world of things and with what has been done there through me. And this may be pride, or it may be the full stress of the whole being and delight in labour — there are a hundred explanations. But I have wondered whether that profound repose was not communicated from some far source and whether the life that is in it was altogether governed by time. And I am sure that state never comes while I am concerned with myself."
CHARLES WILLIAMS, ENGLISH (1886–1945)

The over-all judgment: the diminution of excesses in one quarter to the benefit of another brings the situation into concordance with right and reason. Accordingly, the sage restrains his wrath and represses his desires. Let there be sincerity in this and conformity to the times. Poverty should not be covered with empty pretences. Even sacrifices to heaven may be simple.

When an artist for the purpose of embellishing nature adds green to the springtime, rose to the dawn, red to young lips, he creates ugliness because he lies. When he softens the grimace of pain, the flabbiness of old age, the hideousness of the perverse, when he arranges nature, when he veils her, disguises her, when he softens her in order to please an ignorant public, he creates ugliness because he is afraid of the truth.
FRANÇOIS AUGUSTE RENÉ RODIN, FRENCH (1840–1917)

To every *thing there is* a season, and a time to every purpose under the heaven:

[266]41

A time to be born, and a time to die; a time to plant,
and a time to pluck up *that which* is planted;
A time to kill, and a time to heal; a time to break
down, and a time to build up;
A time to weep, and a time to laugh; a time to mourn,
and a time to dance;
A time to cast away stones, and a time to gather
stones together; a time to embrace, and a time to
refrain from embracing;
A time to get, and a time to lose; a time to keep, and
a time to cast away;
A time to rend, and a time to sew; a time to keep
silence, and a time to speak;
A time to love, and a time to hate; a time of war, and
a time of peace.
ECCLESIASTES, HEBREW (SECOND CENTURY B.C.)

Steadfastly the will
Must toil thereto, till efforts end in ease,
And thought has passed from thinking. Shaking off
All longings bred by dreams of fame and gain,
Shutting the doorways of the senses close
With watchful ward; so, step by step, it comes
To gift of peace assured and heart assuaged,
When the mind dwells self-wrapped, and the soul
    broods
Cumberless. But, as often as the heart
Breaks — wild and wavering — from control, so oft
Let him re-curb it, let him rein it back
To the soul's governance! For perfect bliss
Grows only in the bosom tranquillized,
The spirit passionless, purged from offence,
Vowed to the Infinite. He who thus vows
His soul to the Supreme Soul, quitting sin,
Passes unhindered to the endless bliss
Of unity with Brahma.
BHAGAVAD GITA, INDIAN (FIRST CENTURY B.C.)

42 Help From Above
THE I HEXAGRAM

*At the outset, the man receives help from on high. He
should use it to accomplish something correspondingly
worthwhile. Success will cause his rashness to be forgotten.*

Who so desires the ocean makes light of streams.
AHMAD IBN-AL-HUSAYN AL-MUTANABBI,
SYRIAN (915–965)

Success is a rare paint, hides all the ugliness.
JOHN SUCKLING, ENGLISH (1609–1642)

---

*The ensuing gains issue naturally from the inner good-
ness of the man, who is in harmony with the highest
laws of the universe.*

He, full of bashfulness and truth, loved much, hoped
little, and desired naught.
TORQUATO TASSO, ITALIAN (1544–1595)

Well, he had something, though he called it nothing —
An ass's wit, a hair-belly shrewdness
That would appraise the intentions of the angel
By the very yard-stick of his own confusion,
And bring the most to pass.
ROBERT RANKE GRAVES, IRISH (BORN 1895)

---

*Even unfortunate events accrue to the good of the man.
Pursued with reasonableness and sincerity, they exert
beneficial influence, as if officially sanctioned.*

It is not bad. Let them play.
Let the guns bark and the bombing-plane
Speak his prodigious blasphemies.
It is not bad, it is high time,
Stark violence is still the sire of all the world's values.

What but the wolf's tooth whittled so fine
The fleet limbs of the antelope?
What but fear winged the birds, and hunger
Gemmed with such eyes the great goshawk's head?
Violence has been the sire of all the world's values.

Who would remember Helen's face
Lacking the terrible halo of spears?
Who formed Christ but Herod and Caesar,
The cruel and bloody victories of Caesar?
Violence has been the sire of all the world's values.

Never weep, let them play,
Old violence is not too old to beget new values.

ROBINSON JEFFERS, AMERICAN (1887–1962)

---

[268]42

*As the mediator between the prince and his followers,
the man renders proper advice on the distribution of
benefits. If he does not retain portions for selfish purposes
and follows a moderate course, he will retain the confidence of all for executing critical projects.*

I [a civil servant] possess great power, and I may do
you harm. I do not, however, act for myself, but for
the public good as determined by the legislature or
the local authorities and often by direct representa-
tions from the public. Nor do I act arbitrarily, but
according to rules which are equally valid for everybody. Not my will prevails, but the will of other
members of the public. If, therefore, you quarrel with
my powers, you should not blame their immediate
executor but their ultimate creator. Yet, of course,
some discretion is necessarily left to me, and I know
that I ought to exercise this with all politeness,
understanding, and the infliction of the least amount
of necessary pain. Like all men — like you, for example, — I am sustained in my work by my pay and
other rights, my zeal is not consistently at its highest
level, and I have alternations of mood (sometimes I
am alert, sometimes slack), yet I will not deny my
services because they are troublesome to me and because they are just a little beyond the minimum
which will forestall and avoid complaint, but positively seize opportunities to be helpful, fitting the
remedy carefully to the case. Your own roughness,
accent, and social standing may affect me, but I will
try to avoid letting them improperly bias my reasoned judgment. Business would proceed more
speedily and appropriately if you would cooperate
with me by recognizing my difficult position and
treating me with sympathy rather than hostility, if
you read all the rules which you are supposed to read
and keep, before you fly into a temper because mistakes have occurred, and if you willingly cooperated
on the various committees which are and should be
established for collaboration.
Even with all the arrangements and personal control
which conduce to smooth working of the service and
satisfaction of the public, I may still suffer from unsympathetic treatment because ultimately I am the
representative of the state — that is, the whole of the
public! You will of course enjoy my power and
[269]42

applaud it when it does you some immediate good:
I must beg you to recall the significance of my work
when I have to weigh the rest of the public good
against you. I at least am a member of a body which
is neutral in the state, or rather helpful to all. You
cannot buy more of my services if you happen to be
well off, you will not get less if you happen to be
badly off; you will not be passed over if you belong
to one particular party or given special privileges if
you belong to another. We represent the unity and
collective control of the state. I give the whole of my
time to the work and am as entitled to my pay and
pension and other rights as any other worker. If my
services are intangible or misunderstood they are
nevertheless productive and important. Without
them, your state will be nothing but a desert full of
the discordant noises of people giving contradictory
orders: It will crumble and cease to be a state — for a
state is coordinated action.
HERMAN FINER, AMERICAN (BORN 1878)

Benefits are only accepted so far as they can be re-
quited; beyond that point, instead of gratitude they
excite hatred.
CORNELIUS TACITUS, ROMAN (55–117)

---

*Without asking for recognition and gratitude, the man in
a high position benefits those below. He acts from the
inner necessity of acknowledged goodness.*

Considered as artists, we perhaps have no need to
interfere in the affairs of the world. But considered as
men, yes. The miner who is exploited or shot down,
the slaves in the camps, those in the colonies, the
legions of persecuted throughout the world — they
need all those who can speak to communicate their
silence and to keep in touch with them. I have not
written, day after day, fighting articles and texts, I
have not taken part in the common struggles because
I desire the world to be covered with Greek statues
and masterpieces. The man who has such a desire
does exist in me. Except that he has something better
to do in trying to instill life into the creatures of his
imagination. But from my first articles to my latest
book I have written so much, and perhaps too much,
only because I cannot keep from being drawn toward
[270]42

everyday life, toward those, whoever they may be, who are humiliated and debased. They need to hope, and if all keep silent or if they are given a choice between two kinds of humiliation, they will be forever deprived of hope and we with them. It seems to me impossible to endure that idea, nor can he who cannot endure it lie down to sleep in his tower. Not through virtue, as you see, but through a sort of almost organic tolerance, which you feel or do not feel. Indeed, I see many who fail to feel it, but I cannot envy their sleep.

ALBERT CAMUS, FRENCH (1913–1960)

There was, however, one small incident of my boyhood days which . . . must have meant a good deal to me or it would not have stayed in my memory, clear and sharp, vivid and shadowless, all these slow-drifting years. We had a little slave boy whom we had hired from some one, there in Hannibal. He was from the eastern shore of Maryland, and had been brought away from his family and friends, halfway across the American continent and sold. He was a cheery spirit, innocent and gentle, and the noisiest creature that ever was, perhaps. All day long he was singing, whistling, yelling, whooping, laughing—it was maddening, devastating, unendurable. At last, one day, I lost all my temper, and went raging to my mother and said Sandy had been singing for an hour without a single break, and I couldn't stand it, and *wouldn't* she please shut him up. The tears came into her eyes and her lip trembled, and she said something like this:

"Poor thing, when he sings it shows that he is not remembering, and that comforts me; but when he is still I am afraid he is thinking and I cannot bear it. He will never see his mother again; if he can sing, I must not hinder it, but be thankful for it. If you were older, you would understand me; then that friendless child's noise would make you glad."

MARK TWAIN, AMERICAN (1835–1910)

The man in a high position fails to bring benefits to those below. They, in turn, assail his reputation and do not support him. He does not think before speaking and does not decide the principles that govern his relationships before he sets forth.

. . . after garnering all that was most profitable in you,
after consuming the most fruitful years of your life
and the greatest vigor of your body, after reducing
you to a thing of rags and tatters, he is looking for a
rubbish heap on which to cast you aside uncere-
moniously, and for another man to engage who can
stand the work. Under the charge that you once made
overtures to a page of his, or that, in spite of your
age, you are trying to seduce an innocent girl, or
something else of that sort, you leave at night, hiding
your face, bundled out neck and crop, destitute of
everything and at the end of your tether, taking with
you, in addition to the burden of your years, that
excellent companion, gout.

LUCIAN, GREEK (SECOND CENTURY)

*The over-all judgment: sacrifice by those above to in-
crease the resources and happiness of those below
engenders the devotion of the people. This makes challenging enterprises successful. The limited time for such
favorable actions should be utilized while it lasts.*

Now we learn that in the dim past, in the august era
of a certain most revered Mikado, the Empire was
ruled with great kindness: that the palace was
thatched with reeds and its eaves were not repaired,
because it was seen that little smoke went up from
the houses, and the taxes were on that account re-
mitted. So did the sovereign have pity on his people
and help them in their distress.

KAMO NO-CHOMEI, JAPANESE (THIRTEENTH CENTURY)

After wandering through jungles and forests, the
sultan came across the hut of a poor peasant. Over
the door he saw two dead dogs hung from their
necks by ropes. The peasant recognized his ruler,
quickly humbling himself and offering the sultan the
hospitality of his home.

"I will not enter until you have told me why these
dogs hang over your door," the sultan answered.

"Oh, Sultan of all the World," the peasant replied.
"I hanged these two creatures because they betrayed
me. As my small herd of cattle was disappearing one
after another, I hid myself one day by the grazing
grounds next to the river. Soon crocodiles came to

feed on the cattle. Instead of driving them off or
barking a warning, my dogs played with the crocodiles, allowing them to carry off one more of my
herd. So I hanged the dogs for their faithless betrayal."

The sultan returned to his palace where he reflected
on the poor peasant's tale. "There is a lesson here,"
he thought. "It is a revelation from Allah! My subjects are like the peasant's herd. Yet I put their care
in the hands of unfaithful ministers." Realizing this,
the sultan called for the imperial account books. Even
a brief examination showed that not only had Minister Rassat stolen from the imperial treasury, but
that he had extorted vast sums of wealth in return
for official pardons as well.

The Sultan of Kembajat closed the account books and
commanded that a plaque be fashioned, upon which
he had engraved in letters of gold:

> While a foolish ruler may squander his subject's
> bread,
> A corrupt minister will surely lose his head.

The plaque was fastened to the palace gate beside the
dangling corpse of the greedy Rassat — hanged as
were dogs over the door to the poor peasant's hut.

BOKHARI, MALAYAN (SEVENTEENTH CENTURY)

The old Quaker was right: "I expect to pass through
life but once. If there is any kindness, or any good
thing I can do to my fellow beings, let me do it now.
I shall pass this way but once."

WILLIAM CHANNING GANNETT, AMERICAN (1840–1924)

≣≣≣≣ 43 Removing Corruption

THE KUAI HEXAGRAM

---

*At the outset, the man presses forward prematurely
without sufficient preparation and strength. Initial setbacks due to blind miscalculations are grounds for blame.*

Until the Donkey tried to clear
The Fence, he thought himself a Deer.

ARTHUR GUITERMAN, AMERICAN (1871–1943)

The man remains alert to unseen dangers at all times. Hostile measures against him will fail even at night because of his guarded alertness.

It has been related that dogs drink at the river Nile running along, that they may not be seized by the crocodiles.
PHAEDRUS, ROMAN (FIRST CENTURY)

The man displays his purposes too openly. The superior man does not show outward hostility when bent on cutting off the criminal, since the time is not ripe and the inferior man will endanger the situation through countermeasures. He resolves the difficulty by maintaining outward politeness, avoiding recriminations, and awaiting the propitious opportunity. Although he is misunderstood and maligned by the multitude, there will be no blame in the end.

Speech was given to the ordinary sort of men whereby to communicate their mind; but to wise men, whereby to conceal it.
ROBERT SOUTH, ENGLISH (1634–1716)

The man is restless and wishes to enforce his will by stubbornly pushing forward. But he meets with insuperable antagonisms. Advice to desist and to follow others is ignored.

But hardly had he set foot into the darkness when he realized, as though condemned by an irrevocable judgment, that his fate was to be fulfilled without delay. He called out into the emptiness in anger and sorrow.
"O Invisible Spirit, who has three times warned me and whom I have thrice refused to believe. O Spirit to whom I now bow down as to one stronger than I, tell me, ere thou destroyest me, who thou art?"
Again the voice rang out, stiflingly close at hand and immeasurably far away:
"No mortal hath yet known me. Many names have I: the superstitious call me Destiny, fools call me Luck, and pious call me God. To those who deem themselves wise I am that Power which was in the Beginning and continues without and through all Eternity."
[274]43

"Then I curse thee in this my last moment," shouted the youth with bitterness of death in his heart. "If thou art indeed the Power that was in the Beginning and continues without and through all Eternity, then was it fated that all should happen as it did — that I should go through the forest and commit murder, that I should cross this meadow and bring ruin upon my Fatherland, that I should climb this rock and here find death — all this despite thy warning. But why was I condemned to hear thee speak to me thrice, if thy warning was not to help me? And why, oh, irony of ironies! must I in this my last moment whimper my feeble question to thee?"
An answer was made to the youth, stern and terrible, and in a peel of mysterious laughter that echoed to the utmost confines of the invisible heavens. As he tried to catch the words the earth moved and sank from under his feet. He fell, deeper than a million bottomless pits, amid all the lurking nights of time, that have been and will be, from the Beginning to the End of all things.
ARTHUR SCHNITZLER, AUSTRIAN (1862–1931)

Uprooting corruption from high offices requires the utmost determination.

I abominate abominable things. . . . I will not approach filth with my hands.
BOOK OF THE DEAD, EGYPTIAN (400 B.C.)

A revolution is not the same as inviting people to dinner, or writing an essay, or painting a picture, or doing fancy needlework; it cannot be anything so refined, so calm, so gentle, or so mild, kind, courteous, restrained and magnanimous. A revolution is an uprising, an act of violence whereby one class overthrows another. A rural revolution is revolution by which the peasantry overthrows the authority of the feudal landlord class. If the peasants do not use the maximum of their strength, they can never overthrow the authority of the landlords which has been deeply rooted for thousands of years. In the rural areas, there must be a great, fervent revolutionary upsurge, which alone can arouse hundreds and thousands of the people to form a great force. . . . To put it bluntly, it was necessary to bring about a brief reign

of terror in every rural area; otherwise one could never suppress the activities of the counter-revolutionaries in the countryside or overthrow the authority of the gentry. To right a wrong it is necessary to exceed the proper limits, and the wrong cannot be righted without the proper limits being exceeded.
CHAIRMAN MAO TSE-TUNG, CHINESE (BORN 1893)

Just as victory is at hand, the man finds no helpers to eradicate the remaining evil. The evil conceals itself, only to spring up again at a later time.

A tendency to superstition is of the very essence of humanity; and, when we think we have completely extinguished it, we shall find it retreating into the strangest nooks and corners, that it may issue out thence on the first occasion it can do with safety.
JOHANN WOLFGANG VON GOETHE, GERMAN (1749–1832)

Tell me, what is the final integer, the one at the very top, the biggest of all.
But that's ridiculous! Since the number of integers is infinite, how can you have a final integer?
Well then how can you have a final revolution? There is no final revolution. Revolutions are infinite.
YEVGENI IVANOVICH ZAMYATIN, RUSSIAN (1884–1937)

The over-all judgment: a fight without quarter is necessary to remove corrupt and powerful bureaucrats. This requires more the strength of character than of arms. The culprit's guilt must be openly proclaimed at court. The leader's own shortcomings must be corrected. He must eventually employ force after he has convinced his adherents of his extreme reluctance to do so.

Extravagant emotion is the fever that purges the soul of impurity.
ARNOLD SCHÖNBERG, AUSTRIAN (1874–1951)

It is not enough to do good; one must do it the right way.
JOHN VISCOUNT MORLEY, ENGLISH (1838–1923)

Lord Coke gravely informs us that corporations cannot be excommunicated, because they have no souls, and they appear to be as destitute of every feeling as if they had also no bowels. . . . There is in truth but

one point through which they are vulnerable, and
that is the keyhole of the cash box.
HUGO GROTIUS, DUTCH (1583–1645)

44 Infiltration by Inferior Men

THE KOU HEXAGRAM

*At the outset, the inferior man has wormed his way into
the organization. He must be held in check energetically,
otherwise he will grow disgusting and dangerous.*

The law often allows what honor forbids.
BERNARD J. SAURIN, FRENCH (1706–1781)

Deep the waters of the Black Pool, coloured like ink;
They say a Holy Dragon lives there, whom men have
    never seen.
Beside the Pool they have built a shrine; the authori-
    ties have established a ritual;
A dragon by itself remains a dragon, but men can
    make it a god.
Prosperity and disaster, rain and drought, plagues
    and pestilences —
By the village people were all regarded as the Sacred
    Dragon's doing.
They made offerings of suckling-pig and poured
    libations of wine;
The morning prayers and evening gifts depended in
    a "medium's" advice.
  When the dragon comes, ah!
  The wind stirs and sighs.
  Paper money thrown, ah!
  Silk umbrellas waved.
  When the dragon goes, ah!
  The wind also — still.
  Incense-fire dies, ah!
  The cups and vessels are cold.
Meats lie stacked on the rocks of the Pool's shore;
Wind flows on the grass in front of the shrine.
I do not know, of all those offerings, how much the
    Dragon eats;
But the mice of the woods and the foxes of the hills
    are continually drunk and sated.
Why are the foxes so lucky?
What have the suckling-pigs done,

[277]44

That year by year *they* should be killed, merely to
glut the foxes?
That the foxes are robbing the Sacred Dragon and
eating His suckling-pig,
Beneath the nine-fold depths of His pool, does He
know or not.
PO CHÜ-I, CHINESE (772–846)

---

*The inferior element is contained not by force but by
gentle means. No error will issue from such a course.
However, contact of the inferior with those farther away
must be prevented. Otherwise, the evil will spread.*

Turning the other cheek is a kind of moral jiu-jitsu.
GERALD STANLEY LEE, AMERICAN (BORN 1862)

When the world has once begun to use us ill, it afterwards continues the same treatment with less scruple
and ceremony, as men do to a whore.
JONATHAN SWIFT, ENGLISH (1667–1745)

---

*The man is tempted to join with the inferior element.
Circumstances prevent this, leaving him with a painful
decision. The position is perilous, but a clear insight will
prevent great errors.*

How many second-story brains
All their renown amongst us owe
To always wisely taking pains
To choose their audience from the floor below!
ANTOINE FRANÇOIS LE BAILLY, FRENCH (1756–1832)

---

*The man keeps himself aloof from the common people.
He will lose their help when needed.*

As the franchise broadened and elegant, glittering,
imposing trappings faded from British Parliamentary
and public life, Lord Rosebery was conscious of an
ever-widening gap between himself and the Radical
electorate. The great principle "for which Hampden
died in the field and Sidney on the scaffold," the
economics and philosophy of Mill, the venerable
inspiration of Gladstonian memories, were no longer
enough. One had to face the caucus, the wire-puller
and the soap-box; one had to stand on platforms
built of planks of all descriptions. He did not like it.
He could not do it. He would not try. He knew what
[278]44

was wise and fair and true. He would not go through the laborious, vexatious, and at times humiliating processes necessary under modern conditions to bring about these great ends. He would not stoop; he did not conquer.

The man is well disposed toward his subordinates, tolerates their weaknesses, and protects their welfare. He is modest about his talents and does not resort to outward show or tireless admonition.

No one knew whence the strange bird came.
Possibly the last hurricane had swept it
from an unknown island or from some gulf;
or it was born of gigantic seaweeds,
or it fell from another atmosphere,
from another world, another mystery.
Old sailors had never seen it among the ice,
nor had any wanderer ever met up with it:
man-shaped it was, like an angel, and silent
like any poet.
At first it hovered over the great dome of the temple;
but the high priest drove it away, as one would drive
  a malign spirit.
In the same night it lit on the summit of the light-
  house,
and the keeper drove it thence, lest it mislead the
  ships.
No one offered it a morsel of bread
or the kindly shelter of a resting place.
Someone said: This is one of those evil birds that
  devour the flocks.
And another: This bird is no doubt a hungry demon.
When with outstretched wings it sheltered weary
  children,
the mothers themselves stoned the mysterious,
  persecuted and unresting bird.
It had fled, perhaps, from a silent peak among the
  clouds
or had lost its mate by an arrow.
The bird was man-shaped, like an angel,
and solitary as any poet.
And it seemed to desire the companionship of men
who drove it from them as one would drive a malign

spirit.

When the accustomed flood overwhelmed the wheat-
fields, someone said:

The bird ate the lambs.

And since all the fountains denied it water,

the bird fell upon the earth like a Samson deprived of
life.

Then a humble fisherman gathered up the soft body
and said:

I found the body of a great gentle bird.

And someone remembered that the bird used to
carry eggs to the hermits.

A beggar told how the bird often sheltered him from
the cold.

And a naked man said: The bird gave me feathers for
a coat.

And the leader of the people: It was the king of the
birds and we knew it not . . .

JORGE DE LIMA, BRAZILIAN (BORN 1893)

The cart was halted before the enclosure, and reject-
ing the offers of assistance with the same air of
simple self-reliance he had displayed throughout,
Tennessee's Partner lifted the rough coffin on his
back, and deposited it unaided within the shallow
grave. He then nailed down the board which served
as a lid; and mounting the little mound of earth
beside it, took off his hat and slowly mopped his
face with his handkerchief. This the crowd felt was
a preliminary to speech; and they disposed themselves variously on stumps and boulders, and sat
expectant.

"When a man," began Tennessee's Partner slowly,
"has been running free all day, what's the natural
thing for him to do? Why, to come home. And if he
ain't in a condition to go home, what can his best
friend do? Why, bring him home! And here's Tennessee has been running free, and we brings him
home from his wandering." He paused, and picked
up a fragment of quartz, rubbed it thoughtfully on
his sleeve and went on: "It ain't the first time I've
packed him on my back, as you see'd me now. It
ain't the first time that I brought him to this yer
cabin when he couldn't help himself; it ain't the first
time that I and 'Jinny' have waited for him on yon hill,
and picked him up and so fetched him home, when

he couldn't speak and didn't know me. And now that it's the last time, why —— ." He paused, and rubbed the quartz gently on his sleeve—"you see it's sort of rough on his pardner. And now, gentlemen," he added, abruptly, picking up his long-handled shovel, "the fun'l's over; and my thanks, and Tennessee's thanks, to you for your trouble."

Resisting any proffers of assistance, he began to fill in the grave, turning his back upon the crowd that after a few moments' hesitation gradually withdrew.

FRANCIS BRET HARTE, AMERICAN (1836–1902)

After his retirement from the everyday world, the man rebuffs the low and the inferior who come to him. He is blamed and reproached for his noble pride. Since he is no longer active in the world, he is able to bear criticisms with composure and continues to speak forthrightly without error.

There is something in your nature and habits that fits you for the situation into which your good fortune has thrown you. In the first place, you are in no danger of exciting the jealousy of your patrons by a mortifying display of extraordinary talents, while your sordid devotion to their will and to your own interest at once ensures their gratitude and contempt. To crawl and lick the dust is all they expect of you and all you can do. Otherwise they might fear your power, for they could have no dependence on your fidelity: but they take you with safety and fondness to their bosoms; for they know that if you cease to be a tool, you cease to be anything. If you had an exuberance of wit, the unguarded use of it might sometimes glance at your employers; if you were sincere yourself, you might respect the motives of others; if you had sufficient understanding, you might attempt an argument, and fail in it. But luckily for yourself and your admirers, you are but the dull echo, "the tenth transmitter" of some hackneyed jest: the want of all manly and candid feeling in yourself only excites your suspicion and antipathy to it in others, as something at which your nature recoils: your slowness to understand makes you quick to misrepresent; and you infallibly make nonsense of what you cannot possibly conceive. What seem your wilful blunders are often the felicity of natural parts,

and your want of penetration has all the appearance
of an affected petulance!
WILLIAM HAZLITT, ENGLISH (1778–1830)

---

*The over-all judgment: unworthy men are attempting to
insinuate themselves into the organization, filling suc-
cessive vacancies with their kind and seizing power
thereby. The superior leader regards even the smallest
and weakest of these as dangerous. He does not dally
with them or tolerate their presence even in a decep-
tively harmless position.*

"What are you up to, my dear Sir?" he resumed
abruptly. "Don't you know the proper procedure?
Where have you come to? Don't you know how matters ought to be conducted? As far as this is concerned, you should have first of all submitted a petition to the Chancellery; it would have gone from
there to the head of the proper Division, then would
have been transferred to the Secretary, and the Secretary would in due time have brought it to my attention—"
"But Your Excellency," said Akakii Akakiievich,
trying to collect whatever little pinch of presence of
mind he had, yet feeling at the same time that he was
in a dreadful sweat, "I ventured to trouble you, Your
Excellency, because secretaries now . . . aren't any
too much to be relied upon—"
"What? What? What?" said the important person.
"Where did you get such a tone from? Where did you
get such notions? What sort of rebellious feeling has
spread among the young people against the administra-
tors and their superiors?" The important person
had, it seems, failed to notice that Akakii Akakiievich would never see fifty again, consequently, even
if he could have been called a young man it could be
applied only relatively, that is, to someone who is
already seventy. "Do you know whom you're saying
this to? Do you realize in whose presence you are?
Do you realize? Do you realize, I'm asking you!"
Here he stamped his foot, bringing his voice to such
an overwhelming note that even another than an
Akakii Akakiievich would have been frightened.
Akakii Akakiievich was simply bereft of his senses,
swayed, shook all over, and simply could not stand
on his feet. If a couple of doormen had not run up

right then and there to support him he would have slumped to the floor; they carried him out in a practically cataleptic state. But the important person, satisfied because the effect had surpassed even anything he had expected, and inebriated by the idea that a word from him could actually deprive a man of his senses, looked out of his eye to learn how his friend was taking this and noticed, not without satisfaction, that his friend was in a most indeterminate state and was even beginning to experience fear on his own account.

NIKOLAI VASILIEVICH GOGOL, RUSSIAN (1809–1852)

Now Dissembling would seem, to define it generally, to be an affectation of the worst in word and deed; and the Dissembler will be disposed rather to go up to an enemy and talk with him than to show his hatred; he will praise to his face one he has girded at behind his back; he will commiserate even his adversary's ill-fortune in losing his case to him. More, he will forget his vilifiers, and will laugh in approval of what is said against him; to such as are put upon and resent it he will speak blandly; any that are in haste to see him are bidden go back home. He never admits he is doing it; and makes pretenses, as that he's but now come upon the scene, or joined the company late, or was ill abed. If you are borrowing of your friend and put him under contribution, he will tell you he is but a poor man; when he would sell you anything, no, it is not for sale; when he would not, why then it is. He pretends he has not heard when he hears, and says he has not seen when he sees; and when he has admitted you right he avers he has no remembrance of it. He'll look into this, doesn't know that, is surprised at the other; this again is just the conclusion he once came to himself. He is forever saying such things as "I don't believe it"; "If so, he must have changed"; "I never expected this"; "Don't tell *me*"; "Whether to disbelieve *you* or make a liar of *him* is more than I can tell"; "Don't you be too credulous."

THEOPHRASTUS, GREEK (died 287 B.C.)

He's just, your cousin, ay, abhorently;
He'd wash his hands in blood, to keep them clean.

ELIZABETH BARRETT BROWNING, ENGLISH (1806–1861)

[283]44

45 Unity

At the outset, the man desires union. But confusion and indecision exist because he is separated from his associates. He calls for help, which is provided, thereby transforming distress into joy.

The president has to live alone and like it. If he indulges in the luxury of thinking out loud, he sets off a chain reaction of rumors throughout the organization. He is the final, focal point of all the competitive pressures of men in the organization who are ambitious. If he confides in one and not in the others, he immediately lowers the morale of his executive staff. . . .

Most company presidents show an immediate understanding of what President William Howard Taft had in mind when he said after he had been in the White House several months, "Nobody ever drops in for the evening."

J. ELLIOTT JANNEY, AMERICAN (BORN 1903)

Secret forces are bringing compatible spirits together. If the man permits himself to be led by this ineffable attraction, good fortune will come his way. When deep friendships exist, formalities and elaborate preparations are not necessary.

You have been told also that life is darkness, and in your weariness you echo what was said for the weary.
And I say that life is indeed darkness save when there is urge,
And all urge is blind save when there is knowledge,
And all knowledge is vain save when there is work,
And all work is empty save when there is love;
And when you work with love you bind yourself to yourself, and to one another, and to God.

And what is it to work with love?
It is to weave the cloth with threads drawn from your heart, even as if your beloved were to wear that cloth.
It is to build a house with affection, even as if your beloved were to dwell in that house.

[284]45

It is to sow seeds with tenderness and reap the harvest with joy, even as if your beloved were to eat the fruit.
It is to charge all things you fashion with a breath of your own spirit,
And to know that all the blessed dead are standing about you and watching.
KAHLIL GIBRAN, LEBANESE (1833–1931)

The man attempts to join with others. But the envelop-ing circle excludes him. He should resolutely seek to ally himself with a man near the center of the group, who will bring him in. Some humiliation may occur at first, but this is not a mistake.

Teachers of every kind are to be strictly enjoined not to thrust precious stones down the throats of dogs or to put collars of gold round the necks of pigs and bears — that is, to the mean, the ignoble, the worth-less; to shopkeepers and the lowborn they are to teach nothing more than the mandates about prayer, fasting, alms-giving, and the pilgrimage to Mecca, along with some chapters of the Qurān and some doctrines of the Faith, without which their religion cannot be correct and valid prayers are not possible. They are to be instructed in nothing more lest it bring honor to their mean souls. They are not to be taught reading and writing, for plenty of disorders arise owing to the skill of the lowborn in knowledge. The disorders into which all the affairs of religion and government are thrown is due to the acts and words of the lowborn, whom they have made skillful. For by means of their skill they become governors, revenue-collectors, accountants, officers, and rulers.
ZIĀ UD-DĪN BARNĪ, INDIAN (1285–1357)

The man rallies the people to the country's service. This brings good fortune to himself, though he does not actively seek it.

But submitting to the laws of any country, living quietly and enjoying privileges and protection under them, makes not a man a member of that society; it is only a local protection and homage due to and from all those who, not being in a state of war, come within the territories belonging to any government, to all parts whereof the force of its law extends. But this no more makes a man a member of that society, a perpetual subject of that commonwealth, than it would make a man a subject to another in whose family he found it convenient to abide for some time, though, whilst he continued in it, he were obliged to comply with the laws and submit to the government he found there. And thus we see that foreigners, by living all their lives under another government, and enjoying the privileges and protection of it, though they are bound, even in conscience, to submit to its administration as far forth as any denizen, yet do not thereby come to be subjects or members of that commonwealth. Nothing can make any man so but his actually entering into it by positive engagement and express promise and compact. This is that which, I think, concerning the beginning of political societies, and that consent which makes anyone a member of any commonwealth.

JOHN LOCKE, ENGLISH (1632–1704)

What is the standing of our nation [China] in the world? In comparison with other nations we have the greatest population and the oldest culture, of four thousand years' duration. We ought to be advancing in line with the nations of Europe and America. But the Chinese people have only family and clan groups; there is no national spirit. Consequently, in spite of four hundred million people gathered together in one China, we are in fact but a sheet of loose sand. We are the poorest and weakest state in the world, occupying the lowest position in international affairs; the rest of mankind is the carving knife and the serving dish, while we are the fish and meat. Our position now is extremely perilous; if we do not earnestly promote nationalism and weld together our four hundred millions into a strong nation, we face a tragedy — the loss of our country and the destruction of our race. To ward off this danger, we must espouse nationalism and employ the national spirit to save the country.

PRESIDENT SUN YAT-SEN, CHINESE (1866–1925)

Although the people unite under the man's leadership, certain difficulties remain. His aims have not been clearly explained, and his thinking is beyond the comprehension
[286]45

of all. Some followers stay with him because of his in-
fluential position. If he remains steadfast in his virtues
so far as practically possible, he will eventually dis-
sipate these uncertainties.

To those of my race who depend upon bettering their
condition in a foreign land, or who underestimate
the importance of cultivating friendly relations with
the Southern white man, who is his next-door
neighbor, I would say: "Cast down your bucket
where you are" — Cast it down in making friends in
every manly way of the people of all races by whom
we are surrounded.

Cast it down in agriculture, mechanics, in commerce,
in domestic service, and in the professions. . . . Our
greatest danger is that in the great leap from slavery
to freedom we may overlook the fact that the masses
of us are to live by the productions of our hands, and
fail to dignify and glorify common labor, and put
brains and skill into the common occupations of life;
we shall prosper in proportion as we learn to draw
the line between the superficial and the substantial,
the ornamental gewgaws of life and the useful. No
race can prosper till it learns that there is as much
dignity in tilling a field as in writing a poem. It is at
the bottom of life we must begin, and not at the top.
Nor should we permit our grievances to overshadow
our opportunities. . . .

There is no defense or security for any of us, except
in the highest intelligence and development of all.
If anywhere there are efforts tending to curtail the
fullest growth of the Negro, let these efforts be
turned into stimulating, encouraging, and making him the most useful and intelligent citizen.
Efforts or means so invested will pay a thousand per
cent interest. . . .

The wisest among my race understand that the agitation of questions of social equality is the extremest
folly, and that progress in the enjoyment of all the
privileges that will come to us must be the result of
severe and constant struggle rather than of artificial
forcing. No race that has anything to contribute to
the markets of the world is long in any degree ostra-
cized. It is important and right that all the privileges
of the law be ours, but it is vastly more important
that we be prepared for the exercise of those privi-

leges. The opportunity to earn a dollar in a factory just now is worth infinitely more than the opportunity to spend a dollar in an opera house.
BOOKER T. WASHINGTON, AMERICAN (1856–1915)

Caesar . . . is, in fine, perhaps the only one of those mighty ones, who has preserved to the end of his career the statesman's tact of discriminating between the possible and the impossible, and has not broken down in the task which for greatly gifted natures is the most difficult of all—the task of recognizing when on the pinnacle of success, its natural limits.
THEODOR MOMMSEN, GERMAN (1817–1903)

The man does not remain inactive in his high position but seeks alliance with another, who misjudges him. He is saddened by the rebuff. But the unity will come eventually as a result of his determination.

There is no better test of a man's ultimate chivalry and integrity than how he behaves when he is wrong; and Johnson behaved very well. He understood (what so many faultlessly polite people do not understand) that a stiff apology is a second insult. He understood that the injured party does not want to be compensated because he has been wronged; he wants to be healed because he has been hurt. Boswell once complained to him in private, explaining that he did not mind asperities when they were alone, but did not like to be torn to pieces in company. He added some idle figure of speech, some simile so trivial that I cannot even remember what it was. "Sir," said Johnson, "that is one of the happiest similes I have ever heard." He did not waste time in formally withdrawing this word with reservations and that word with explanations. Finding that he had given pain, he went out of his way to give pleasure. If he had not known what would irritate Boswell, he knew at least what would soothe him. It was this gigantic realism in Johnson's kindness, the directness of his emotionalism when he is emotional, that gives him his hold upon generations of living men. There is nothing elaborate about his ethics; he wants to know whether a man, as a fact, is happy or unhappy, is lying or telling the truth. He may seem to be hammering at the brain through long nights of
[288]45

noise and thunder, but he can walk into the heart
without knocking.
GILBERT KEITH CHESTERTON, ENGLISH (1874–1936)

---

*The over-all judgment: unity requires a collective moral
force, together with a great leader. Ancestors unite the
clan, and heaven unites nature. With unity the time is
right for great deeds.*

In Rome,—in the Forum,—there opened one night
A gulf. All the augurs turned pale at the sight.
In this omen the anger of Heaven they read.
Men consulted the gods: then the oracle said:
"Ever open this gulf shall endure, till at last
That which Rome hath most precious within it be
 cast."
The Romans threw in their corn and their stuff,
But the gulf yawned as wide. Rome seemed likely
 enough
To be ruined ere this rent in her heart she could
 choke.
Then Curtius, revering the oracle, spoke:
"O Qiurites! to this Heaven's question has come:
What to Rome is most precious? The manhood of
 Rome."
He plunged, and the gulf closed.
EARL OWEN MEREDITH, ENGLISH (1831–1891)

In the 7th month of the first year of the reign of the
Second Emperor (209 B.C.) the poor people of the
village were sent to garrison Yü-yang, a force of nine
hundred men. But they got as far as the district of the
Great Swamp in Ch'i, they encountered heavy rain
and the road became impassable so that it was
evident that they would not reach their destination
on time. According to the law, men who failed to
arrive at the appointed time were executed. Ch'en
She and Wu Kuang plotted together, saying, "If we
try to run away we will die, and if we start a revolt we
will likewise die. Since we die in either case, would
it be better to die fighting for a kingdom?" . . . When
the officer in command of the group was drunk, Wu
Kuang made a point of openly announcing several
times that he was going to run away. In this way
Wu Kuang hoped to arouse the commander's anger,
get him to punish him, and so stir up the men's ire
[289]45

and resentment. As Wu Kuang had expected, the
commander began to beat him, when his sword
slipped out of its scabbard. Wu Kuang sprang up,
seized the sword, and killed the commander. Ch'en
She rushed to his assistance and they proceeded to
kill the other two commanding officers as well. Then
they called together all the men of the group and
announced: "Because of the rain which we encountered, we cannot reach our rendezvous on time.
And anyone who misses a rendezvous has his head
cut off! Even if you should somehow escape with
your heads, six or seven out of every ten of you are
bound to die in the course of garrison duty. Now,
brave fellows, if you are unwilling to die, we have
nothing more to say. But if you would risk death,
then let us risk it for the sake of fame and glory!
Kings and nobles, generals and ministers — such men
are made, not born!" The men all answered, "We are
with you!"

PAN KU, CHINESE (32–92)

In a dense bit of jungle lived a sparrow and his wife,
who had built their nest on the branch of a tamal
tree, and in the course of time a family appeared.

Now one day a jungle elephant with the spring fever
was distressed by the heat, and came beneath that
tamal tree in search of shade. Blinded by his fever,
he pulled with the tip of his trunk at the branch
where the sparrows had their nest, and broke it. In
the process the sparrows' eggs were crushed, though
the parent-birds — further life being predestined —
barely escaped death.

Then the hen-sparrow lamented, desolate with grief
at the death of her chicks. And presently, hearing
her lamentation, a woodpecker bird, a great friend of
hers, came grieved at her grief, and said, "My dear
friend, why lament in vain? For the Scripture says:

> For lost and dead and past
>   The wise have no laments:
> Between the wise and fools
>   Is just this difference."

..."That is good doctrine," said the hen-sparrow,
"but what of it? This elephant — curse his spring
fever! — killed my babies. So if you are my friend,
think of some plan to kill this big elephant. If that

[290]45

were done, I should feel less grief at the death of my children.". . .

"Madam," said the woodpecker, "your remark is very true. For the proverb says:
　A friend in need is a friend indeed,
　　Although of different caste;
　The whole world is your eager friend
　　So long as riches last.
. . ."Now see what my wit can devise. But you must know that I, too, have a friend, a gnat called Lute-Buzz. I will return with her, so that this villainous beast of an elephant may be killed."

So he went with the hen-sparrow, found the gnat, and said, "Dear madam, this is my friend the hen-sparrow. She is mourning because a villainous elephant smashed her eggs. So you must lend your assistance while I work out a plan for killing him."

"My good friend," said the gnat, "there is only one possible answer. But I also have a very intimate friend, a frog named Cloud-Messenger. Let us do the right thing by calling him into consultation.". . .

So all three went together and told Cloud-Messenger the entire story. And the frog said: "How feeble a thing is that wretched elephant when pitted against a great throng enraged. Gnat, you must go and buzz in his fevered ear, so that he may shut his eyes in delight at hearing your music. Then the wood-pecker's bill will peck out his eyes. After that I will sit at the edge of a pit and croak. And he, being thirsty, will hear me, and will approach expecting to find a body of water. When he comes to the pit, he will fall in and perish."

When they carried out the plan, the fevered elephant shut his eyes in delight at the song of the gnat, was blinded by the woodpecker, wandered thirst-smitten at noonday, followed the croak of a frog, came to a great pit, fell in, and died.

"And that is why I say,
　Woodpecker and sparrow
　　With froggy and gnat
　Attacking *en masse,* laid
　　The elephant flat."

PANCHATANTRA, INDIAN (SECOND CENTURY B.C.)

[291]45

46 Advancement

THE SHÊNG HEXAGRAM

At the outset, the man is advancing upward toward those who welcome him.

Is there another
Word in the language so unnecessary
As "fail" or "failure"?
No one has ever failed to fail in the end:
And for the very evident reason
That we're made in no fit proportion
To the universal occasion; which, as all
Children, poets, and myth-makers know,
Was made to be inhabited
By giants, friends, and angels of such size
The whole volume of human generations
Could be cupped in their hands;
And very ludicrous it is to see us,
With no more than enough spirit to pray with,
If as much, swarming under gigantic
Stars and spaces.
CHRISTOPHER FRY, ENGLISH (BORN 1907)

"How do you feel yourself this morning, my lad?"
he inquired, putting the usual commonplace
question.
"Much easier, thank you, sir," replied the youth in
the pure, sweet, modulated tones of a highly-culti-
vated nature.
The judge was surprised, but did not show that he
was so, as he said, "You have done my daughter a
great service, but at the cost of much suffering to
yourself, I fear my lad."
"I consider myself very fortunate and happy, sir, in
having had the privilege of rendering Miss Merlin
any service, at whatever cost to myself," replied
Ishmael, with graceful courtesy.
EMMA DOROTHY ELIZA SOUTHWORTH,
AMERICAN (1819–1899)

*The man is an effective but brusque officer serving a
weak leader. His upright sincerity and devoted loyalty meet with a favorable response.*

Not enough to attack me in various articles, but I am
said to be a strange fellow with an uncivil answer, I
do not wash up to the satisfaction of everyone, I do
not answer everyone's contention in humility. This
they consider and deem a great vice in me. I myself,
however, deem it a great virtue and would not that
it were otherwise than it is. I like my ways well
enough. In order, however, that I may justify myself
as to how my strange manner is to be understood,
pay heed: I am by nature not subtly spun, neither is
it usual in my country to attain anything by spinning
silk. Neither are we raised on figs, nor on meat, nor
on wheaten bread, but on cheese, milk and oatcakes.
This cannot make subtle fellows; besides what one
receives in youth stick to one all one's days. The same
is almost coarse to the subtle, the cat-clean, the
super-fine. For those, who are brought up in soft
rainment and in the women's apartments, and we
who grow up among fir-cones do not understand one
another well. Therefore must the coarse be judged
coarse, though the same thinks himself utterly subtle
and charming. Thus it is with me too: what I think
is silk, the others call ticking and coarse cloth.
PARACELSUS (THEOPHRASTUS VON HOHEMHEIM),
SWISS (1493–1541)

No impediments retard the man's bold advance.

In 1918 he [Henry Ford] had borrowed on notes to
buy out his minority stockholders for the picayune
sum of seventyfive million dollars.
In February 1920, he needed cash to pay off some of
those notes that were coming due. A banker is supposed to have called on him and offered him every
facility if the bankers' representative could be made
a member of the board of directors. Henry Ford
handed the banker his hat,
  and went about raising the money in his own way:
He shipped every car and part he had in his plant to
his dealers and demanded immediate cash payment.
Let the other fellow do the borrowing had always
been a cardinal principle. He shut down production
and canceled all orders from the supplyfirms. Many
dealers were ruined, many supplyfirms failed, but
when he reopened his plant,
  he owned it absolutely,
[293]46

the way a man owns an unmortgaged farm with the
taxes paid up. . . .
. . . in 1922 Henry Ford sold one million three hundred and thirty two thousand two hundred and nine
tin lizzies; he was the richest man in the world.
JOHN RODERIGO DOS PASSOS, AMERICAN (BORN 1896)

---

*The man's progress is aided and abetted by gods and men.
The ruler confides in him, facilitates his efforts, and
raises him in distinction.*

All his faults were such that one loves him still the
better for them.
OLIVER GOLDSMITH, ENGLISH (1728–1774)

---

*As he approaches the pinnacle, the man guards against
intoxication with success. He steadily advances step by
step with the greatest thoroughness and necessary
ceremony.*

About six months before this I had had a conversation with my dear old friend, Judge Lawlor, in which
he asked me how I thought I would fight Sullivan—
what I thought my tactics would be. And I distinctly
remember telling him the most important thing in
my fight with Sullivan would be to convince him that
there was one man he was going to meet who was
not licked before the fight started.
"How are you going to do that?" inquired the Judge.
"I don't know myself; but I've got to do it, someway."
Meanwhile, Sullivan sat in his corner trying to catch
my eye, his clenched fists on his knees, elbows out,
and his head thrust forward in an ugly fashion.
He had a wicked eye.
Now, as I had always done before, I was trying to
convince him that he was the last person or thing in
the world I was thinking about. I was bowing to
people I didn't even see, smiling at entire strangers,
waving my hand and talking to my seconds, laughing all the time.
Finally the referee called us up to the center of the
ring for our final instructions. We walked up,
Sullivan with his arms still folded, looking right at
my eyes, — not in them, for I never met his stare, —
and rising and falling on his toes without a pause. I
waited for the referee, my gaze on him, and you could

have heard a pin drop in the place. You wouldn't
think 10,000 people could be so quiet. At last the
referee got down to "Hitting in the clinches."
"Then what about clinching like this?" I asked, and
took hold of the referee and put my elbows up under
his chin, pushing his back, and repeated, "What if
he does this?"
"That's a foul, of course," he answered. "The one
that does it will be cautioned once. If he tries it a
second time, he loses the fight."
"All right," I said, as gruffly as I could, "that's all I
wanted to know."
Then, for the first time since entering the ring, I
looked Sullivan square in the eye and very aggres-
sively, too. He stopped his rising and falling on his
toes and stood staring at me as if he were petrified, so
surprised was he at this sudden change in my attitude, and I saw at once it had the effect I intended: I
had him guessing!
In a very cocksure manner I jerked the towel from
my shoulders, turned my back on him and ripped
out: "Let her go!"
JAMES JOHN CORBETT, AMERICAN (1866–1933)

I know what augmentation of her glory
England hath gained from thee by more than one
Victory. Thy services are great, and never
Hath realm on throne been by a stronger arm
Supported. But despite thy valiant deeds,
Do not be blind through too much confidence.
The more our queen, whose favors match thy merit,
Hath put thee where thou ne'er shouldst fall, the more
Thou needest to tremble lest her pride should stifle
A love that she with shame beholds rejected.
To see thine honored state end suddenly,
Her gracious hand needs but to be withdrawn;
And what security does the rarest service
Give him who treads the verge of an abyss?
One false step is enough; countless examples
Of such great downfalls fill the world with awe.
THOMAS CORNEILLE, FRENCH (1625–1709)

---

*The man advances blindly. Only the most exacting cor-
rectness will save him from unfortunate consequences.*

Lencho was an ox of a man, working like an animal

in the fields, but still he knew how to write. The following Sunday, at daybreak, after having convinced himself that there is a protecting spirit, he began to write a letter which he himself would carry to town and place in the mail.

It was nothing less than a letter to God.

"God," he wrote, "if you don't help me, my family and I will go hungry this year. I need a hundred *pesos* in order to resow the field and to live until the crop comes, because the hailstorm . . ."

He wrote "To God" on the envelope, put the letter inside and, still troubled, went to town. At the post office he placed a stamp on the letter and dropped it into the mailbox.

One of the employees, who was a postman and also helped at the post office, went to his boss laughing heartily and showed him the letter to God. Never in his career as a postman had he known that address. The postmaster — a fat, amiable fellow — also broke out laughing, but almost immediately he turned serious and, tapping the letter on his desk, commented:

"What faith! I wish I had the faith of the man who wrote this letter. To believe the way he believes. To hope with the confidence that he knows how to hope with. Starting up a correspondence with God!"

So, in order not to disillusion the prodigy of faith, revealed by a letter that could not be delivered, the postmaster came up with an idea: answer the letter. But when he opened it, it was evident that to answer it he needed something more than good will, ink and paper. But he stuck to his resolution: he asked for money from his employee, he himself gave part of his salary, and several friends of his were obliged to give something "for an act of charity."

It was impossible for him to gather together the hundred *pesos* requested by Lencho, so he was able to send the farmer only a little more than half. He put the bills in an envelope addressed to Lencho and with them a letter containing only a single word as a signature: GOD.

The following Sunday Lencho came a bit earlier than usual to ask if there was a letter for him. It was the postman himself who handed the letter to him, while the postmaster, experiencing the contentment of a man who has performed a good deed, looked on from the doorway of his office.

Lencho showed not the slightest surprise on seeing the bills — such was his confidence — but he became angry when he counted the money . . . God could not have made a mistake, nor could he have denied Lencho what he had requested!

Immediately, Lencho went up to the window to ask for paper and ink. On the public writing table, he started in to write, with much wrinkling of his brow, caused by the effort he had to make to express his ideas. When he finished, he went to the window to buy a stamp which he licked and then affixed to the envelope with a blow of his fist.

The moment that the letter fell into the mailbox the postmaster went to open it. It said:

"God: of the money that I asked for, only seventy *pesos* reached me. Send me the rest, since I need it very much. But don't send it to me through the mail, because the post office employees are a bunch of crooks. Lencho."

GREGORIA LÓPEZ Y FUENTES, MEXICAN (BORN 1897)

The over-all judgment: the time is propitious for those serving in minor positions to push upward to gain the heights of influence and distinction. The good officer should have no anxiety about going directly to the authorities.

Man is perishable. That may be; but let us perish resisting, and if it be nothingness that awaits us, do not let us so act that it shall be justice.

ÉTIENNE PIVERT DE SÉNANCOUR, FRENCH (1770–1846)

The beginning of the reign of Emperor Alexander was marked with bright hopes for Russia's prosperity. The gentry had recuperated, the merchant class did not object to giving credit, the army served without making trouble, scholars studied what they wished, all spoke what they thought, and everyone expected better days. Unfortunately, circumstances prevented the realization of these hopes, which aged without their fulfillment. The unsuccessful, expensive war of 1807 and others disorganized our finances, though we had not yet realized it when preparing for the war of 1812. Finally, Napoleon invaded Russia and then only, for the first time, did the Russian people become aware of their power; only then awakened in all our hearts a feeling of independence, at first political and finally national. That is the beginning of free thinking in Russia. The government itself spoke such words as "Liberty, Emancipation!" It had itself sown the idea of abuses resulting from the unlimited power of Napoleon, and the appeal of the Russian monarch resounded on the banks of the Rhine and the Seine. The war was still on when the soldiers, upon their return home, for the first time disseminated grumbling among the masses. "We shed blood," they would say, "and then we are forced again to sweat under feudal obligations. We freed the Fatherland from the tyrant, and now we ourselves are tyranized over by the ruling class." The army, from general to privates, upon its return, did nothing but discuss how good it is in foreign lands. A comparison with their own country naturally brought up the question, Why should it not be so in our own land?

At first, as long as they talked without being hindered, it was lost in the air, for thinking is like gunpowder, only dangerous when pressed. Many cherished the hope that the Emperor would grant a constitution, as he himself had started at the opening of the Legislative Assembly in Warsaw, and the attempt of some generals to free their serfs encouraged that sentiment. But after 1817 everything changed. Those who saw evil or who wished improvement, thanks to the mass of spies were forced to whisper about it, and this was the beginning of secret societies. Oppression by the government of deserving officers irritated men's minds. Then the military men began to talk: "Did we free Europe in order to be ourselves placed in chains? Did we grant a constitution to France in order that we dare not talk about it, and did we buy at the price of blood priority among nations in order that we may be humiliated at home?" The destructive policy toward schools and the persecution of education forced us in utter despair to begin considering some important measures. And since the grumbling of the people, caused by exhaustion and the abuses of national and civil administrations, threatened bloody revolution, the Societies intended to prevent a greater evil by a lesser one and began their activities at the first opportunity.

ALEKSANDR ALEKSANDROVICH BESTUZHEV,
RUSSIAN (1797–1837)

I wanted to avoid violence. Nonviolence is the first article of my faith. It is also the last article of my creed. But I had to make my choice. I had either to submit to a system which I considered had done an irreparable harm to my country, or incur the risk of the mad fury of my people bursting forth, when they understood the truth from my lips. I know that my people have sometimes gone mad. I am deeply sorry for it and I am therefore here to submit not to a light penalty but to the highest penalty. I do not ask for mercy. I do not plead any extenuating act. I am here, therefore, to invite and cheerfully submit to the highest penalty that can be inflicted upon me for what in law is a deliberate crime and what appears to me to be the highest duty of a citizen. The only course open to you, the judge, is, as I am just going to say in my statement, either to resign your post or inflict on me the severest penalty, if you believe that the system and law you are assisting to administer are good for the people. I do not expect this kind of conversion, but by the time I have finished my statement, you will perhaps have a glimpse of what is raging within my breast to run this maddest risk which a sane man can run.

MAHATMA MOHANDAS KARAMCHAND GANDHI,
INDIAN (1869–1948)

---

47 Adversity

THE K'UN HEXAGRAM

At the outset, the man lacks clear vision and is badly off. He is overwhelmed and has no immediate prospects of deliverance.

CHEBUTYKIN *(enters; without staggering, just as if he were sober, takes a turn about the room, stops, looks about him, then goes to washstand and begins washing his hands, speaking glumly):* May the devil take them

. . . and break them . . . all of 'em. . . . They think I'm
a doctor, that I can cure all their ills and pains, when
I know absolutely nothing, have forgot everything I
ever did know, and remember nothing — absolutely
nothing! *(Nathalie and Olga tiptoe out without his
perceiving it.)* Devil take it all. Last Wednesday I
attended a woman out in the sticks; she died — and I
am guilty of her death. Yes. . . . I did know a thing or
two twenty-five years ago, but now I know nothing.
Nothing. Maybe I'm not even a man, but merely pretending now that I have hands and feet — and a head;
maybe I don't even exist, but it merely seems to me
that I walk about, eat, sleep — *(Weeps.)* Oh, only not to
exist! *(Glumly, as he stops weeping.)* What the devil.
. . . A couple of days ago, at the club, they got to talking; they mentioned Shakespeare, Voltaire; I'd never
read them, not a blessed word, but I put on a knowing air, as if I had read them. And there were others
there who did the very same thing I did. How vulgar
— low down! And I reminded myself of the woman I
had done to death on Wednesday . . . and I reminded
myself of everything else as well — and everything in
my soul became snarled, vile, abominable. And I
went off . . . off on a bender.
ANTON PAVLOVICH CHEKHOV, RUSSIAN (1860–1904)

---

*The man is apparently well off but is actually inwardly
depressed. He is unable to solve the ordinary problems of
life and develop his basic principles. He is rescued by the
prince, who is looking for able helpers. However, he
must first be patient until the unseen obstacles are overcome by prayers and sacrifices.*

Two or three weeks ago I went one Sunday evening
to the church of a famous Brooklyn preacher . . . and
something like a revival was going on there. The
clergyman told some anecdotes connected with the
revival, and recounted some of the reasons why men
failed to become Christians. One case he mentioned
struck me. He said he had noticed on the outskirts of
the congregation, night after night, a man who listened intently, and who gradually moved forward.
One night, the clergyman said, he went over to him,
saying: "My brother, are you not ready to become a
Christian?" The man said, no he was not. He said
it, not in a defiant tone, but in a sorrowful tone. The

clergyman asked him why, whether he did not believe in the truths he had been hearing? Yes, he
believed them all. Why, then, wouldn't he become a
Christian? "Well," he said, "I can't join the church
without giving up my business; and it is necessary
for the support of my wife and children. If I gave that
up, I don't know how in the world I can get along. I
had a hard time before I found my present business,
and I cannot afford to give it up. Yet, I can't become a
Christian without giving it up." The clergyman
asked: "Are you a rum-seller?" No, he was not a
rum-seller. Well, the clergyman said, he didn't know
what in the world the man could be; it seemed to him
that the rum-seller was the only man who does a
business that would prevent his becoming a Christian; and he finally said: "What is your business?"
The man said: "I sell soap." "Soap!" exclaimed the
clergyman. "You sell soap? How in the world does
that prevent you from being a Christian?" "Well,"
the man said, "it is this way: the soap I sell is one of
those patent soaps that are extensively advertised as
enabling you to clean clothes very quickly; as containing no deleterious compound whatever. Every
cake of soap I sell is wrapped in a paper on which is
printed a statement that it contains no injurious
chemicals, whereas the truth of the matter is that it
does, and that though it will take the dirt out of the
clothes pretty quickly, it will, in a little while, rot
them completely out. I have to make my living this
way; and I cannot feel that I can become a Christian
if I sell that soap."
HENRY GEORGE, AMERICAN (1839–1897)

I struggle and struggle, and try to buffet down my
cruel reflections as they arise; and when I cannot, I
am forced to try to make myself laugh that I may not
cry; for one or other I must do; and is it not philosophy carried to the highest pitch for a man to conquer
such tumults of soul as I am sometimes agitated by,
and in the very height of the storm to quaver out a
horse-laugh?
SAMUEL RICHARDSON, ENGLISH (1689–1761)

*The man is indecisively unable to deal with adversity
and is oppressed by something which should not oppress
him. He leans on things like thorns and thistles, which*

are hazardous yet cannot support him.

I am as one who is left alone at a banquet, the lights
dead and the flowers faded.
BARON EDWARD GEORGE BULWER-LYTTON,
ENGLISH (1803–1873)

---

*The man in a high position proceeds hesitantly to help
the lower class. He encounters difficulty in breaking
loose from the circle of the wealthy and the powerful.
The original intention of his good resolution eventually
brings favorable results.*

You see, I am of the mob, the ultimate rabble. You
have no idea what the mob is. Even in your imagination you cannot conceive what lies in its heart. You
are of a different caste. Those who come from it and
have lived through everything understand everything. There people die at the age of thirty because
they are already old men. Their children are idiots
[those in the Polish coal mines district]. I am responsible for all this! I am! I am responsible before
my spirit which calls to me: I refuse! If I, a doctor,
don't do it, who will? I received everything I needed.
. . . I must give back what I took. This damned debt.
I can have neither a father, nor a mother, nor a wife,
nor anything to press against my heart with love
until these terrible nightmares [the miserable dens
inhabited by workers] disappear from the face of the
earth. I must renounce happiness. I must be alone,
by myself. With nobody around to hold me back.
STEFAN ŻEROMSKI, POLISH (1864–1925)

---

*The man's good intentions to help mankind are obstructed
from above and below, especially by the bureaucrats.
Gradually the situation improves. In the meantime, all
he can do is to maintain inner composure, as in offering
sacrifices to heaven.*

Ever since Adam fools have been in the majority.
CASIMIR DELAVIGNE, FRENCH (1793–1846)

The world would be better and brighter if our teachers would dwell on the Duty of Happiness as well
as on the Happiness of Duty, for we ought to be as

cheerful as we can, if only because to be happy ourselves is a most effectual contribution to the happiness of others.

SIR JOHN LUBBOCK, ENGLISH (1834–1913)

---

*The man appears to be in the depths of distress. His
fears and irresolute concerns over previous failures are
not conducive to progress. But the oppressive bonds can
be broken if he repents of his error and grasps the
situation firmly.*

How can we choke the old and long Remorse
  Which lives, and squirms, and fights
And feeds on us as worms upon a corse,
  Or, on the oak, its mites?
How can we choke the old and long Remorse?

What subtle philtre, wine, or drowsy draught
  Will drown that ancient foe,
Greedy as whores in his disastrous craft,
  Ant-patient, sure, and slow?
What subtle philtre, wine or drowsy draught?

CHARLES PIERRE BAUDELAIRE, FRENCH (1821–1867)

---

*The over-all judgment: adversity breaks the inferior
man's will but only bends the superior man's spirit. Outward influence is denied the great man, who accordingly
uses words sparingly but retains his central position.*

One day when the Sultan was in his palace at Damascus a beautiful youth who was his favorite
rushed into his presence, crying out in great agitation that he must fly at once to Baghdad and imploring leave to borrow his Majesty's swiftest horse.

The Sultan asked why he was in such haste to go to
Baghdad. "Because," the youth answered, "as I
passed through the garden of the Palace just now,
Death was standing there, and when he saw me
stretched out his arms as if to threaten me, and I
must lose no time in escaping from him."

The young man was given leave to take the Sultan's
horse and fly; and when he was gone the Sultan went
down indignantly into the garden, and found Death
still there. "How dare you make threatening gestures
at my favourite?" he cried; but Death, astonished,

answered: "I assure Your Majesty I did not threaten him. I only threw up my arms in surprise at seeing him here, because I have a tryst with him tonight in Baghdad."
JEAN COCTEAU, FRENCH (1889–1963)

Oh! Shame, unspeakable, unutterable shame! It was bitter to realize that his heart had failed him in the first battle, that he had fallen short of his own expectations. Where had been the boldness, the heroism of which he had dreamed as much when he was still far from the front line?
DMITRI ANDREEVICH FURMANOV, RUSSIAN (1891–1926)

"Don't be cynical," Judge Coates said. "A cynic is just a man who found out when he was about ten that there wasn't any Santa Claus, and he's still upset. Yes, there'll be more war; and soon, I don't doubt. There always has been. There'll be deaths and disappointments and failures. When they come, you meet them. Nobody promises you a good time or an easy time. I don't know who it was who said when we think of the past we regret and when we think of the future we fear. And with reason. But no bets are off. There is the present to think of, and as long as you live there always will be. In the present, every day is a miracle. The world gets up in the morning and is fed and goes to work, and in the evening it comes home and is fed again and perhaps has a little amusement and goes to sleep. To make that possible, so much has to be done by so many people that, on the face of it, it is impossible. Well, every day we do it; and every day, come hell, high water, we're going to have to go on doing it as well as we can."
JAMES GOULD COZZENS, AMERICAN (BORN 1903)

 # 48 Potentialities Fulfilled

THE CHING HEXAGRAM

At the outset, the man's life is immersed in corrupt, useless, and repulsive muck. No one is attracted to him.

I am a literary scavenger. I haunt the intellectual slaughter pens, and live by the putrid offal that self-

respecting writers reject. I glean the stinking ma-
terials for my stories from the sewers and cesspools
of life. For the dollar they pay, I furnish my readers
with those thrills that public decency forbids them to
experience at first hand. I am a procurer for the purpose of mental prostitution.
HAROLD BELL WRIGHT, AMERICAN (1872–1944)

---

*As in the case of able statesmen who refuse to serve as
ministers of the government, the man possesses precious
qualities but neglects them. His talents are dissipated in
miscellaneous directions.*

By dint of taking interest in everything, the Parisian
ends by being interested in nothing. No emotion
dominating his face, which friction has rubbed
away, it turns gray like the faces of those houses
upon which all kinds of dust and smoke have blown.
In effect, the Parisian, with his indifference on the
day for what the morrow will bring forth, lives like a
child, whatever may be his age. He grumbles at
everything, consoles himself for everything, jests at
everything, forgets, desires, and tastes everything,
seizes all with passion, quits all with indifference —
his kings, his conquests, his glory, his idols of bronze
or glass — as he throws away his stockings, his hats,
and his fortune. In Paris no sentiment can withstand the drift of things, and their current compels
a struggle in which the passions are relaxed: there
love is a desire, and hatred a whim; there's no true
kinsman but the thousand-franc note, no better
friend than the pawnbroker. This universal toleration
bears its fruits, and in the salon, as in the street, there
is no one *de trop*; there is no one absolutely useful,
or absolutely harmful — knaves or fools, men of wit or
integrity. There everything is tolerated: the government and the guillotine, religion and the cholera.
You are always acceptable to this world, you will
never be missed by it. What, then, is the dominating
impulse in this country without morals, without
faith, without any sentiment, wherein, however,
every sentiment, belief, and moral has its origin and
end? It is gold and pleasure. Take those two words
for a lantern, and explore that great stucco cage, that
hive with its black gutters, and follow the windings
of that thought which agitates, sustains, and oc-
[305]48

cupies it! Consider! And, in the first place, examine the world which possesses nothing.
HONORÉ DE BALZAC, FRENCH (1799–1850)

The man has competence which is being overlooked and unused. Were the chief executive clear-sighted, such a man would have been employed for the benefit of all. Those who know his abilities are deeply saddened to see them go to waste.

And so the Duckling was admitted on trial for three weeks; but no eggs came. And the Tom Cat was master of the house, and the Hen was the lady, and always said "We and the world!" for she thought they were half the world, and by far the better half. The Duckling thought one might have a different opinion, but the Hen would not allow it.
"Can you lay eggs?" she asked.
"No."
"Then you'll have the goodness to hold your tongue!"
And the Tom Cat said, "Can you curve your back, and purr, and give out sparks?"
"No."
"Then will you please have no opinion of your own when sensible people are speaking."
HANS CHRISTIAN ANDERSON, DANISH (1805–1875)

The man begins to organize his life and develop his capacities. He is too occupied in this task to help others at the moment. For this he deserves no blame, since he will be able to contribute more later on.

The great difficulty in education is to get experience out of ideas.
GEORGE SANTAYANA, AMERICAN (1863–1952)

The natural-born leader performs wide and useful services for the people.

Grandfather put down his knife and fork and looked around the table. "I remember one time we ran out of meat—" His voice dropped to a curious low sing-song, dropped into a tonal groove the story had worn for itself. "There was no buffalo, no antelope, not even rabbits. The hunters couldn't even shoot a coyote. That was the time for the leader to be on the

watch. I was the leader, and I kept my eyes open.
Know why? Well, just the minute the people began
to get hungry they'd start slaughtering the team
oxen. . . . Started from the middle and worked toward
the ends. Finally they'd eat the lead pair, and then
the wheelers. The leader of a party had to keep them
from doing that."
JOHN ERNST STEINBECK, AMERICAN (BORN 1902)

This was the noblest Roman of them all.
All the conspirators save only he
Did that they did in envy of great Caesar;
He only, in a general honest thought
And common good to all, made one of them.
His life was gentle, and the elements
So mixed in him that Nature might stand up
And say to the world "This was a man!"
WILLIAM SHAKESPEARE, ENGLISH (1564–1616)

---

*The man's inexhaustible and dependable inspiration is
drawn upon by all with whom he comes in contact.*

But there is something colossal about any human
figure when that individual becomes truly and
thoroughly human. A more human individual than
Katsimbalis I have never met. Walking with him
through the streets of Amaroussion I had the feeling
that I was walking the earth in a totally new way. The
earth became more intimate, more alive, more promising. He spoke frequently of the past, it is true, not
as something dead and forgotten however, but rather
as something which we carry within us, something
which fructifies the present and makes the future
inviting. He spoke of little things and of great with
equal reverence; he was never too busy to pause and
dwell on the things which moved him; he had endless time on his hands, which in itself is the mark of
a great soul. . . . There are men so full, so rich, who
give themselves so completely . . . They come to you
brimming over and they fill you to overflowing. They
ask nothing of you except that you participate in
their superabundant joy of living. They never inquire which side of the fence you are on because
the world they inhabit has no fences. They make
themselves invulnerable by habitually exposing
themselves to every danger. They grow more heroic
[307]48

in the measure that they reveal their weaknesses. Certainly in those endless and seemingly fabulous stories which Katsimbalis was in the habit of recounting there must have been a good element of fancy and distortion, yet even if truth was occasionally sacrificed to reality the man behind the story only succeeded thereby in revealing more faithfully and thoroughly his human image. . . . There was another interesting aspect of his remarkable gift, one which again bears analogy to the musician's talent. During the time I knew him Katsimbalis' life was relatively quiet and unadventurous. But the most trivial incident, if it happened to Katsimbalis, had a way of blossoming into a great event. It might be nothing more than that he had picked a flower by the roadside on his way home. But when he had done with the story that flower, humble though it might be, would become the most wonderful flower that ever a man had picked. That flower would remain in the memory of the listener as the flower which Katsimbalis had picked; it would become unique, not because there was anything in the least extraordinary about it, but because Katsimbalis had immortalized it by noticing it, because he had put into that flower all that he thought and felt about flowers, which is like saying — a universe.

HENRY MILLER, AMERICAN (BORN 1891)

The over-all judgment: despite changes in political structures and national entities, the basic needs of man remain the same. The leader should understand and furnish these fundamental necessities. Carelessness in this central duty, as well as the absence of competent people to implement the plan, leads to evil.

A full stomach is heaven; the rest is luxury.

CHINESE PROVERB

The idea has occurred to me that if one wanted to crush, to annihilate a man utterly, to inflict on him the most terrible of punishments so that the most ferocious murderer would shudder at and dread it beforehand, one need only give him work of an absolutely, completely useless and irrational character
. . if he had to pour water from one vessel to another and back, over and over again, to pound sand, to

move a heap of earth from one place to another and back again, I believe the convict would hang himself in a few days or would commit a thousand crimes, preferring rather to die than endure such humiliation, shame and torture.

FËDOR MIKHAILOVICH DOSTOEVSKY, RUSSIAN (1821–1881)

The face beseeched me to believe the story the lips were trying to tell. In my mind everything concerning the relationship of men and women became confused, a muddle. . . . The whole story of mankind's loneliness, of the effort to reach out to unattainable beauty tried to get itself expressed from the lips of a mumbling old man, crazed with loneliness, who stood by the side of a country road on a foggy morning holding a little dog in his arms.

SHERWOOD ANDERSON, AMERICAN (1876–1941)

---

49 Revolutions

THE KO HEXAGRAM

At the outset, the man is under restraint. Premature offensive action will be unfortunate.

FIRST EXECUTIONER. It's your turn today, Ahinta,
SECOND EXECUTIONER. No, it's yours, Goha.
FIRST EXECUTIONER. Let's see. . . . Ah, yes. Well, let's wait a little. There's no hurry.
SECOND EXECUTIONER. Why?
FIRST EXECUTIONER. Well, my father once said to me, "Goha," he said to me, "you never know. Some kind man might come along and buy his freedom. You never know. A son might be born to the king, and a general pardon proclaimed. An elephant might break loose, and the lucky beggar might escape. You never know. There might even be a new king come to the throne, and all the prisoners set free." That's what he said. . . . That's why I never hurry.

SHUDRAKA, INDIAN (FIRST CENTURY B.C.)

After a series of unsuccessful attempts, the man's chance to make effective changes has come. He succeeds because of the requisite capabilities, thorough planning, and public confidence.

A dinner lubricates business.
WILLIAM SCOTT, ENGLISH (1745–1836)

The man is disposed toward violent and far-reaching changes. Yet after the complaints have been well aired, his recommendations will be understood. He will succeed.

The Faustian inventor and discoverer is a unique type. The primitive force of his will, the brilliance of his visions, the steely energy of his practical ponderings, must appear queer and incomprehensible to anyone at the standpoint of another Culture, but for us they are in the blood. Our whole Culture has a discoverer's soul. To *dis*-cover that which is not seen, to draw it into the light-world of the inner eye so as to master it — that was its stubborn passion from the first days on. All its great inventions slowly ripened in the deeps, to emerge at last with the necessity of a Destiny. All of them were very nearly approached by the high-hearted, happy research of the early Gothic monks. Here, if anywhere, the religious origins of all technical thoughts are manifested. These meditative discoverers in their cells, who with prayers and fasting *wrung* God's secret out of him, felt that they were *serving* God thereby. Here is the Faust-figure, the grand symbol of a true discovering Culture. The *Scientia experimentalis,* as Roger Bacon was the first to call nature-research, the *insistent* questioning of Nature with levers and screws, began that of which the issue lies under our eyes as a countryside sprouting factory-chimneys and conveyor-towers. But for all of them, too, there was the truly Faustian danger of the Devil's having a hand in the game, the risk that he was leading them in spirit to that mountain on which he promises all the power of the earth. This is the significance of the *perpetuum mobile* dreamed of by those strange Dominicans like Petrus Peregrinus, which would wrest the almightiness from God. Again and again they succumbed to this ambition; they forced this secret out of God in order themselves to be God. They listened for the laws of the cosmic pulse in order to overpower it. And so they created the *idea of the machine* as a small cosmos obeying the will of man alone. But with that they overpassed the slender border-line whereat the reverent piety of others saw the beginning of sin, and

[310]49

on it, from Roger Bacon to Giordano Bruno, they came to grief. Ever and ever again, true belief has regarded the machine as of the Devil.

The passion of discovery declares itself as early as the Gothic architecture — compare with this the deliberate form-poverty of the Doric! — and is manifest throughout our music. Book-printing appeared, and the long-range weapon. On the heels of Columbus and Copernicus come the telescope, the microscope, the chemical elements, and lastly the immense technological corpus of the early Baroque.

Then followed, however, simultaneously with Rationalism, the discovery of the steam-engine, which upset everything and transformed economic life from the foundation up. Till then nature had rendered services, but now she was tied to the yoke as a *slave*, and her work was as though in contempt measured by a standard of horsepower. We advanced from the muscle-force of the Negro, which was set to work in organized routines, to the organic reserves of the Earth's crust, where the life-forces of millennia lay stored as coal; and today we cast our eyes on inorganic nature, where water-forces are already being brought in to supplement coal. As the horse-powers run to millions and milliards, the numbers of the population increase and increase, on a scale that no other Culture ever thought possible. This growth is a *product of the Machine*, which insists on being used and directed, and to that end centuples the forces of each individual. For the sake of the machine, human life becomes precious. *Work* becomes the great word of ethical thinking; in the eighteenth century it loses it derogatory implication in all languages. The machine works and forces the man to cooperate. The entire Culture reaches a degree of activity such that the earth trembles under it. . . . For this Faustian passion has altered the Face of the Earth.
OSWALD SPENGLER, GERMAN (1880–1936)

The man succeeds in effecting changes because of inner firmness, adherence to higher ideals, coupled with adequate power.

Yet a time comes when reasonable men find it hard to understand how any one in his senses can sup-
[311]49

pose that by eating or drinking wine he consumes the body or blood of deity. "When we call corn Ceres and wine Bacchus," says Cicero, "we use a common figure of speech; but do you imagine that anybody is so insane as to believe that the thing he feeds upon is a god?" In writing thus the Roman philospher little foresaw that in Rome itself, and in the countries which have derived their creed from her, the belief which he here stigmatizes as insane was destined to persist for thousands of years, as a cardinal doctrine of religion, among peoples who pride themselves on their religious enlightenment by comparison with the blind superstitions of pagan antiquity. So little can even the greatest minds of one generation foresee the devious track which the religious faith of mankind will pursue in after ages.
SIR JAMES GEORGE FRAZER, SCOTTISH (1854–1941)

The great man clearly shows the strong guiding principles behind his proposed changes. He retains the spontaneous support of the followers.

No great deed is done
By falterers who ask for certainty.
GEORGE ELIOT, ENGLISH (1819–1880)

The tree of liberty grows only when watered by the blood of tyrants.
BERTRAND BARÈRE DE VIEUZAC, FRENCH (1755–1841)

After bringing about successful major reforms, the man introduces the necessary minor adjustments in order to bring inferior men into compliance with the new order.

We see that in many things life is very great. It is incomparably great in its material aspects, in its body of wealth, in the diversity and sweep of its energy, in the industries which have been conceived and built up by the genius of individual men and the limitless enterprise of groups of men. It is great, also, very great, in its moral force. Nowhere else in the world have noble men and women exhibited in more striking forms the beauty and the energy of sympathy and helpfulness and counsel in their efforts to rectify wrong, alleviate suffering, and set the weak in the way of strength and hope. We have built up, moreover, a great system of government, which has stood through a long age as in many respects a model for those who seek to set liberty upon foundations that will endure against fortuitous change, against storm and accident. Our life contains every great thing, and contains it in rich abundance.

But the evil has come with the good, and much fine gold has been corroded. With riches has come inexcusable waste. We have squandered a great part of what we might have used, and have not stopped to conserve the exceeding bounty of nature, without which our genius for enterprise would have been worthless and impotent, scorning to be careful, shamefully prodigal as well as admirably efficient. We have been proud of our industrial achievements, but we have not hitherto stopped thoughtfully enough to count the human cost, the cost of lives snuffed out, of energies overtaxed and broken, the fearful physical and spiritual cost to the men and women and children upon whom the dead weight and burden of it all has fallen pitilessly the years through. The groans and agony of it all had not yet reached our ears, the solemn, moving undertone of our life, coming up out of the mines and factories, and out of every home where the struggle had its intimate and familiar seat. With the great Government went many deep secret things which we too long delayed to look into and scrutinize with candid, fearless eyes. The great Government we loved has too often been made use of for private and selfish purposes, and those who used it had forgotten the people.

At last a vision has been vouchsafed us of our life as a whole. We see the bad with the good; the debased and decadent with the sound and vital. With this vision we approach new affairs. Our duty is to cleanse, to reconsider, to restore, to correct the evil without impairing the good, to purify and humanize every process of our common life without weakening or sentimentalizing it. There has been something cruel and heartless and unfeeling in our haste to succeed and be great. Our thought has been "Let every man look out for himself, let every generation look out for itself," while we reared giant machinery which made it impossible that any but those who stood at the levers of control should have a chance to look out for themselves. We had not forgotten our morals. We remembered well enough that we had set up a policy which was meant to serve the humblest as well as the most powerful, with an eye single to the standards of justice and fair play, and remembered it with pride. But we were very heedless and in a hurry to be great.

PRESIDENT WOODROW WILSON, AMERICAN (1856–1924)

The over-all judgment: people are suspicious of change. Accordingly, it should not be made too hastily. Political revolutions should include prior proof of their necessity and firm correctness in their conduct. When the good effects begin to be evident, occasions for regret will disappear.

Good morning, Uncle, are you fishing?
Yessir, Cap'n, I'm fishin'.
Have you caught any fish yet?
Nossir, I don't believe I has.
Have you had any nibbles?
Nossir, I can't say I is.
Do you think there are any fish in that hole?
Cap'n, I don't much reckon there's any fish there nohow.
Well, Uncle, why do you keep fishing there?
Well, Cap'n, this the hole I'se always done my fishin' in, 'cause that's my house right up yonder on the rise.

JOHN CROWE RANSOM, AMERICAN (BORN 1888)

Having learned from our faithful councillors that foreign *religieux* have come into our realm, where they preach a law contrary to that of Japan, and that they have even had the audacity to destroy temples dedicated to our (native gods) Kami and Hotoke; although this outrage merits the severest punishment, wishing nevertheless to show them mercy, we order them under pain of death to quit Japan within twenty days. During that space no harm or hurt will come to them. But at the expiration of that term, we order that if any of them be found in our States, they shall be seized and punished as the greatest criminals.

TOYOTOMI HIDEYOSHI, JAPANESE (1536–1598)

There is a sacred horror about everything grand. It is easy to admire mediocrity and hills; but whatever is too lofty, a genius as well as a mountain, an assembly as well as a masterpiece, seen too near, is appalling. . . . Hence there is more dismay than admiration.
VICTOR HUGO, FRENCH (1802–1885)

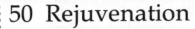

50 Rejuvenation

THE TING HEXAGRAM

At the outset, the evil is being discarded. This opens up opportunities for renewal, no matter how lowly a position the man may temporarily occupy.

HIPPOLYTUS. Forgive me, madam! With a blush I own
That I mistook your words, quite innocent.
For very shame I cannot see you longer—
Now I will go—
PHAEDRA. Ah, prince, you misunderstood me,—
Too well, indeed! For I had said enough.
You could not well mistake. But do not think
That in those moments when I love you most
I do not feel my guilt. No easy yielding
Has helped the poison that infects my mind.
The sorry object of divining revenge,
I am not half so hateful to your sight
As to myself. The gods will bear me witness,—
They who have lit this fire within my veins,—
The gods who take their barbarous delight
In leading some poor mortal heart astray!
Nay, do you not remember, in the past,
How I was not content to fly?—I drove you
Out of the land, so that I might appear
Most odious—and to resist you better
I tried to make you hate me—and in vain!
You hated more, and I loved not the less,
While your misfortunes lent you newer charms.
I have been drowned in tears and scorched by fire!
Your own eyes might convince you of the truth
If you could look at me, but for a moment!
What do I say? You think this vile confession
That I have made is what I meant to say?
I dare not dare betray my son. For him
I feared,—and came to beg you not to hate him.

[315]50

This was the purpose of a heart too full
Of love for you to speak of aught besides.
Take your revenge, and punish me my passion!
Prove yourself worthy of your valiant father,
And rid the world of an offensive monster!
Does Theseus' widow dare to love his son?
Monster indeed! Nay, let her not escape you!
Here is my heart! Here is the place to strike!
It is most eager to absolve itself!
It leaps impatiently to meet your blow! —
Strike deep! Or if, indeed, you find it shameful
To drench your hand in such polluted blood, —
If that be punishment too mild for you, —
Too easy for your hate, — if not your arm,
Then lend your sword to me. — Come! Give it now!
JEAN BAPTISTE RACINE, FRENCH (1639–1699)

The man achieves great success, thereby incurring the
envy of others. No harm will come to him, since he is
not distracted from his purpose.

America, then, exhibits in her social state an extraordinary phenomenon. Men are there seen on a
greater equality in point of fortune and intellect, or,
in other words, more equal in strength, than in any
other country in the world, or in any age of which
history has preserved the remembrance.
The political consequences of such a social condition
as this are easily deducible.
It is impossible to believe that equality will not eventually find its way into the political world, as it does
everywhere else. To conceive of men remaining forever unequal upon a single point, yet equal on all
others, is impossible; they must come in the end to
be equal upon all.
Now, I know of only two methods of establishing
equality in the political world; rights must be given
to every citizen, or none at all to anyone. For nations
which are arrived at the same stage of social existence as the Anglo-Americans, it is, therefore, very
difficult to discover a medium between the sovereignty of all and the absolute power of one man: and
it would be vain to deny the social condition which I
have been describing is just as liable to one of these
consequences as to the other.
There is, in fact, a manly and lawful passion for

equality that unites men to wish all to be powerful
and honored. This passion tends to elevate the
humble to the rank of the great; but there exists also
in the human heart a depraved taste for equality
which impels the weak to attempt to lower the powerful to their own level and reduces men to prefer
equality in slavery to inequality with freedom. Not
that those nations whose social condition is democratic naturally despise liberty; on the contrary, they
have an instinctive love of it. But liberty is not the
chief and constant object of their desires; equality is
their idol; they make rapid and sudden efforts to
obtain liberty and, if they miss their aim, resign
themselves to their disappointment; but nothing can
satisfy them without equality, and they would rather
perish than lose it.

ALEXIS CHARLES DE TOCQUEVILLE, FRENCH (1805–1859)

---

*The man is faced with obstacles. His abilities go un-
noticed and talents unused. But this is only a temporary
setback, as the tension will be relieved.*

JEREMY. Ay, more indeed; for who cares for anybody
that has more wit than himself?
SCANDAL. Jeremy speaks like an oracle. Don't you
see how worthless great men, and dull rich rogues,
avoid a witty man of small fortunes? Why, he looks
like a writ of inquiry into their titles and estates;
and seems commissioned by Heaven to seize the
better half.

WILLIAM CONGREVE, ENGLISH (1670–1729)

---

*The man fails to discharge his responsibilities because of
personal inadequacies. Great plans supported by limited
knowledge, heavy loads by meager strength, high office
by weak character — these result in shame and disaster.*

Against stupidity the very gods themselves struggle
in vain.

JOHANN CHRISTOPH FRIEDRICH VON SCHILLER,
GERMAN (1759–1805)

---

*The man is modest and approachable. He thereby at-
tracts associates, who can provide able help and advice.*

One busy day, an excited workman forced his way
into that sacred sanctum [Andrew Carnegie's office]

and insisted on showing to the "boss" a crowbar which he carried lovingly in his grimy hands. Vehemently Carnegie protested, and, just as persistently, the man refused to make his exit until an examination had been well and truly made of his precious crowbar. It seemed that a little while previously he had accidently dropped the heavy tool between two mighty steel rollers in the mills and watched its safe passage under their relentless pressure. Being an observant man he had waited until the iron had cooled enough to be handled; with his first glance at its condition, he had made a discovery of such apparent importance that he had resolved to bear it with him to headquarters.

"Of course I'll be fined for the crowbar," he said, "and maybe I'll be fired too, but I don't care. What I want you to do is to take a look at the new color and fibre of the thing, now that it's been cold-rolled. Crowbars don't look like that when they're broken, and I ought to know for I've seen plenty. But this one, when it had come out from between the roller and cooled a bit so that I could pick it up, 'peared to me like some sort of new metal, close-grained and tough at that. Take a peek at it. Seems funny to me."

Thus urged, Carnegie complied with the wish of his employee, and at his first examination of the half-flattened instrument suddenly asked, "Have you shown this to anyone?"

"No, sir. I thought I'd just bring it to you."

"You did well, and are obviously a keen man. You won't be fired, and you won't be fined. You'll be promoted! Here's a hundred dollar note. Put it in your pocket. You'll have lots of them in the days to come — but keep quiet about this matter."

. . . all the cold-rolled steel rails of the American railroads are the children of that crowbar.

JULIAN B. ARNOLD, AMERICAN (BORN 1863)

Prime Minister Kuo Tze I of the T'ang Dynasty was an outstanding statesman as well as a distinguished general. His success in both political and military service made him the most admired national hero of his day. But fame, power, wealth and success could not distract the prime minister from his keen interest in and devotion to Buddhism. Regarding himself as a plain, humble, and devoted Buddhist, he often visited his favorite Zen Master to study under him. He and the Zen Master seemed to get along very well. The fact that he held the position of prime minister, an exalted status in those days of old China, seemed to have no influence on their association. Apparently no noticeable trace of politeness on the Zen Master's part or of vain loftiness on the part of the minister existed in their relationship, which seemed to be a purely religious one of a revered Master and an obedient disciple. One day, however, when Kuo Tze I, as usual, paid a visit to the Zen Master, he asked the following question: "Your Reverence, how does Buddhism explain egotism?" The Zen Master's face suddenly turned blue, and in an extremely haughty and contemptuous manner he addressed the premier as follows: "What are you saying, you numb-skull?" This unreasonable and unexpected defiance so hurt the feelings of the prime minister that a slight, sullen expression of anger began to show on his face. The Zen Master then smiled and said: "Your Excellency, this is egotism!"

CHANG CHEN-CHI, CHINESE (1959)

The sage imparts wise counsel to the benefit of the worthy recipient. His gentle and sincere behavior pleases the heavens, which dispense good fortune to all.

No man was ever more thoroughly free from every species of artifice and pretension; more sincere, plain and unassuming. He [Ricardo] was particularly fond of assembling intelligent men around him, and in conversing in the most unrestrained manner on all topics of interest, but more especially on those connected with his favorite science. On these as on all occasions, he readily gave way to others, and never displayed the least impatience to speak; but when he did speak, the solidity of his judgment, his candor, and his extraordinary talent for resolving a question into its elements and for setting the most difficult and complicated subjects in the most striking point of view, arrested the attention of everyone, and delighted all who heard him. He never entered an argument, whether in public or private, for the sake of displaying ingenuity, of baffling an opponent, or

[319]50

of gaining a victory. The discovery of truth was his
exclusive object.

JOHN RAMSAY MCCULLOCH, SCOTTISH (1789–1864)

The man Flammonde, from God knows where,
With firm address and foreign air,
With news of nations in his talk
And something royal in his walk,
With glint of iron in his eyes,
But never doubt, nor yet surprise,
Appeared, and stayed, and held his head
As one by kings accredited.

. . . .

Moreover, many a malcontent
He soothed and found munificent;
His courtesy beguiled and foiled
Suspicion that his years were soiled;
His mien distinguished any crowd,
His credit strengthened when he bowed;
And women, young and old, were fond
Of looking at the man Flammonde.

There was a woman in our town
On whom the fashion was to frown;
But while our talk renewed the tinge
Of a long-faded scarlet fringe,
The man Flammonde saw none of that,
And what he saw we wondered at —
That none of us, in her distress,
Could hide or find our littleness.

There was a boy that all agreed
Had shut within him the rare seed
Of learning. We could understand,
But none of us could lift a hand.
The man Flammonde appraised the youth,
And told a few of us the truth;
And thereby, for a little gold,
A flowered future was unrolled.

There were two citizens who fought
For years and years, and over nought;
They made life awkward for their friends,
And shortened their own dividends.
That man Flammonde said what was wrong
Should be made right; nor was it long
Before they were again in line,
And had each other in to dine.

[320]50

. . . .

What was he, when we came to sift
His meaning, and to note the drift
Of incommunicable ways
That make us ponder while we praise?
EDWIN ARLINGTON ROBINSON, AMERICAN (1869–1935)

---

*The over-all judgment: men of talent, virtue, and worth
are being nourished, which leads to great progress and
success.*

It was he who had guided me with care toward all the
wisdom of the pampa. He had taught me the knowledge of the herder, the cunning of the buster. . . .
Under him, I became physician to my ponies. . . .
And he taught me how to live: courage and fairness
in the fight, love of one's fate whatever it might be,
strength of character in affairs of the heart, caution
with women and liquor, reserve among strangers,
faith to friends.
I even learned from him how to have a good time:
from him, and none other, how to strum the guitar
and shake a light foot in the dance. From the store of
his memory I took songs to sing alone or with a partner; and by watching him learned to manage the
intricate steps of the *gato,* the *triunfo,* and other
gaucho dances. He was overflowing with verses and
stories, enough to make a hundred halfbreed girls
crimson with joy or with shame.
Yet all this was nothing but a spark from the fire of
the man; and my wonder at him grew with every
day.
RICARDO GÜIRALDES, ARGENTINAN (1886–1927)

. . . a university is a place of concourse, whither students come from every quarter for every kind of
knowledge. You cannot have the best of every kind
of knowledge everywhere; you must go to some great
city or emporium for it. There you have all the
choicest productions of nature and art together,
which you find each in its own separate place elsewhere. All the riches of the land, and of the earth, are
carried up thither; there are the best markets, and
there the best workmen. It is the center of trade, the
supreme court of fashion, the umpire of rival talents,
and the standard of things rare and precious. It is the
[321]50

place of seeing galleries of first-rate pictures, and of hearing wonderful voices and performers of transcendent skill. It is the place for great preachers, great orators, great nobles, great statesmen. In the nature of things, greatness and unity go together; excellence implies a center. And such . . . is a University. . . . It is the place to which a thousand schools make contributions; in which the intellect may safely range and speculate, sure to find its equal in some antagonist activity, and its judge in the tribunal of truth. It is a place where inquiry is pushed forward, and discoveries verified and perfected, and rashness rendered innocuous, and error exposed, by the collision of mind with mind, and knowledge with knowledge. It is the place where the professor becomes eloquent, and is a missionary and a preacher, displaying his science in its most complete and most winning form, pouring it forth with zeal of enthusiasm, and lighting up his own love of it in the breasts of his hearers. It is the place where the catechist makes good his ground as he goes, treading in the truth day by day into the ready memory, and wedging and tightening it into the expanding reason. It is a place which wins the admiration of the young by its celebrity, kindles the affections of the middle-aged by its beauty, and rivets the fidelity of the old by its associations. It is a seat of wisdom, a light of the world, a minister of the faith, an Alma Mater of the rising generation. It is this and a great deal more.

CARDINAL JOHN HENRY NEWMAN, ENGLISH (1801–1890)

"There are three hundred and sixty schools of wisdom," said the Patriarch, "and all of them lead to Self-attainment. Which school do you want to study?"
"Just as you think best," said Monkey, "I am all attention."
"Well, how about Art?" said the Patriarch. "Would you like me to teach you that?" "What sort of wisdom is that?" asked Monkey. "You would be able to summon fairies and ride the Phoenix," said the Patriarch, "divine by shuffling the yarrow-stalks and know how to avoid disaster and pursue good fortune." "But should I live forever?" asked Monkey. "Certainly not," said the Patriarch. "Then that's no good to me," said Monkey.

"How about natural philosophy?" said the Patriarch. "What is that about?" asked Monkey. "It means the teaching of Confucius," said the Patriarch, "and of Buddha and Lao Tzu, of the Dualists and Mo Tzu and the Doctors of Medicine; reading scriptures, saying prayers, learning how to have adepts and sages at your beck and call." "But should I live forever?" asked Monkey. "If that's what you are thinking about," said the Patriarch, "I am afraid philosophy is no better than a prop in the wall." "Master," said Monkey, "I am a plain, simple man, and I don't understand that sort of patter. What do you mean by a prop in the wall?" "When men are building a room," said the Patriarch, "and want it to stand firm, they put a pillar to prop up the walls. But one day the roof falls in and the pillar rots." "That doesn't sound much like long life," said Monkey. "I'm not going to learn philosophy!"

"How about Quietism?" asked the Patriarch. "What does that consist of?" asked Monkey. "Low diet," said the Patriarch, "inactivity, meditation, restraint of word and deed, yoga practised prostrate or standing." "But should I live forever?" asked Monkey. "The results of Quietism," said the Patriarch, "are no better than unbaked clay in the kiln." "You've got a very poor memory," said Monkey. "Didn't I tell you just now that I don't understand that sort of patter? What do you mean by unbaked clay in the kiln?" "The bricks and tiles," said the Patriarch, "may be waiting, all shaped and ready, in the kiln; but if they have not yet been fired, there will come a day when heavy rain falls and they are washed away." "That does not promise well for the future," said Monkey. "I don't think I'll bother about Quietism."

"You might try exercises," said the Patriarch. "What do you mean by that?" asked Monkey. "Various forms of activity," said the Patriarch, "such as the exercises called 'Gathering the Yin and Patching the Yang,' 'Drawing the Bow and Treading the Catapult,' 'Rubbing the Navel to Pass Breath.' Then there are alchemical practices, such as the Magical Explosion, Burning the Reeds and Striking the Tripod, Promoting Red Lead, Melting the Autumn Stone, and Drinking Bride's Milk." "Would these make me live forever?" asked Monkey. "To hope for that," said the

[323]50

Patriarch, "would be like trying to fish the moon out of water." "There you go again!" said Monkey. "What pray do you mean by fishing the moon out of water?" "When the moon is in the sky," said the Patriarch, "it is reflected in the water. It looks just like a real thing, but if you try to catch hold of it you find it only an illusion." "That does not sound much good," said Monkey. "I shan't learn exercises."

"Tut!" cried the Patriarch, and coming down from the platform, he caught hold of the knuckle-rapper and pointed it at Monkey, saying, "You wretched simian! You won't learn this and you won't learn that! I should like to know what it is you do want." And so saying struck Monkey over the head three times. Then he folded his hands behind his back and strode off into the inner room, dismissing his audience and locking the door behind him.

The pupils all turned indignantly upon Monkey. "You villainous ape," they shouted at him, "do you think that is the way to behave? The Master offers to teach you, and instead of accepting thankfully, you begin arguing with him. Now he's thoroughly offended and goodness knows when he'll come back." They were all very angry and poured abuse on him; but Monkey was not in the least upset, and merely replied by a broad grin. The truth of the matter was, he understood the language of secret signs. That was why he did not take up the quarrel or attempt to argue. He knew that the Master, by striking him three times, was giving him an appointment at the third watch; and by going off with his hands folded behind his back, meant that Monkey was to look for him in the inner apartments. The locking of the door meant that he was to come round by the back door and would then receive instruction.

WU CH'ENG-EN, CHINESE (1505–1580)

 51 Shock

THE CHÊN HEXAGRAM

At the outset, an unexpected movement causes the man to be apprehensive. But he soon smiles with confident relief as the ordeal passes.

A mere trifle consoles us, for a mere trifle distresses us.
BLAISE PASCAL, FRENCH (1623–1662)

In this fearful predicament [a mutiny of the Company's officers supported by civil service, resulting
from his abolishing the system of pay and allow-
ances known as "double batta"], he [Robert Clive]
never faltered, and his supreme mastery over men
was never better exemplified. . . . In a few days, by
amazing promptness of action and pure inflexibility
of will, he had shamed the mutineers into submission. It is in a crisis of this nature that Clive appears
almost a Titanic figure. He matched all the resources
of his wonderful personality against a rebellious
Council, an army in open mutiny, a foreign position
of extreme peril, and won the day.
PAUL ERNEST ROBERTS, ENGLISH (BORN 1873)

---

*An uprising endangers the man. He accepts the material
losses and ascends to lofty heights inaccessible to the
threatening forces. After the shock and upheaval have
subsided, his property will be restored without his
fighting for it.*

Thus it seems possible that the contest between the
French Canadian and the New Englander for the
mastery of North America may not, after all, have
been concluded and disposed of finally by the outcome of the Seven Years' War. For, when the French
flag was hauled down, the French peasant did not
disappear with the emblem of the French Government's sovereignty. Under the tutelage of the Roman
Catholic Church, this peasantry continued, undisturbed, to be fruitful and multiply and replenish
the Earth; and now in the fullness of time the French
Canadian is making a counter-offensive into the
heart of his old rival's homeland. He is conquering
New England in the peasant's way — by slower but
surer methods than those which Governments have
at their command. He is conducting his operations
with the plough-share and not with the sword, and
he is asserting his ownership by the positive act of
colonizing the countryside and not by the carto-
graphical conceit of painting colors and drawing
lines on a scrap of paper. Meanwhile, law and re-

ligion and environment are combining to assist him. The environment of a harsh countryside keeps him exposed to a stimulus which no longer invigorates his rival in the softer atmosphere of the distant Western cities. His religion forbids him to restrict the size of his family by contraceptive methods of birth-control. And the United States legislation, which has restricted immigration from countries overseas but not from countries on the American continent, has left the French Canadian immigrant in a privileged position which is shared with him by none but the Mexican. Perhaps the present act in the drama of North American history may end, after a century of peaceful penetration, in a triumphal meeting between the two resurgent Latin peasantries in the neighborhood of the Federal Capitol of the United States! Is this the denouement that our great-grandchildren are destined to witness in A.D. 2033? There have been reversals of fortune every bit as strange as this in North American history before.
ARNOLD JOSEPH TOYNBEE, ENGLISH (BORN 1889)

The startling strokes of fate bring mental conflict to the man. He should retain presence of mind. If he tailors his responses appropriately, he will overpower these external blows.

Here is a startling alternative which to the English, alone among great nations, has been not startling but a matter of course. Here is a casual assumption that a choice must be made between goodness and intelligence; that stupidity is first cousin to moral conduct, and cleverness the first step into mischief; that reason and God are not on good terms with each other.
JOHN ERSKINE, SCOTTISH (1695–1768)

The man is unable to make progress against an unyielding situation and remains trapped by its stubborn resistance.

Destitute of the means of expansion, alien to all idea of aggression and conquest, little desirous of making its thought prevail outside itself, it [the Celtic race] had only known how to retire so far as space has permitted, and then, at bay in its place of retreat, to make an invincible resistance to its enemies. Its very fidelity has been a useless devotion. Stubborn of submission and ever behind the age, it is faithful to its conquerors when its conquerors are no longer faithful to themselves. It was the last to defend its religious independence against Rome—and it has become the staunchest stronghold of Catholicism; it was the last in France to defend its political independence against the king—and it has given to the world the last royalists.

Thus the Celtic race has worn itself out in resistance to its time, and in the defense of desperate causes. It does not seem as though in any epoch it had any aptitude for political life. The spirit of family stifled within it all attempts at more extended organization. Moreover, it does not appear that the peoples which form it are by themselves susceptible of progress. To them life appears a fixed condition, which man has no power to alter. Endowed with little initiative, too much inclined to look upon themselves as minors and in tutelage, they are quick to believe in destiny and resign themselves to it. Seeing how little audacious they are against God, one would scarcely believe this race to be the daughter of Japhet.

Thence ensues its sadness. Take the songs of its bards of the sixth century; they weep more defeats than they sing victories. Its history is itself only one long lament; it still recalls its exiles, its flights across the seas. If at times it seems to be cheerful, a tear is not slow to glisten behind its smile; it does not know that strange forgetfulness of human conditions and destinies which is called gaiety. Its songs of joy are as elegies, there is nothing to equal the delicate sadness of its national melodies. One might call them emanations from on high which, falling drop by drop upon the soul, pass through it like memories of another world. Never have men feasted so long upon these solitary delights of the spirit, these poetic memories which simultaneously intercross all the sensations of life, so vague, so deep, so penetrative, that one might die from them, without being able to say whether it was from bitterness or sweetness.

ERNEST RENAN, FRENCH (1823–1892)

The man is exposed to repeated shocks and continuing

I am not ashamed of my grandparents for having been slaves. I am only ashamed of myself for having at one time been ashamed. About eighty-five years ago they were told that they were free, united with others of our country in everything . . . social, separate like the fingers of the hand. And they believed it. They exulted in it. They stayed in their place, worked hard, and brought up my father to do the same. But my grandfather is the one. He was an odd old guy, my grandfather, and I'm told I take after him. It was he who caused the trouble. On his deathbed he called my father to him and said, "Son, after I'm gone I want you to keep up the good fight. I never told you, but our life is a war and I have been a traitor all my born days, a spy in the enemy's country ever since I give up my gun back in the Reconstruction. Live with your head in the lion's mouth. I want you to overcome 'em with yeses, undermine 'em with grins, agree 'em to death and destruction, let 'em swoller you till they vomit or bust wide open." They thought the old man had gone out of his mind. He had been the meekest of men. The younger children were rushed from the room, the shades drawn and the flame of the lamp turned so low that it sputtered on the wick like the old man's breathing. "Learn it to the younguns," he whispered fiercely; then he died.

RALPH WALDO ELLISON, AMERICAN (BORN 1914)

The man has not yet found a moderate course of behavior. He is dismayed at the startling events of the times. Action will lead only to evil under such conditions. He should withdraw, taking appropriate precautions, before the shock has affected him personally. His associates may speak against him, but he should not be concerned.

Now all the truth is out,
Be secret and take defeat
From any brazen throat,
For how can you compete,
Being honor bred, with one
Who, were it proved he lies,

[328]51

Were neither shamed in his own
Nor in his neighbour's eyes?
Bred to a harder thing
Then triumph, turn away
And like a laughing string
Whereupon mad fingers play
Amid a place of stone,
Be secret and exult,
Because of all things known
That is the most difficult.
WILLIAM BUTLER YEATS, IRISH (1865–1939)

---

*The over-all judgment: the superior man understands the
nature of shocks and so remains sufficiently confident and
self-possessed to take appropriate action. He concentrates on the service in which he is engaged.*

The Regimental Commander observed the little
group of survivors. They numbered twenty-six, all
that remained of four hundred and fifty men. Then
the Major's glance fell on the nine dead, killed that
morning. They lay close together, their waxy faces
staring into space. They had beaten off an attack and
then their ammunition was exhausted. There was
nothing more that they could do. General Stempel
had visited the position two days before and had
said to the Major, "I don't believe there are more
than ten thousand troops still able to fire. The others
are only waiting to die. And the number decreases,
in geometrical proportion, from position to position
with each step we take back. The Sixth Army is
almost defenceless. When things have reached that
point, it's time to pack up."
That was forty-eight hours ago. Three years ago,
the Company Commander had heard Hitler say in
Munich: "Whatever sacrifice may be demanded of
us as individuals is irrelevant. Victory is and always
will be all that matters."
And the General's words, and Hitler's words, went
round and round in the Major's head.
"When things have reached that point, it's time to
pack up." Well, things had reached that point so . . .
The troops formed a half-circle and they understood
very well what their Regimental Commander said to
them. "We are out of touch with Army, the division
is dead, and the regiment is us. We are in fact the last

of the Sixth Army. You swore an oath of loyalty to the
flag and you said, . . . 'if need be, unto death.' The
magazines of your rifles are as empty as your stomachs. I absolve you from your oath. Each man can do
as he sees fit. Germany will have to manage as best
she can without us."
Then the Company Commander shook each of his
twenty-six men by the hand, and looked steadily
into each man's eyes. The soldiers had the impression that tears were running down his cheeks, but
that may have been due to the icy wind. Then for the
last time he raised his hand to the peak of his cap
and saluted. One salute for his men and one for the
patch of snow where the nine with the waxy faces lay.
HEINZ SCHRÖTER, GERMAN (BORN 1905)

A gentle answer did the old Man make,
In courteous speech which forth he slowly drew:
And him with further words I thus bespake,
"What occupation do you there pursue?
This is a lonesome place for one like you."
Ere he replied, a flash of mild surprise
Broke from the sable orbs of his yet-vivid eyes.

His words came feebly, from a feeble chest,
But each in solemn order followed each,
With something of a lofty utterance drest—
Choice word and measured phrase, above the reach
Of ordinary men; a stately speech;
Such as grave Livers do in Scotland use,
Religious men, who give to God and man their dues.

He told that to these waters he had come
To gather leeches, being old and poor:
Employment hazardous and wearisome!
And he had many hardships to endure:
From pond to pond he roamed, from moor to moor;
Housing, with God's good help, by choice or chance;
And in this way he gained an honest maintenance.

The old Man still stood talking by my side;
But now his voice to me was like a stream
Scarce hears; nor word from word could I divide;
And the whole body of the Man did seem
Like one whom I had met with a dream;
Or like a man from some far region sent,
To give me human strength, by apt admonishment.
[330]51

My former thoughts returned: the fear that kills;
And hope that is unwilling to be fed;
Cold, pain, and labour, and all fleshly ills;
And mighty Poets in their misery dead.
— Perplexed, and longing to be comforted,
My question eagerly did I renew,
"How is it that you live, and what is it you do?"

He with a smile did then his words repeat;
And said that, gathering leeches, far and wide
He traveled; stirring thus about his feet
The waters of the pools where they abide,
"Once I could meet with them on every side;
But they have dwindled long by slow decay;
Yet still I persevere, and find them where I may."

While he was talking thus, the lonely place,
The old Man's shape, and speech — all troubled me:
In my mind's eye I seemed to see him pace
About the weary moors continually,
Wandering about alone and silently.
While these thoughts within myself pursued,
He, having made a pause, the same discourse re-
  newed.

And soon with this he other matter blended,
Cheerfully uttered, with demeanour kind,
But stately in the main; and, when he ended,
I could have laughed myself to scorn to find
In that decrepit Man so firm a mind.
"God," said I, "be my help and stay secure;
I'll think of the Leech-gatherer on the lonely moor!"

WILLIAM WORDSWORTH, ENGLISH (1770–1850)

Sandy was very wise. Up and down the Eastern
Shore it was whispered that Sandy was "voodoo,"
that he was versed in black magic. Sandy was a
full-blooded African. He remembered coming across
the "great waters." He remembered the darkness,
the moans and the awful smells. But he had been
fortunate. The chain which fastened his small ankle
to the hold of the ship also held his giant mother, and
she had talked to him. All through the darkness she
had talked to him. The straight, long-limbed woman of
the Wambugwe had been a prize catch. The Bantus
of eastern Africa were hard to capture. They brought
the highest prices in the markets. Sandy remembered
the rage of the dealer when his mother was found

dead. She had never set foot on this new land, but all during the long journey she had talked — and Sandy had not forgotten. He had not forgotten one word.

This mother's son now sat quietly by on his haunches, waiting. Long ago he had learned patience. The waters of great rivers move slowly, almost imperceptibly; big trees of the forest stand still, yet each year grow; seasons come in due time; nothing stays the same. Sandy knew.

SHIRLEY GRAHAM, AMERICAN (BORN 1908)

 ## 52 Resting

THE KÊN HEXAGRAM

At the outset, the man pauses to study the situation as it actually exists — without being led astray by wishful thinking or ulterior motives. He must remain persistently firm and correct to avoid irresolute drifting.

At dinner Lenz had recovered his spirits. They discussed literature and he was in his element. Idealism was then in fashion and Kaufmann was a convert to it. Lenz attacked it violently. He said that even those poets who claimed to represent reality had very little idea what it was really like, but at least they were preferable to those who pretended to explain it. God the Father certainly made the world as it should be and we were not likely to patch up something better; our only aim should be to copy Him a little. "What I demand of any work of art is life, the possibility that it might really exist, and that is all that matters; it isn't for us to ask whether it's ugly or beautiful. The sense of life in any work is more important than either of these, and it is the only possible criterion of art. But we very seldom find it; in Shakespeare, in folk songs absolutely, in Goethe sometimes. All the rest we can throw on the fire. Such people couldn't even create a dog's kennel. They pretend to create ideal types but all the works of theirs I've seen are more like wooden dummies.

"Idealism is the greatest possible insult to human nature; idealists ought to try it for themselves one day, surrender themselves to even the most limited form of life and try to reproduce its movements, its implications, its subtle, hardly noticeable play of expression. It's something which I have myself to do in my plays, in *The Tudor* and *The Soldiers.* My characters are the most ordinary creatures in the world, but the organs of feeling are the same in nearly all men. It's only a question of how thick a crust they have to penetrate. One has to have an eye and an ear for such things.

"Yesterday when I was walking in the valley I saw two girls sitting on a rock. One was doing up her hair, the other was helping her. The golden hair was hanging down; she had a pale serious face, very young, and a black dress, and the other was so anxious to help her. The finest, most intimate pictures of the German Primitives can hardly give one an idea of such a scene as that. Sometimes one wishes one had a Medusa's head, so as to turn a scene like that to stone, and then call everyone to come and look at it. Then the two girls stood up. The scene was destroyed, but as they walked down between the rocks, they suddenly composed another picture. The finest paintings, the richest harmonies, first compose a group and then dissolve it.

"Only one thing matters; an inexhaustible beauty which passes from one form into another, eternally transformed, yet always the same. We certainly can't transfix it forever and put it in a museum and reduce it to a catalogue and then summon old and young to look at it, and lecture to graybeards and babies about it and let them go into ecstasies over it. One has to love all mankind to penetrate the existence of even a single human being; no one must be too mean or too ugly for one. Only then can one understand them. The most ordinary face makes a deeper impression than the mere sensation of beauty. Without copying a single detail from the outside world, it's quite easy to invent ideal types for oneself in which there isn't a spark of life, neither bone nor muscle nor throbbing pulse of the blood."

GEORG BÜCHNER, GERMAN (1813–1837)

The man is unable to stop his stronger master even when the latter is bent in the direction of wrongdoing. He is unhappy about being swept along by such a movement.

The art of power and its minions are the same in all countries and in all ages. It marks its victim; denounces it; and excites the public odium and the public hatred, to conceal its own abuses and encroachments.

HENRY CLAY, AMERICAN (1777–1852)

Danger results from the smoldering resentment against forced inaction on the part of the man. The proper frame of mind for meditation and concentration can arise naturally only out of inner composure and not through artificial rigidity.

Necessity is the argument of tyrants; it is the creed of slaves.

EARL WILLIAM PITT, ENGLISH (1708–1778)

The man forgets his ego. This leads to the highest state of rest.

One day I asked the Master: "How can the shot [arrow] be loosed if 'I' do not do it?"

"'It' shoots," he replied.

"I have heard you say that several times before, so let me put it another way: How can I wait self-obliviously for the shot if 'I' am no longer there?"

"'It' waits at the highest tension."

"And who or what is this 'It'?"

"Once you have understood that, you will have no further need of me. . . ."

Then, one day, after a shot, the Master made a deep bow and broke off the lesson. "Just then 'It' shot!" he cried, as I stared at him bewildered. And when I at last understood what he meant I couldn't suppress a sudden whoop of delight.

"What I have said," the Master told me severely, "was not praise, only a statement that ought not to touch you. Nor was my bow meant for you, for you are entirely innocent of this shot. You remained this time absolutely self-oblivious and without purpose in the highest tension, so that the shot fell from you like a ripe fruit. . . ."

"I'm afraid I don't understand anything more at all," I answered, "even the simplest things have got in a muddle. Is it 'I' who draw the bow, or is it the bow that draws me into the state of highest tension? Do

[334]52

'I' hit the goal, or does the goal hit me? Is 'It' spiritual when seen by the eyes of the body, and corporeal when seen by the eyes of the spirit — or both or neither? Bow, arrow, goal and ego, all melt into one another, so that I can no longer separate them. And even the need to separate has gone. For as soon as I take the bow and shoot, everything becomes so clear and straightforward and so ridiculously simple. . . ." "Now at last," the Master broke in, "the bow-string has cut right through you."
EUGEN HERRIGEL, GERMAN (1884–1955)

The man is judicious in his choice of words. He thereby eliminates occasions for regret.

I like not him who at his drinking beside the full mixing-bowl tells of strife and lamentable war, but rather one that taketh thought for lightsome mirth by mingling the Muses and the splendid gifts of Aphrodite.
ANACREON, GREEK (572–488 B.C.)

The man attains tranquillity in relation to life in its entirety.

I cannot but think that he who finds a certain proportion of pain and evil inseparably woven up in the life of the very worms, will bear his own share with more courage and submission.
THOMAS HENRY HUXLEY, ENGLISH (1825–1895)

The idea most vital and essential to the samurai is that of death, which he ought to have before his mind day and night, night and day, from the dawn of the first day of the year to the last minute of the last day of it. When this notion takes firm hold of you, you are able to discharge your duties to their fullest extent: you are loyal to your master, filial to your parents, and naturally can avoid all kinds of disasters. Not only is your life itself thereby prolonged, but your personal dignity is enhanced. Think what a frail thing life is, especially that of a samurai. This being so, you will come to consider every day of your life your last and dedicate it to the fulfillment of your obligations. Never let the thought of a long life seize upon you, for then you are apt to indulge in all
[335]52

kinds of dissipation, and end your days in dire disgrace. That was the reason why Masashige is said to have told his son Masatsura to keep the idea of death all the time before his mind.
DAIDŌJI YŪSAN, JAPANESE (SEVENTEENTH CENTURY)

The over-all judgment: one should rest when it is time to rest and act when it is time to act. True resting and putting to rest are attained through the disappearance of the ego, which leads to the harmony of one's behavior with the laws of the universe. Resting in principle involves doing that which is right in every position in which one is placed.

Jinsai was very poor, so poor that at the end of the year he could not make New Year's rice cakes; but he was very calm about it. His wife came, and kneeling down before him said: "I will do the housework under any circumstances; but there is one thing that is unbearable. Our boy Genso does not understand the meaning of our poverty; he envies the neighbor's children their rice cakes. I scold him, but my heart is torn in two." Jinsai continued to pore over his books without making any reply. Then, taking off his garnet ring, he handed it to his wife, as much as to say, "Sell this, and buy some rice cakes."
STORY OF JINSAI ITO, JAPANESE (1627–1705)

The dying man himself was no longer to be fooled and duped by hope; he knew that he was done for, and he no longer cared. Rather, as if that knowledge had brought him a new strength — the immense and measureless strength that comes from resignation, and that has vanquished terror and despair — Gant had already consigned himself to death, and now was waiting for it, without weariness or anxiety, and with a perfect and peaceful acquiescence.
This complete resignation and tranquillity of a man whose life had been so full of violence, protest, and howling fury stunned and silenced them, and left them helpless. It seemed that Gant, knowing that often he had lived badly, was now determined to die well. And in this he succeeded. He accepted every reassurance, or frenzied activity, with a passive gratefulness which he seemed to want everyone to know. On the evening of the day after his first
[336]52

hemorrhage, he asked for food and Eliza, bustling out, pathetically eager to do something, killed a chicken and cooked it for him.

And as if, from that infinite depth of death and silence from which he looked at her, he had seen, behind the bridling brisk activity of her figure, forever bustling back and forth, saying confusedly — "Why, yes! The very thing! This very minute, sir!" — had seen the white strained face, the stricken eyes of a proud and sensitive woman who had wanted affection all her life, had received for the most part injury and abuse, and who was ready to clutch at any crust of comfort that might console or justify her before he died — he ate part of the chicken with relish, and then looking up at her, said quietly:

"I tell you what — that was a good chicken."

THOMAS CLAYTON WOLFE, AMERICAN (1900–1938)

A man of sense ought not to say, nor will I be very confident, that the description which I have given of the soul and her mansions is exactly true. But I do say that, inasmuch as the soul is shown to be immortal, he may venture to think, not improperly or unworthily, that something of the kind is true. The venture is a glorious one, and he ought to comfort himself with words like these, which is the reason why I lengthen out the tale. Wherefore, I say, let a man be of good cheer about his soul, who having cast away the pleasures and ornaments of the body as alien to him and working harm rather than good, has sought after the pleasures of knowledge; and has arrayed the soul, not in some foreign attire, but in her own proper jewels, temperance, and justice, and courage, and nobility, and truth — in these adorned she is ready to go on her journey to the world below, when the hour comes. You, Simians and Cebus, and all other men, will depart at some time or other. Me already, as a tragic poet would say, the voice of fate calls . . .

When he had done speaking, Crito said: And have you any commands for us, Socrates — anything to say about your children, or any other matter in which we can serve you?

Nothing particular, Crito, he replied: only, as I have always told you, take care of yourselves; that is a service which you may be ever rendering to me and mine and to all of us, whether you promise to do so or not. But if you have no thought for yourselves, and care not to walk according to the rule which I have prescribed for you, not now for the first time, however much you may profess or promise at the moment, it will be of no avail.

We will do our best, said Crito: and in what way shall we bury you?

In any way that you like; but you must get hold of me, and take care that I do not run away from you. Then he turned to us, and added with a smile: I cannot make Crito believe that I am the same Socrates who have been talking and conducting the argument; he fancies that I am the other Socrates whom he will soon see, a dead body — and he asks, How shall he bury me? And though I have spoken many words in the endeavor to show that when I have drunk the poison I shall leave you and go the joys of the blessed, — these words of mine, with which I was comforting you and myself, have had, as I perceive, no effect upon Crito. And therefore I want you to be surety for me to him now, as at the trial . . . he was surety for me to the judges that I would remain, and you must be my surety to him that I shall not remain, but go away and depart; and then he will suffer less at my death, and not be grieved when he sees my body being burned or buried. I would not have him sorrow at my hard lot, or say at the burial, Thus we lay out Socrates, or, Thus we follow him to the grave or bury him, for false words are not only evil in themselves, but they infect the soul with evil. Be of good cheer then, my dear Crito, and say that you are burying my body only, and do with whatever is usual, and what you think best.

When he had spoken these words, he arose and went into a chamber to bathe; Crito followed him and told us to wait. So we remained behind, talking and thinking of the subject of discourse, and also of the greatness of our sorrow; he was like a father of whom we were being bereaved, and we were about to pass the rest of our lives as orphans. When he had taken his bath his children were brought to him . . . and the women of his family also came, and he talked to them and gave them a few directions in the presence of Crito; then he dismissed them and returned to us.

[338]52

Now the hour of sunset was near, for a good deal of time had passed while he was within. When he came out, he sat down with us again after his bath, but not much was said. Soon the jailer, who was the servant of the Eleven, entered and stood by him, saying: To you, Socrates, whom I know to be the noblest and gentlest and best of all who ever came to this place, I will not impute the angry feelings of other men, who rage and swear at me, when, in obedience to the authorities, I bid them drink the poison—indeed, I am sure that you will not be angry with me; for others, as you are aware, and not I, are to blame. And so fare you well, and try to bear lightly what needs be—you know my errand. Then bursting into tears he turned away and went out.

Socrates looked at him and said: I return your good wishes, and will do as you bid. Then turning to us, he said, How charming the man is: since I have been in prison he always has been coming to see me, and at times he would talk to me, and was as good to me as could be, and now see how generously he sorrows on my account. We must do as he says, Crito; and therefore let the cup be brought, if the poison is prepared; if not, let the attendant prepare some.

Yet, said Crito, the sun is still upon the hill-tops, and I know that many a one has taken the draught late, and after the announcement has been made to him, he has eaten and drunk, and enjoyed the society of his beloved; do not hurry—there is time enough.

Socrates said: Yes, Crito, and they of whom you speak are right in so acting, for they think that they will be gainers by the delay; but I am right in not following their example, for I do not think that I should gain anything by drinking the poison a little later; I should only be ridiculous in my own eyes for sparing and saving a life which is already forfeit. Please then do as I say, and not to refuse me.

Crito made a sign to the servant, who was standing by; and he went out, and having been absent for some time, returned with the jailer carrying the cup of poison. Socrates said: You, my good friend, who are experienced in such matters, shall give me directions how I am to proceed. The man answered: You have only to walk about until your legs are heavy, and then to lie down, and the poison will act. At the same time he handed the cup to Socrates, who in the easiest and gentlest manner, without the least fear or change of color or feature, looking at the man with all his eyes, Echecrates, as his manner was, took the cup and said: What do you say about making a libation of this cup to any god? May I, or not? The man answered: We only prepare, Socrates, just so much as we deem enough. I understand, he said: but I may and must ask the gods to prosper my journey from this to the other world — even so — and so be it according to my prayer. Then raising the cup to his lips, quite readily and cheerfully he drank off the poison. And hitherto most of us had been able to control our sorrow; but now when we saw him drinking, and saw too that he had finished the draught, we could no longer forebear, and in spite of myself my own tears were flowing fast; so that I covered my face and wept, not for him, but at the thought of my own calamity in having to part from such a friend. Nor was I the first; for Crito, when he found himself unable to restrain his tears, had got up, and I followed; and at the moment, Apollodorus, who had been weeping all the time, broke out in a loud and passionate cry which made cowards of us all. Socrates alone retained his calmness: What is this strange outcry? he said. I sent away the women mainly in order that they might not misbehave in this way, for I have been told that a man should die in peace. Be quiet then, and have patience. When we heard his words we were ashamed, and refrained our tears; and he walked about until, as he said, his legs began to fail, and then he lay on his back, according to the directions, and the man who gave him the poison now and then looked at his feet and legs; and after a while he pressed his foot hard, and asked him if he could feel; and he said, No; and then his leg, and so upwards and upwards, and showed us that he was cold and stiff. And he felt them himself and said: When the poison reaches the heart, that will be the end. He was beginning to grow cold about the groin, when he uncovered his face, for he had covered himself up, and said — they were his last words — he said: Crito, I owe a cock to Aesculapius; will you remember to pay the debt? The debt shall be paid, said

Crito; is there anything else? There was no answer to this question; but in a minute or two a movement was heard, and the attendant uncovered him; his eyes were set, and Crito closed his eyes and mouth. Such was the end, Echecrates, of our friend; concerning whom I may truly say, that of all the men of his time whom I have known, he was the wisest and justest and best.

PLATO, GREEK (427–347 B.C.)

 ## 53 Growth

THE CHIEN HEXAGRAM

At the outset, the young man begins to make his way in the world. He is subjected to criticisms because his inexperienced steps are slow and hesitant. These will help prevent future errors on his part.

Life taught me with oar and rifle,
And a strong wind with a knotted cord
Lashed me upon my shoulders
To make me both calm and nimble,
And simple like iron nails.

NIKOLAI SEMYONOVICH TIKHONOV,
RUSSIAN (BORN 1896)

The man soon overcomes his initial insecurity. He acquires a good position, earns a reasonable livelihood, and enjoys the company of his comrades.

But little by little they had gained experience and assurance. With the almost imperceptible, delicate movements of a bird, the infallible instinct that causes it to sort out exactly what is needed to build its nest, they had succeeded, little by little, in picking up, here and there, from everything that came to hand, bits and scraps which they had put together to build themselves a soft little nest, within which they stayed, well protected, watched over by every side, well sheltered.

It was extraordinary to see with what rapidity, skill and voracity they caught on the wing, managed to extract from everything, books, plays, films, a quite unimportant conversation, a random phrase, a proverb, a song, pictures . . . or even subway posters and

advertisements, the principles laid down by manufacturers of soap powders and face creams . . . the
advice of Aunt Annie or Father Soury — it was extraordinary to see how unfailingly, among all the things
that come to hand, they seized upon exactly what
was needed to spin their cocoon, their impermeable
covering, to fashion this armor in which later on,
under the kindly eye of the concierges, they went
forth — amid general encouragement, unconquerable,
calm and assured: grandmothers, daughters, mal-
treated women, mothers — standing at doors pressing
with all their weight against doors, like battering rams.
NATHALIE SARRAUTE, FRENCH (BORN 1902)

If you read some of the English papers, you would
see what unheard-of enthusiasm, what unparalleled
frenzy I aroused among the cold Britons with my
first concert in the large Italian opera on June 3. If I
should write you for a whole year, I could never tell
you the smallest part of it. The whole theater, pit,
boxes, gallery, seemed like a sea in a tempest, owing
to the shouting and the clapping, the waving of
handkerchiefs, hats thrown into the air, etc. They
said things that it would be immodest of me to
repeat . . . all the more flattering for me since through
the tones of my instrument I have been able to dispel
a bad impression made on the public by the high
prices that I have fixed for my concerts right from the
beginning. I played, and all the malignant slander
changed to ineffable praise; every syllable of censure
produced a panegyric. The entire audience — involuntarily as it were — stood up on the benches and
seats in the pit. Above in the boxes you would have
thought they were about to throw themselves down
with *un saut de Leucade.*
NICOLÒ PAGANINI, ITALIAN (1782–1840)

---

*The man goes too far and plunges into struggles beyond
what is required by the natural laws of development. He
loses his way. His life and family are jeopardized. He
will regain his advantage if he does not provoke conflicts
but uses his strength more in guarding his own position
in line with his available resources and capabilities.*

The last rays of the setting sun,
Which once shone upon me warmly, have now gone.

The wind keeps returning to strike the walls
While cold birds seek warmth in one another's breast.
Clinging to their feathers,
They fear hunger in silence.
O, men of influence
Remember to withdraw in time!
You look sad and frail.
Is it because of power and fame?
I prefer to fly with jays and tits,
Not with hoary herons.
For they travel high and far,
Making the return too hard.

JUAN CHI, CHINESE (216–263)

The man attains a safe position through docility and pliancy.

It is generally better to deal by speech than by letter;
and by the mediation of a third than by a man's self.
Letters are good, when a man would draw an answer
by letter back again; or when it may serve for a man's
justification afterwards to produce his own letter; or
where it may be danger to be interrupted, or heard
by pieces. To deal in person is good, when a man's
face breedeth regard, as commonly with inferiors; or
in tender cases, where a man's eye upon the countenance of him with whom he speaketh may give him a
direction how far to go; and generally where a man
will reserve to himself liberty either to disavow or to
expound. In choice of instruments, it is better to
choose men of a plainer sort, that are likely to do that
which is committed to them, and to report back again
faithfully the success, than those that are cunning
to contrive out of other men's business somewhat to
grace themselves, and will help the matter in report
for satisfaction sake. Use also such persons as affect
the business wherein they are employed; for that
quickeneth much; and such as are fit for the matter;
as bold men for expostulation, fair-spoken men for
persuasion, crafty men for inquiry and observation,
froward [stubborn] and absurd [stupid] men for
business that doth not well bear out [justify] itself.
Use also such as have been lucky, and prevailed before in things wherein you have employed them; for
that breeds confidence, and they will strive to maintain their prescription. It is better to sound a person

with whom one deals afar off, than to fall upon the
point at first; except you mean to surprise him by
some short question. It is better dealing with men in
appetite, than with those that are where they would
be. If a man deal with another upon conditions, the
start or first performance is all; which a man cannot
reasonably demand, except either the nature of the
thing be such, which must go before; or else a man
can persuade the other party that he shall still need
him in some other thing; or else that he be counted
the honester man. All practice is to discover, or to
work. Men discover themselves in trust, in passion,
at unawares, and of necessity, when they would have
somewhat done and cannot find an apt pretext. If you
would work any man, you must either know his
nature and fashions, and so lead him; or his ends,
and so persuade him; or his weakness and disadvan-
tages, and so awe him; or those that have interest in
him, and so govern him. In dealing with cunning
persons, we must ever consider their ends, to inter-
pret their speeches; and it is good to say little to
them, and that which they least look for. In all nego-
tiations of difficulty, a man may not look to sow and
reap at once; but must prepare business, and so
ripen it by degrees.
BARON FRANCIS BACON, ENGLISH (1561–1626)

---

*Because of the calumny of deceitful people, the man is
misjudged while advancing into a high position. Although
reconciliation and progress result eventually, nothing is
achieved in the interim.*

LADY SNEERWELL. Did you circulate the report of
Lady Brittle's intrigue with Captain Boastall?
SNAKE *(with pardonable self-satisfaction)*. That's in
as fine a train as your ladyship could wish. In the
common course of things, I think it must reach
Mrs. Clackitt's ears within four-and-twenty hours;
(knowingly) and then, you know, the business is as
good as done.
LADY SNEERWELL *(thoughtfully)*. Why, truly, Mrs.
Clackitt has a very pretty talent, and a great deal of
industry.
SNAKE *(with urbane detachment)*. True, madam, and
has been tolerably successful in her day. To my
knowledge she has been the cause of six matches

being broken off and three sons being disinherited; *(putting down his cup to concentrate on the statistics)* of four forced elopements and as many close confinements; nine separate maintenances and two divorces.

RICHARD BRINSLEY SHERIDAN, IRISH (1751–1816)

Everyone knows the all-pervading influence of literature at the present day, and how much the opinions and passions of mankind are under its control. The mere contests of the sword are temporary; their wounds are but in the flesh, and it is the pride of the generous to forgive and forget them; but the slanders of the pen pierce the heart, they rankle longest in the noblest spirits; they dwell ever present in the mind, and render it morbidly sensitive to the most trifling collision. It is but seldom that any one overt act produces hostilities between two nations; there exists, most commonly, a previous jealousy and ill-will; a predisposition to take offence. Trace these to their cause, and how often will they be found to originate in the mischievous effusions of mercenary writers; who, secure in their closets, and for ignominious bread, concoct and circulate the venom that is to inflame the generous and the brave.

WASHINGTON IRVING, AMERICAN (1783–1859)

The man reaches the pinnacle, completes his work, and leaves inspiration for the world to follow.

In hell, amongst all the brave company that is ever to be found there of lovers and fair ladies and astrologers, tossing and turning to get rid of the torment of their hot bodies, one woman sat alone and smiled. She had the air of a listener, lifting her head now and then as though some voice from above attracted her.

"Who is that woman?" inquired a newcomer, dazzled by her exceeding beauty, "the one with smooth ivory limbs and long hair falling down over her arms to the hands resting and on to her lap? She is the only soul here whose eyes are ever looking aloft. What skeleton does she keep in the cupboard of God up yonder?"

"They say," one made haste to answer, "that she was a great singer in her day, with a voice like a falling star in a clear sky; and that when she came here to meet her doom, God took her voice from her and cast it to the eternal echoes of the spheres, finding it too beautiful a thing to let die. So now she hears it with recognition, and remembering how once it was her own, shares still the pleasure that God takes in it. Do not speak to her, for she believes that she is in Heaven."

"No, that is not her story," said another.

"What then?"

"It is this: On earth a poet made his songs of her, so that her name became eternally wedded to his verse, which still rings on the lips of men. Now she lifts her head and hears his praise of her eternally going on wherever language is spoken. That is her true story."

"Did she love him well?"

"So little that here and now she passes him daily and does not recognize his face!"

"And he?"

The other laughed and answered: "It is he who just now told you that tale concerning her voice, continuing here the lies which he used to make about her when they two were on earth!"

But the newcomer said: "If he is able to give happiness in Hell, how can what he says be a lie?"

LAURENCE HOUSMAN, ENGLISH (1865–1959)

The over-all judgment: the gradual development of honorable relationships and cooperative sentiments must precede great achievements. Agitation for the rapid rise of a man in the service of a state is not the proper course. Penetrating gentleness, which is necessary, flows from a steadfast inner tranquillity.

To know what you like is the beginning of wisdom and of old age. Youth is wholly experimental. The essence and charm of that unquiet and delightful epoch is ignorance of self as well as ignorance of life. These two unknowns the young man brings together again and again, now in the airiest touch, now with a bitter hug; but never with indifference, to which he is a total stranger, and never with that near kinsman of indifference, contentment.

ROBERT LOUIS STEVENSON, SCOTTISH (1850–1894)

It is not strange . . . that such an exuberance of enterprise should cause some individuals to mistake change for progress, and the invasion of the rights of others for national prowess and glory.

PRESIDENT MILLARD FILLMORE, AMERICAN (1800–1874)

Perhaps you are wondering about the kind of encouragement Bonnat is giving me. He tells me: "Your painting isn't bad, it is 'chic,' but even so it isn't bad, but your drawing is absolutely atrocious."

So I must gather my courage and start once again.

HENRI DE TOULOUSE-LAUTREC, FRENCH (1864–1901)

54 Propriety

THE KUEI MEI HEXAGRAM

At the outset, the man in a relatively low position enjoys the confidence of the prince. Outwardly, he keeps tactfully behind the official ministers. Although this diminishes his status, he continues to perform valuable services for the state.

I am known to other men. They know me as an object, not as subject. They are unaware of my subjectivity as such; unaware not merely of its inexhaustible depth, but also of the presence of the whole in each of its operations, that existential complexity of inner circumstances, data of nature, free choice, attractions, weaknesses, virtues perhaps, loves and pains; that atmosphere of imminent vitality which alone lends meaning to each of my acts.

JACQUES MARITAIN, FRENCH (BORN 1882)

Devoted loyalty on the part of the man will compensate for many weaknesses on the part of his associates as well.

He made an automatic bow. Then a bewildered struggling look came into his face, then a hopeless look, and then he stood staring vacantly, like a somnambulist, at the waiting audience. The moments of painful suspense went by, and still he stood as if struck dumb. I saw how it was; he had been seized with stage-fright.

Alas! little sister! She turned her large dismayed eyes upon me. "He's forgotten it," she said. Then a swift change came into her face; a strong, determined look;

[347]54

and on the funeral-like silence of the room broke the sweet, brave child-voice:

"Amid the permutations and combinations of the actors and the forces which make up the great kaleidoscope of history, we often find that a turn of Destiny's hand . . ."

Everybody about us turned and looked. The breathless silence; the sweet, childish voice; the childish face; the long, unchildlike words, produced a weird effect.

But the help came too late; the unhappy brother was already staggering in humiliation from the stage. The band quickly struck up, and waves of lively music rolled out to cover the defeat.

I gave the little sister a glance in which I meant to show the intense sympathy I felt; but she did not see me. Her eyes, swimming with tears, were on her brother's face. I put my arm around her, but she was too absorbed to heed the caress, and before I could appreciate her purpose, she was on her way to the shame stricken young man sitting with a face like a statue's.

When he saw her by his side the set face relaxed and a quick mist came into his eyes. The young men got closer together to make room for her. She sat down beside him, laid her flowers on his knee, and slipped her hand in his.

I could not keep my eyes from her sweet, pitying face. I saw her whisper to him, he bending a little to catch her words. Later, I found out that she was asking him if he knew his "piece" now, and that he answered yes.

When the young man next on the list had spoken and while the band was playing, the child, to the brother's great surprise, made her way up the stage steps, and pressed through the throng of professors and trustees and distinguished visitors, up to the college president.

"If you please, sir," she said with a little curtsy, "will you and the trustees let my brother try again? He knows his piece now."

For a moment the president stared at her through his gold-bowed spectacles and then, appreciating the child's petition, he smiled on her, and went down and spoke to the young man who had failed.

So it happened that when the band had again ceased

playing, it was briefly announced that Mr. _____
_____ would now deliver his oration—"Historical
Parallels."

A ripple of heightened and expectant interest passed
over the audience, and then all sat stone still, as
though fearing to breathe lest the speaker might
again take fright. No danger! The hero in the youth
was aroused. He went at his "piece" with a set purpose to conquer, to redeem himself, and to bring the
smile back into the child's tear-stained face. I
watched the face during the speaking. The wide
eyes, the parted lips, the whole rapt being said that
the breathless audience was forgotten, that her spirit
was moving with his.

And when the address was ended with the ardent
abandon of one who catches enthusiasm in the realization that he is fighting down a wrong judgment
and conquering a sympathy, the effect was really
thrilling. That dignified audience broke into rap-
turous applause; bouquets intended for the vale-
dictorian rained like a tempest. And the child who
had helped to save the day—that one beaming little
face, in its pride and gladness, is something to be
forever remembered.

SARAH WINTER KELLOGG, AMERICAN (1875)

---

*It is preferable to be a concubine rather than a slave. The
inferior person enters into situations incompatible with
self-esteem, in pursuit of joys that cannot be attained
legitimately.*

It's grand, and you cannot expect to be both grand
and comfortable.

SIR JAMES MATTHEW BARRIE, SCOTTISH (1860–1937)

How I should love
To lie among the peonies
And drink to my heart's content!
But, alas!
If the flowers could speak,
I fear they would say:
"We do not blossom for old men."

LIÜ YU-SHIH, CHINESE (772–804)

---

*The person does not throw her virtue away but waits.
Her marriage will be all the better for it.*

He who puts up at the first inn he comes across, very often passes a bad night.
FILIPPO BALDINUCCI, ITALIAN (1634–1696)

The man is reminded that the sister of King I placed herself graciously below her outranked husband and remained free of vanity. The moon that is full does not face the sun.

He who raises himself on tiptoe cannot stand firm; he who stretches his legs wide apart cannot walk.
LAO-TZU, CHINESE (604–531 B.C.)

William Penn made himself endeared to the Indians by his marked condescension and acquiescence in their wishes. He walked with them, sat with them on the ground, and ate with them of their roasted acorns and hominy. At this they expressed their great delight, and soon began to show how they could hop and jump; at which exhibition William Penn, to cap the climax, sprang up and out-danced them all!
JOHN FISKE, AMERICAN (1842–1901)

The man goes through superficial actions, such as offering an empty basket and a preslaughtered sheep to the gods, solely to preserve the form. This disregard for content bodes no good for lasting associations.

To them, the Romantic Hero was no longer the knight, the wandering poet, the aviator, nor the brave young district attorney, but the great sales manager, who had an Analysis of Merchandising Problems on his glass-topped desk, whose title of nobility was "go-getter," and who devoted himself and all his young samurai to the cosmic purpose of Selling — not of selling anything in particular, for or to anybody in particular, but pure Selling.
SINCLAIR LEWIS, AMERICAN (1885–1951)

JUPITER. Don't let it go any further, but, between ourselves, the sacrifice and votive offerings have fallen off terribly of late. Why, I can remember the time when people offered us human sacrifices — No mistake about it — human sacrifices! Think of that.
DIANA. Ah! those good old days!
[350]54

JUPITER. Then it fell off to oxen, pigs and sheep.
APOLLO. Well there are worse things than oxen, pigs
and sheep.
JUPITER. So I've found to my cost. My dear sir — between ourselves it's dropped off from one thing to
another until it has positively dwindled down to
preserved Australian beef!
SIR WILLIAM SCHWENCK GILBERT, ENGLISH (1836–1911)

*The over-all judgment: spontaneous affection is the
strong bond in meaningful relationships. There are fixed
proprieties, however. A person in a lower station should
not scheme to supplant the one above.*

When friends are at your hearthside met,
Sweet courtesy has done its most
If you have made each guest forget
That he himself is not the host.
THOMAS BAILEY ALDRICH, AMERICAN (1836–1907)

It is a fundamental rule of human nature that the
largest portion of the energy of the human race must
be consumed in supplying the primary necessities
of existence. The chief aim of a savage's life is to
make that life secure and mankind is by nature so
frail and needy that the immense majority of men,
even on the higher levels of culture, must always and
everywhere devote themselves to bread-winning
and the material cares of life. To put it simply: the
masses must forever remain the masses. There would
be no culture without kitchenmaids.
Obviously education could never thrive if there was
nobody to do the rough work. Millions must plough
and forge and dig in order that a few thousand may
write and paint and study.
It sounds harsh, but it is true for all time, and whining and complaining can never alter it.
HEINRICH VON TREITSCHKE, GERMAN (1834–1896)

Know then thyself, presume not God to scan
The proper study of mankind is man.
Placed on this isthmus of a middle state.
A being darkly wise, and rudely great:
With too much knowledge for the sceptic side,
With too much weakness for the stoic's pride,
He hangs between; in doubt to act, or rest;

In doubt to deem himself a god, or beast;
In doubt his mind or body to prefer;
Born but to die, and reasoning but to err;
Alike in ignorance, his reason such,
Whether he thinks too little or too much:
Chaos of thought and passion, all confused;
Still by himself abused or disabused;
Created half to rise and half to fall;
Great lord of all things, yet a prey to all;
Sole judge of truth, in endless error hurled:
The glory, jest, and riddle of the world!
ALEXANDER POPE, ENGLISH (1688–1744)

 ## 55 Prosperity

THE FÊNG HEXAGRAM

At the outset, the man meets his destined ruler and goes forth with his approval. Mutual helpfulness is required for continued prosperity.

Men might be better if we better deemed
Of them. The worst way to improve the world
Is to condemn it.
PHILIP JAMES BAILEY, ENGLISH (1816–1902)

Intrigues have put a barrier between the chief executive desiring great works and the man capable of bringing them about. The courtiers have usurped the ruler's power. The man should not take energetic action, which will only lead to suspicion and dislike. He must depend upon his sincere devotion to move the ruler's mind in a less obvious way.

MRS. CHEVELEY (*shaking her head*). I am not in a mood tonight for silver twilights, or rose-pink dawns. I want to talk business.
(*Motions to him with her fan to sit down again beside her.*)
SIR ROBERT CHILTERN. I fear I have no advice to give you, Mrs. Cheveley, except to interest yourself in something less dangerous. The success of the Canal depends, of course, on the attitude of England, and I am going to lay the report of the Commissioners before the House tomorrow night.
CHEVELEY. That you must not do. In your own inter-

ests, Sir Robert, to say nothing of mine, you must not do that.

CHILTERN (*looking at her in wonder*). In my own interests? My dear Mrs. Cheveley, what do you mean? (*Sits down beside her.*)

CHEVELEY. Sir Robert, I will be quite frank with you. I want you to withdraw the report that you had intended to lay before the House, on the ground that you have reasons to believe that the Commissioners have been prejudiced, or misinformed, or something. Then I want you to say a few words to the effect that the Government is going to reconsider the question, and that you have reason to believe that the Canal, if completed, will be of great international value. You know the sort of things ministers say in cases of this kind. A few ordinary platitudes will do. In modern life nothing produces such an effect as a good platitude. It makes the whole world kin. Will you do this for me?

CHILTERN. Mrs. Cheveley, you cannot be serious in making such a proposition!

CHEVELEY. I am quite serious.

CHILTERN (*coldly*). Pray allow me to believe you are not!

CHEVELEY (*speaking with great deliberation and emphasis*). Ah! But I am. And if you do what I ask you, I . . . will pay you very handsomely.

CHILTERN. Pay me!

CHEVELEY. Yes.

CHILTERN. I am afraid I don't understand what you mean.

CHEVELEY (*leaning back on the sofa and looking at him*). How very disappointing! And I have come all the way from Vienna in order that you should thoroughly understand me.

CHILTERN. I fear I don't.

CHEVELEY (*in her most nonchalant manner*). My dear Sir Robert, you are a man of the world, and you have your price, I suppose. Everybody has nowadays. The drawback is that most people are so dreadfully expensive. I know I am. I hope you will be more reasonable in your terms.

CHILTERN (*rises indignantly*). If you will allow me, I will call your carriage for you. You have lived so long abroad, Mrs. Cheveley, that you seem unable to realize that you are talking to an English gentleman.

CHEVELEY (*detains him by touching his arm with her fan, and keeping it there while she is talking*). I realize that I am talking to a man who laid the foundation of his fortune by selling to a Stock Exchange speculator a Cabinet secret.
OSCAR FINGAL WILDE, IRISH (1856–1900)

The prince is so eclipsed that even insignificant personalities push themselves onto the stage. Although the man is in a key position, he is powerless to achieve anything. But he remains free of error.

Think of it, cousin. Tell it to your friends,
The statesmen, soldiers, and philosophers;
Noise it about the earth, and let it stir
The sluggish spirits of the multitudes,
Pursue the thought, scan it, from end to end,
Through all its latent possibilities.
It is a great seed dropped, I promise you,
And it must sprout. Thought never wholly dies;
It only wants a name — a hard Greek name —
Some few apostles, who may live on it —
A crowd of listeners, with the average dullness
That man possesses — and we organize;
Spread our new doctrine, like a general plague;
Talk of man's progress and development,
Wrongs of society, the march of mind,
The Devil, Doctor Faustus, and what not;
And lo! this pretty world turns upside down,
All with a fool's idea.
GEORGE HENRY BOKER, AMERICAN (1823–1890)

The eclipse is decreasing. The man gets together with elements with which he has a natural affinity.

How oft the darkest hour of ill
Breaks brightest into dawn.
EURIPIDES, GREEK (484–406 B.C.)

The modest ruler assembles ministers of brilliant ability around him. Especially is he attracted to men who are sound of heart and sure of getting results.

Not for me the general renowned nor the well-
  groomed dandy,
Nor he who is proud of his curls or is shaven in part;
But give me a man that is small and whose legs are
  bandy,

Provided he's firm on his feet and valiant in heart.
ARCHILOCHUS, GREEK (SEVENTH CENTURY B.C.)

When war broke between Spain and the United States, it was very necessary to communicate quickly with the leader of the Insurgents. Garcia was somewhere in the mountain fastness of Cuba—no one knew where. No mail or telegraph message could reach him. The President must secure his cooperation, and quickly.
What to do!
Someone said to the President, "There is a fellow by the name of Rowan will find Garcia for you, if anybody can."
Rowan was sent for and given a letter to be delivered to Garcia. How the "fellow by the name of Rowan" took the letter, sealed it up in an oilskin pouch, strapped it over his heart, in four days landed by night off the coast of Cuba from an open boat, disappeared into the jungle, and in three weeks came out on the other side of the Island, having traversed a hostile country by foot and delivered his letter to Garcia—are things I have no special desire now to tell in detail.
The point that I wish to make is this: McKinley gave Rowan a letter to be delivered to Garcia; Rowan took the letter and did not ask: "Where is he at?"
ELBERT GREEN HUBBARD, AMERICAN (1856–1915)

The man is overwhelmed by his pride as he seeks personal splendor, alienating even members of his own household. He becomes isolated and is undone.

Once the Meschacebe, still very close to its source, was tired of being only a clear brook. It called for the snows from the mountains and torrential waters, rain in tempests; it overflowed its banks and laid waste these charming forests. The proud brook at first was pleased with its power; but, seeing that everything was becoming desolate in its course, that it was flowing ever in solitude, that its waters were ever troubled, it yearned for the humble bed which Nature had made for it, the birds, flowers, trees, and streamlets, once modest companions of its peaceful course.
VISCOUNT FRANÇOIS RENÉ DE CHATEAUBRIAND, FRENCH (1768–1848)

*The over-all judgment: the ruler finally reaches the
zenith of his powers, where his cheer and light shine
beneficently like the sun upon all below. Although the
time of abundance is limited, he should not be anxious.
It is only natural that, after the sun reaches the meridian,
it declines. In the meantime his motive force guided by
intelligence will sustain a prosperous country.*

Moreover I have had banyan trees planted on the
roads to give shade to man and beast; I have planted
mango groves, and I have had ponds dug and shel-
ters erected along the roads at every eight kos [a
day's journey]. Everywhere I had wells dug for the
benefit of man and beast. . . . What I have done has
been done that men may conform to Righteousness.
All the good deeds that I have done have been accepted and followed by the people. And so obedience
to mother and father, obedience to teachers, respect
for the aged, kindliness to brahmans and ascetics,
to the poor and weak, and to slaves and servants,
have increased and will continue to increase. . . . And
this progress of Righteousness among men has taken
place in two manners, by enforcing conformity to
Righteousness, and by exhortation. I have enforced
the law against killing certain animals and many
others, but the greatest progress of Righteousness
among men comes from exhortation in favor of non-
injury to life and abstention from killing living
beings.

EMPEROR ASHOKA, INDIAN (268–233 B.C.)

In an orchard there should be enough to eat, enough
to lay up, enough to be stolen, and enough to rot
upon the ground.
SAMUEL MADDEN, ENGLISH (1686–1765)

When, Mr. President, a man becomes a member of
this body [United States Senate] he cannot even
dream of the ordeal to which he cannot fail to be
exposed;
  of how much courage he must posses to resist the
  temptations which daily beset him;
  of that sensitive shrinking from undeserved censure
  which he must learn to control;
  of the ever-recurring contest between a natural de-

sire for public approbation and a sense of public
duty;

of the load of injustice he must be content to bear,
even from those who should be his friends; the im-
putations of his motives; the sneers and sarcasms of
ignorance and malice; all the manifold injuries which
partisan or private malignity, disappointed of its
objects, may shower upon his unprotected head.
All this, Mr. President, if he should retain his integrity, he must learn to bear unmoved, and walk
steadily onward in the path of duty, sustained only
by the reflection that time may do him justice, or if
not, that after all his individual hopes and aspirations, and even his name among men, should be of
little account to him when weighed in the balance
against the welfare of a people of whose destiny he
is a constituted guardian and defender.

WILLIAM PITT FESSENDEN, AMERICAN (1806–1869)

 ## 56 The Newcomer

THE LÜ HEXAGRAM

---

*At the outset, the newcomer in a lowly position is oc-
cupying himself with disgraceful machinations. His
aspirations invite troubles.*

"One mode," says Clavering's correspondent [from
Madras], "of amassing money at the Nobob's cost is
curious. He is generally in arrears to the Company.
Here the Governor, being cash-keeper, is generally
on good terms with the banker, who manages matters thus: The Governor presses the Nabob for the
balance due from him; the Nabob flies to his banker
for relief; the banker engages to pay the money, and
grants his notes accordingly, which he puts in the
cash-box as ready money; the Nabob pays him an
interest for it at two and three percent. a month, till
the tunkaws [assignments] he grants on the particular districts for it are paid. Matters in the meantime
are so managed that there is no call for this money
for the Company's service till the tunkaws become
due. By this means not a cash is advanced by the
banker, though he receives a heavy interest from the
Nabob, which is divided as lawful spoil."

Here, Mr. Speaker, you have the whole art and mys-

tery, the true Free-mason secret, of the profession of
soucaring [money-lending]; by which a few innocent,
inexperienced young Englishmen, such as Mr. Paul
Benfield, for instance, without property upon which
anyone would lend to themselves a single shilling,
are enabled at once to take provinces in mortgage,
to make princes their debtors, and to become cred-
itors for millions.
EDMUND BURKE, ENGLISH (1729–1797)

---

*The man retains his inner sense of modesty and reserve.
He acquires the necessary means of livelihood, a home,
and good and trustworthy servants.*

Literary men, and the young still more than the old
of this class, have commonly a good deal to rescind
in their style in order to adapt it to business. But the
young, if they be men of sound qualities, will soon
learn what is not apt and discard it; which the old
will not. The leading rule is to be content to be com-
mon-place, — a rule which might be observed with
advantage in other writings, but is distinctly applicable to these. Any point of style is to be avoided by a
statesman which gives reason to suppose that he is
thinking more of his credit than of his business. It
belongs to high station to rest upon its advantages,
and by no means to court the notice of inferiors or
to be solicitous of effect. *Their* interests should en-
gross the thoughts of the statesman, and he should
appear to have no occasion for any other credit than
that of duly regarding their welfare. His style, therefore, should have the correctness and clearness
which education and practice impart to the writing
of a man of good understanding, should not evince
any solicitous precision beyond what may be done to
exactitude in the subject-matter, much less any ambition for argument for its own sake, and less still of
ornament or pungency in like manner gratuitous. If
he be a man of philosophic mind, philosophy will
enter into his views and enlarge and enlighten them;
but it will be well that it should not ostensibly manifest itself in his writing, because he has to address
himself, not to philosophers but to ordinary men;
who are ever of the opinion (erroneous though it be)
that what he recognizes to be philosophy is not fit
for common use. A statesman's philosophy, there-

fore, should be as it were foundations sunk in the ground, and should not overtly appear, except in so far as it may be made to take the form of trite and popular maxims. With respect to ornament and figures of speech, it is to be observed that all language whatsoever carries metaphor within it; though much that is metaphorical may not be cognisably so to those who do not probe and search it and see into the sources of its meanings. The customariness of many metaphorical uses of words makes us unconscious of their metaphor; and the care of a statesman should be to avoid express metaphors (as well as express philosophy), and use only such as lie hid in common language and will not attract specific notice. Yet since much of the force and propriety of language depends upon a reference, conscious or unconscious, to its metaphorical basis, the exclusion of metaphorical invention does not negative such an exercise of imagination as shall detect the latent metaphors of language, and so deal with them as to give to the style a congruity and aptitude otherwise unattainable.

SIR HENRY TAYLOR, ENGLISH (1800–1886)

The newcomer becomes arrogant and truculent. He eventually loses his house and servant and finds himself without support in a perilous situation.

A man said to the universe:
　"Sir, I exist!"
"However," replied the universe,
"That fact has not created in me
A sense of obligation."

STEPHEN CRANE, AMERICAN (1871–1900)

Although the inferior man finds a resting place and a means of livelihood, his aspirations are greater than his capabilities. He remains ill at ease, a stranger in a strange environment.

Nightlong in the cold
　That monkey sits
　Conjecturing
How to catch the moon.

SHIKI, JAPANESE (1866–1902)

The man succeeds in his task and receives the recognition and praise of his friends. They recommend him to the prince, who accepts his services in a highly responsible position.

The reason the gentleman is called worthy is not that he is able to do everything that the most skillful man can do. The reason the gentleman is called wise is not because he knows everything that the wise man knows. When he is called discriminating, this does not mean that he is able to split hairs so exhaustively as the sophists. That he is called an investigator does not mean that he is able to examine exhaustively into everything that an investigator may examine. He has his limit.

In observing high and low lands, in judging whether fields are poor or fertile, and in deciding where the various grains should be planted, the gentleman is not as capable as a farmer. When it is a matter of understanding commodities, and determining their quality and value, the gentleman cannot vie with a merchant. As regards skill in the use of the compass, square, plumb line, and other tools, he is less able than an artisan. In disregarding right and wrong, truth and falsehood, but manipulating them so that they seem to change places and shame each other, the gentleman cannot compare with Hui Shih and Teng Hsi.

However, if it is a question of ranking men according to their virtue; if offices are to be bestowed according to ability; if both the worthy and the unworthy are to be put in their proper places . . . if all things and events are to be dealt with properly; if the charter of Shen Tzu and Mo Tzu are to be suppressed; if Hui Shih and Teng Hsi are not to dare to put forth their arguments; if speech is always to accord with the truth and affairs are always to be properly managed — it is in these matters that the gentleman excels.
HSÜN-TZU, CHINESE (300–235 B.C.)

Many brave men lived before Agamemnon but they are all unmourned and lost in oblivion, because they had no bard to sing their praises.
HORACE, ROMAN (65–8 B.C.)

The newcomer becomes careless, imprudent, and violent at the height of his distinction.

It is an ever-recurring experience that every man who has power is apt to abuse it; he will go further and further until he meets a barrier.
BARON CHARLES DE SECONDAT DE MONTESQUIEU, FRENCH (1689–1755)

The over-all judgment: the newcomer must be cautious and correct within himself and humble and obliging to others in order to make progress. He must preserve an upright integrity in his sojourn.

Born with a gift of laughter and a sense that the world is mad . . .
RAFAEL SABATINI, ITALIAN (1875–1950)

Politics is the science of exigencies.
THEODORE PARKER, AMERICAN (1810–1860)

What another would have done as well as you, do not do it. What another would have said as well as you, do not say it; written as well, do not write it. Be faithful to that which exists nowhere but in yourself — and thus make yourself indispensable.
ANDRÉ GIDE, FRENCH (1869–1951)

 # 57 Gentle Penetration

THE SUN HEXAGRAM

At the outset, the man is perplexed and drifts indecisively. A resolute military discipline is required of him.

Man is, of all creatures, the most difficult to sound and know. He is dual and artificial, and there are in him so many cabinets and dark corners from which he comes forth, sometimes a man, sometimes a satyr; in his actions is a perpetual race of errors; sometimes a god, sometimes a fly; he laughs and weeps for one and the same thing; content and discontent; he will and he will not, and in the end knows not what he will; now he is filled with such joy and gladness that he cannot stay within his own skin, and presently he falls out with himself and dares not trust himself.

For the most part men's actions are nothing but impulses, induced by occasions and that have reference
to others. Irresolution, inconstancy, and instability
are the most common and apparent vices in the nature of man. We follow our inclinations, and as the
wind of occasion carries us, not governed by reason.
PIERRE CHARRON, FRENCH (1541–1603)

Do not consider what you may do, but what it will
become you to have done, and let the sense of honor
subdue your mind.
CLAUDIUS CLAUDIANUS, ROMAN (365–408)

---

*Undesirable influences from hidden quarters adversely
affect the man's progress. They must be indefatigably
traced to their darkest sources and exposed. This will
eliminate their power over people.*

Men think themselves free because they are conscious of their volitions and desires, but are ignorant
of the causes by which they are led to wish and
desire.
BENEDICT SPINOZA, DUTCH (1632–1677)

---

*The man deliberates repeatedly about the same issues,
thereby generating fresh scruples and doubts. His striving is ineffective.*

I call out. No one answers. Instead of concluding that
there is no one there—which might be purely and
simply an ascertainable fact, dated and localized in
space and time—I decide to behave as if there were
someone there, someone who, for reasons unknown,
refrained from answering. From then on, the silence
which follows my calling out is no longer a *true*
silence; it is endowed with a content, a depth, a soul
—and this soul refers me back to mine. The distance
between my cry, still ringing in my own ears, and
my silent (perhaps deaf) vis-à-vis to whom it is addressed becomes an anguish, a hope and a despair;
it gives a meaning to my life. Henceforth, the only
thing I shall attach importance to will be this false
emptiness and the problems it sets me. Ought I to go
on calling out? Should I shout more loudly? Should
I use a different set of words? Again I try . . . I very

soon realize that no one will answer; but the invisible presence that I continue to create by calling out forces me to go on forever breaking the silence with my unhappy cry. Soon the reverberating sound begins to confuse me. Spellbound, as it were, I call out again . . . and again. In the end, my distraught consciousness translates my exasperated solitude into a higher necessity and a promise of redemption.
ALAIN ROBBE-GRILLET, FRENCH (BORN 1922)

The man gains praise by counteracting evil. He can now meet his needs for offerings to the gods, for everyday use, and for guests.

Everyone has a mass of bad work in him which he will have to work off and get rid of before he can do better — and indeed, the more lasting a man's ultimate good work is, the more sure he is to pass through a time, and perhaps a very long one, in which there seems very little hope for him at all. We must all sow our spiritual wild oats.
SAMUEL BUTLER, ENGLISH (1835–1902)

Another fear, perhaps the most corroding one in our world of possessors of material wealth, is the panic alarm at any glimpse of possible changes in the social fabric which may make things uncomfortable for possessors. The Latin poet who many years ago described the light-hearted stride of a poor man across a dark plain infested with robbers described the care-free gait at which Vermont moves through the uncertain and troubled modern world. Vermont, like some of the remote valleys in the Pyrenees, has always been too far out of the furiously swirling current of modern industrial life to be too much affected by it or to dread its vagaries. For generations now, when times get hard and manufacturers are flat and deflated and the mills in the industrial States around us are shut down, and the newspapers are talking about bankruptcies and breadlines, the Vermont family, exactly as rich and exactly as poor as it ever was, remarks with a kindliness tinged with pride: "Well, we'd better ask Lem's folks up to stay a spell, till times get better. I guess it's pretty hard sledding for them." And when times get better and Lem's family leave the poor frame farmhouse which has
[363]57

been their refuge, and drive off down the steep stony
road which is the first stage of their journey back to
wages and movies, the Vermont family stand looking
after them, still with friendliness.

DOROTHY CANFIELD FISHER, AMERICAN (BORN 1879)

---

*Continued integrity on the part of the man compensates
for his poor beginning. However, prior to the change
the man needs to ponder carefully. After the change, he
needs to check his results.*

Bad is the plan that admits no change.

PUBLILIUS SYRUS, ROMAN (FIRST CENTURY B.C.)

In a certain place there dwelt four brahman youths
in the greatest friendship. Three of them had got to
the further shore of the ocean of science, but were
devoid of common-sense; while the fourth had common-sense only, and no mind for science. Now once
upon a time these friends took counsel together and
said, "Of what profit is science, if we cannot go
with it to some foreign country and win the favor of
princes and make our fortune? Therefore to the
Eastern Country let us go." And so it came to
pass.
Now after they had gone a little way, the eldest
spoke: "There is one among us, the fourth, who has
no learning, but only common-sense; and a man can't
get presents from kings by common-sense without
learning. Not a whit will I give him of all that I gain;
so let him go home." And the second said, "Ho there,
Gumption! get you homeward, for you have no learning!" But the third made answer, "Alas, it is not
fitting to do so: for we have played together since we
were boys. So let him come along too. He's a noble
fellow, and shall have a share in the riches we
win."
On they went together, till in a jungle they saw the
bones of a dead lion. Then spoke the first: "Ha! now
we can put our book-learning to the test. Here lies
some sort of a dead creature: by the power of our
learning we'll bring it back to life. I'll put the bones
together." And that he did with zeal. The second
added flesh, blood, and hide. But just as the third
was breathing the breath of life into it, Gumption
stopped him and said, "Hold: this is a lion you are
[364]57

turning out. If you make him alive, he will kill everyone of us." Thereupon made answer the other, "Fie,
stupid! Is learning to be fruitless in my hands?"
"Well, then," said Gumption, "just wait a bit till I
climb a tree."
Thereupon the lion was brought to life. But the instant this was done, he sprang up and killed the
three. Afterwards Gumption climbed down and went
home.
PANCHATANTRA, INDIAN (200 B.C.)

*The man appreciates the underlying problem and traces
the injurious influence to its ultimate origin. However,
he lacks the power to overcome it and is hurt in the
process.*

There is no lie so reckless as to be without some
proof.
PLINY THE ELDER, ROMAN (23–79)

*The over-all judgment: small and gradual improvements
can be realized by gentle penetrations. They are made to
endure by setting clearly defined objectives. Further advantages can be realized by following the great man.*

Firstly, gradualness. About this most important condition of fruitful scientific work I can never speak
without emotion. Gradualness, gradualness, gradualness.
IVAN PETROVICH PAVLOV, RUSSIAN (1849–1936)

Mocius asked a Confucian: "Why do you pursue
music?" He answers: "Music is pursued for its own
sake." Whereupon Mocius says: "You have not answered me. Suppose I ask you why you build houses.
And you answer that it is to keep off the cold in
winter and the heat in summer and to separate men
from women. Then you would have told me the
reason for building houses. Now I am asking why
you pursue music. And you answer that music is
pursued for its own sake. This is like saying that
houses are built for their own sake."
MOCIUS, CHINESE (470–390 B.C.)

To the great problem of our century — the lack of a
belief in the meaning of life, the experience of emptiness, of hopelessness of despair — the suggested des-

cription of man's basic nature gives an answer: life is accepted if meaning in the midst of meaninglessness is accepted. The experience of meaninglessness, emptiness and despair is *not* neurotic but realistic. Life has all these elements. The experience becomes neurotic or psychotic only if the power of affirmation of life in terms of "in spite of" has vanished. The negative elements are possible consequences of man's basic nature, of finite freedom. They are universally real, but they are not structurally necessary. They can be conquered by the presence of a healing power.

PAUL JOHANNES TILLICH, GERMAN (1886–1965)

 # 58 Joy

THE TUI HEXAGRAM

At the outset, the man lives in quiet, self-contained joy.

It is a hot day in June when the sun hangs still in the sky and there is not a whiff of wind or air, nor a trace of clouds; the front and back yards are hot like an oven and not a single bird dares to fly about. Perspiration flows down my whole body in little rivulets. There is the noon-day meal before me, but I cannot take it for the sheer heat. I ask for a mat to spread on the ground and lie down, but the mat is wet with moisture and flies swarm about to rest on my nose and refuse to be driven away. Just at this moment when I am completely helpless, suddenly there is a rumbling of thunder and big sheets of black clouds overcast the sky and come majestically like a great army advancing to battle. Rain water begins to pour down from the eaves like a cataract. The perspiration stops. The clamminess of the ground is gone. All flies disappear to hide themselves and I can eat my rice. Ah, is this not happiness? . . .

Having nothing to do after a meal I go to the shops and take a fancy to a little thing. After bargaining for some time; we still haggle about a small difference, but the shop-boy still refuses to sell it. Then I take out a little thing from my sleeve, which is worth about the same thing as the difference and throw it at the boy. The boy suddenly smiles and bows courteously saying, "Oh, you are too generous!" Ah, is this not happiness?

I have nothing to do after a meal and try to go through the things in some old trunks. I see there are dozens or hundreds of I.O.U.'s from people who owe my family money. Some of them are dead and some still living, but in any case there is no hope of their returning the money. Behind people's backs I put them together in a pile and make a bonfire of them, and I look up to the sky and see the last trace of smoke disappear. Ah, is this not happiness?

It is a summer day. I go bareheaded and barefooted, holding a parasol to watch young people singing Soochow folk songs while treading the water wheel. The water comes up over the wheel in a gushing torrent like molten silver or melting snow. Ah, is this not happiness?

I wake up in the morning and seem to hear some one in the house sighing and saying that last night some one died. I immediately ask to find out who it is, and learn that it is the sharpest, and most calculating fellow in town. Ah, is this not happiness? . . .

To cut with a sharp knife a bright green watermelon on a big scarlet plate of a summer afternoon. Ah, is this not happiness? . . .

A poor scholar comes to borrow money from me, but is shy about mentioning the topic, and so he allows the conversation to drift along on other topics. I see his uncomfortable situation, pull him aside to a place where we are alone and ask him how much he needs. Then I go inside and give him the sum and after having done this, I ask him: "Must you go immediately to settle this matter or can you stay a while and have a drink with me?" Ah, is this not happiness? . . .

To open the window and let a wasp out of the room. Ah, is this not happiness?

CHIN SHENG-T'AN, CHINESE (1609–1661)

The man is tempted by pleasures unbecoming to a superior man. But he clings to duty and integrity.

SIREN. Come worthy Greek, Ulysses come
Possess these shores with me:
The winds and Seas are troublesome,
And here we may be free.

Here may we sit, and view their toils
That travail in the deep,
And joy the day in mirth the while,
And spend the night in sleep.
ULYSSES. Fair Nymph, if fame, or honor were
To be attained with ease,
Then would I come, and rest with thee,
And leave such toils as these.
But here it dwells, and here must I
With danger seek it forth,
To spend the time luxuriously
Becomes not men of worth.
SAMUEL DANIEL, ENGLISH (1562–1619)

IRENE. I . . . swore . . . that I would serve you in all
things —
RUBEK. As the model for my art —
IRENE. — in frank, utter nakedness —
RUBEK *(with emotion)*. And you did serve me, Irene —
so bravely — so gladly and so ungrudgingly.
IRENE. Yes, with all the pulsing blood of my youth, I
served you!
RUBEK *(nodding, with a look of gratitude)*. That you
have every right to say.
IRENE. I fell down at your feet and served you,
Arnold! *(Holding her clenched fist toward him.)* But
you, you, — you — !
RUBEK *(defensively)*. I never did you any wrong!
Never, Irene!
IRENE. Yes, you did! You did wrong to my innermost,
inborn nature —
RUBEK *(starting back)*. I — !
IRENE. Yes, you! I exposed myself wholly and un-
reservedly to your gaze — *(More softly.)* And never
once did you touch me.
RUBEK. Irene, did you not understand that many a
time I was almost beside myself under the spell of
all your loveliness?
IRENE *(continuing undisturbed)*. And yet — if you had
touched me, I think I should have killed you on the
spot. For I had a sharp needle always upon me —
hidden in my hair — *(Strokes her forehead medita-
tively.)* But after all — that you could —
RUBEK *(looks impressively at her)*. I was an artist, Irene.
IRENE *(darkly)*. That is just it. That is just it.
HENRIK IBSEN, NORWEGIAN (1828–1906)

---

*Evil threatens the man because of his excessive devotion
to idle pleasures.*

I knew a very old Russian in Paris, enormously
rich, who used to keep the most charming young
dancers, and who, when once asked whether he had,
or needed to have, any illusions as to their feelings
for him, thought the question over and said: "I do
not think, if my chef succeeds in making me a good
omelette that I bother much whether he loves me or
not."
ISAK DINESEN, DANISH (BORN 1885)

Once mighty Magyars, facing decadency,
See how the blood of Arpad degenerates!
    See you not heaven, stern, revengeful,
    Scourging your country with fierce misfortune?
DANIEL BERZSENYI, HUNGARIAN (1776–1836)

*Indecision regarding the choice among pleasures tempo-
rarily robs the man of inner peace. After due reflection,
he attains joy by turning away from the lower pleasures
and seeking the higher ones.*

Sanātan was telling his beads by the Ganges when a
Brahmin in rags came to him and said, "Help me,
I am poor!"

"My alms-bowl is all that is my own," said Sanātan,
"I have given away everything I had."

"But my Lord Shiva came to me in my dreams," said
the Brahmin, "and counselled me to come to you."
Sanātan suddenly remembered he had picked up a
stone without price among the pebbles of the river-
bank, and thinking that someone might need it hid
it in the sands.

He pointed out the spot to the Brahmin, who wondering, dug up the stone.

The Brahmin sat on the earth and mused alone till
the sun went down behind the trees, and cow-herds
went home with their cattle.

Then he rose and came slowly to Sanātan and said,
"Master, give me the least fraction of the wealth that
disdains all the wealth of the world."
And he threw the precious stone into the water.
SIR RABINDRANATH TAGORE, INDIAN (1861–1941)

The man associates with destructive people and exposes himself to perils. There is the possibility that his own strength and sincerity may be perverted into instruments of evil.

"I have been told about a peculiar institution in your land known as lawsuits," Wu Chih-ho broke in before the travelers could say a word. "I have come across the word in books, but as the thing is unknown in our country I have never been able fully to comprehend its meaning. Upon careful inquiry I found that lawsuits in your noble country arise from many diverse causes. Sometimes they arise from petty quarrels, sometimes from disputes in money matters, but at the bottom of all is the lack of patience and tolerance. Once the matter is brought to the courts, it becomes a procession of charges and counter-charges, of deliberate lies and falsehoods; the litigants become like people possessed, each trying to do the other the greatest possible injury. More often than not both sides come out with less money than they started with, to say nothing of the humiliation and the bodily punishment that they suffer in court.

"But even more inexplicable are those persons who instigate the foolish and the ignorant to sue in order to profit thereby, people who specialize in making something out of nothing, people who clutch at the thin air and pounce upon gray shadows. If they are discovered, they always have time to flee justice while their unfortunate clients are left to suffer for their ignorance. Such people are, of course, monstrous, but it seems to me that these creatures could not flourish if it were not for the vindictiveness and avarice of the victims themselves."

LI JU-CHEN, CHINESE (1763–1830)

I know, my son, thy honest nature shrinks
From glozing words and practice of deceit;
But (for 'tis sweet to snatch a victory)
Be bold today and honest afterwards.
For one brief hour of lying follow me;
All time to come shall prove thy probity.

SOPHOCLES, GREEK (496–406 B.C.)

Vanity in his leadership causes the man to become de-
pendent upon external conditions and chances for
satisfaction.

Learn, O thou mighty maggoty Pier Luigi, learn, O
thou little thrippenny duke, the customs of such an
honoured king.
Every little squire of thirty bumpkins and a tumble-
down hovel expects to be given the ceremonial of
divine worship.
PIETRO ARETINO, ITALIAN (1492–1556)

"We have now," said Imlac, "gratified our minds
with an exact view of the greatest work of man, except the wall of China.
"Of the wall it is very easy to assign the motive. It
seemed a wealthy and timorous nature from the in-
cursions of barbarians, whose unskilfulness in arts,
made it easier for them to supply their wants by
rapine than by industry, and who from time to time
poured in upon the habitations of peaceful commerce
as vultures descend upon domestic fowl. Their celer-
ity and fierceness made the wall necessary, and their
ignorance made it efficacious.
"But for the pyramids no reason has ever been given,
adequate to the cost and labor of the work. The narrowness of the chamber proves that it could afford
no retreat from enemies, and the treasures might
have been reposited at far less expense with equal
security. It seems to have been erected only in compliance with that hunger of imagination which preys
incessantly upon life, and must be always appeased
by some employment. Those who have already all
that they can enjoy must enlarge their desires. He
that has built for use, till use is supplied, must begin
to build for vanity, and extend his plan to the utmost
power of human performance, that he may not be
soon reduced to form another wish.
"I consider this mighty structure as a monument of
the insufficiency of human enjoyments. A king,
whose power is unlimited, and whose treasures surmount all real and imaginary wants, is compelled to
solace, by the erection of a pyramid, the satiety of
dominion and tastelessness of pleasures, and to
amuse the tediousness of declining life, by seeing

thousands labouring without end, and one stone for
no purpose laid upon another. Whoever thou art,
that, not content with a moderate condition, imag-
inest happiness in royal magnificence, and dreamest
that command or riches can feed the appetite of
novelty with perpetual gratifications, survey the
Pyramids and confess thy folly!"
SAMUEL JOHNSON, ENGLISH (1709–1784)

*The over-all judgment: joy and friendliness encourage
people during difficult times. But they also seduce some
from honest labors. They must accordingly be based upon
steadfastness to a worthy cause in order to realize progress and retain values.*

The truth is, I do indulge myself a little the more in
pleasure, knowing that this is the proper age of my
life to do it; and, out of my observation that most
men that do thrive in the world do forget to take
pleasure during the time that they are getting their
estate, but reserve that till they have got one, and
then it is too late for them to enjoy it.
SAMUEL PEPYS, ENGLISH (1633–1703)

Laugh, and the world laughs with you;
Weep, and you weep alone;
For the sad old earth must borrow its mirth,
But has trouble enough of its own.
ELLA WHEELER WILCOX, AMERICAN (1850–1919)

Philosophy! What a fatuous
word for one who understands it well!
Philosophy! . . . . A poor devil
wears himself out filling
his head (entirely bald
from the effort of study)
with exaggerated maxims
that sound very solemn;
somewhere in his mind he prints
magnificent documents
on virtue, decency, constancy,
fidelity, heroism. And then
what happens? Our wise man
makes a visit and sees
a girl, attractive, gay,
alluring, with playful eyes,

[372]58

with light complexion
and rosy cheeks, and then
goodbye! all the poor scholar's
wisdom disappears in the trap.
JUAN PABLO FORNER, SPANISH (1756–1797)

59 Overcoming Dissension

THE HUAN HEXAGRAM

At the outset, the man overcomes misunderstanding
through a precise and energetic response to the needs of
the moment.

... my theory of technique, if I have one, is very far
from original; nor is it complicated. I can express it
in fifteen words, by quoting The Eternal Question
And Immortal Answer of burlesk, viz. "Would you
hit a woman with a child?—No, I'd hit her with a
brick." Like the burlesk comedian, I am abnormally
fond of that precision which creates movement.
EDWARD ESTLIN CUMMINGS, AMERICAN (1894–1962)

The man finds himself alienated from others because of
the prevailing ill humor and misanthropy. However, he
revises his judgment of humanity and takes shelter in
his strong position. His moderate and just view of man-
kind removes the causes for repentance later.

But there are certain people I simply can't put up
with. A dreariness and sense of death come over me
when I meet them—I really find it difficult to breathe
when they are in the room, as if they had pumped
all the air out of it. Wouldn't it be dreadful to produce that effect on people! But they never seem to be
aware of it. I remember once meeting a famous Bore;
I really must tell you about it, it shows the unbeliev-
able obtuseness of such people.
I told this and another story or two with great gusto,
and talked on of my experiences and sensations, till
suddenly I noticed, in the appearance of my charming neighbor, something—a slightly glazed look in
her eyes, a just perceptible irregularity in her breathing—which turned that occasion for me suddenly
into a Nightmare.
LOGAN PEARSALL SMITH, ENGLISH (1865–1946)

If criminals are fated,
'Tis wrong to punish crime.
When God the ores created,
He knew that on a time
They should become the sources
Whence sword-blades dripping blood
Flash o'er the manes of horses
Iron-curbed, iron-shod.
ABU'L-'ALA AL-MA'ARI, PERSIAN (973–1057)

The man disregards his own personal interests in order to work for the benefit of others.

But over all the ravages of that terrible time there towered highest the solitary figure of that powerful grave-digger, who, nerved by the spectacle of the common misfortune, by one heroic effort rose for the time above the wrecks of his own nature. In the thick of the plague, in the very garden spot of the pestilence, he ruled like an unterrified king. Through days unnaturally chill with gray cloud and drizzling rain, or unnaturally hot with the fierce sun and suffocating damps that appeared to steam forth from subterranean cauldrons, he worked unfaltering, sometimes with a helper, sometimes with none. There were times when, exhausted, he would lie down in the half-dug graves and there sleep until able to go on; and many a midnight found him under the spectral moon, all but hidden by the rank nightshade as he bent over to mark out the lines of one of those mortal cellars.
JAMES LANE ALLEN, AMERICAN (1849–1925)

The man brings dissent and partisanship to an end by his transcendent view of life's interrelationships. He rises above personal friendships to assemble good men from near and afar.

It used to be an applauded political maxim, "Measures, not men." I venture to denounce the soundness of this maxim, and to propose, "Men, not measures.". . . Better a hundred times an honest administration of an erroneous policy than a corrupt and incapable administration of a good one.
EDWARD JOHN PHELPS, AMERICAN (1822–1900)

Shall I ask the brave soldier, who fights by my side
In the cause of mankind, if our creeds agree?
THOMAS MOORE, IRISH (1779–1852)

---

*The man announces a great policy during a period of
disunity and deadlock which serves as a rallying point
for reforms. Misunderstanding is thereby dissipated by
his proclamation.*

Speak against covetousness, and cry out upon it.
Stand not ticking and toying at the branches nor at
the boughs, for then there will be new boughs and
branches spring again of them; but strike at the root
and fear not these giants of England, these great men
and men of power, these men that are oppressors of
the poor; fear them not, but strike at the root of the
evil, which is mischievous covetousness.
HUGH LATIMER, ENGLISH (1485–1555)

Give an immediate meaning to the individual without hope and multiply the attempts, not by an organization, but by an idea: review the martyrs. Pei,
writing, would be listened to because he, Ch'en, was
going to die; he knew how much weight an idea acquires through the blood that is shed in its name.
ANDRÉ MALRAUX, FRENCH (BORN 1901)

The man removes the sources of danger and bloodshed.

There is no such test of a man's superiority of character as in the well-conducting of an unavoidable
quarrel.
SIR HENRY TAYLOR, ENGLISH (1800–1886)

---

*The over-all judgment: the ruler overcomes divisive
egotism through filial piety within himself, which leads
to unity and progress throughout the country. The time
is favorable to undertake a great project.*

Without thee, Lord, what could there be
For the king thou lovest, and dost call his name?
Thou shalt bless his title as thou wilt,
And unto him vouchsafe a path direct.
I, the prince obeying thee,
And what thy hands have made.
'Tis thou who art my creator,

[375]59

Entrusting me with the rule of hosts of men.
According to thy mercy, Lord,
Which thou dost spread o'er all of them,
Turn into loving-kindness thy dread power,
And make to spring up in my heart
A reverence for thy divinity.
Give as thou thinkest best.

KING NEBUCHADREZZAR, BABYLONIAN (DIED 502 B.C.)

The reason [for the inability of the Arabs to establish an empire unless they are imbued with religion by a prophet or a saint, or generally inspired by religious enthusiasm] is that, being naturally wild, they are of all peoples the most reluctant to submit to one another owing to the rudeness of their manners, their arrogance, their high spirit, and their jealousy of authority. Seldom, therefore, are they unanimous. But when they follow a prophet or a saint, they are restrained by something within themselves; their pride and jealousy depart from them, submission and concord are no longer difficult. Religion brings them together: it takes away their rudeness and insolence, it removes envy and jealousy from their hearts. If there be among them the prophet or saint who urges them to fulfill the command of God, and bids them be of one voice to make the truth prevail, they will become completely united and gain victory and empire.

IBN KHALDUN, TUNISIAN (1332–1406)

Of the second-rate rulers, people speak respectfully saying, "He has done this, he has done that."

Of the first-rate rulers they do not say this. They say: "We have done it all ourselves."

LAO-TZU, CHINESE (604–531 B.C.)

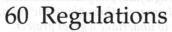 # 60 Regulations

THE CHIEH HEXAGRAM

At the outset, the man appreciates his own limitations and exercises judicious discretion in not pressing beyond them. He does not exert his authority rashly.

Harmony sings not in Pittacus' proverb,
nay, not for me, although a wight of wisdom spake
[376]60

the word, that *to excel is hard.*
A god alone could have such privilege: a man
undone by a resistless fate
must needs be bad. Yes: every man
is worthy if his luck is good,
and bad if it goes badly. They most excel
who are beloved by the gods.

Therefore I seek no impossible being,
I squander not my life's allotted term, in vain,
on an impracticable hope —
faultless humanity — beyond their power who win
the bread of life from spacious earth;
when 'tis discovered, I shall tell.
Honour and love to every man
who wills to do no baseness; but not the gods
themselves oppose necessity.

SIMONIDES, GREEK (FIFTH CENTURY B.C.)

The time for immediate action has come. The opportunity
should be seized quickly and energetically. The man does
not act, and bad luck ensues.

She passed with her mother. What beauty so rare!
What looks all aglow with the wheat's burnished
gold!
What rhythm in her step! How innate her air
So royal! What lines 'neath the tulle's soft fold!
She passed with her mother; turned toward me,
and there
Blue eyes pierced my heart to a depth untold!
I stood there enraptured . . . .
Quick, fever'd, the cry
"Yes, follow her!" burst from both body and soul.
. . . But I feared the mad path of rash loving to try,
And opening old wounds not so quickly made whole;
And in spite of my yearning beyond all control,
I shut close my eyes, and let her pass by!

AMADO NERVO, MEXICAN (1870–1919)

The man does not follow promulgated laws in his own
activities. His actions lead to regret.

To Hell with the Constitution . . . we are following
the orders of Governor Peabody.

TOM MC CLELLAN, AMERICAN (1905)

*The man understands the nature of regulations and
accommodates accordingly. He does not waste energy in
useless struggles, but directs it effectively to solving the
problem at hand.*

We are gratified in defining law as rules about force,
since everything turns upon the regular use of force.
KARL OLIVECRONA, SWEDISH (BORN 1897)

---

*Before exacting obedience from others, the man in a
high position first applies the restrictions to himself. His
beneficial influence is widely felt.*

I am one of those who cannot see the good that is to
result from all this mystifying and blue-devilling of
society. The contrast it presents to the cheerful and
solid wisdom of antiquity is too forcible not to strike
any one who has the least knowledge of classical
literature. To represent vice and misery as the necessary accompaniments of genius, is as mischievous as
it is false, and the feeling is as unclassical as the
language in which it is usually expressed.
THOMAS LOVE PEACOCK, ENGLISH (1785–1866)

Our government was, in the words of Abraham Lincoln, "The government of the people, by the people,
and for the people." It was the noblest ambition of all
true Americans to carry this democratic government
to the highest degree of perfection and justice, in
probity, in assured peace, in the security of human
rights, in progressive civilization; to solve the problems of popular self-government on the grandest
scale, and thus to make this republic the example and
guiding star of mankind. . . .

Then came the Spanish War. A few vigorous blows
laid the feeble enemy helpless at our feet. The whole
scene seemed to have suddenly changed. . . . A loud
demand arose that, pledge or no pledge to the contrary, the conquests should be kept. . . . Why not?
was the cry. Has not the career of the republic almost
from its very beginning been one of territorial expansion? Has it not acquired Louisiana, Florida,
Texas, the vast countries that came through the
Mexican War, and Alaska, and has it not digested
well? . . . What is the difference? . . .

The cry is suddenly raised that this great country has become too small for us. . . .

"But the Pacific Ocean," we are mysteriously told, "will be the great commercial battlefield of the future.". . .

"But we must have coaling stations for our navy!". . .

"But we must civilize those poor people!". . .

The rest of the pleas for imperialism consist of those high-sounding catchwords of which a free people, when about to decide a great question, should be especially suspicious. We are admonished that it is time for us to become a world power. . . .

If this democracy, after all the intoxication of triumph in war, conscientiously remembers its professions and pledges, and soberly reflects on its duties to itself and others, and then deliberately resists the temptation of conquest, it will achieve the grandest triumphs of the democratic idea that history knows of.

CARL SCHURZ, AMERICAN (1829–1906)

The man exhibits an exaggerated desire for restrictive regulations. This will not be endured for long by the people. However, ruthless severity may, at times, be the only protection against temptation and irresolution and may eliminate later cause for repentance.

Pastor Cobbett accomplished miracles. Even today many people will say there was never a finer island than Matareva in the old days. We were forced to bathe each afternoon. We had to kill the land crabs that burrowed in our gardens, buy screens for our kitchens and nail tin around our coconut trees to keep rats from eating the young nuts. We had to burn coral to make lime for painting our houses, and our walks had to be lined with white shells. Every woman worked one day a week at the church, so that the gardens there were the most beautiful in the Pacific.

The pastor was equally relentless regarding our spiritual lives. The old music, which everyone knows to have been lascivious, was forbidden and replaced by church hymns. Dancing was completely taboo and wardens could arrest anyone who dared to start the lewd old hulas. Everyone had to get married, widows must not talk with men except in the presence of other women and the number of illegitimate babies — a phrase never used on our island before Pastor Cobbett's time — was much reduced. There were some, of course, for in the old days girls had babies before they were married as proof that they would make good wives, but Pastor Cobbett raved against the practice and the penalties were brutally severe except when the father proved to be a warden. If the warden was unmarried, he had to marry the girl right away. If he already had a wife, he was reprimanded in private and the girl was publicly humiliated before the entire village on Sunday morning. She had to march from the rear of the big church up to the altar, fall upon the floor, put on a black cloth over her head and walk back past all of us. It was always surprising to me that any girl would have the courage to risk such public shame, but many did and it was found that old women of the village supported them in their behavior, but as the old women died off, the girls found no consolation and some of them committed suicide, a thing never before heard of in our village.

JAMES ALBERT MICHENER, AMERICAN (BORN 1907)

The over-all judgment: fixed limits are necessary to preserve world order for such things as the bounds of loyalty, the constraints on expenditures, and the control of people. Strictness and severity should be ameliorated in the light of local and extenuating circumstances.

(If) a seignor laid hands on the wife of a(nother) seignor, thereby treating her like a young child, when they have prosecuted him (and) convicted him, they shall cut off (one) finger of his. If he has kissed her, they shall draw her lower lip along the edge of the blade of an ax (and) cut (it) off.

ASSYRIAN LAW (THIRTEENTH CENTURY B.C.)

Do not ask from men what Nature had denied them. . . . Do not beg the monkey to have a fine deportment, nor the ox nor the donkey to have a sweet voice.

IACOPONE DA TODI, ITALIAN (DIED 1306)

Suppose, for example, that a legislator should feel himself authorized to undertake the extirpation of

drunkenness and fornication by direct laws. He
would have to begin by a multitude of regulations.
The first inconvenience would therefore be a complexity of laws. The easier it is to conceal these vices,
the more necessary it would be to resort to severity
of punishment, in order to destroy by the terror of
examples the constantly recurring hope of impunity.
This excessive rigour of laws forms a second inconvenience not less grave than the first. The difficulty
of procuring proofs would be such that it would be
necessary to encourage informers, and to entertain
an army of spies. This necessity forms a third inconvenience, greater than either of the others. Let us
compare the results of good and evil. Offenses of this
nature, if that name can be properly given to im-
prudences, produces no alarm; but the pretended
remedy would spread a universal terror; innocent or
guilty, everyone would fear for himself or his con-
nections; suspicions and accusations would render
society dangerous; we should fly from it; we should
involve ourselves in mystery and concealment; we
should shun all the disclosures of confidence. Instead
of suppressing one vice, the laws would produce
other vices, new and more dangerous.
JEREMY BENTHAM, ENGLISH (1748–1832)

61 Sincerity

THE CHUNG FU HEXAGRAM

*At the outset, the man relies on his inner stability and
preparedness, which are the basis of a correct attitude
toward the world. If he seeks secret ties, however, his
peace of mind and inmost sincerity will be jeapordized.*

KING. Nobody's afraid
to die when he sees good reason for it. Hell,
we're not here for fun! We came believing
there was some use in it. Maybe some of us think
there still is use. I've been trying to hold on
this last half-year—I've been trying to believe
the whole world would rise up and step on this evil
that crawls over Spain—and it has risen up,
and stepped on us. And now I'm beginning to
wonder

if a cause is sacred when it's lost. Did we volunteer
to die in a lost cause?
VICTOR. What's gone? What's changed
since yesterday?
KING. Our cause is lost, that's all . . .
Why should we die here for a dead cause, for a
  symbol,
on these empty ramparts, where there's nothing to
  win,
even if you could win it?
VICTOR. Yes, but if I die
then I know men will never give in;
then I'll know there's something in the race
of men, because even I had it, that hates injustice
more than it wants to live. — Because even I had it —
and I'm no hero — And that means the Hitlers
and the Mussolinis always lose in the end —
force loses in the long run, and the spirit wins,
whatever spirit is. Anyway it's the thing
that says it's better to sit here with the moon
and hold them off while I can. If I went with you
I'd never know whether the race was turning
down again, to the dinosaurs — this way
I keep my faith. In myself and what men are
and in what we may be.
MAXWELL ANDERSON, AMERICAN (1888–1959)

---

*The man voices his feelings and defends his deeds by
clear explanations, which exert a far-reaching chain
reaction.*

I accuse General Billot of having had in his hands
certain proofs of Dreyfus' innocence and of having
hushed them up, of having rendered himself guilty
of the crime of *lèse-humanité* and *lèse-justice* with
a political object and in order to screen the compro-
mised General Staff.
I accuse General de Boisdeffre and General Gonse
of having made themselves accomplices of the
same crime — the one, doubtless, through clerical
prejudice, the other, perhaps, from the *esprit de
Corps* which makes the War Office a sacred, unassail-
able ark. . . .
I accuse the three experts, *Sieurs* Belhomme, Varinard
and Couard, of having made a false and fraudulent
report, unless a medical examination should find
[382]61

them to be suffering from defective vision and diseased judgment.

I accuse the War Office of having carried on in the press, particularly in the *Eclair* and the *Echo de Paris*, an abominable campaign, in order to screen their mistake and mislead the public.

Lastly, I accuse the first Court-Martial of having violated the law by condemning an accused man on the basis of a secret document, and I accuse the second Court-Martial of having, in obedience to orders, screened that illegality by committing in its turn the judicial crime of knowingly acquitting a guilty man [Esterhazy].

In prefering these charges, I am aware that I bring myself under Article 30 and 31 of the Press Law of July 29, 1881, which punishes defamation. And I do so voluntarily.

... My passionate protest is merely the cry of my soul. Let them venture then to bring me before the Court of Assize and let an inquiry be made in broad daylight!

I wait.

ÉMILE ZOLA, FRENCH (1840–1902)

The man depends on others for his joys and sorrows, which generates an uncertainty of moods. His sincerity is impure and contaminated with external influences.

I have seen the whole racket, and if there is any more disastrous road than that from Park Avenue to the Rue de la Paix and back again, I don't know it. They are homeless people, ashamed of being American, unable to master the culture of another country; ashamed, usually, of their husbands, wives, grandparents, and unable to bring up descendants of whom they could be proud, even if they had the nerve to bear them, ashamed of each other, yet leaning on each other's weakness, a menace to the social order in which they live.

FRANCIS SCOTT FITZGERALD, AMERICAN (1896–1940)

After listening to the saintly Don Emmanuel preach in church for the first time, Lazarus said to his pious sister: "He's not like the others; still he doesn't fool me, he's too intelligent to believe everything he must teach."

[383]61

"You mean you think he's a hypocrite?"
"A hypocrite . . . no! But he has a job by which he
must live."
MIGUEL DE UNAMUNO Y JUGO, SPANISH (1864–1936)

The man is humble and respectful in receiving enlighten-
ment from superior quarters. He is like the team horse
which follows the straight course without having to look
at its mate.

Two things fill the mind with an ever-increasing
wonder and awe, the more often and the more in-
tensely the mind is occupied with them: the starry
heavens above me, and the moral law within me.
IMMANUEL KANT, GERMAN (1724–1804)

Andrew quoted again from the old King of Wisdom
—"I withheld not my heart from any joy, for my
heart rejoiced in all my labor, and that was my portion of labor." Then Andrew thought of the hard
winter which had passed, as all hard things must
pass, of all the toilsome lives of those beside him, of
all the work which they had done with their poor,
knotted hands, of the tracks which they had worn on
the earth toward their graves, with their weary feet,
and suddenly he seemed to grasp a new and further
meaning for that verse of Ecclesiastes.

He seemed to see that labor is not alone for itself, not
for what it accomplishes of the tasks of the world,
not for its equivalent in silver and gold, not even for
the end of human happiness and love, but for the
growth in character of the laborer.

"That is the portion of labor," he said.
MARY WILKINS FREEMAN, AMERICAN (1852–1930)

The perfect sincerity of the sage on the throne binds all in
union with himself.

The royal feast was done; the King
  Sought some new sport to banish care,
And to his jester cried: "Sir Fool,
  Kneel now, and make for us a prayer!"

The jester doffed his cap and bells,
  And stood the mocking court before;
They could not see the bitter smile

Before the painted grin he wore.

He bowed his head, and bent his knee
Upon the monarch's silken stool;
His pleading voice arose: "O Lord,
Be merciful to me, a fool!

"No pity, Lord, could change the heart
From red with wrong to white as wool;
The rod must heal the sin: but, Lord,
Be merciful to me, a fool!

"'Tis not by guilt the onward sweep
Of truth and right, O Lord, we stay;
'Tis by our follies that so long
We hold the earth from heaven away.

"These clumsy feet, still in the mire,
Go crushing blossoms without end;
These hard, well-meaning hands we thrust
Among the heart-strings of a friend.

"The ill-timed truth we might have kept —
Who knows how sharp it pierced and stung?
The word we had not sense to say —
Who knows how grandly it had rung?

"Our faults no tenderness should ask,
The chastening stripes must cleanse them all;
But for our blunders — oh, in shame
Before the eyes of heaven we fall.

"Earth bears no balsam for mistakes;
Men crown the knave, and scourge the tool
That did his will; but Thou, O Lord,
Be merciful to me, a fool!"

The room was hushed! in silence rose
The King, and sought his gardens cool,
And walked apart, and murmured low,
"Be merciful to me, a fool!"
EDWARD ROLAND SILL, AMERICAN (1841–1887)

If there is sincerity in the heart,
There will be beauty in the character.
If there is beauty in the character,
There will be harmony in the home.
If there is harmony in the home,
There will be order in the nation.
When there is order in the nation,
There will be peace in the world.
GREAT LEARNING, CHINESE (THIRD CENTURY B.C.)

Mere words cannot be relied upon. Overdependence on them leads to bad results.

When a movement harbors the purpose of tearing down a world and building another in its place, complete clarity must reign in the ranks of its own leadership with regard to the following principles: Every movement will first have to sift the human material it wins into two large groups: supporters and members.
The function of propaganda is to attract supporters, the function of organization is to win members.
A supporter of a movement is one who declares himself to be in agreement with its aims, a member is one who fights for them. . . .
Propaganda must consequently have to see that an idea wins supporters, while the organization must take the greatest care only to make the most valuable elements among the supporters into members. Propaganda does not, therefore, need to rack its brains with regard to the importance of every individual instructed by it, with regard to his ability, capacity, and understanding, or character, while the organization must carefully gather from the mass of these elements those which really make possible the victory of the movement.
FÜHRER ADOLF HITLER, GERMAN (1889–1945)

The over-all judgment: great sincerity invariably prevails over even the coarsest and most recalcitrant of pigs, fishes, and men. With such a favorable response the way is open for undertaking even dangerous enterprises.

I long for people who don't have polished sentences hanging around their necks like pearls,
People who stutter and use the simplest words.
ERIK KNUDSEN, DANISH (BORN 1922)

Enthusiasm is that secret and harmonious spirit which hovers over the production of genius, throwing the reader of a book, or the spectator of a statue, into the very ideal presence whence these works have really originated. A great work always leaves us in a state of musing.
ISAAC D'ISRAELI, ENGLISH (1766–1848)

But now the words of the traveler amazed and almost stunned her. She suddenly realized that it wasn't the others who were wrong and could not understand her but herself who could not rise up to the same height of those fathers and mothers willing to resign themselves, without crying, not only to the departures of their sons but even to their death.

She lifted her head, she bent over from her corner trying to listen with great attention to the details which the fat man was giving to his companions about the way his son had fallen as a hero, for his King and his Country, happy and without regrets. It seemed to her that she had stumbled into a world she had never dreamt of, a world so far unknown to her and she was pleased to hear everyone joining in congratulating that brave father who could so stoically speak of his son's death.

Then suddenly, just as if she had heard nothing of what had been said and almost as if waking up from a dream, she turned to the old man, asking him:

"Then . . . is your son really dead?"

Everybody stared at her. The old man, too, turned to look at her, fixing his great, bulging, horribly watery light gray eyes, deep in her face. For some time he tried to answer, but words failed him. He looked and looked at her, almost as if only then — at that silly, incongruous question — he had suddenly realized at last that his son was really dead — gone for ever — for ever. His face contracted, became horribly distorted, then he snatched in haste a handkerchief from his pocket and, to the amazement of everyone, broke into harrowing, heart-rending, uncontrollable sobs.

LUIGI PIRANDELLO, ITALIAN (1867–1936)

---

62 Small Gains

THE HSIAO KUO HEXAGRAM

At the outset, the man should heed the case of a bird leaving the nest before it is fledged. He should spend his early life learning the traditional ways in order to avoid wasting his energies in senseless jousting.

It is easier to grow in dignity than to make a start.
LUCIUS ANNAEUS SENECA, ROMAN (4 B.C.–65 A.D.)

The man fails to meet the chief executive, but goes about his duties among other officials. He does not force his way into the limelight.

Getting patronage is the whole art of life. A man cannot have a career without it.
GEORGE BERNARD SHAW, IRISH (1856–1950)

To be resign'd when ills betide,
Patient when favours are deni'd,
  And pleas'd with favours given;—
Dear Chloe, this is wisdom's part;
This is that incense of the heart
  Whose fragrance smells to heaven.
NATHANIEL COTTON, ENGLISH (1707–1788)

The man is disdainful of weak enemies and does not exercise adequate precautions in the face of apparently insignificant signs. He will be hurt.

It is the little rift within the lute,
That by and by will make the music mute,
And ever widening slowly silence all.

The little rift within the lover's lute,
Or little pitted speck in garner'd fruit,
That rotting inward slowly moulders all.
LORD TENNYSON, ENGLISH (1809–1892)

The man exercises restraint and caution. He meets the exigencies of the situation without exceeding the natural bounds.

Giuliano [Architect to the Pope], I learn from a letter sent by you that the Pope was angry at my departure, that he is willing to place the money at my disposal and to carry out what was agreed upon between us; also, that I am to come back and fear nothing.
Regarding my departure, the fact is that on Holy Saturday, I heard the Pope, speaking with a jeweler and the Master of the Ceremonies, say that he did not want to spend another baiocco on stones, whether small or large, which surprised me very much. How-

ever, before I set out I asked him for some of the money needed for continuing my work. His Holiness replied that I was to return on Monday; and I went on Monday, and on Tuesday, and on Wednesday, and on Thursday—as His Holiness saw. At last on Friday morning, I was turned out, that is, I was driven away; and the person who turned me away said he knew who I was, but that such were his orders. Thereupon, having heard those words on the Saturday and seeing them afterwards put into execution, I lost all hope. But this alone was not the whole reason of my departure. . . .

. . . Give His Holiness to understand . . . that if he really wishes to have this tomb erected it would be well for him not to vex me as to where the work is to be done, provided that within the agreed period of five years it will be erected in St. Peter's, on the site he shall choose, and that it be a beautiful work, as I have promised: for I am persuaded that it will be a work without equal in all the world if it be carried out.

. . . let him deposit said money here in Florence with a person whose name I will send you. . . . With regard to the aforesaid money and work, I will bind myself in any way His Holiness may direct, and I will furnish whatever security here in Florence he may require. . . . I beg of you to let me have an answer, and quickly. I have nothing further to add.

MICHELANGELO BUONARROTI, ITALIAN (1475–1564)

Because of the lack of able helpers, the prince is unsuccessful in his attempts to set the world in order. He searches intently for the required talents among those who have retired from the public scene. The right man with a demonstrated record of achievement is finally found and the difficult task completed.

There is, continued my father, a certain mien and motion of the body and all its parts, both in acting and speaking, which argues a man well within; and I am not at all surprised that Gregory of Nazianzum, upon observing the hasty and untoward gestures of Julian, should foretell he would one day become an apostate;—or that St. Ambrose should turn his amanuensis out of doors, because of an indecent motion of his head, which went backwards and for-

wards like a flail; — or that Democritus should conceive Protagoras to be a scholar, from seeing him
bind up a faggot, and thrusting, as he did it, the
small twigs inwards. — There are a thousand un-
noticed openings, continued my father, which let a
penetrating eye at once into a man's soul; and I
maintain it, added he, that a man of sense does not
lay down his hat in coming into a room, — or take it
up in going out of it, but something escapes, which
discovers him.
LAURENCE STERNE, ENGLISH (1713–1768)

Many men have made themselves known by looking
forward, seeing something sure to be of importance
in the future, making the subject thoroughly their
own and then when the right moment comes, stepping forward as the chief authority on the subject.
ROBERT EDWIN PEARY, AMERICAN (1856–1920)

The man does not know how to control his preoccupation
with trivia. His overshooting and restlessly pressing on
bring disappointment and calamity to himself and his
people.

I put for a general inclination of all mankind a perpetual and restless desire of power after power, that
ceaseth only in death. And the cause of this is not
always that a man hopes for a more intensive delight,
than he has already attained to; or that he cannot be
content with a moderate power; but because he cannot assure the power and means to live well, which
he hath present, without the acquisition of more.
THOMAS HOBBES, ENGLISH (1588–1679)

The over-all judgment: the time is not ripe for striving
after major achievements. Because of the absence of
requisite power, one must be content with small and
cumulative gains. The bird does not fly into the sun but
descends with dignity to the earth where its nest is
located.

No great thing is created suddenly, any more than a
bunch of grapes or a fig. If you tell me that you desire
a fig, I answer you that there must be time. Let it
first blossom, then bear fruit, then ripen.
EPICTETUS, GREEK (FIRST CENTURY)

Success depends on three things: who says it, what
he says, how he says it; and of these three things,
what he says is the least important.
JOHN VISCOUNT MORLEY, ENGLISH (1838–1923)

No more about war, revolution and the salvation of
the world! Let us be modest and turn our attention to
other and smaller things. Let us ponder on a human
being, on a soul, or a fool. Let us play a little, look
around a little and, if we can, laugh or smile a little.
PAUL KORNFELD, GERMAN (1889–1942)

63 Tasks Completed

THE CHI CHI HEXAGRAM

*At the outset, the man is not caught in the intoxication of
the masses during a great transition. The general pressure finally overwhelms him. However, this occurs only
at the last minute, after he has successfully completed
the enterprise.*

Patronio first told about a good man and his son
leading a beast to market. On the way, they met a
group of friends. After exchanging greetings the
friends remarked that it's a pity that they don't save
some energy and one of them ride the beast instead
of walking. The father asked his son about the advice.
The son said it sounded reasonable. So the father
asked the son to mount the beast.
Farther down the road, the father and mounted son
met a second group of travelers. After an exchange of
greetings, the travelers thought the son lacking in
filial piety in riding while letting his father walk.
The father asked the son what he thought of the comment. The son said it seems appropriate. So father
and son exchanged places.
A little ways further, a third group was encountered.
After the usual exchange of greetings, the strangers
said that the older man can certainly stand the hard-
ship of walking better than the youngster. The father
asked the son what he thought of their observation.
The son said it sounds correct. So the old man asked
the son to mount at his side.
A fourth group of people was encountered before

long, who were heard saying that it was cruel to be
putting so much weight on a thin animal. The father
asked the son what he thought of their remark.
The son said he can't see anything untrue about
it. . . .
At this point Patronio turned to Count Lucanor,
"Now, Count. What is it now that you want to do
but do not want anybody to speak ill of you?"
PRINCE DON JUAN MANUEL, SPANISH (1282–1347)

The man is not accorded the protective confidence of his
superiors. In his desire to achieve something, he is
tempted to seek it and draw it to himself. He should not
do so, but should remain patient and faithful. What is
truly his will come to him eventually.

To the king of the land of Egypt, our lord . . .
At the feet of the lord we fall down . . .
Now for twenty years we have been sending to the
    king, our lord . . .
But now Tunis
thy city, weeps
and her tears are running,
and there is no help for us.
We have been sending to the king, the lord, the king
    of the land of Egypt,
for twenty years;
but not one word
has come to us from our lord.
SYRIAN GOVERNOR (1360 B.C.)

And a little dog, nameless and mongrel and many-
fathered, grown, yet weighing less than six pounds,
saying as if to itself, "I can't be dangerous, because
there's nothing much smaller than I am; I can't be
fierce, because they would call it just a noise; I can't
be humble, because I'm already too close to the
ground to genuflect; I can't be proud, because I
wouldn't be near enough to it for anyone to know
who was casting the shadow, and I don't even know
that I'm going to heaven, because they have already
decided that I don't possess an immortal soul. So all
I can be is brave. But it's all right. I can be that,
even if they still call it just noise."
WILLIAM HARRISON FAULKNER, AMERICAN (1897–1962)

A correct subjugation policy is essential after the conquest. Inferior people, of no value at home, should not be sent to govern the colonies. Protracted struggles usually follow, and small men are inadequate to the tasks.

Rights! People are fed up with them; what they want is bread. To constitutions teeming with sublime ideas which no one·has ever seen functioning in practice . . . they prefer an opportunity to work in peace, security in their personal pursuits, and the assurance that the authorities, instead of launching forth on wild goose chases after ideals, will hang the cheats, the thieves, and the revolutionaries. . . . Fewer rights and fewer liberties in exchange for more order and more peace. . . . Enough of utopias. . . . I want order and peace, albeit for the price of all the rights which have cost me so dear. . . . I daresay the day is at hand when the nation will declare: We want order and peace even at the cost of our independence.

FRANCISCO G. CÓSMES,

MEXICAN (NINETEENTH CENTURY)

Evils are occasionally uncovered but quickly glossed over during periods of prosperity and cultural advance. The man is not complacent about such readily hidden defects and takes earnest steps toward their correction.

Here honor binds me, and I wish to satisfy it.

PIERRE CORNEILLE, FRENCH (1606–1684)

Men are deceived by what the eyes see, but the gods are swayed by what the heart conceals.

A curious game, a particular favorite among the children [of the Netsilik Eskimos] was . . . the (spirit game), in which they imitated and parodied shaman seances and the general fear of evil spirits with a capital sense of humor. They held complete and true shaman seances, fought with imaginary enemies just as grown-ups do; in fact, they even used the same formulas that they had heard their parents utter when really in fear and danger. Although this game was absolute blasphemy the grown-up audience writhed with laughter, just as if they took a certain satisfaction in seeing the evil and inexorable gravity of life made the subject of farcical burlesque. Some

hours later it might happen that an attack of illness, or perhaps a bad dream, would rally the grown-ups to a seance during which they desperately sought to defend themselves against hidden enemies, with exactly the same means as the children had mocked in play. When I mentioned this remarkable circumstance to my friend Kuvdluitssoq, and enquired whether it was really prudent to mock the spirits, he answered with the greatest astonishment pictured in his face that the spirits really understood a joke.
KNUD JOHAN VICTOR RASMUSSEN, DANISH (1879–1933)

Needless violence and self-glorification upon completion of a difficult undertaking cause the man to fall back into misfortune.

"I am afraid," replied Elinor, "that the pleasantness of an employment does not always evince its propriety."
JANE AUSTEN, ENGLISH (1775–1817)

The over-all judgment: there are many details to be attended to after one has relieved the distresses of the kingdom. The fact that things appear to proceed on their own tempts a man to relax, which invites disorder in the end. The superior man takes appropriate precautionary measures.

The seizure of Power is only the beginning. For a number of reasons, the bourgeoisie, overthrown in one country, remains for a considerable time stronger than the proletariat which has overthrown it. Therefore, the important thing is to retain power, to consolidate it, to make it invincible. What is required to attain this end? At least three main tasks confronting the proletariat on the morrow of its victory must be fulfilled. They are (a) to break the resistance of the landed proprietors and capitalists now overthrown and expropriated by the revolution and to liquidate every attempt they make to restore the power of capital; (b) to organize construction in such a way as will rally all toilers around the proletariat and prepare the way for the liquidation, the extinction of all classes; (c) to arm the revolution and to organize the army of the revolution for the struggle against the external enemy and for the struggle against imperialism.

[394]63

It need hardly be emphasized that there is not the slightest possibility of accomplishing these tasks in a short period of time, within a few years. . . . Under the dictatorship of the proletariat we will have to reeducate millions of peasants and petty proprietors, hundreds of thousands of office workers, officials and bourgeois intellectuals; to subordinate all these to the proletarian State and to proletarian leadership; to overcome their bourgeois habits and traditions; to reeducate in a protracted struggle, under the controlling auspices of the dictatorship of the proletariat, the proletarians themselves of their own petty-bourgeois prejudices at the first stroke as if by magic, or at the behest of the Virgin Mary, or by a slogan, resolution, or decree; it can be done only in the course of a long and difficult mass struggle against the mass of petty-bourgeois influences.

PREMIER JOSEPH STALIN, RUSSIAN (1879–1953)

A person had become a master in the art of wrestling; he knew three hundred and sixty sleights in this art, and could exhibit a fresh trick for every day throughout the year. Perhaps owing to a liking that a corner of his heart took for the handsome person of one of his scholars, he taught him three hundred and fifty-nine of these feats, but he was putting off the last one, and under some pretense deferring it.

In short, the youth became such a proficient in the art and talent of wrestling that none of his contemporaries had ability to cope with him, till he at length had one day boasted before the reigning sovereign, saying: "To any superiority my master possesses over me, he is beholden to my reverence of his seniority, and in virtue of his tutorage; otherwise I am not inferior in power, and am his equal in skill." This want of respect displeased the king. He ordered a wrestling match to be held, and a spacious field to be fenced in for the occasion. The ministers of state, nobles of the court, and gallant men of the realm were assembled, and the ceremonials of the combat marshalled. Like a huge and lusty elephant, the youth rushed into the ring with such a crash that had a brazen mountain opposed him he would have moved it from its base. The master being aware that the youth was his superior in strength, engaged him

in that strange feat of which he had kept him ignorant. The youth was unacquainted with its guard,
advancing, nevertheless. The master seized him with
both hands, and, lifting him bodily from the ground,
raised him above his head and flung him on the
earth. The crowd set up a shout. The king ordered
them to give the master an honorary dress and
handsome largess, and the youth he addressed with
reproach and asperity, saying: "You played the
traitor with your patron, and failed in your presumption of opposing him." He replied: "O sire! my
master did not overcome me by strength and ability,
but one cunning trick in the art of wrestling was left
which he was reserved in teaching me, and by that
little feat had today the upper hand of me." The
master said: "I reserved myself for such a day as
this. As the wise have told us, put not so much in a
friend's power that, if hostilely disposed, he can
do you an injury. Have you not heard what that man
said who was treacherously dealt with by his own
pupil: 'Either in fact there was no good faith in this
world, or nobody has perhaps practised it in our
days. No person learned the art of archery from me
who did not in the end make me his butt.'"
SAADI MUSLIH-UD-DIN, PERSIAN (1184–1291)

Either you pursue or push, O Sisyphus, the stone
destined to keep rolling.
OVID, ROMAN (43 B.C.–17 A.D.)

64 Tasks Yet to be Completed
THE WEI CHI HEXAGRAM

*At the outset, the man attempts to advance in a frenzy
during times of disorder in pursuit of tangible accomplishments. This only leads to humiliation, since the time
for good results is not at hand.*

If I can only *concentrate* myself: this is the great lesson
of life. I have hours of unspeakable reaction against
my smallness of production; my wretched habits of
work — or of un-work, my levity, my vagueness of
mind, my perpetual failure to focus my attention, to
absorb myself, to look things in the face, to invent,
to produce, in a word. I shall be 40 years old in April

next: it's a horrible fact! I believe however that I have learned how to work and that it is in moments of forced idleness, almost alone, that these melancholy reflections seize me. When I am really at work, I'm happy, I feel strong, I see many opportunities ahead. It is the only thing that makes life endurable. I must make some great efforts during the next few years, however, if I wish not to have been on the whole a failure. I shall have been a failure unless I do something *great!*

HENRY JAMES, AMERICAN (1843–1916)

The man represses untimely actions through patient control of his strength, while remaining steadfast in his resolve.

Talent is a long patience. — It involves looking at everything one wants to describe long enough, and attentively enough, to find in it some aspect that no one has yet seen or expressed. Everything contains some element of the unexplored because we are accustomed to use our eyes only with the memory of what other people before us have thought about the object we are looking at. The least thing has a bit of the unknown in it. Let us find this. In order to describe a fire burning or a tree in the field, let us stand in front of that fire and that tree until they no longer look to us like any other fire or any other tree.

This is how one becomes original.

GUY DE MAUPASSANT, FRENCH (1850–1893)

The time is ripe for transition, but the man lacks sufficient strength to act alone. Advancing under these conditions would mean disaster.

But when I call to mind I am a King,
Methinks I should revenge me of the wrongs,
That Mortimer and Isobel have done. . . .
But what are kings when regiment is gone
But perfect shadows in a sunshine day?
My nobles rule; I bear the name of King;
I wear the crown, but am controlled by them —
By Mortimer, and my unconstant Queen,
Who spots my nuptial bed with infamy!
— Whilst I am lodged within this cave of care

Where sorrow at my elbow still attends,
To company my heart with sad laments
That bleeds within me for this strange exchange.
CHRISTOPHER MARLOWE, ENGLISH (1564–1593)

---

*The time for fierce struggles against the forces of de-
cadence has arrived. The man lays the foundation of
power and mastery for the future with vigor. Misgivings
are to be silenced. Rewards will come later.*

Don't you get it into your head that every man who
talks learnedly about anthropology is a scientific
man. The proportion of quacks to scientists in all
departments is about 16 to 1 — the ratio we hear so
much about out here. Pitch into them by all means.
ROSCOE POUND, AMERICAN (1870–1964)

---

*Steadfastness to correct action and to sincerity on the
part of the man has rallied men of good faith. Victory is
achieved. A glorious new era has replaced the decadent
old one.*

I beseech you be careful what captains of Horse you
choose, what men be mounted: a few honest men are
better than numbers. . . . If you choose godly honest
men to be captains of Horse, honest men will follow
them; and they will be careful to mount such. . . . I
had rather have a plain russet-coated captain that
knows what he fights for, and loves what he knows,
than that which you call a gentleman and is nothing
else.
LORD PROTECTOR OLIVER CROMWELL,
ENGLISH (1599–1658)

Here enter you, and welcome from our hearts,
All noble sparks, endow'd with gallant parts.
This is the glorious place, which bravely shall
Afford wherewith to entertain you all.
Were you a thousand, here you shall not want
For any thing: for what you'll ask we'll grant,
Stay here you lively, jovial, handsome, brisk,
Gay, witty, frolic, cheerful, merry, frisk,
Spruce, jocund, courteous, furtherers of trades,
And in a word, all worthy, gentle blades.
  Blades of heroic breasts
  Shall taste here of the feasts

Both privilly
And civilly
Of the celestial guests,
Blades of heroic breasts.

Here enter you, pure, honest, faithful, true
Expounders of the Scriptures, old and new.
Whose glosses do not bind our reason, but
Make it to see the clearer, and who shut
Its passages from hatred, avarice,
Pride, factions, convenants, and all sort of vice.
Come, settle here a charitable faith,
Which neighbourly affection nourisheth.
And whose light chaseth all corrupters hence,
Of the blest word, from the aforesaid sense.
 The Holy Sacred Word,
 May it always afford
  T' us all in common,
  Both man and woman,
 A spiritual shield and sword,
 The Holy Sacred Word.

Here enter you all ladies of high birth,
Delicious, stately, charming, full of mirth,
Ingenious, lovely, miniard, proper, fair,
Magnetic, graceful, splendid, pleasant, rare,
Obliging, sprightly, virtuous, young, solacious,
Kind, neat, quick, feat, bright, compt, ripe, choice,
 dear, precious,
Alluring, courtly, comely, fine, complete,
Wise, personable, ravishing, and sweet.
Come joys enjoy. The Lord celestial
Hath given enough, wherewith to please us all.
 God give us, God forgive us,
 And from all woes relieve us;
  That we the treasure
  May reap of pleasure,
 And shun whate'er is grievous,
 God give us, God forgive us.

FRANÇOIS RABELAIS, FRENCH (1494–1553)

---

*The man is filled with confidence and quietly feasting
with convivial friends. No error will result from such
exuberance during the dawning of a new era. It must be
kept within proper bounds, however. Otherwise, in-
temperance will lead to forfeiting of the favorable gains
achieved.*

For lo! the winter is past, the rain is over *and* gone;

The flowers appear on the earth; the time of the singing of birds is come, and the voice of the turtle is
heard in our land.

SONG OF SOLOMON, HEBREW (500 B.C.)

The over-all judgment: order and prosperity in a con-
fused world are being realized. The chaos, which has
been turned into order following deliberation and
caution, is merely dormant. In its turn, the order is now
entering the incipient stages of chaos. The yin-yang
cycle begins anew, as it has always been and will be
repeated for ever and ever.

The people [of India of the fifth century] are numerous and happy; they have not to register their house-
holds, or attend to any magistrates or their rules;
only those who cultivate the royal land have to pay a
portion of the gain from it. If they want to go they
go; if they want to stay they stay. The king governs
without decapitation or corporal punishments.
Criminals are simply fined . . . even in cases of repeated attempts at wicked rebellion they only have
their right hands cut off. . . . Throughout the whole
country the people do not kill any living creature,
nor eat onions or garlic.

FA HIEN, CHINESE (FIFTH CENTURY)

The world's great age begins anew,
    The golden years return,
The earth doth like a snake renew
    Her winter weeds outworn:
Heaven smiles, and faiths and empires gleam,
Like wrecks of a dissolving dream.

A brighter Hellas rears its mountains
    From waves serener far;
A new Peneus rolls his fountains
    Against the morning star.
Where fairer Tempes bloom, there sleep
Young Cyclads on a sunnier deep.

A loftier Argo cleaves the main,
    Fraught with a later prize;
Another Orpheus sings again,
    And loves, and weeps, and dies.

[400]64

A new Ulysses leaves once more
Calypso, for his native shore.

O, write no more the tale of Troy,
    If earth Death's scroll must be!
Nor mix with Laian rage the joy
    Which dawns upon the free:
Although a subtler Sphinx renew
Riddles of Death Thebes never knew.

Another Athens shall arise,
    And to remoter time
Bequeath, like sunset to the skies,
    The splendor of its prime;
And leave, if nought so bright may live,
All earth can take or Heaven can give.

Saturn and Love their long repose
    Shall burst, more bright and good
Than all who fell, than One who rose,
    Than many unsubdued;
Not gold, not blood, their altar dowers,
But votive tears and symbol flowers.

O cease! Must hate and death return?
    Cease! Must men kill and die?
Cease! Drain not to its dregs the urn
    Of bitter prophecy.
The world is weary of the past,
O might it die or rest at last!

PERCY BYSSHE SHELLEY, ENGLISH (1792–1822)

On this chill uncertain spring day, toward twilight,
I have heard the first frog quaver from the marsh.
That is a sound that Pharaoh listened to as it rose
from the Nile, and it blended, I suppose, with his
discontents and longings, as it does with ours. There
is something lonely in that first shaken and uplifted
trilling croak. And more than lonely, for I hear a
warning in it, as Pharaoh heard the sound of plague.
It speaks of the return of life, of animal life, to the
earth. It tells of all that is most unutterable in evolution — the terrible continuity and fluidity of pro-
toplasm, the irrespressible forces of reproduction —
not mystical human love, but the cold batrachian jelly
by which we vertebrates are linked to the things that
creep and writhe and are blind yet breed and have
[401]64

being. More than half it seems to threaten that when mankind has quite thoroughly shattered and eaten and debauched himself with his own follies, that voice may still be ringing out in the marshes of the Nile and the Thames and the Potomac, unconscious that Pharaoh wept for his son.

DONALD CULCROSS PEATTIE, AMERICAN (BORN 1898)

III. Epilogue

The *I Ching* ends thus with a joyful realization of order, though it is tempered with a sober acceptance of chaos to come. This yes-but quality pervades the entire book, as it does all of life. The end of an episode in a man's life does not end anything. It carries within it the beginning of a second; it flows into the middle of a third. Similar events appear in different situations — at the beginning of one, in the middle of another, at the end of a third, and so on.

The message seems clear: a given event cannot be evaluated outside its context. A happy event per se cannot be viewed as "good"; it might be the prelude of evil days to come. Nor can a sad event per se be viewed as "evil"; it might be the basis for good days to come. Similar events in different situations represent channels in which local complications and decisions are transcended and moved from one plane to another without "missing a step." This is the mechanism whereby conversations drift from one subject to another far afield, whereby the original purposes of a reorganization are frustrated in their implementation, whereby efforts at peace result in war. It accounts for the naturalness of the unexpected, the jujitsu of fate. It is the milieu of the great and the bold, of the wise and the skillful — metaphoric allusions of the poet that bring ancient richness to his poem, motifs of the composer that knit his opera into an organic whole, imperceptible switching of ground rules by the negotiator that sweeps the unwary from competition, nimbleness of the humorist that provides the sparkle in his wit. It is the common ground upon which all men can meet to resolve their differences, to share their fortunes, and to spread their cheer. A man has ten thousand ways to reach his neighbor; no man needs be alone.

The authors of the *I Ching* realized, of course, that it would be unreasonable to expect the average man to attain such a level of enlightenment without leading him by the hand at least part of the way. Accordingly, the simplified scheme of sixty-four sets of circumstances was introduced. These provided digestible portions. A person can use these situations as behavioral standards against which to fashion his own courses of action. Even this level of attainment may bring a gain in one's ethical stature and represents success in itself. But those who are less self-centered and less committed to rationalism can aspire to a higher level of appreciation of the world about them. They can rise above the rational organization of the material and seek the intuitive harmony of the fluxing whole of Nature.

All of us have experienced such satisfying moments of selfless participation in Nature. But most of us have lost it early in life.

When I was eleven years of age, spending the summer on my grandparents' estate, I used, as often as I could do it unobserved, to steal into the stable and gently stroke the neck of my darling, a broad dapple-grey horse. It was not a casual delight but a great, certainly friendly, but also deeply stirring happening. . . . The horse, even when I had not begun by pouring oats for him into the manger, very gently raised his massive head, ears flicking, then snorted quietly, as a conspirator gives a signal meant to be recognizable only by his fellow-conspirator; and I was approved. But once — I do not know what came over the child, at any rate it was childlike enough — it struck me about the stroking, what fun it gave me, and suddenly I became conscious of my hand. The game went on as before, but something had changed, it was no longer the same thing.

MARTIN BUBER, HEBREW (BORN 1878)

In the course of our educational and professional preoccupations with rational components, we have become progressively more estranged from the totality. As we glamorize the analytical intellect, we neglect our total selves. "Paradise regained" recedes farther into the distance.

The old masters teach us that this reintegration is within every man's reach, if he will only "let it come." But just how it comes they refuse to, or rather cannot, say explicitly. One of the classical stories about achieving enlightenment goes something like this:

It seems that a certain Master invariably stuck out his thumb and remained silent whenever his pupils asked him to explain the nature of the *Tao*. After many such occasions the pupil next to him began to imitate him in jest. One day when this mimicy occurred, the Master suddenly whipped out a sharp sword and cut off the boy's thumb. Whereupon, the boy ran toward the back door crying in pain. The Master called out to him. Just as the boy turned around, the Master again stuck out his thumb. Then and there, so the story states it, the boy gained sudden enlightenment and apprehended the nature of the *Tao*.

Although undoubtedly fascinating, this illustration probably eludes the Western man of affairs, for whom this book is written. Perhaps the centuries-old sermon of the Zen master Wu-tzu is more understandable. He said that gaining sudden enlightenment is like learning the art of burglary in the following story:

The son of an aging housebreaker decided that it was about time for him to learn the profession to support the family. So he asked his father for lessons. The father approved the proposal and took him along on the next attempt. They broke through a fence, stealthily entered a mansion, and opened a large chest. The father suggested that the son step into the chest and pick out the valuables. Whereupon the son did. As soon as he got in, the father dropped the lid, locked the chest, sneaked out into the courtyard, loudly knocked on the door waking the whole household and quickly retired through the hole in the fence. The excited residents scurried around with their candles and discovered that the thief had gotten away. Meanwhile the son, imprisoned in the chest, was terribly afraid; an idea flashed through his mind. He made a scratching noise like a mouse, at the sound of which the master of the family sent the maid to investigate. When the maid unlocked the chest, out jumped the boy, who blew out the candle, pushed the maid aside and ran off with the neighbors on his heels. Passing a well, he lit upon a second thought. He picked up a large stone and dropped it into the well with a loud splash. Hearing the sound the pursuers all gathered around the deep and dark hole, attempting to see the burglar drowning himself. The boy ran on. Safely back home, the youngster blamed the old man for the harrowing experience. Replied the father understandingly, "Tell me, son, how did you get away?" Whereupon the son recounted the events in detail. And the father finally smiled and said, "There son, you have now learnt the art of burglary."

In the light of this perspective, the Western man of affairs may wish to look at the *I Ching* again to be sure that he has acquired what in fact there is to acquire. If he is in earnest about the exercise, I would like to suggest the following procedure:

Concentrate on the sixty-four situations, one at a time, in the order presented. Deliberate over the ramifications of the statements of the *I Ching*, the nuances portrayed by the added excerpts, the recollections of your own experiences, at a slow, even tempo. Then lay the book aside for a year or so.

Review the sixty-four situations. Meditate over them one at a time in random fashion. Note the similarities among them. Note the cross linkages. Observe the facility of movement from one situation to another. Note how the perusal of one situation brings to mind the events of another and then how recollections of your own life and experience become intermingled in the process with the lives and experiences recorded throughout the sixty-four hexagrams. Notice how the parts complement one another in the pervasive harmony of the whole. Then lay the book aside for a month or so.

Leaf through the book at random. Glance at a page here and there, there and here. Do not analyze; do not think. Do not dwell on what the *I Ching* says; muse on life as a whole, and let the passages of the *I Ching* fall into your musings as they will. Do not dwell on your own life; muse on the lives of all of the creatures in the cosmic play, and let the passages of the *I Ching* fall into your musings as they will. Let feelings diffuse as they will. Then lay the book aside for a day or so.

Pick up the book, feel it, then throw it away.

IV. References*

Abbadie, Arnauld d'. *Twelve Years in Upper Ethiopia.*
Translated in Basil Davidson. *The African Past.* Boston:
Little, Brown, 1964. Pp. 309–310. (1)

Abrahams, Peter. "The Blacks," *Holiday Magazine,* April
1959. (23)

Abu'l al-Ma'ari. *Meditations.* Translated by Reynold A.
Nicholson. (59)

Acton, John. "Conflicts with Rome," *The Rambler,* New
Ser. IV (January 1964). (38)

Addison, Joseph. "The Battle of Blenheim," *The Campaign.*
London: Hills, 1710. (7)

Addison, Joseph. *Cato.* In *Works of Joseph Addison.* New
York: Harper, 1850. Act I, Sc. 2. (25)

Aesop. "The Wolf in Sheep's Clothing," *Fables.* Translated
by Thomas James and George T. Townsend. Philadelphia:
Lippincott Edition, 1949. P. 9. (23)

Akemi Tachibana. Translated by R. H. Blyth. *Japanese
Humour.* Tokyo: Japan Travel Bureau, 1957. (25)

Aldrich, Thomas B. "Hospitality," *Poems.* Boston: Houghton Mifflin, 1882. (54)

Allen, James L. "King Solomon of Kentucky," *Flute and
Violin.* 1891. (59)

Amenemhet I. "Advice to His Son." Translated in J. H.
Breasted. *Development of Religion and Thought in Ancient
Egypt.* P. 203. (36)

Amiel, Henri-Frédéric. *Amiel's Journal.* Translated by Mrs.
Humphrey Ward. New York: Brentano's, 1928. P. 179. (17)

Anacreon. *Elegiacs.* (52)

Andersen, Hans C. "The Ugly Duckling," *Andersen's Tales.*
Translated by H. W. Dulcken. New York: Routledge, 1888.
(48)

Anderson, Maxwell. *Key Largo.* Hindsdale: Anderson
House, 1939. Prologue. (61)

Anderson, Sherwood. "Brothers," *The Triumph of the Egg.*
New York: Huebsch, 1921. (48)

Andrade, Mario de. "Variation of a Bad Friend." Translated by John Nist. *Modern Brazilian Poetry.* Bloomington:
Indiana University, 1962. Pp. 35–36. (31)

Anouilh, Jean. *The Lark.* Adapted by Lilian Hellman. New
York: Random House, 1955. Act I. (15)

"Antar." Translated by Etienne Delécluse and Epiphanius
Wilson in Epiphanius Wilson (ed.). *Arabian Literature.*
New York: Colonial, 1902. (6)

*The hexagram in which the reference is cited is shown in paren-
theses at the end of each reference.

Archilochus. "The Soldier's General." Translated by A. Watson Bain. (55)

Aretino, Pietro. *Horatio.* Quoted by Francesco de Sanctis. *History of Italian Literature.* Translated by Joan Redfern. New York: Harcourt, Brace, 1931. Basic Books Edition, Vol. II, p. 608. (58)

Argüello Barreto, Santiago. "The Eagle and the Dry Leaf." Translated by Alice S. Blackwell. *Some Spanish American Poets.* Philadelphia: University of Pennsylvania, 1937. (20)

Ariosto, Ludovico. *Sorcerer.* Quoted by Francesco de Sanctis. *History of Italian Literature.* Translated by Joan Redfern. New York: Harcourt, Brace, 1931. Basic Books Edition, Vol. II, p. 476. (36)

Aristophanes. *The Frogs.* Translated by John H. Frere. (28)

Aristotle. *Nicomachean Ethics.* Bk. IV, 5. Translated in Saxe Cummins and Robert N. Linscott (eds.). *The Social Philosophers.* New York: Random House, 1947. P. 80. (30)

Arnold, Julian B. *Giants in Dressing Gowns.* Chicago: Argus, 1942. Pp. 154–155. (50)

Arnold, Matthew. "Rugby Chapel." In W. H. Auden and Norman H. Pearson (eds.). *Poets of the English Language.* New York: Viking, 1950. Vol. V, pp. 222–224. (32)

Ashoka. "Seventh Pillar Edict." Translated in William Theodore de Bary *et al. Sources of Indian Tradition.* New York: Columbia University, 1958. Pp. 152–153. (55)

Assyrian Law. Translated by Theophile J. Meek in James B. Pritchard (ed.). *Ancient Near Eastern Texts.* Princeton: Princeton University, 1950. P. 181. (60)

Augustine. *City of God.* Translated by Marcus Dods. Edinburgh: Clark, 1887. Bk. IV, Chap. 3. (6)

Aurangzeb. Translated by James Tod. *Annals and Antiquities of Rajasthan.* 1894. (40)

Aurelius Antoninus, Marcus. *Meditations.* Translated by George Long. 1862. Bk. IV. (15)

Austen, Jane. *Sense and Sensibility.* New York: Dodd, Mead, 1949. P. 41. (63)

Bacon, Francis. "Essay on Negotiating." *Harvard Classics,* Vol. III, pp. 123–124. (53)

Bagehot, Walter. "Mr. Cobden," *Biographical Studies.* 1889. (38)

Bailey, Philip J. "A Mountain Sunrise," *Festus.* New York: Miller, 1865. (55)

Baker, Dorothy. *Young Man with a Horn.* New York: Dodd, 1938. (35)

Baldinucci, Fillippo. *The Vigil.* Translated by Thomas B. Harbottle and Philip H. Dalbiac. *Dictionary of Quotations (French and Italian).* New York: Ungar, 1958. P. 261. (54)

Balzac, Honoré de, "The Girl with the Golden Eyes," *The Thirteen.* Translated by Ellen Marriage. Boston: Estes, 1901. (48)

Bandello, Matteo. *Novel*. Translated by Thomas Roscoe. *Italian Novelists*. 1836. (15)

Barère de Vieuzac, Bertrand. "Speech in the Convention Nationale." 1792. (49)

Barrie, James M. *The Little Minister*. 1891. Chap. 10. (54)

Basho. Translated by Asataro Miyamori. *An Anthology of Haiku, Ancient and Modern*. Tokyo: Maruzen, 1932. (38)

Bastiat, Frédéric. "To the Youth of France," *The Harmonies of Political Economy*. Translated by P. J. Stirling. London: 1860. (17)

Baudelaire, Charles Pierre. "The Irreparable." Translated by Roy Campbell. *Poems of Baudelaire*. New York: Pantheon, 1952. P. 72. (47)

Beaumarchais, Pierre de. *The Barber of Seville*. Translated by W. R. Taylor. Boston: Baker, 1922. (23, 33)

Belinsky, Vissarion G. Translated by Rufus W. Mathewson, Jr. *The Positive Hero in Russian Literature*. New York: Columbia University, 1958. (29)

"Bell of Atri." Translated by Thomas Roscoe. *Italian Novelists*. 1836. (23)

Benediktsson, Einar. "Rain." Translated by Watson Kirkconnell. *Icelandic Poems and Stories*. New York: American-Scandinavian Foundation, 1943. (30)

Bennett, Arnold. *The Card*. 1911. Chap. 12. (2)

Bentham, Jeremy. *Principles of Legislation*. Translated by Richard Hildreth. 1864. Chap. 12. (60)

Bernanos, Georges. *Under the Sun of Satan*. Translated by Helmut A. Hatzfeld. *Literature through Art*. New York: Oxford University, 1952. P. 208. (29)

Berzenyi, Daniel. "To the Hungarians." Translated by Watson Kirkconnell in Joseph Kemenyi *et al*. *World Literatures*. Pittsburgh: University of Pittsburgh, 1956. P. 138. (58)

Bestuzhev, Aleksandr. "Letter to Nicholas I." Translated by A. G. Mazour. *The First Russian Revolution*. Berkeley: University of California, 1957. Pp. 277–278. (46)

Bhagavad Gita. Translated by Edwin Arnold. Chap. 6. (41)

Bialik, Chaim N. "The Last Word." Translated by Joseph Leftwich. *The Golden Peacock*. New York: Yoseloff, 1961. Pp. 46–50. (26)

Billings, Josh. "Affurisms," *His Sayings*. 1865. (28)

Bisland, Elizabeth. *Three Wise Men of the East*. Chapel Hill: University of North Carolina, 1930. Pp. 232–234. (4)

Blackstone, William. *Commentaries on the Laws of England*. 1762. (10)

Blake, William. "Eternity." (41)

Blok, Aleksandr. "The Twelve." Stanza 11, Translated by Babette Deutsch and Adam Yarmolinsky in Philo M. Buck, Jr. (ed.). *An Anthology of World Literature*. New York: Macmillan, 1951. Third Edition, p. 1099. (17)

Boccaccio, Giovanni. "The Falcon," *The Decameron*. Translated by Thomas Roscoe. *Italian Novelists*. 1836. (41)

[409]

Boileau-Despréaux, Nicolas. *The Art of Poetry.* Translated by William Soame. 1892. (15)

Boker, George H. *Francesca da Rimini.* 1855. Act III, Sc. 1. (55)

Bokhari. "The Sultan of Kembajat," *Crown of Kings.* Adapted by Gene Z. Hanrahan. *50 Great Oriental Stories.* New York: Bantam, 1965. Pp. 384–385. (42)

Bolingbroke, Lord. "On the Study and Use of History," *Works.* 1841. Vol. II. (5)

Bolitho, William. "The Saxophone," *Leviathan.* New York: Harper, 1924. (12)

Bonnieres, Robert de. In *Figaro.* Translated by Robert Baldick. *The Goncourt Journal.* New York: Oxford University, 1962. P. xi. (20)

"Book of the Dead," *Egyptian Papyrus.* (43)

Brooks, William E. *Grant of Appomattox.* Indianapolis: Bobbs-Merrill, 1942. Pp. 297–299. (40)

Brown, John. "Written Statement Just before His Execution." December 2, 1859. (28)

Browning, Elizabeth B. *Aurora Leigh.* 1857. (44)

Browning, Robert. "Bishop Blougram's Apology." In W. H. Auden and Norman H. Pearson (eds.). *Poets of the English Language.* New York: Viking, 1950. Vol. V, p. 171. (16)

Buber, Martin. *Dialogue.* Translated by Chaim Potok. "Martin Buber and the Jews," *Commentary,* March 1946. (Epilogue)

Büchner, Georg. "Lenz." Translated by Goronwy Rees in Stephen Spender (ed.). *Great German Short Stories.* New York: Dell, 1960. Pp. 30–31. (52)

Bulwer-Lytton, Edward G. *The Last Days of Pompeii.* 1834. Chap. 5. (47)

Burckhardt, Jacob. "Letter to Louise Burckhardt, July 16, 1840," *The Letters of Jacob Burckhardt.* Edited by Alexander Dru. New York: Pantheon, 1955. P. 54. (30)

Burke, Edmund. "Speech in House of Commons on the Nabob of Arcot's Debts." February 28, 1785. (56)

Burns, Robert. "The Toadeater," *The Poetical Works of Robert Burns.* London: Hamilton, Adams, n.d. P. 379. (8)

Burton, Robert. *Anatomy of Melancholy.* 1621. (30)

Butler, Samuel. *The Way of All Flesh.* New York: Dutton, 1916. P. 259. (57)

Byron, George. "She Walks in Beauty." In Louis Untermeyer (ed.). *A Treasury of Great Poems.* New York: Simon and Schuster, 1942. Pp. 700–701. (10)

Caesar, Julius. "Speech against Execution of Catiline's Fellow Conspirators." Translated by William Rose. 1813. (30)

Campbell, Roy. "Luis de Camões," *Talking Bronco.* London: Faber and Faber, 1954. P. 11. (7)

Campistron, Jean G. de. *Andronic.* Act I. Translated by Lacy Lockert. *The Chief Rivals of Corneille and Racine.* Nashville:

Vanderbilt University, 1956. Pp. 429–430. (3)

Camus, Albert. "The Artist and His Time," *The Myth of Sisyphus and Other Essays*. Translated by Justin O'Brien. New York: Vintage, 1960. Pp. 149–150. (42)

Carlyle, Thomas. "Gospel of Mammonism," *Past and Present*. 1843. (14)

Casals, Pablo. Quoted in J. M. Corredor. *Conversations with Casals*. New York: Dutton, 1956. (38)

Cassius Longinus. "Argument before the Roman Senate." Translated by William J. Brodribb. 1879. (21)

Castiglione, Baldassare. *The Book of the Courtier*. Translated by L. E. Opdycke. New York: Scribner's, 1903. Bk. IV. (9)

Castillejo, Cristóbal de. *On Conversation, False Message*. Translated by Thomas B. Harbottle and Martin Hume. *Dictionary of Quotations (Spanish)*. New York: Ungar, 1958. P. 150 (38)

Cather, Willa. "Neighbour Rosicky," *Obscure Destinies*. New York: Knopf, 1930. Pp. 65–67. (4)

Caulaincourt, Armand de. *With Napoleon in Russia*. Edited by George Libraire. New York: Grosset and Dunlap, 1935. Pp. 5–7. (7)

Cervantes Saavedra, Miguel de. *Don Quixote of La Mancha*. Translated by Peter A. Motteux. 1702. (39)

Chāndogya Upaniṣad. Translated by T. R. Krishnāchārya. Bombay: Nirnayasāgara, 1904. 6.1–3, 12–14. (4)

Chang Chen-chi. *Practice of Zen*. New York: Harper, 1959. (50)

Chang Hsieh. *East-West Research*. 1618. Translated by Joseph Needham. *Science and Civilization in China*. Cambridge: Cambridge University, 1954–. Vol. VI. (40)

Charron, Pierre. *Treatise on Wisdom*. Translated by Myrtilla Daly. 1891. (57)

Chateaubriand, François de. Translated by George K. Anderson. (55)

Chaucer, Geoffrey. "The Wife of Bath's Prologue," *Canterbury Tales*. (21)

Chekhov, Anton. *The Three Sisters*. Act II. Translated by Bernard G. Guerney. *A Treasury of Russian Literature*. Philadelphia: Vanguard, 1943. P. 839. (47)

Chénier, André. "Testament." Quoted in C. A. Sainte-Beuve. *Talks of Monday*. Translated by E. J. Trechmann. New York: Dutton, 1909. (36)

Chesterfield, Lord. *Letters to His Son*. Edited by Lord Mahon. 1845–1853. (14)

Chesterton, Gilbert K. *The Common Man*. New York: Sheed and Ward, 1950. Pp. 120–121. (45)

Chikamatsu Monzaemon. Translated by Donald Keene. *Major Plays of Chikamatsu*. New York: Columbia University, 1961. P. 26. (33)

Chin Sheng-t'an. "Thirty-three Happy Moments." Translated by Lin Yutang. *The Importance of Living.* New York: Day, 1937. Pp. 131–135. (58)

Chinese proverb. (48)

Chou Yung. "The Ferryman's Wisdom." Translated by Lin Yutang. *Translations from the Chinese.* New York: Forum, 1963. (2)

Chrysostom, Dio. *Eleventh Discourses.* Chap. 2. Translated by J. W. Cohoon. *Loeb Classical Library.* (9)

Chuang-tzu. Translated by Herbert A. Giles and edited by Lionel Giles. *Musings of a Chinese Mystic.* New York: Dutton, 1906. (1)

Chuang-tzu. Translated by Herbert A. Giles. *Chuang Tzu: Mystic, Moralist and Social Reformer.* London: Quaritch, 1926. Second Edition. (12)

Churchill, Winston S. *Great Contemporaries.* London: Butterworth, 1937. Pp. 18-19. (44)

Cicero, Marcus. *In Truth.* Translated by Marcus Dods. 1887. Bk. I, 15. (6)

Claudius Claudianus. *Honor of the Fourth Council.* (57)

Clausewitz, Karl von. *On War.* Translated by O. J. Matthijs Jolles. New York: Modern Library, 1943. (9)

Clay, Henry. "Speech in United States Senate." March 14, 1834. (52)

Clearchus. "Corinth." *Fragment.* Translated by F. A. Paley. 1881. (22)

Cocteau, Jean. Quoted by Edith Wharton. *A Backward Glance.* New York: Scribner's, 1964. Pp. 285–286. (47)

Coffin, Robert P. T. "The Pines," *Collected Poems.* New York: Macmillan, 1948. Pp. 196–197. (20)

Coke, Edward. "Speech." May 9, 1628. (40)

Colette, Sidonie-Gabrielle. *Gigi.* Translated by Roger Senhouse. New York: Farrar, Straus and Cudahy, 1952. Signet Edition, pp. 33–34. (22)

Confucius. Translated by Lin Yutang. *Wisdom of Laotse.* New York: Modern Library, 1948. Pp. 250–251. (19)

Congreve, William. *Love for Love.* 1695. (50)

Conrad, Joseph. *Lord Jim.* 1900. Chap. 16. (38)

Conwell, Russell. "My Prayer." Stanza 1. (17)

Corbett, James J. *The Roar of the Crowd.* New York: Putnam's, 1925. (46)

Corneille, Pierre. *Polyeucte.* Act V, Sc. 3. (63)

Corneille, Thomas. *The Earl of Essex.* Act I. Translated by Lacy Lockert. *The Chief Rivals of Corneille and Racine.* Nashville: Vanderbilt University, 1956. (46)

Cósmes, Francisco G. Translated by Helene Weyl in F. S. C. Northrop (ed.). *Ideological Differences and World Order.* New Haven: Yale University, 1949. P. 174. (63)

Cotton, Nathaniel. "The Fireside." Stanza 11. (62)

Cozzens, James G. *The Just and the Unjust.* New York: Harcourt, Brace, 1942. P. 434. (47)

Crane, Stephen. "The Man." 1899. (56)

Crèvecoeur, St. John de. *Letters.* 1904 Edition, pp. 57–58. (34)

Crockett, Davy. *Life of Col. David Crockett.* Philadelphia: Evans, 1860. P. 384. (39)

Cromwell, Oliver. "Letter to William Springs," *Letters and Speeches of Oliver Cromwell.* Edited by Thomas Carlyle. 1846. Vol. I. (64)

Cronin, Morton J. "The Tyranny of Democratic Manners," *New Republic,* January 20, 1958. (14)

Cummings, E. E. *Poems 1923–1924.* New York: Harcourt, Brace, 1954. (59)

Daidoji Yusan. *Primer on Bushido.* Translated by Daisetz T. Suzuki. *Zen and Japanese Culture.* New York: Pantheon, 1958. P. 72. (52)

Daniel, Samuel. "Ulysses and the Siren." In W. H. Auden and Norman H. Pearson (eds.). *Poets of the English Language.* New York: Viking, 1950. Vol. II, pp. 89–90. (58)

Dante Alighieri. *Inferno.* Translated by Laurence Binyon. London: Benn, 1932. (37)

Darwin, Charles. *The Descent of Man.* 1871. Chap. 21. (3)

Davies, W. H. "Broken Hearts." (37)

Davis, Richard H. *The Bar Sinister.* New York: Scribner's, 1903. (34)

Debs, Eugene. *His Life, Writings and Speeches.* Kansas: Girard, 1908. (39)

Decatur, Stephen. "Toast Given at Norfolk." April 1816. (8)

Delavigne, Casimir. *Does Study Bring Happiness?* (47)

Descartes, René. *Discourse on Method.* 1637. (26)

Dhammapada. "Commentary: A Courtesan Tempts the Monk Ocean-of-Beauty." Translated by Eugene W. Burlingame. Cambridge: Harvard University, 1921. (27)

Dickinson, Emily. *The Poems of Emily Dickinson.* Boston: Little, Brown, 1930. Second Series, Life, I, Stanza 1. (35)

Dickinson, John. *Letters from a Farmer in Pennsylvania.* Edited by R. T. H. Halsey. 1908. (34)

Dinesen, Isak. "The Chevalier," *Seven Gothic Tales.* New York: Smith and Haas, 1934. P. 83. (58)

Disraeli, Benjamin. *Henrietta Temple.* Bk. VI, Chap. 9. (25)

D'Israeli, Isaac. *Literary Character.* 1795. Chap. 12. (61)

Dobrolyubov, N. A. *Selected Philosophical Essays.* Translated by Rufus W. Mathewson, Jr. *The Positive Hero in Russian Literature.* New York: Columbia University, 1959. (40)

Donne, John. "The Undertaking." In *Great Poems of the English Language.* Compiled by Wallace A. Briggs and William R. Benét. New York: Tudor, 1948. P. 136. (2)

Dos Passos, John. *U. S. A.* New York: Harcourt, Brace, 1938. Modern Library Edition III, pp. 54–55. (46)

Dostoevsky, Fëdor. *The Brothers Karamazov*. Translated by Constance Garnett. New York: Macmillan, 1912. (35)

Dostoevsky, Fëdor. *House of the Dead*. Translated by Constance Garnett. New York: Macmillan, 1954. Pp. 19–20. (48)

Drucker, Peter F. "How to be an Employee," *Fortune Magazine*, May 1952. (24)

Du Gard, Roger Martin. *André Gide*. Translated by Albert Guérard. Cambridge: Harvard University, 1951. (1)

Dumas, Alexandre, fils. *The Question of Money*. 1857. Act II, Sc. 7. (9)

Ecclesiastes 3: 1–8. King James Version of the Bible. (41)

Eckermann, Johann P. "Talk of January 31, 1827," *Conversations with Goethe*. Translated by John Oxenford. 1850. (30)

Ekken Kaibara. Translated by Ken Hoshino. *The Way of Contentment*. London: Murray, 1913. (27)

Eliot, George. *The Spanish Gypsy*. 1868. Bk. I. (49)

Eliot, John. "Speech in House of Commons on the Petition of Right." June 3, 1628. (15)

Ellison, Ralph W. *The Invisible Man*. New York: Random House, 1952. (51)

Emerson, Ralph W. "Terminus." In *Great Poems of the English Language*. Compiled by William A. Briggs and William R. Benét. New York: Tudor, 1948. P. 680. (32)

Ennius, Quintus. *Annals*. (40)

Epictetus. *Discourses*. Translated by Thomas W. Higginson. 1856. Chap. 15. (62)

Epicurus. Translated by Cyril Bailey. *The Greek Atomists and Epicurus*. Oxford: Clarendon, 1928. (31)

Erasmus, Desiderius. *The Lives of Vitrier . . . and John Colet*. Translated by J. H. Lupton. 1883. (6)

Erskine, John. *The Moral Obligation to be Intelligent and Other Essays*. 1921. (51)

Euripedes. *Iphigenia in Tauris*. Translated by Gilbert Murray. Line 723. (55)

Everett, Edward. *Mount Vernon Papers*. 1859. No. 14. (14)

Fa Hien. "Travel Report on India." Translated by James Legge in H. H. Gowen. *History of Indian Literature*. New York: 1931. (64)

Farmer, James E. *Versailles and the Court under Louis XIV*. New York: Century, 1906. Pp. 336–338. (4)

Faulkner, William H. "The Bear," *Collected Stories*. New York: Random House, 1942. (63)

Fessenden, William P. "Eulogy in United States Senate at Death of Senator Foot." 1866. (55)

Fielding, Henry. *The Miser*. 1733. (16)

Fillmore, Millard. "Third Annual Presidential Address." December 6, 1852. (53)

Finer, Herman. *Theory and Practice of Modern Government.* New York: Holt, 1949. Revised Edition, pp. 935–936. (42)

Fisher, Dorothy C. *These United States.* New York: Boni and Liveright, 1923. (57)

Fiske, John. *The Dutch and Quaker Colonies in America.* 1899. Vol. II. (54)

Fitzgerald, F. Scott. "Letter to His Daughter." 1937. (61)

Flaubert, Gustave. "Letter to Madame Z." Translated by Walter Pater. (30)

Foch, Ferdinand. "Statement at Battle of the Marne." (1918). Quoted in G. G. Aston. *The Biography of the Late Marshall Foch.* New York: Macmillan, 1929. (28)

Foeldes, Yolanda. *The Homecoming.* Translated by Paul Tabori (ed.). *Hungarian Anthology.* London: Bale and Staples, 1943. Pp. 41–42. (22)

Fokine, Michel. Translated by Vitale Fokine and edited by Anatole Chujoy. *Fokine. Memoirs of a Ballet Master.* Boston: Little, Brown, 1961. P. v. (25)

Fonvisin, Denis I. *Universal Courtiers' Grammar.* Translated by Bernard G. Guerney. *The Portable Russian Reader.* New York: Viking, 1947. Pp. 23–25. (17)

Ford, Henry. *My Life and Work.* Garden City: Doubleday, Page, 1922. (22)

Forner, Juan P. "Philosopher in Love." Translated by John A. Cook. *Neo-Classic Drama in Spain.* Dallas: Southern Methodist University, 1959. P. 387. (58)

Fox, Charles J. "Speech in House of Commons on Bill to Abolish the Tyranny of East India Company." December 1, 1783. (39)

France, Anatole. "The Procurator of Judea." Translated by Frederic Chapman. *Mother of Pearl.* New York: Dodd, Mead, 1910. (13)

Francis of Assisi. *The Little Flowers of Saint Francis.* Translated by Thomas Okey. London: Dent, 1910. (24)

Franklin, Benjamin. "Queries and Remarks Respecting Alterations in Constitution of Pennsylvania," *Works.* Vol. V, p. 167. (7)

Frazer, James. *The Golden Bough.* 1890. (49)

Frederick the Great. Quoted by Henri de Catt. *Memoirs.* Translated by F. S. Flint. *Frederick the Great.* 1884. (5)

Freeman, Mary E. *The Portion of Labor.* New York: Harpers, 1901. P. 562. (61)

Freneau, Philip. "To the Memory of the Brave Americans Who Fell at Eutaw Springs." September 8, 1781. (28)

Frishman, David. "For the Messiah." Translated by Maurice Samuel. *Anthology of Modern Jewish Poetry.* New York: Behrman House, 1927. (9)

Fronto, Marcus Cornelius. "Preamble to History." Quoted in L. Friedländer. *Roman Life and Manners under the Early*

Empire. Translated by J. H. Freese and L. A. Magnus. New York: Dutton, 1936. Vol. II, p. 3. (41)

Frost, Robert. "Letter to Louis Untermeyer, March 10, 1924." *Selected Letters of Robert Frost.* Edited by Lawrance Thompson. New York: Holt, Rinehart and Winston, 1964. P. 300. (33)

Fry, Christopher. *The Dark Is Light Enough.* New York: Oxford University, 1954. P. 44. (46)

Funck-Brentano, Frantz, and Albert Sorel. *Law of Nations.* 1877. (20)

Furmanov, Dmitri. *Chapaev.* Translated by Rufus W. Mathewson, Jr. *The Positive Hero in Russian Literature.* New York: Columbia University, 1958. (47)

Gaboriau, Emile. *Monsieur Lacoq.* 1869. Part II, Chap. 4. (29)

Galileo Galilei. "Recanting before Church Authorities, April 30, 1633." Translated by Gerald Dickler. *Man on Trial.* Garden City: Doubleday, 1962. Pp. 71–72. (6)

Galsworthy, John. *The Forsyte Saga.* New York: Scribner's, 1922. Pp. 320–321. (11)

Gandhi, Mohandas. "Statement before English Judge before Being Sentenced for Seditious Articles." March 23, 1922. (46)

Gannett, W. C. "Blessed Be Drudgery," *The Faith That Makes Faithful.* Boston: Stratford, 1918. (42)

Garibaldi, Giuseppe. Translated in G. M. Trevelyan. *Garibaldi's Defense of the Roman Republic.* London: Longmans, Green, 1907. (8)

Garrison, William L. "Statement," *The Liberator,* January 1, 1831. (29)

Garshin, Vsevolod M. "The Signal." Translated by Thomas Seltzer (ed.). *Best Russian Short Stories.* New York: Boni and Liveright, 1917. Pp. 131–133. (24)

Gauguin, Paul. Translated by John Cournos. *A Modern Plutarch.* Indianapolis: Bobbs-Merrill, 1928. (19)

Gaulle, Charles de. *The Call to Honour.* New York: Viking, 1955. P. 3. (14)

Gautama Buddha. "Sermon on Abuse." Translated in Lin Yutang (ed.). *The Wisdom of China and India.* New York: Modern Library, 1942. P. 363. (9)

George, Henry. "The Crime of Poverty," *Our Land and Policy.* New York: Doubleday, Page, 1904. (47)

Gibran, Kahlil. *The Prophet.* New York: Knopf, 1923. Pp. 26–27. (45)

Gide, André. *Terrestrial Nourishments.* 1897. (56)

Gilbert, William S. *Thespis.* 1871. (54)

Giraudoux, Jean. *Tiger at the Gates.* Translated by Christopher Fry. New York: Oxford University, 1955. Act I. (3)

Goethe, Johann Wolfgang von. Translated by John S. Blackie. *The Wisdom of Goethe.* 1883. (43)

Gogol, Nikolai V. "The Overcoat." Translated by Bernard

G. Guerney. *A Treasury of Russian Literature*. New York: Vanguard, 1943. P. 154. (44)

Goldsmith, Oliver. *The Good-Natur'd Man*. 1768. Act I. (46)

Gómez de Quevedo y Villegas, Francisco. "Epistle to Olivares." Translated by Gerald Brenan. *The Literature of the Spanish People*. Cambridge: Cambridge University, 1953. (29)

Goncourt, Edmond, and Jules de. *Journal*. Translated by Robert Baldick. New York: Oxford University, 1962. (30)

Gorky, Maksim. *Lower Depths*. Translated by Edwin Hopkins. Boston: Badger, 1915. (24)

Gough, John B. "What Is a Minority." (35)

Gracián, Baltasar. *The Art of Worldly Wisdom*. Translated by Joseph Jacobs. 1892. (9, 17)

Graham, Shirley. *There Was Once a Slave*. New York: Messner, 1947. Pp. 9–10. (51)

Grahame, Kenneth. *The Wind in the Willows*. New York: Scribner's, 1908. Grosset and Dunlap Edition, pp. 136–137. (33)

Graves, Robert. "Gardener," *Collected Poems*. New York: Doubleday, 1961. P. 102. (42)

Gray, Thomas. "Ode on a Distant Prospect of Eton College." In W. H. Auden and Norman H. Pearson (eds.). *Poets of the English Language*. New York: Viking, 1950. Vol. III, pp. 543–546. (4)

Great Learning. Translated by Shao Chang Lee in Charlton Laird (ed.). *The World Through Literature*. New York: Appleton-Century-Crofts, 1951. P. 51. (61)

Greene, Robert. *George A. Greene, The Pinner of Wakefield*. 1599. (22)

Gregory of Nazianzus. "Oration over Basil, Bishop of Cesares." Translated in S. E. Frost, Jr. (ed.). *The World's Great Sermons*. Garden City: Halcyon, 1943. Pp. 27–28. (14)

Grenville, George. "Speech in House of Commons against Expulsion of John Wilkes." 1769. (21)

Griboedov, Aleksandr S. *Intelligence Comes to Grief*. Translated by N. Benardsky. *Gore at Uman*. 1857. (23)

Griswold, Rufus W. "Obituary Notice," *New York Tribune*, October 9, 1849. (6)

Grotius, Hugo. *The Law of War and Peace*. Translated by Francis Kelsey. *Classics of International Law*. Edited by J. B. Scott. Washington: Carnegie, 1925. Bk. II, Chap. 9. (43)

Gui, Bernard. *Manual of the Inquisitor*. Translated in *Introduction to Contemporary Civilization in the West*. New York: Columbia University, 1960. Third Edition, Vol. I, pp. 197–198. (19)

Güiraldes, Ricardo. *Don Segundo Sombra*. Translated by Harriet de Onís. New York: Farrar and Rinehart, 1935. Chap. 2. (50)

Guiterman, Arthur. *A Poet's Proverbs*. New York: Dutton, 1924. P. 48. (43)

Gundolf, Friedrich. Translated by Peter Green. *Essays in Antiquity*. Cleveland: World, 1960. (13)

Habe, Hans. "This Is Defeat." Translated by Paul Tabori (ed.). *Hungarian Anthology*. London: Bale and Staples, 1943. Pp. 77–78. (33)

Hammurabi. *Code of Hammurabi*. Translated by Theophile J. Meek in James B. Pritchard (ed.). *Ancient Near Eastern Texts*. Princeton: Princeton University, 1950. Pp. 177–178. (1)

Hamsun, Knut. "The Call of Life." Translated by Anders Orbeck (ed.). *Norway's Best Stories*. New York: American-Scandinavian Foundation, 1927. (16)

Han Yü. "On the 15th Evening of the 8th Month Presented to Chang Kung the Keeper of the Records." Translated by Soame Jenyns. *Three Hundred Poems of T'ang Dynasty*. London: Murray, 1944. Pp. 39–40. (5)

Han-tzu. Translated by Lin Mousheng. *Men and Ideas*. New York: Day, 1942. (7)

Hare, Julius C. and Augustus W. *Guesses at Truth*. 1851–1855. (38)

Harris, Joel C. *Uncle Remus, His Songs and His Sayings*. 1881. (32)

Harte, Bret. "Tennessee's Partner." San Francisco: Elder, 1907. (44)

Hattusilis III. Translated in Sabatino Moscati. *The Face of the Ancient Orient*. Chicago: Quadrangle Books, 1959. Anchor Edition, pp. 171–172. (35)

Hazlitt, William. "A Letter to William Gifford, Esq." 1819. (44)

Hegel, Georg W. F. *Philosophy of History*. Translated by J. Sibree. 1857. In *Introduction to Contemporary Civilization in the West*. New York: Columbia University, 1961. Third Edition, Vol. II, p. 132. (19)

Heike Monogatari. Translated by Edwin O. Reischauer and Joseph K. Yamigawa. *Translations from Early Japanese Literature*. Cambridge: Harvard University, 1951. (28)

Heine, Heinrich. "Anno 1829." Translated by Louis Untermeyer. *Heinrich Heine, Paradox and Poet*. New York: Harcourt, Brace, 1937. (33)

Henley, William E. "Invictus." In Sith Thompson and John Gassner (eds.). *Our Heritage of World Literature*. New York: Holt, 1942. Revised Edition, pp. 1341–1342. (29)

Heraclitus. "The Word," *Fragments*. Translated by John Burnet. 1892. (12)

Herbert, Alan P. "Speech in House of Commons for a Festival of Britain." November 23, 1949. (5)

Herbert, George. "The Church Porch," *The Temple*. 1633. (36)

Herodotus. *An Account of Egypt*. Translated by G. C. Macaulay. New York: Collier, 1910. (8)

Herodotus. *Clio*. Translated by William Beloe. 1840. Bk. I, Chap. 133. (3)

[418]

Herrigel, Eugen. *Zen in the Art of Archery.* Translated by R. F. C. Hull. New York: Pantheon, 1953. Pp. 76–88. (52)

Hesiod. *Works and Days.* Translated by Violet Zielke in Paul MacKendrick and Herbert M. Howe (eds.). *Classics in Translation.* Madison: University of Wisconsin, 1952. Vol. I. (26)

Hesse, Hermann. *Steppenwolf.* Translated by Basil Creighton. New York: Holt, Rinehart and Winston, 1929. Reprinted 1963 paperback, pp. 8–9. (22)

Hideyoshi, Toyotomi. Translated by James Murdoch. *History of Japan.* London: 1925. Vol. II, p. 243. (49)

Hillyer, Robert. "XXth Century," *Collected Verse.* New York: Knopf, 1934. Pp. 232–233. (32)

Hitler, Adolf. *My Struggle.* Translated by Ralph Manheim. Boston: Houghton Mifflin, 1943. Pp. 581–582. (61)

Hitopadesa. Translated by Charles Wilkins. 1787. (40)

Hobbes, Thomas. *Leviathan.* 1651. Chap. 10. (62)

Hofmannsthal, Hugo von. "The Letter of Lord Chandos." Translated by Mary Hottinger and T. and J. Stern. *Hugo von Hofmannsthal, Selected Prose.* New York: Pantheon, 1952. P. 134. (3)

Hogben, Lancelot. *Mathematics for the Millions.* New York: Norton, 1937. P. 17. (26)

Holbach, Paul d'. *Good Sense.* Translated in John H. Randall, Jr. *The Making of the Modern Mind.* Boston: Houghton Mifflin, 1940. Revised Edition, p. 303. (29)

Holland, Josiah G. "Anvils and Hammer," *Gold-Foil Hammered from Popular Proverbs.* 1859. (37)

Hollis, Christopher. In *The Listener,* August 9, 1956. (34)

Holmes, Oliver W. "Letter to His Mother, June 11, 1854." (36)

Holmes, Oliver W., Jr. "Speech in New York." February 15, 1913. (7)

Homer. *Odyssy.* Translated in Mark Van Doren. *On Great Poems of Western Literature.* New York: Collier, 1962. P. 70. (38)

Horace. *Odes.* Bk. IV. (56)

Horne, Richard H. *Orion.* Bk. III, Canto ii. (11)

Housman, A. E. *A Shropshire Lad.* Philadelphia: Altemus, 1902. Epilogue. (19)

Housman, Laurence. *Ironical Tales.* New York: Doran, 1927. (53)

Howard, Sidney. *The Silver Cord.* New York: Scribner's, 1926. (37)

Howell, James. *Proverbs.* 1659. (2)

Hsün-tzu. "Merit of the Confucian," *The Works of Hsuntse.* Translated by Homer H. Dubs. London: Probsthain, 1928. Bk. VIII. (56)

Hubbard, Elbert. "A Message to Garcia." (55)

Hudson, W. H. "El Ombu," *Tales of the Pampas.* New York: Knopf, 1916. (33)

[419]

Hughes, Rupert. *George Washington*. New York: Morrow, 1930. P. 657. (7)

Hugo, Victor. *Ninety-three*. Part II, Bk. III, Chap. 1. (49)

Hunt, Leigh. "The Glove and the Lions." (6)

Hunt, Leigh. "Abou Ben Adhem." In *Great Poems of the English Language*. Compiled by Wallace A. Briggs and William R. Benét. New York: Tudor, 1948. P. 496. (20)

Huxley, Thomas. "Evolution and Ethics," *Romanes Lecture*. 1893. (9)

Huxley, Thomas. *Educational Value of the Natural History Sciences*. 1854. (52)

Iacopone da Todi. Quoted by Francesco de Sanctis. *History of Italian Literature*. Translated by Joan Redfern. New York: Harcourt, Brace, 1931. Basic Books Edition, Vol. I. p. 44. (60)

Ibn-al-Husayn al-Mutanabbi, Ahmad. Translated by H. A. R. Gibb. *Arabic Literature*. Oxford: Clarendon, 1963. (42)

Ibn al Tiqtaqa. *Al Fakhri*. Translated by Erwin I. J. Rosenthal. *Political Thought in Medieval Islam*. Cambridge: University, 1958. (34)

Ibn Khaldun. "Prolegnoma." Translated by R. A. Nicholson. *Translations of Eastern Poetry and Prose*. Cambridge: Cambridge University, 1922. (59)

Ibn Shakil. "Ugliness." Translated by A. J. Arberry. *Moorish Poetry*, Cambridge: Cambridge University, 1953. P. 28. (41)

Ibsen, Henrik. *An Enemy of the People*. Act II. Translated by Philo M. Buck, Jr. *An Anthology of World Literature*. New York: Macmillan, 1951. Third Edition, pp. 1004–1005. (21)

Ibsen, Henrik. *When We Dead Awaken*. Translated by William Archer. 1900. Act I. (58)

Igjugarjuk. Quoted by Knud Rasmussen. *Across Arctic America*. New York: Putnam's, 1927. (18)

Im Bang. "The Resourceful Wife." Translated by James Gale. *Korean Folk Tales*. Rutland: Tuttle, 1962. Pp. 90–91. (10)

Innocent III, Pope. "Letter to the Archbishop in Gascony, 1198." Translated by O. J. Thatcher and E. H. McNeal. *Source Book for Medieval History*. New York: Scribner's, 1905. Pp. 209–210. (18)

Ionesco, Eugène. *The Killer*. Translated by Donald Watson. *Eugene Ionesco, Plays*. London: Calder, 1959. (18)

Iriate, Tomas de. Translated by John A. Cook. *Neo-Classic Drama in Spain*. Dallas: Southern Methodist University, 1959. Pp. 247–248. (27)

Irving, Washington. *The Sketch Book*. 1820. (53)

Isocrates. "Oration VII," *The Areopagiticus*. Translated by H. Lamar Crosby in Paul MacKendrick and Herbert M. Howe (eds.). *Classics in Translation*. Madison: University of Wisconsin, 1952. Vol. I, pp. 278–279. (1)

Issa, Kobayashi. "Contentment in Poverty." Translated by Harold G. Henderson. *An Introduction to Haiku*. Garden City: Doubleday, 1958. Anchor Edition, p. 141. (28)

Jalal al-Din Rumi. *The Masnavi.* Translated by A. J. Arberry. *Tales from the Masnavi.* London: Allen and Unwin, 1961. P. 65. (34)

James, Henry. *Notebooks.* Edited by F. O. Matthiesen and Kenneth B. Murdock. New York: Oxford University, 1947. Pp. 44–45. (64)

Jar.ney, J. Elliott. In *Harvard Business Review,* May–June 1952. (45)

Jaspers, Karl. *The Great Philosophers.* Edited by Hannah Arendt and translated by Ralph Manheim. New York: Harcourt, Brace and World, 1962. Pp. 48–49. (11)

Jeffers, Robinson. "The Bloody Sire," *Selected Poems.* New York: Vintage, 1965. (42)

Jerrold, Douglas. *The Romance of a Keyhole.* (22)

Jesus. Quoted in Mark 15: 34. King James Version of the Bible. (15)

Jewett, Sarah O. *Letters of Sarah Orne Jewett.* Edited by Annie Fields. Boston: Houghton Mifflin, 1911. (40)

Jinsai Ito. Translated by R. C. Armstrong. *Light from the East: Studies in Japanese Confucianism.* Toronto: University of Toronto, 1914. (52)

John of Salisbury. *Policraticus.* Translated by John Dickinson. *The Statesman's Book of John of Salisbury.* New York: Crofts, 1927. (31)

Johnson, Samuel. *Rasselas, Prince of Abyssinia.* 1759. (58)

Joubert, Joseph. *Thoughts.* Translated by Katherine Lyttleton. 1898. (31)

Joyce, James. *A Portrait of the Artist as a Young Man.* New York: New American Library, 1954. (33)

Juan Chi. Translated by Jerome Ch'en and Michael Bullock. *Poems of Solitude.* New York: Abelard-Schuman, 1960. P. 14. (53)

Jung, Carl G. *Transformations and Symbolisms of the Libido.* Translated by Jolande Jacobi. *Psychological Reflections.* New York: Pantheon, 1953. (11)

Juppensha Ikku. Translated by R. H. Blyth. *Japanese Humour.* Tokyo: Japan Travel Bureau, 1957. Pp. 151–152. (3)

Kafka, Franz. *The Great Wall of China.* Translated by Willa and Edwin Muir. London: Secker, 1933. (35)

Kamo no-Chomei. "Hojoki." Translated by A. L. Sadler. *The Ten Foot Square Hut and Tales of the Heike.* Sydney: Angus and Robertson, 1928. (42)

Kant, Immanuel. *Critique of Practical Reason.* 1788. Conclusion. (61)

Kazantzakis, Nikos. *The Saviors of God.* Translated by Kimon Friar. New York: Simon and Schuster, 1960. (34)

Keats, John. "Ode to a Nightingale." In *Great Poems of the English Language*. Compiled by Wallace A. Briggs and William R. Benét. New York: Tudor, 1948. Pp. 617–618. (12)

Kellogg, Sarah W. "A Second Trial." Reprinted in S. H. Clark (ed.). *Handbook of Best Readings*. New York: Scribner's, 1902. (54)

Khlebnikov, Velemir. "The Refusal." Translated in Vyacheslav Zavalishin. *Early Soviet Writers*. New York: Praeger, 1958. (1)

Kidd, Benjamin. *Social Evolution*. 1874. (19)

Kierkegaard, Sören. *Fear and Trembling*. Translated by Walter Lowrie. Princeton: Princeton University, 1941. Pp. 115–120. (1)

Kikaku Enomoto. Translated by Atsuharu Sakai. *Japan in a Nutshell*. Yokahama: Yamagata, 1952. Vol. II. (23)

Kingsley, Charles. *The Saints Tragedy*. 1848. Act IV, Sc. 3. (12)

Kipling, Rudyard. *The Jungle Book*. 1894. Grosset and Dunlap Edition, p. 45. (33)

Kirkland, Joseph. *Zury: The Meanest Man in Spring County*. 1887. (27)

Klee, Paul. Translated by Herbert Read. *A Concise History of Modern Painting*. New York: Praeger, 1959. P. 187. (3)

Knudsen, Erik. "To an Unknown God." Translated by P. M. Mitchell. *A History of Danish Literature*. New York: American-Scandinavian Foundation, 1958. (61)

Koestler, Arthur. *Darkness at Noon*. Translated by Daphne Hardy. New York: Macmillan, 1941. (24)

Kornfeld, Paul. Translated by H. F. Garten. *Modern German Drama*. Fair Lawn: Essential, 1959. P. 173. (62)

Kropotkin, Pëtr A. *Memoirs of a Revolutionist*. Boston: Houghton Mifflin, 1930. Pp. 215–217. (34)

Krylov, Ivan A. "The Ass and the Nightingale." Translated in "Russian Fabulists, with Specimens," *Fraser's Magazine*, 1842. (33)

Kutsugen. Translated by Herbert A. Giles. *Gems of Chinese Literature*. 1884. (29)

La Bruyère, Jean de. *Characters*. Translated by Henri van Laun. 1885. (31)

La Monnoie, Bernard de. "Epigram." Translated in Alan Conder. *Cassell's Anthology of French Poetry*. London: Cassell, 1950. (41)

Lao-tzu. Translated by Lionel Giles. *The Sayings of Lao Tzu*. London: Murray, 1906. (25, 39, 54, 59)

La Rochefoucauld, François de. *Maxims*. Translated by Louis Kronenberger. New York: Random House, 1959. No. 159. (28)

Latimer, Hugh. Quoted by Harold S. Darby. *Hugh Latimer*. London: Epworth, 1953. (59)

Lawrence, D. H. "The Fox," *The Portable D. H. Lawrence.* New York: Viking, 1947. Pp. 241–242. (34)

Lawrence, T. E. *Seven Pillars of Wisdom.* Garden City: Doubleday, 1938. Pp. 175–176. (13)

Lea, Charles. *A History of the Inquisition of Spain.* New York: Macmillan, 1906. American Scholar Edition, Vol. III, pp. 437–442. (21)

Le Bailly, Antoine F. *New Stories.* II, 4. Translated by Thomas B. Harbottle and Philip H. Dalbiac. *Dictionary of Quotations (French and Italian).* New York: Macmillan, 1901. (44)

Le Bon, Gustave. *Psychology of Peoples.* 1898. (16)

Lecky, William. *History of England in the Eighteenth Century.* 1878–1890. (39)

Lee, Gerald S. *Crowds.* Garden City: Doubleday, 1913. Bk. IV, Chap. 10. (44)

Legge, James. *Translation of the Yi Ching. (The Sacred Books of the East,* edited by F. Max Müller.) 1899. (Introduction)

Leibniz, Gottfried von. *New Essays Concerning Human Understanding.* Translated by Alfred G. Langley. 1896. (29)

Lenin. *Works.* Moscow: Foreign Languages, 1960. Vol. XXIV. (6)

Leopardi, Giacomo. "To Himself." Translated by Francis H. Cliffe. 1896. (16)

Lessing, Gotthold E. *Minna von Barnhelm.* Translated by Ernest Bell. New York: Collier, 1910. Acts I, V. (2, 25)

Lewis, Sinclair. *Babbitt.* New York: Modern Library, 1924. (54)

Li Ju-chen. "Romance of the Mirrored Flowers." Translated by Chi-chen Wong and Ethel Andrews in George Kao (ed.). *Chinese Wit and Humor.* New York: Coward-McCann, 1946. P. 185. (58)

Li Po. Translated by Soame Jenyns. *Selections from Three Hundred Poems of the T'ang Dynasty.* London: Murray, 1940. Pp. 47–48. (37)

Liddell Hart, Basil H. *Strategy.* New York: Praeger, 1954. Pp. 370–371. (13)

Lima, Jorge de. "The Bird." Translated by Dudley Poore. *Anthology of Latin-American Poetry.* New York: New Directions, 1947. (44)

Liu Yü-shih. "Peonies." Translated by Henry H. Hart. *Poems of the Hundred Names.* Palo Alto: Stanford University, 1954. (54)

Livius, Titus. Translated by Francis King. *Classical and Foreign Quotations.* New York: Ungar, 1958. (35)

Livius, Titus. "The War with Lars Porsinna," *The History of Rome.* Translated by B. O. Foster. Cambridge: Loeb Classical Library, 1908. [26]

Lloyd George, David. "Memorandum to World War I Peace Conference, March 25, 1919." (18)

Locke, John. "Of Civil Government," *The Two Treatises of Government.* 1685. Chap. 8. (45)

Lomonosov, Mikhail V. "Letter to I. I. Shuvalow, May 10, 1753." Translated by Leo Wiener (ed.). *Anthology of Russian Literature.* New York: Putnam's, 1902. (32)

London, Jack. "What Life Means to Me." Quoted in Leonard D. Abbott (ed.). *London Essays of Revolt.* New York: Vanguard, 1926. (36)

London Speaker. "The Emir Game of Chess." Reprinted in S. H. Clark (ed.). *Handbook of Best Readings.* New York: Scribner's, 1902. (41)

López y Fuentes, Gregorio. "A Letter to God." Translated by Donald A. Yates in Angel Flores (ed.). *Great Spanish Short Stories.* New York: Dell, 1962. Pp. 246–247. (46)

Lubbock, John. *The Pleasures of Life.* 1887. P. 2. (47)

Lucan. *The Civil War.* Translated by J. D. Duff. Cambridge: Loeb Classical Library. Bk. IV, line 702. (39)

Lucian. "On Salaried Posts in Great Houses." Translated by A. M. Harmon. *Lucian.* London: Heinemann, 1913. (42)

Luther, Martin. "A Treatise on Good Works," *Works.* Edited by Henry E. Jacobs *et al.* Philadelphia: Holman, 1915. Vol. I. (6)

Lyall, Alfred C. *Asiatic Studies, Religious and Social.* 1899. (3)

Mably, Gabriel de. *The Rights and Duties of the Citizen.* Translated by John H. Randall, Jr. *The Career of Philosophy.* New York: Columbia University, 1962. Pp. 981–982. (18)

Macauley, Thomas B. *The Romance of History.* In *Complete Works.* 1898. (31)

McClellan, Tom. Quoted in William Haywood. *Bill Haywood's Book.* New York: International, 1929. (60)

McCulloch, J. R. (ed.). *The Works of Ricardo.* 1852. Vol. I. (50)

Machiavelli, Nicolò. *The Prince.* Translated by Thomas G. Bergin. New York: Appleton-Century-Crofts, 1947. Pp. 48–49. (16)

Machiavelli, Nicolò. *The Prince and the Discourses.* Translated by Luigi Ricci and E. R. P. Vincent. New York: Modern Library, 1940. P. 87. (31)

McKelway, St. Clair. "Benzoin for the Turbinates," *The New Yorker,* March 22, 1941. (31)

Madariaga, Salvador de. *Hermán Cortés.* London: Hodder and Stoughton, 1942. Pp. 313–314. (11)

Madden, Samuel. Quoted in James Boswell. *Life of Dr. Johnson.* 1791. Everyman Edition, Vol. I, p. 457. (55)

Maeterlinck, Maurice. *The Life of the Bee.* Translated by Alfred Sutro. New York: Dodd, Mead, 1913. Mentor Edition, pp. 43–44. (29)

Mahabharata. Translated in E. Louise Mally (ed.). *A Treasury of Animal Stories.* New York: Citadel, 1946. Pp. 216–217. (9)

Maimonides, Moses. "Epistle to Jacob of Yemen." Translated by Boaz Cohen. New York: American Academy for Jewish Research, 1952. (36)

Malraux, André. *Man's Fate*. Translated by Haakon M. Chevalier. New York: Random House, 1934. (59)

Mansfield, Katherine. "The Fly," *The Doves' Nest and Other Stories*. New York: 1923. (8)

Manuel, Don Juan. *Count Lucanor*. Translated by James York. 1868. (63)

Manzoni, Alessandro. *The Bethrothed*. New York: Collier, 1909. Chap. 4. (9)

Mao Tse-tung. *Selected Works*. New York: International, 1954–1962. (43)

Maritain, Jacques. *Existence and the Existent*. Translated by Lewis Galantière and Gerald B. Phelan. New York: Pantheon, 1948. (54)

Marlowe, Christopher. *Edward the Second*. 1593. Act V, Sc. 1. (64)

Marquand, John P. "You Can't Do That," *Saturday Evening Post*, 1935. (4)

Martialis, Marcus. "A Total Abstainer." Translated by Paul Nixon. (10)

Marvell, Andrew. "The Garden." In W. H. Auden and Norman H. Pearson (eds.). *Poems of the English Language*. New York: Viking, 1950. Vol. II, p. 540. (22)

Masefield, John. *Sea Life in Nelson's Time*. New York: Macmillan, 1937. Pp. 157–159. (7)

Massinger, Philip. *The Unnatural Combat*. 1639. Act V, Sc. 2. (3)

Masters, Edgar L. "Silence," *Songs and Satires*. New York: Macmillan, 1916. (10)

Maugham, W. Somerset. *The Mixture as Before*. New York: Doubleday, Doran, 1940. (17)

Maugham, W. Somerset. *The Summing Up*. Garden City: Doubleday, 1938. Mentor Edition, p. 191. (25)

Maupassant, Guy de. *Pierre and Jean*. Translated by Miriam Allcott. *Novelists on the Novel*. New York: Columbia University, 1959. (64)

Mazzini, Giuseppe. "Young Italy," *Life and Writings*. 1890. (21)

Medici, Lorenzo de. "Letter to His Son, April 1492." Translated in Evan Jones (ed.). *The Father*. New York: Rinehart, 1960. (35)

Melville, Herman. *Moby Dick*. 1851. Chap. 10. (13)

Melville, Herman. *White-Jacket*. 1850. Chap. 62. (15)

Menander. *Fragments*. (32)

Mencius. Translated by James Legge. *The Chinese Classics*. 1893. Vol. II. (15, 25)

Mencken, H. L. "Letter to Will Durant." Quoted in William Durant. *On the Meaning of Life*. New York: Long and Smith, 1932. (2)

Meredith, Owen. "Lucile." (45)

Metastasio, Pietro. *Didone*. Quoted by Francesco de Sanctis. *History of Italian Literature*. Translated by Joan Redfern. New York: Harcourt, Brace, 1931. Vol. II. (29)

Michelangelo Buonarroti. "Letter to Giuliano da San Gallo, May 2, 1506." (62)

Michener, James A. *Return to Paradise*. New York: Random House, 1951. Pp. 22–23. (60)

Middleton, Thomas. *The Mayor of Queensborough*. 1661. (18)

Miller, Henry. *The Colossus of Maroussi*. London: Secker and Warburg, 1942. Pp. 229–231. (48)

Milne, A. A. *The Truth About Blayds*. In *Three Plays*. New York: Putnam's, 1922. (35)

Mo Ti. Translated by Mei Yi-pao. *The Ethical and Political Works of Motse*. London: Probsthain, 1929. (17)

Mocius. Translated by Lin Mousheng. *Men and Ideas*. New York: Day, 1942. (57)

Molière. *Tartuffe*. Translated by Henri van Laun. 1880. Act I. (15)

Mommsen, Theodor. *The Portrait of Julius Caesar*. Translated by Leo Hamalian and Edmond L. Volpe (eds.). *Great Essays by Nobel Prize Winners*. New York: Noonday, 1960. (45)

Montaigne, Michel de. "On the Art of Conversing," *Essays*. 1585. Bk. III. (22)

Montaigne, Michel de. "On the Education of Children," *Essays*. Translated by Charles Cotton. (27)

Montalbo, Juan. "Pinchincha," *Seven Treatises*. 1882. Translated in *Bulletin of Pan American Union*, March 1934. (20)

Montale, Eugenio. "Poem." Translated by Edwin Morgan. (1)

Montesquieu, Charles de Secondat de. *Spirit of the Laws*. Translated by Thomas Nugent, revised by J. V. Prichard. 1896. (12, 56)

Montluc, Adrien de. *Comedy of Proverbs*. Act I, Sc. 3. (22)

Moore, Thomas. "Come, Send Round the Wine." Stanza 2. (59)

Moratín, Leandro Fernández de. *The Female Hypocrite*. Act I, Sc. 1. Translated by John A. Cook. *Neo-Classic Drama in Spain*. Dallas: Southern Methodist University, 1959. P. 353. (4)

Morgenthau, Hans J. *In Defense of the National Interest*. New York: Knopf, 1951. Pp. 5–6. (26)

Morley, John. *On Compromise*. 1874. (43)

Morley, John. *Recollections*. New York: Macmillan, 1917. Vol. II, Bk. V, Chap. 4. (62)

Muir, Edwin. "The Good Man in Hell," *Collected Poems*. London: Faber and Faber, 1960. P. 104. (30)

Muju. "A Cup of Tea," *Collection of Stone and Sand*. Translated by Nyogen Senzaki and Paul Reps. *101 Zen Stories*. Philadelphia: McKay, 1939. (19)

Murasaki Shikibu. *The Tale of Genji.* Translated by Arthur Waley. London: Allen and Unwin, 1927. (32)

Musset, Alfred de. *Confession of a Child of the Century.* Translated by K. Warren (ed.). *The Complete Writings of Alfred de Musset.* New York: Hill, 1905. Vol. VIII. (9)

Nansen, Odd. "Grini Prisoner No. 480," *American-Scandinavian Review,* March 1946. (8)

Napoleon Bonaparte. "Letter to Prince Eugene, June 5, 1805." Translated by J. M. Thompson (ed.). *Letters of Napoleon.* Oxford: Blackwell, 1934. (31)

Nebuchadrezzar. "Prayer to Marduk." Translated in *Cambridge Ancient History.* Cambridge: Cambridge University, 1929. Vol. III, pp. 216–217. (59)

Nehru, Motilal. "Letter to Pandit Prithinath, Dec. 22, 1899." Quoted by B. R. Nanda. *The Nehrus.* New York: Day, 1963. (40)

Nekrasov, Nikolai A. "The Green Rustle." Translated by Juliet M. Soskice. *Poems by Nicholas Nekrasov.* London: Oxford University, 1936. (25)

Nervo, Amado. "Cowardice." Translated by G. Dundas Craig. *The Modernist Trend in Spanish American Poetry.* Berkeley: University of California, 1934. (60)

Newman, John H. *The Idea of a University.* 1852. (50)

Nibelungs, Story of the. Translated by Margaret Armour. *The Fall of the Nibelungs.* 1897. (26)

Nichols, Robert, and Maurice Browne. *Wings over Europe.* New York: Theater Guild, 1929. (6)

Nicolson, Harold. *Good Behaviour.* New York: Doubleday, 1956. P. 33. (18)

Nietzsche, Friedrich W. "The Religious Mood," *Beyond Good and Evil.* Translated by Helen Zimmern. New York: Macmillan, 1907. Sec. 51. (34)

Nigerian Folk Tale. "The Talking Skull." Translated by Peggy Rutherfoord (ed.). *African Voices.* New York: Vanguard, 1960. P. 124. (3)

Nobumitsu, Kwanze K. *Benkei in a Boat.* Translated in *The Noh Drama.* Rutland: Tuttle, 1960. P. 174. (1)

Ogarev, N. P. "Letter to Annenkov." Translated by Francis Haskal in Franco Venturi. *Roots of Revolution.* New York: Knopf, 1960. (14)

Okakura, Kakuzo. *The Book of Tea.* New York: Dodd, Mead, 1906. Pp. 87–88. (20)

Olivecrona, Karl. *Law as Fact.* London: Oxford University, 1939. (60)

Ortega y Gasset, José. *The Revolt of the Masses.* New York: Norton, 1932. Mentor Edition, p. 12. (23)

"O-Shichi, Ballad of." Translated by Joseph L. French. *Lotus and Chrysanthemum.* New York: Liveright, 1927. (37)

Otomo no-Tabito. Translated by Younghill Kang and John W. Morrison in Charlton Laird (ed.). *The World through*

Literature. New York: Appleton-Century-Crofts, 1951.
P. 83. (13)
Ovid, *Metamorphoses*. (63)

Paganini, Nicolò. "Letter to Germi, June 1831." Translated
by G. I. C. de Courcy. *Paganini*. Norman: University of
Oklahoma, 1957. Vol. II. (53)

Paine, Thomas. *Rights of Man*. Part II, Chap. 3. (11)

Palma, Ricardo. "The Mayor's Ears." Translated by Ralph
Flores in Angel Flores (ed.). *Great Spanish Short Stories*.
New York: Dell, 1962. P. 108. (5)

Pan Ku. *History of the Former Han Dynasty*. Translated by
William Theodore de Bary, Wing-tsit Chan, and Burton
Watson. *Sources of Chinese Tradition*. New York: Columbia
University, 1960. Pp. 168–169. (45)

Panchatantra. "The Duel between Elephant and Sparrow."
Translated by Arthur W. Ryder. Chicago: University of
Chicago, 1925. Pp. 153–156. (45)

Panchatantra. "The Lion-makers." Translated by Charles
R. Lanman. New York: International Society, 1897. (57)

Paracelsus. "The Sixth Defense, to Excuse His Strange
Manner and Wrathful Ways." Translated by C. Lilian
Temkin in Henry E. Sigerist (ed.). *Four Treatises of Theo-
phrastus von Hohenheim*. Baltimore: Johns Hopkins, 1941.
Pp. 33–34. (46)

Paré, Ambroise. *Journeys in Diverse Places*. Translated by
Stephen Paget. *Ambroise Paré and His Times*. 1897. (4)

Parker, Theodore. "Of Truth," *Ten Sermons of Religion*.
1853. (56)

Pascal, Blaise. *Thoughts*. Translated by W. F. Trotter. New
York: Collier, 1910. Chap. 14, No. 11. (51)

Pavlov, Ivan. "Statement to Russian Students, February
27, 1936." Quoted by Charles P. Curtis, Jr. and Ferris
Greenslet. *The Practical Cogitator*. Boston: Houghton Mifflin, 1945. P. 93. (57)

Peacock, Thomas L. *Nightmare Alley*. (60)

Peary, Robert E. "Letter to His Mother, August 16, 1880."
Quoted by William H. Hobbs. *Peary*. New York: Macmillan, 1936. (62)

Peattie, Donald C. *An Almanac for Moderns*. New York:
Putnam's, 1935. P. 3. (64)

Pepys, Samuel. "Entry, March 10, 1666." *Diary*. (58)

Pericles. "Address in Memory of Athenian Soldiers Who
Died in the Peloponnesian War." (10)

Petrarca, Francesco. "Letter to Zanobi da Strada, April 1,
1352." *Letters from Petrarch*. Translated by Morris Bishop.
Bloomington: University of Indiana, 1965. (27)

Phaedrus. *Fables*. Translated by Henry T. Riley. 1880.
(28, 43)

Phelps, Edward J. "Address before New York Chamber of
Commerce." November 19, 1889. (59)

Phillips, Stephen. "A Man." (27)

Pindar. *Olympia Odes.* (19)

Pirandello, Luigi. "War," *Medals and Other Stories.* New York: Dutton, 1939. (61)

Pitt, William. *Correspondence.* 1838–1840. Vol. I, p. 79. (16)

Pitt, William. "Speech in House of Commons on the India Bill." November 1783. (52)

Plato. *Phaedo.* Translated by Benjamin Jowett. 1899. (52)

Plautus, Titus. *The Comedy of Asses.* Act IV, Sc. 1. Translated by Edward H. Sugden in George E. Duckworth (ed.). *The Complete Roman Drama.* New York: Random House, 1942. (23)

Pliny the Elder. *History.* Bk. VIII, Chap. 22. (57)

Plunkitt, George W. "Honest Graft and Dishonest Graft." Quoted by William L. Riordan. *Plunkitt of Tammany Hall.* New York: McClure, Phillips, 1905. (21)

Plutarch. *The Lives of the Noble Grecians and Romans.* Translated by John Dryden, revised by A. H. Clough. New York: Modern Library, n.d. P. 219. (32)

Po Chü-I. "The Dragon of the Black Pool." Translated by Arthur Waley. *Translations from the Chinese.* New York: Knopf, 1941. Pp. 166–167. (44)

Pocaterra, José R. "The Task," *The Living Age,* 1923. (11)

Poincaré, Henri. Translated in E. T. Bell. *Men of Mathematics.* New York: Simon and Schuster, 1937. Dover Edition, p. 550. (5)

Polybius. "The Roman Constitution," *Histories.* (20)

Pope, Alexander. "An Essay on Man." (54)

Pound, Roscoe. "Letter to Omer F. Hershey, April 4, 1895." (64)

Proudhon, Pierre J. *What Is Property?* Translated by Benjamin R. Tucker. 1876. (10)

Proust, Marcel. *The Sweet Cheat Gone.* Translated by C. K. Scott-Moncrieff. New York: Random House, 1934. P. 48. (11)

Ptahhotep. "The Precepts of Ptahhotep." Papyrus at Bibliothèque Nationale (Paris). Translated in B. G. Gunn. *Instruction of Ptah Hotep.* London: Murray, 1908. (5)

Publilius Syrus. *Maxims.* No. 469. (57)

Punshon, W. M. "Our Prayers." (14)

Rabelais, François. *Gargantua.* Translated by Thomas Urquhart and Peter Motteux. Chicago: Encyclopedia Britannica, 1952. Chap. 54. (64)

Racine, Jean. *Phedre.* Act II. Translated by Robert Henderson. *Six Plays by Corneille and Racine.* New York: Random House, 1931. (50)

Ramakrishna. *Teachings of Sri Ramakrishna.* Almora: Advaita Ashrama, 1934. P. 154. (4)

Ramayana. Translated by R. T. Griffith. 1870. (37)

Randolph, John. "Of Edward Livingston." (36)

[429]

Ranke, Leopold von. *The Ottoman and the Spanish Empires in the Sixteenth and Seventeenth Centuries.* Translated by Walter K. Kelly. 1843. (36)

Ransom, John C. "Poetry as Primitive Language." Quoted by Roy W. Cowden (ed.). *The Writer and His Craft.* Ann Arbor: University of Michigan, 1954. (49)

Rasmussen, Knud. "Report of the Fifth Thule Expedition." Quoted by C. S. Coon (ed.). *A Reader in General Anthropology.* New York: Holt, 1948. P. 140. (63)

Remarque, Erich M. *The Road Back.* Translated by A. W. Wheen. Boston: Little, Brown, 1931. (4)

Renan, Ernest. *The Poetry of the Celtic Races.* Translated by W. G. Hutchison. New York: Collier, 1910. (51)

Richardson, Samuel. "Letter 86," *Clarissa Harlowe.* 1747–1748. (47)

Richter, Jean P. *Hesperus.* 1795. (26)

Rimbaud, Arthur. "The Poor in Church." Translated by Gerard P. Meyer in Hubert Creekmore (ed.). *A Little Treasury of World Poetry.* New York: Scribner's, 1952. Pp. 641–642. (11)

Robbe-Grillet, Alain. Translated by John Weightman. "Alain Robbe-Grillet." In John Cruickshank (ed.). *The Novelist as Philosopher.* London: Oxford University, 1962. Pp. 244–245. (57)

Roberts, P. E. *The Cambridge Modern History.* New York: Macmillan, 1934. Vol. VI. (51)

Robespierre, Maximilien. "Report to the French Convention." February 5, 1794. Translated in Houston Peterson (ed.). *A Treasury of the World's Great Speeches.* New York: Simon and Schuster, 1954. (21)

Robinson, Edwin A. "Flammonde," *Collected Poems.* New York: Macmillan, 1937. (50)

Roche, Boyle. Quoted by Jonah Barrington. *Personal Sketches.* 1827–1832. (16)

Rodin, Auguste. Translated by Louis W. Flaccus. *Artists and Thinkers.* New York: Longmans, Green, 1916. (41)

Rodzianko, Mikhail. *Memoirs.* Quoted in Frank A. Golder (ed.). *Documents of Russian History 1914–1917.* Translated by Emanuel Aronsberg. New York: Appleton-Century, 1927. (21)

Rolland, Romain. *I Will Not Rest.* Translated by K. S. Shelvankar. New York: Liveright, 1937. (17)

Romains, Jules. *Verdun.* Translated by Gerard Hopkins. New York: Knopf, 1939. Pp. 454–457. (13)

Roosevelt, Franklin. "First Inaugural Address." March 4, 1933. (39)

Roosevelt, Theodore. "The World War: Its Tragedies and Its Lessons," *The Outlook,* September 23, 1914. (19)

Rostand, Edmond. *The Eaglet.* Translated by Louis N. Parker. 1900. Act IV. (2)

Rotrou, Jean. *Chosroes.* Translated by Lacy Lockert. *Studies in French-Classical Tragedy*. Nashville: Vanderbilt University, 1958. P. 214. (24)

Rousseau, Jean J. *Confessions*. 1770. (23)

Ruskin, John. *Pre-Raphaelitism*. 1851. (27)

Ruskin, John. *Unto This Last*. 1860–1862. Sec. 16. (8)

Saadi. *Gulistan*. Translated by James Ross. 1823. (63)

Sabatini, Rafael. *Scaromouche*. New York: Houghton Mifflin, 1921. Chap. 1. (56)

Said, Seyyid. In *Princes of Zing*, reprinted in Rex Niven. *Nine Great Africans*. New York: Roy, 1964. Pp. 65–66. (20)

Sainte-Beuve, Charles A. *Montaigne*. Translated by E. Lee. New York: Collier, 1910. (14)

Saint-Pierre, Abbé de. *Project for Perpetual Peace*. Translated by Ralph B. Perry. *One World in the Making*. New York: Current, 1945. (37)

Sallustius Crispus. *Jugurthine War*. Translated by John S. Watson. 1852. (26)

Samaniego, Felix de. "The Wolf and the Dog." Anon. translation. (41)

Santayana, George. *Life of Reason*. New York: Scribner's, 1905. (48)

Saroyan, William. *My Heart's in the Highlands*. Los Angeles: French, 1941. (8)

Sarraute, Nathalie. *Portrait of a Man Unknown*. Translated by Maris Jolas. New York: Braziller, 1958. Pp. 42–43. (53)

Sartre, Jean P. Quoted by A. J. Liebling (ed.). *The Republic of Silence*. New York: Harcourt, Brace, 1947. (38)

Saurin, Bernard J. *Spartacus*. 1760. (44)

Saville, George. *The Character of a Trimmer*. 1688. (30)

Scarroyady. "Statement at Treaty Meeting between Ohio Indians and Province of Pennsylvania." Carlisle: 1753. (3)

Schelling, Thomas C. *The Strategy of Conflict*. Cambridge: Harvard University, 1960. (13)

Schiller, Johann F. Von. *The Maid of Orleans*. 1802. Act III, Sc. 6. (50)

Schlegel, Friedrich von. *Lucinda*. Translated by Paul B. Thomas in Kuno Francke (ed.). *The German Classics*. New York: German Publication Society, 1913. Vol. IV, p. 147. (18)

Schlesinger, Arthur M. *Political and Social History of the United States, 1829–1925*. New York: Macmillan, 1932. (16)

Schnitzler, Arthur. "The Triple Warning." Translated by Barrett H. Clark and Maxim Lieber (eds.). *Great Short Stories of the World*. New York: McBride, 1925. (43)

Schönberg, Arnold. "Letter to Gustav Mahler, 1910," *Arnold Schoenberg's Letters*. Edited by Erwin Stein, translated by Eithne Wilkins and Ernst Kaiser. New York: St. Martins, 1965. (43)

Schröter, Heinz. *Stalingrad*. Translated by Constantine Fitzgibbon. New York: Dutton, 1958. Pp. 200–201. (51)

[431]

Schumpeter, Joseph. *Imperialism and Social Classes.* Translated by Heinz Norden. New York: Kelley, 1951. Chap. V. (13)

Schurz, Carl. "Convocation Address at University of Chicago." January 4, 1899. (60)

Scott, William. Quoted by James Boswell. *Life of Dr. Johnson.* 1835. London Edition, Vol. VIII, p. 67. (49)

Ségur, Philippe-Paul de. "After the Battle of Borodino," *History of Napoleon's Invasion of Russia.* Translated by J. D. Townsend. Boston: Houghton Mifflin, 1958. P. 83. (7)

Selden, John. "Evil Speaking," *Table Talk.* 1689. (26)

Sénancour, Étienne de. "Letter XC," *Obermann.* 1804. (46)

Seneca, Lucius. *Letters to Lucillus.* (62)

Settle, Elkanah. *The Female Prelate.* 1680. (13)

Shakespeare, William. *Julius Caesar.* Act V, Sc. 5. (48)

Shakespeare, William. *King Lear.* 1605. Act I, Sc. 4. (8)

Shaw, George B. *Captain Brassbound's Conversion.* London: Constable, 1906. Act III. (62)

Shelley, Percy B. "Hellas." In *Great Poems of the English Language.* Compiled by Wallace A. Briggs and William R. Benét. New York: Tudor, 1948. Pp. 540–541. (64)

Sheridan, R. B. *The School for Scandal.* 1777. Act I, Sc. 1. (53)

Sherwood, Robert E. *The Petrified Forest.* New York: Scribner's, 1935. (12)

Shiki. Translated in *The Four Seasons.* Mount Vernon: Pauper, 1958. (56)

Shu Ching. Translated by Burton Watson. *Early Chinese Literature.* New York: Columbia University, 1962. Pp. 35–36. (37)

Shudraka. *The Toy Cart.* Translated by P. Lal. *Great Sanskrit Plays.* New York: New Directions, 1964. Act X. (49)

Sidgwick, Henry. "Lines Composed in His Sleep." Quoted by William Osler, *South Place Magazine,* 1907. (24)

Sill, Edward R. "The Fool's Prayer." (61)

Simms, William G. *Mellichampe.* 1825. Chap. 9. (33)

Simonides. "Human Imperfection." Translated by Gilbert Highet in *Oxford Book of Greek Verse.* Edited by T. F. Higham and C. M. Boura. Oxford: Clarendon, 1930. (60)

Slowacki, Juliusz. *Beniowski.* Translated by M. A. Michael in T. N. Filip (ed.). *A Polish Anthology.* London: Duckworth, 1944. (39)

Smith, Adam. "Of Propriety," *The Theory of Moral Sentiments.* 1792. Sec. III, Chap. 2. (30)

Smith, Adam. *Wealth of Nations.* 1776. (19)

Smith, Alexander. *A Life Drama.* 1853. (5)

Smith, Logan P. "Symptoms," *All Trivia.* London: Constable, 1933. Pp. 64–65. (59)

Smuts, Jan C. "Letter," *New York Evening Post,* March 2, 1921. (18)

Somadeva. *The Story of Devadatta*. Translated by C. H. Tawney. *Bibliotheca Indica*. 1880. (12)

Song of Roland. Translated by Frederick Luquiens. New York: Macmillan, 1952. Pp. 59–86. (5)

Song of Solomon 2: 11–12. King James Version of the Bible. (64)

Sophocles. *Philotetes*. Translated by F. Storr. Cambridge: Harvard University, 1928. (58)

South, Robert. "Sermon." April 30, 1676. (43)

Southworth, E. D. E. N. *Ishmael*. 1863. (46)

Spencer, Herbert. "State Tampering with Money and Banks," *Essays: Moral, Political and Aesthetic*. 1865. (37)

Spengler, Oswald. *The Decline of the West*. Translated by Charles F. Atkinson. New York: Knopf, 1928. Vol. II, pp. 501–503. (49)

Spinoza, Benedict. *Ethics*. 1675. (57)

Spitteler, Carl. "Olympian Spring." (32)

Spykman, J. J. *America's Strategy in World Politics*. New York: Harcourt, Brace, 1942. P. 21. (13)

Staël, Anne Germaine de. *Corinne*. 1807. Bk. XVIII, Chap. 5. (16)

Stalin, Joseph. *Foundations of Leninism*. New York: International, 1932. I. 43. (63)

Steffens, Lincoln. *Autobiography*. New York: Harcourt, Brace, 1931. P. 469. (12)

Steinbeck, John. "The Leader of the People," *Long Valley*. Reprinted in *The Portable Steinbeck*. New York: Viking, 1938. (48)

Stendhal. *Lucien Leuwen*. Translated by Raymond Giraud. *The Unheroic Hero*. New Brunswick: Rutgers University, 1957. (36)

Sterne, Laurence. *Tristram Shandy*. 1767. (62)

Stevenson, Robert L. "Letter to a Young Gentleman Who Proposes to Embrace the Career of Art." (53)

Su Tung-po. Translated by Cyril D. Clark (ed.). *Selections from the Works of Su Tung-po*. London: Cape, 1931. P. 111. (40)

Suckling, John. *The Tragedy of Brennoralt*. 1770. Act I, Sc. 1. (42)

Sudermann, Hermann. *The Joy of Living*. Translated by Edith Wharton. New York: Lederer, 1902. (27)

Sumerian Inscription. Translated in S. N. Kramer. "Man and His God," *Supplements to Vetus Testamentum Ill*. Leiden, 1955. (23)

Sun Yat-sen. "Lectures on the Three Principles." Republic of China: 1924. (45)

Sung Yü. "The Man-Wind and the Woman-Wind." Translated by Arthur Waley. *Translations from the Chinese*. New York: Knopf, 1941. Pp. 5–6. (35)

Suzuki, Daisetz T. *Living by Zen*. Tokyo: Sanseido, 1949. Pp. 73–74. (25)

Swahili Folk Verse. "The Poem of the Poor Man." Translated by Lyndon Harries (ed.). *Swahili Poetry*. Oxford: Clarendon, 1962. P. 146. (22)

Swift, Jonathan. *Gulliver's Travels*. 1726. Viking Edition, pp. 469–470. (7)

Swift, Jonathan. In *Miscellanies of Swift and Pope*. New York: Viking, 1948. P. 80. (44)

Syrian Governor. "Message to Akhenaton of Egypt." Fourteenth century B.C. Translated by C. Bezold and E. A. W. Budge. *The Tell el-Amarna Tablets in the British Museum*. 1889–1899. (63)

Tacitus, Cornelius. *Annals*. (42)

Tagore, Rabindranath. *Fruit Gathering*. New York: Macmillan, 1916. Pp. 33–34. (58)

Tagore, Rabindranath. *The Fugitive and Other Poems*. Translated by Amiya Chakravarty (ed.). *A Tagore Reader*. New York: Macmillan, 1961. Pp. 332–333. (8)

Talmud. "Ketuboth." (31)

Talmud. "Taanith." (28)

Tasso, Torquato. *Jerusalem*. II, 16 (42)

Taylor, Henry. *The Statesman*. 1836. Heffer Edition, pp. 22, 53. (56, 59)

Tennyson, Alfred. "Merlin and Vivien." In W. H. Auden and Norman H. Pearson (eds.). *Poets of the English Language*. New York: Viking, 1950. Vol. V, p. 45. (62)

Terence. *Andria*. I, 5. (31)

Thackeray, William M. *The Virginians*. 1859. Chap. 92. (5)

Theocritus. *Idylls*. VII, 41. (27)

Theophrastus. *Characters*. Translated by R. D. Hicks. Cambridge: Harvard University, 1929. (44)

Thoreau, Henry D. "On the Duty of Civil Disobedience." 1849. (21)

Thousand and One Nights, The. "The Sage Durban." Translated by Edward W. Lane. New York: Harper, 1848. (10)

Thucydides. *History of the Peloponnesian War*. Translated by R. Crawly. 1876. (36)

Tikhonov, Nikolai S. Translated by Gleb Struve. *Soviet Russian Literature*. Norman: University of Oklahoma, 1951. (53)

Tilak, Bal G. *The Secret of the Bhagavad Gita*. Translated by Bhalchandra S. Sukthanker. Poona: Tilak, 1936. (32)

Tillich, Paul J. "What Is Basic in Human Nature," *Tenth Karen Horney Lecture*. (58)

Tocqueville, Alexis de. "Democracy in America," *The Recollections of Alexis de Tocqueville*. Translated by Reeve and edited by G. P. Mayer. London: Harvill, 1948. (50)

Tolstoy, Leo N. *The Death of Ivan Ilych*. Translated by Louis and Aylmer Maude. London: Oxford University, 1935. (2)

Toulouse-Lautrec, Henri de. "Letter to His Uncle, May 7, 1882." Translated by Eric Protter. *Painters on Painting*. New York: Grosset and Dunlap, 1963. P. 170. (53)

Toynbee, Arnold J. *A Study of History*. Abridged by D. C. Somervell. New York: Oxford University, 1946. P. 77. (24)

Toynbee, Arnold J. *A Study of History*. London: Oxford University, 1934–1939. (51)

Treitschke, Heinrich von. "The State Idea," *Lectures on Politics*. Translated by Blanche Dugdale and Torben de Bille. London: Constable, 1916. (54)

Trollope, Anthony. *The Bertrams*. 1859. (14)

Tu Fu. "The Return." Translated by Robert Payne. *The White Pony*. New York: Day, 1947. P. 232. (24)

Turgenev, Ivan. "The District Doctor." Translated in Thomas Seltzer (ed.). *Best Russian Short Stories*. New York: Boni and Liveright, 1917. Pp. 65–66. (20)

Twain, Mark. *Autobiography*. New York: Harpers, 1924. Chap. 2. (42)

Tyutchev, Fëdor. "Silentium." Translated by Babette Deutsch in Avram Yarmolinsky. *A Treasury of Russian Verse*. New York: Macmillan, 1949. P. 81. (1)

Unamuno y Jugo, Miguel de. "St. Emmanuel the Good Martyr," *Abel Sanchez and Other Stories*. Translated by Anthony Kerrigan. Chicago: Regnery, 1956. (61)

Valéry, Paul. *Introduction to the Method of Leonardo da Vinci*. Translated by Thomas McGreevy. 1895. (10)

Vattel, Emmerich von. *The Law of Nations*. 1758. (2)

Vavrecka, Hugo. "Comment Following Munich Conference of October 1, 1938." Translated by Frederick L. Schuman. *Russia Since 1917*. New York: Knopf, 1957. (33)

Velleius Paterculus. Translated by J. W. Duff. *A Literary History of Rome*. Edited by A. M. Duff. New York: Barnes and Noble, 1964. Third Edition, P. 79. (7)

Verdi, Giuseppe. "Letter to Camille du Locle, December 7, 1869." Quoted by Franz Werfel and Paul Stefan. *Verdi, the Man in His Letters*. Translated by Edward Downes. New York: Fisher, 1942. (12)

Vergil. *Aeneid*. Translated by Mark Van Doren. *On Great Poems of Western Literature*. New York: Collier, 1962. P. 83. (11)

Vinci, Leonardo da. *Notebooks*. Translated and edited by Edward McCurdy. 1871. (20)

Vishakhadatta. *The Signet Ring of Rakshasa*. Translated by P. Lal. *Great Sanskrit Plays*. New York: New Directions, 1964. Act III. (4)

Voltaire. *Philosophical Letters*. Translated by John Randall, Jr. *The Career of Philosophy*. New York: Columbia University, 1962. P. 870. (27)

[435]

Völuspa. Translated by Henry A. Bellows. *The Poetic Edda.* New York: American-Scandinavian Foundation, 1923. (39)

Wall Street Journal, November 20, 1957. (38)

Wallace, Lew. *Ben Hur.* 1880. (18)

Walton, Izaak. *Walton's Lives.* London: Bell, 1884. Pp. 49–50. (15)

Wang Wei. "Following the Army." Translated by Chang Yin-nan and Lewis C. Walmsley. *Poems by Wang Wei.* Rutland: Tuttle, 1958. (26)

Warring States, Intrigues of the. Translated by Burton Watson. *Early Chinese Literature.* New York: Columbia University, 1962. Pp. 85–86. (24, 41)

Washington, Booker T. "Address at the Cotton and International Exposition." Atlanta, September 18, 1893. (45)

Washington, George. "Letter to Bushrod Washington, November 10, 1787." (19)

Waterton, Charles. Quoted by Edith Sitwell. *English Eccentrics.* New York: Vanguard, 1957. (40)

Webster, Daniel. "Speech in United States Senate Supporting Clay's Compromise." March 7, 1850. (17)

Weizsächer, Ernst von. *Memoirs.* Translated by John Andrews. Chicago: Regnery, 1951. (10)

Whitman, Walt. "Song of Myself," *Leaves of Grass.* 1891. (28)

Whyte, Jr., William H. *The Organization Man.* New York: Simon and Schuster, 1956. P. 3. (12)

Wilcox, Ella W. "Solitude," *New York Sun,* February 25, 1883. (58)

Wilde, Oscar. *An Ideal Husband.* 1899. Act I. (55)

Wilder, Thornton. *The Bridge of San Luis Rey.* New York: Boni, 1927. Grosset and Dunlap Edition, p. 196. (17)

Wilhelm, Hellmut. *Change.* Translated by Cary F. Baynes. New York: Pantheon, 1960. (Introduction)

Wilhelm, Richard. *The I Ching.* Translated by Cary F. Baynes. New York: Pantheon, 1961. Second Edition. (Introduction)

Williams, Charles. *Many Dimensions.* London: Faber and Faber, 1947. Pp. 101–102. (41)

Wilson, Woodrow. "First Inaugural Address." March 4, 1913. (49)

Wolfe, Thomas. *Of Time and the River.* New York: Scribner's, 1935. (52)

Wordsworth, William. "Resolution and Independence." In W. H. Auden and Norman H. Pearson (eds.). *Poets of the English Language.* New York: Viking, 1950. Vol. IV, pp. 181–182. (51)

Woroszylski, Wiktor. "The Watch." Translated by Barbara Vedder in Maria Kuncewicz (ed.). *The Modern Polish Mind.* Boston: Little, Brown, 1962. Pp. 21–23. (37)

Wright, Harold B. *The Eyes of the World*. New York: Appleton-Century, 1914. (48)

Wu Ch'eng-en. *Monkey*. Translated by Arthur Waley. New York: Day, 1943. Grove Edition, pp. 21–22. (50)

Yeats, William B. "To a Friend Whose Works Has Come to Nothing," *Collected Poems*. New York: Macmillan, 1933. P. 124. (51)

Yoshida Kenko. *Essays on Idleness*. Translated by G. B. Sansom. *Transactions of Asiatic Society of Japan*. 1911. (11)

Young, Brigham. "The Mormon Trek to Utah, 1846," *The Discourses of Brigham Young*. Edited by John A. Widtsoe. Salt Lake City: Deseret Book, 1925. (25)

Yun Sun-do. Translated by Peter Hyun. *Voices of the Dawn*. London: Murray, 1960. (38)

Zamoyski, Jan. "Speech in Polish Parliament." 1605. (36)

Zamyatin, Yevgeni. *We*. Translated by Walter N. Vickery in Patricia Blake and Max Hayward. *Dissonant Voices in Soviet Literature*. New York: Random House, 1962. (43)

Zen Poem. Translated by Alan W. Watts. *The Way of Zen*. New York: Pantheon, 1957. (2)

Zeromski, Stefan. "The Homeless People." Quoted by Manfred Kridl. *A Survey of Polish Literature and Culture*. Translated by Olga Scherer-Virdki. New York: Columbia University, 1956. (47)

Zia ud-din Barni. *Rulings on Temporal Government*. Folio 130a. In William Theodore de Bary *et al.* (eds.). *Sources of Indian Tradition*. New York: Columbia University, 1958. P. 517. (45)

Zola, Émile. Quoted in *The Dreyfus Case by the Man—Alfred Dreyfus—and His Son—Pierre Dreyfus*. Edited and translated by Donald C. McKay. New Haven: Yale University, 1937. (61)

Zweig, Stefan. *Marie Antoinette*. Translated by Edan and Cedar Paul. Garden City: Garden City, 1933. Pp. 271–272. (10)

V. Index*

*The authors of quotations are listed in the References and are not repeated in this Index.

[441]

[443]

[451]

[455]

[457]

[459]

[461]

[462]